FUNDAMENTALS OF GUITAR

A WORKBOOK FOR BEGINNING, INTERMEDIATE, OR ADVANCED STUDENTS

MILES OKAZAKI

1st edition (2015)

www.melbay.com

TABLE OF CONTENTS

PREFACE

Why I wrote this book:
While writing, my goal was to produce something to inspire beginners, train intermediate students, and organize information for more advanced players. The approach is heavily visual, because I've often found images to be more efficient and inviting than long verbal descriptions. The content is based on performance experience, using techniques that have led to positive results for myself and other students. There is a good amount of theory, but the focus is on application. The topic is the study of fundamentals, which are useful to revisit at every stage of development, applicable to any style, and infinite in scope.

Who it's for:
This book is meant to serve a multiplicity of personalities and skill levels - the reader is invited to skip around and explore it at any point, according to what seems interesting. There is no reference to the correctness of any particular approach - a primary goal here is to recognize and enjoy that the creative process is different for every individual. We choose the tools that best fit our needs. Think of this book as a creative toolbox - no two people will use it the same way. There is no preferred system for representing musical concepts on the page - I've used or invented whatever notation seems most effective for any particular purpose. This includes Western staff notation, fretboard diagrams, pitch and rhythm circles, graphs, and geometric visualizations. This decreases the cultural and intellectual biases inherent to various notation systems, reduces language barriers, and provides a point of entry for a wider variety of people. There are a fair number of advanced concepts here, but I've made an effort to avoid academic language and theoretical jargon, explaining things the way I understand them using plain language. The overall aim is to present the maximum amount of information in as clear and efficient a manner as possible.

What's in it:
The book is divided into two parts: Pitch (Part I) and Rhythm (Part II). Part I is concerned primarily with the positions and movements of the fretting hand, and Part II with the possibilities of sound production with the picking hand. Part I begins the study of pitch locations and formations the fretboard, from natural harmonics to sets of 1, 2, 3 and 4 pitches. Part II addresses the often neglected topic of rhythm, beginning with a complete course in my approach to symmetrical picking and continuing with studies of multiple notes per stroke on one string (slurs, slides, and ornaments) and playing on multiple strings (rhythmic counterpoint).

How to use it:
The level of difficulty depends entirely on the approach of the reader. The main idea is that thorough study of fundamentals is necessary for freedom on the instrument, which in turn is necessary for creative work. It's very difficult to invent new things without a sense of what is possible and a solid foundation to stand on. This is not the same as accumulating information or having a lot of technical facility. It means being able to decide what information or techniques are useful for your particular creative direction and knowing how to use the tools you have selected. In the world of instructional books there are plenty of encyclopedic listings of chord voicings, compendiums of scales, and exhaustive lists of rhythmic patterns. This is not such a book. It's designed to be practical and achieve results. When a comprehensive list is required, it is given. The focus is on clear language, intuitive illustrations, and avoidance of redundancies. The amount of material may seem overwhelming, but the student is encouraged to treat this book like a creative sketchpad, marking up and customizing its pages. Take what is useful and discard the rest. Add your own improvements. A deep, personal knowledge of a few chosen things will serve creativity better than superficial knowledge of a huge amount of material.

Miles Okazaki
Brooklyn, New York
December, 2014

INTRODUCTION

There is a label in the upper left corner of each page of this book. This is to make it easy for the reader to focus on what is most interesting to them. Below are descriptions of each label:

Illustration A visual display of information. These pages are meant to inspire further study in an area if they seem interesting, or to serve as visual summaries of concepts. The goal is to provide alternative points of entry for different types of musicians.

Concept A verbal explanation of a musical idea. These pages deal with music theory, with an emphasis on simple language. A glossary is provided at the end of the book for the definitions of technical terms that were necessary in the text.

Exercise A description of a physical process to work on a concept on the guitar. These pages are useful as a "quick start." If the material is confusing or difficult, the reader can review nearby pages to understand the context.

Notes An array of empty staves, fretboard diagrams, pitch circles, or other notation devices. These pages are inserted here and there to encourage readers to interact with the book with their own thoughts.

Use these labels as a guide to navigate through the book in whatever way seems useful.
The diagram below shows a map of the book according to page type, for quick reference:

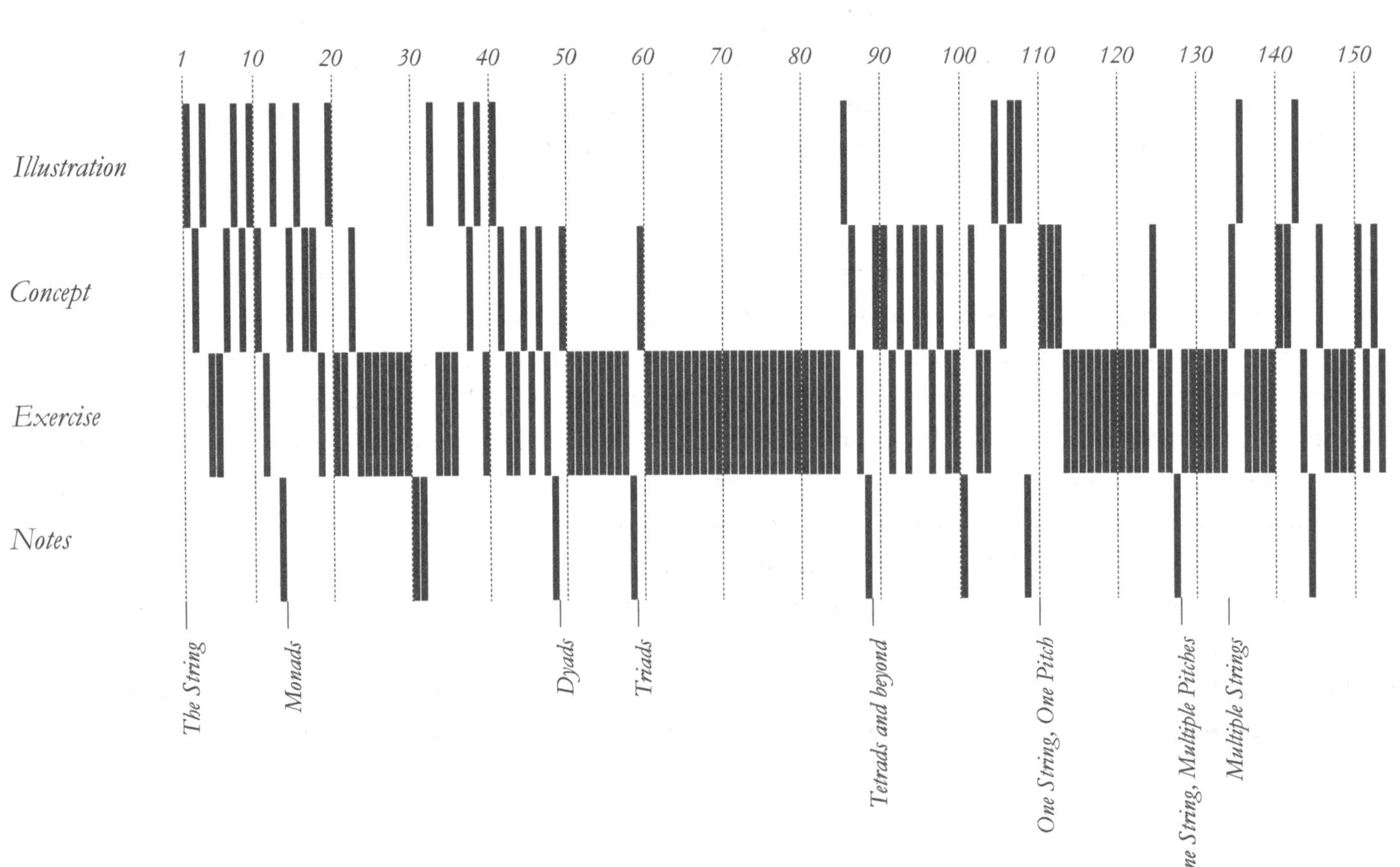

PART I

Pitch

This page intentionally left blank.

NATURAL HARMONICS OF THE STRING

Illustration

Showing:

All locations of Partials 2-12 in relation to the guitar fretboard. (drawn to scale)

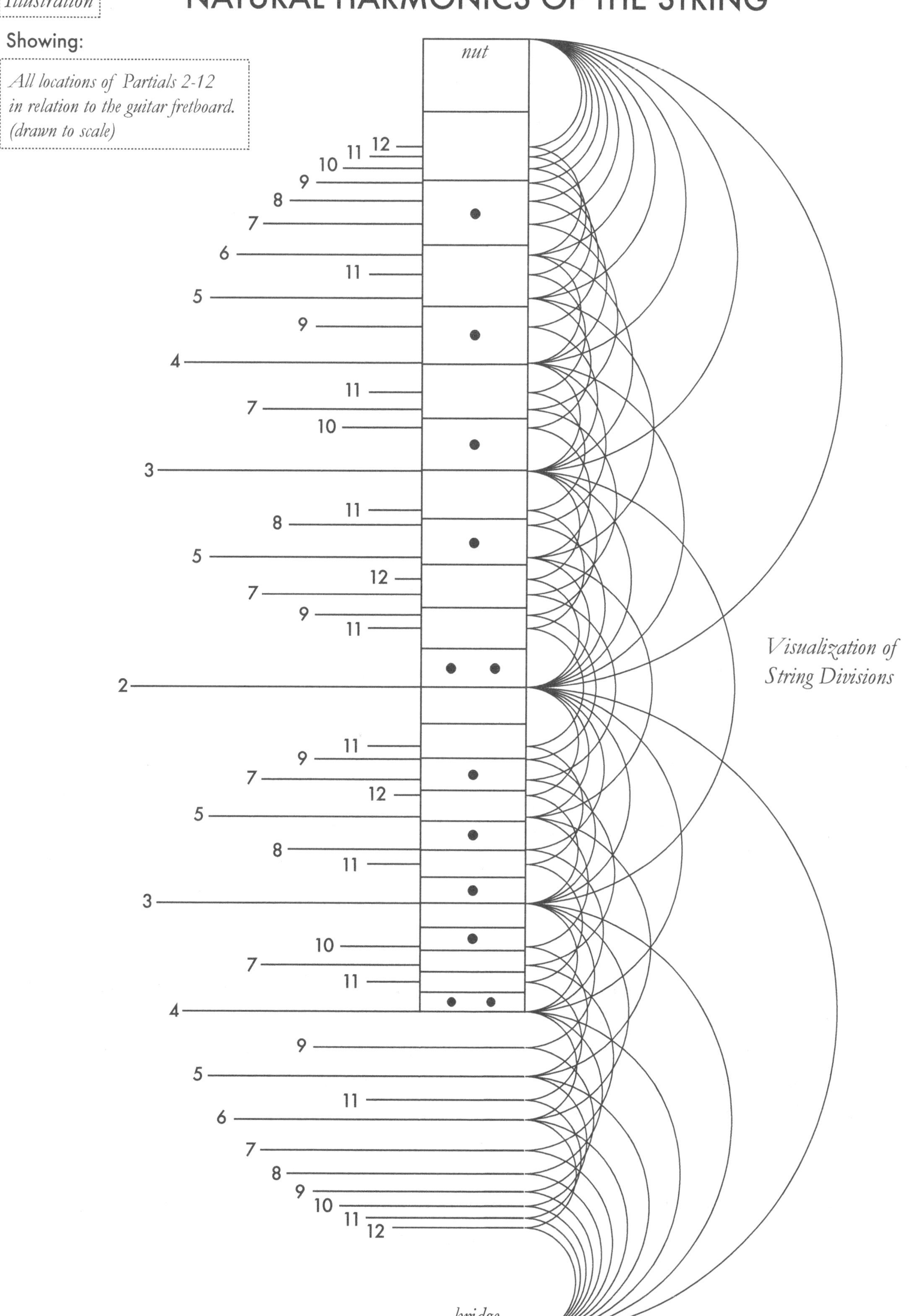

Concept

THE STRING

In order to better understand how the guitar works, it's helpful to take a look how a string works. Here are two strings - one still, and one vibrating:

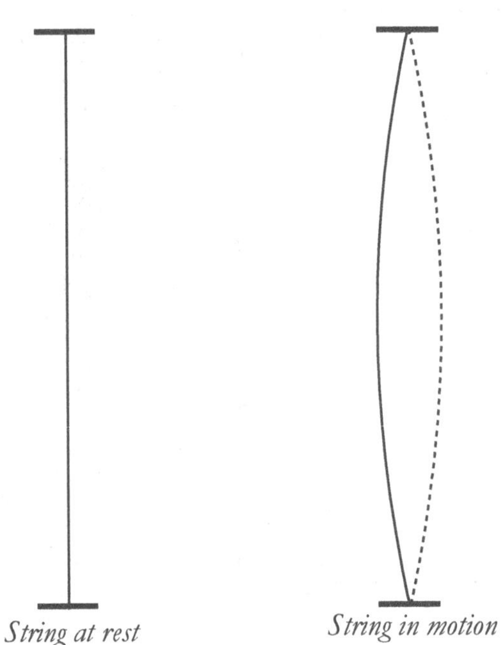

The still string is silent, and the vibrating string produces a pitch, called the *fundamental*.

The fundamental is the pitch that we hear most clearly, and the *timbre* of the sound is determined by the interaction of *overtones* which are found in that fundamental's harmonic series. The vibrating string has a natural tendency to divide its length into equal sections, called *partials*. The entire string (fundamental) is the first partial, the string divided into two parts (1st harmonic) is the second partial, division into three parts (2nd harmonic) is the 3rd partial, and so on. While the entire length of the string is vibrating, these smaller sections are also in motion, producing higher tones that contribute to the color of the sound.

The sounds of these partials can be forced out of hiding through the production of *harmonics,* which dampen the fundamental and bring the overtone into the foreground. This can be done easily on the guitar by lightly placing a finger on a harmonic node (where the string divides evenly by some number) and plucking the string. This effectively divides the string into discrete vibrating sections, producing a higher pitch related to the length of the section. The locations of harmonic nodes on the guitar up to the 12th partial are shown on the previous page.

The following page visualizes the harmonics of an open A string. There is one place to produce the 2nd partial, two places to produce the 3rd partial, 3 places to play the 4th partial, and so on. The series stops at the 12 partial for practical purposes.

Illustration

NATURAL HARMONICS OF THE STRING

Showing:

All locations of partials 1-12, pictured as nodes on a vibrating string tuned to A 110 Hz (open 5th string on guitar). Pictured are the Partial number, string visualization, fretboard reference, frequency, and closest equal tempered pitch in staff notation. If the tuning of the equal tempered pitch does not match the harmonic, the correction to the staff note is shown in cents.

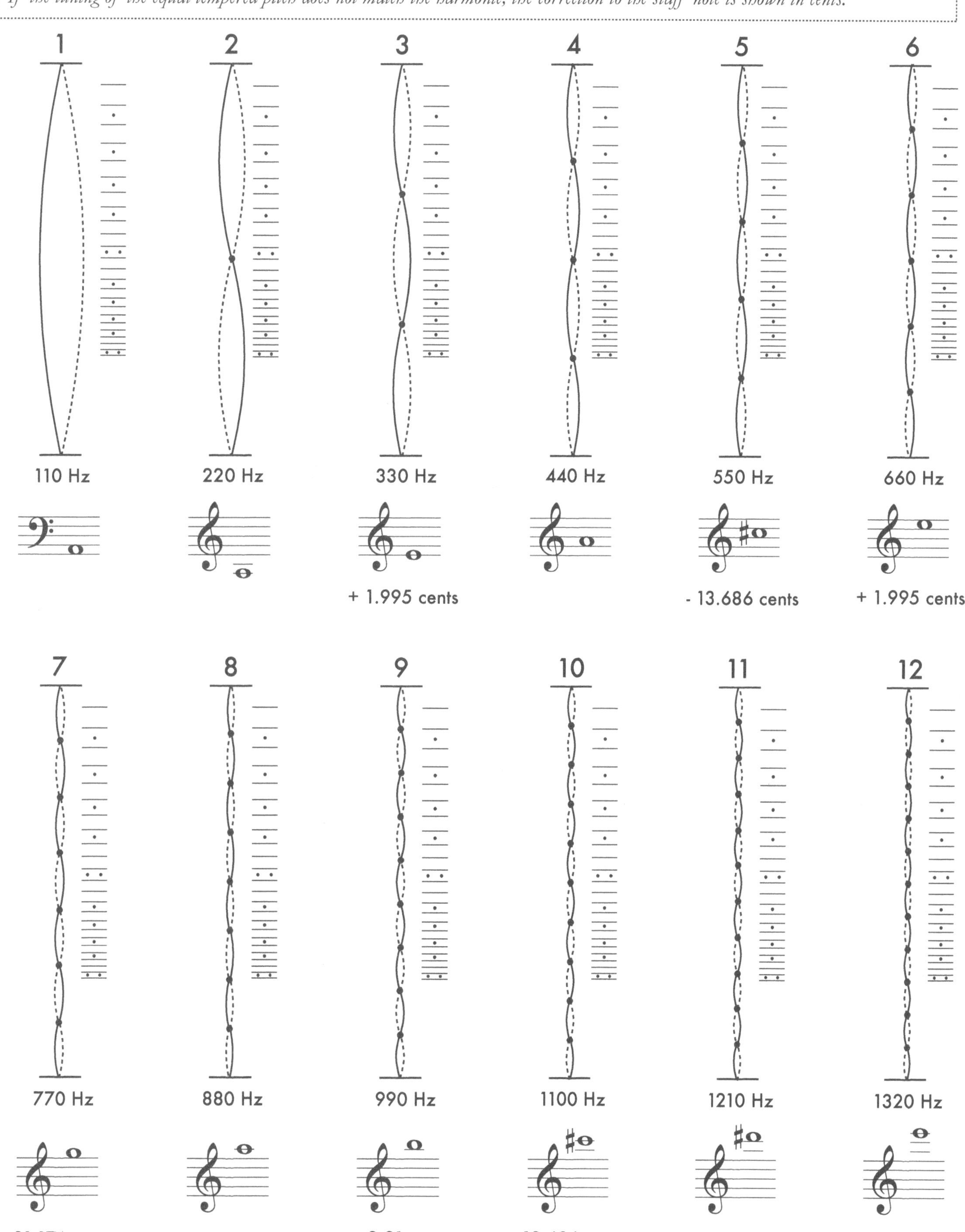

Exercise

HARMONIUM

A study of partials 2 - 7.
This is a composite scale created by all of the natural harmonics of the six strings, up to the 7th partial.
String numbers and partials are given above the staff (strings in circles, partials on top), and skill level below the staff.
When harmonics on more than one string can produce the same pitch, the most convenient fingering is chosen.
Fretboard diagram shows one possible fingering, with the sequence in numbers.
Lower staff notation shows the full set of harmonics up to the 7th partial for all six open strings.
(piches written at concert pitch, with fundamentals as whole notes and harmonics as diamond noteheads).
Pitches on staff notation are only an approximation of the sounded pitch. The only pitch not listed is Bb.

- Play the sequence of natural harmonics shown on the first staff, ascending and descending.
- Try different angles of the finger touching the string, try different ways of plucking, including the thumb (higher partials will require a precise touch and harder stroke).
- Work slowly and produce clear, ringing tones with even dynamics.
- Explore other possible fingerings, combine the pitches to create melodies and chords.

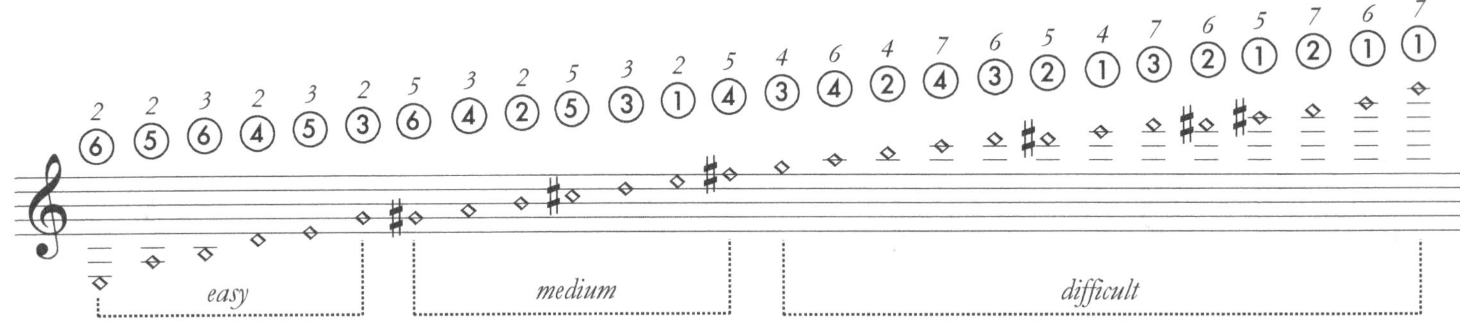

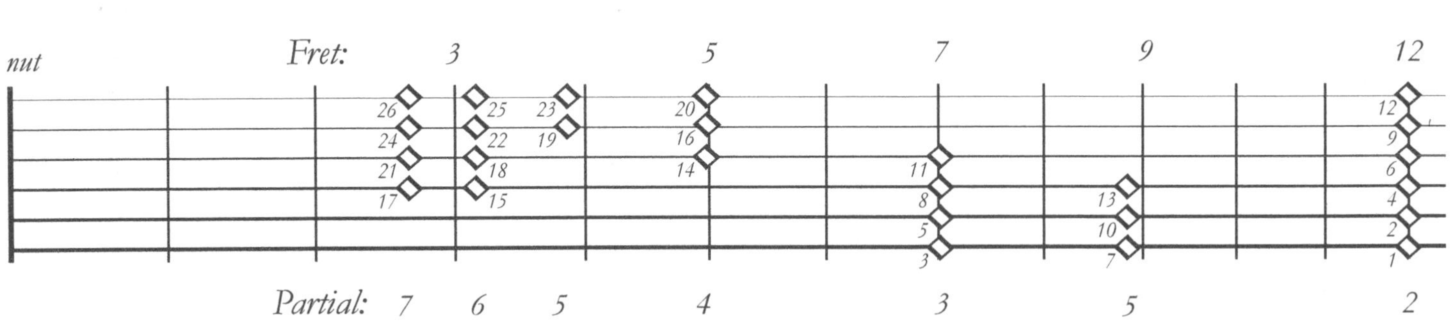

Top Staff: Partials 2-7 of the six strings on the guitar
Bottom Staff: Fundamentals

⑥ ⑤ ④ ③ ② ①

Exercise

CHROMATIC HARMONICS

A study of partials 4 - 11.
This is the longest series of chromatic pitches that can be found in the harmonics of the open strings up to the 11th partial.
String numbers and partials are given (strings in circles, partials above).
When a harmonic on more than one string can produce the same pitch, the most convenient partial is chosen.
Fretboard diagram shows one possible fingering, with the sequence in numbers.
Note the differences of these pitches from an equal tempered chromatic scale (fretted notes), which are approximately:
5th and 10th partials: 14 cents flat
6th partial: 2 cents sharp
7th partial: 31 cents flat
9th partial: 4 cents sharp
11th partial: 49 cents flat

- Play the sequence of natural harmonics shown on the first staff, ascending and descending.
- Try different angles of the finger touching the string, try different ways of plucking, including the thumb (higher partials will require a precise touch and harder stroke).
- If the pitches can't be heard, try first on a bass guitar or a normal guitar with overdrive.
- Work slowly and produce clear, ringing tones with even dynamics.

This is a very difficult exercise.

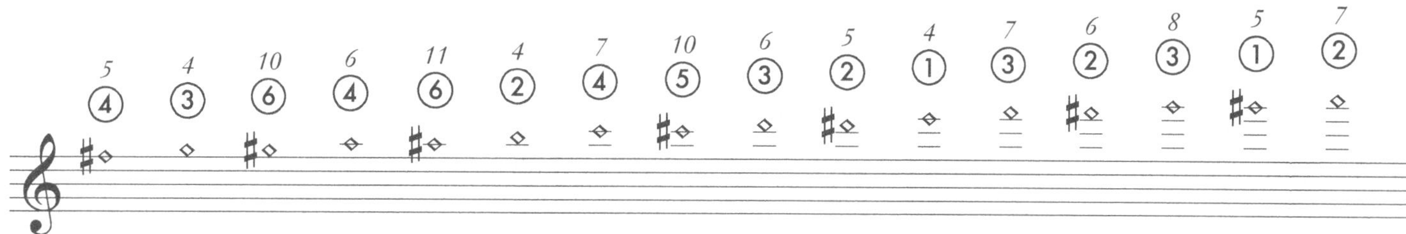

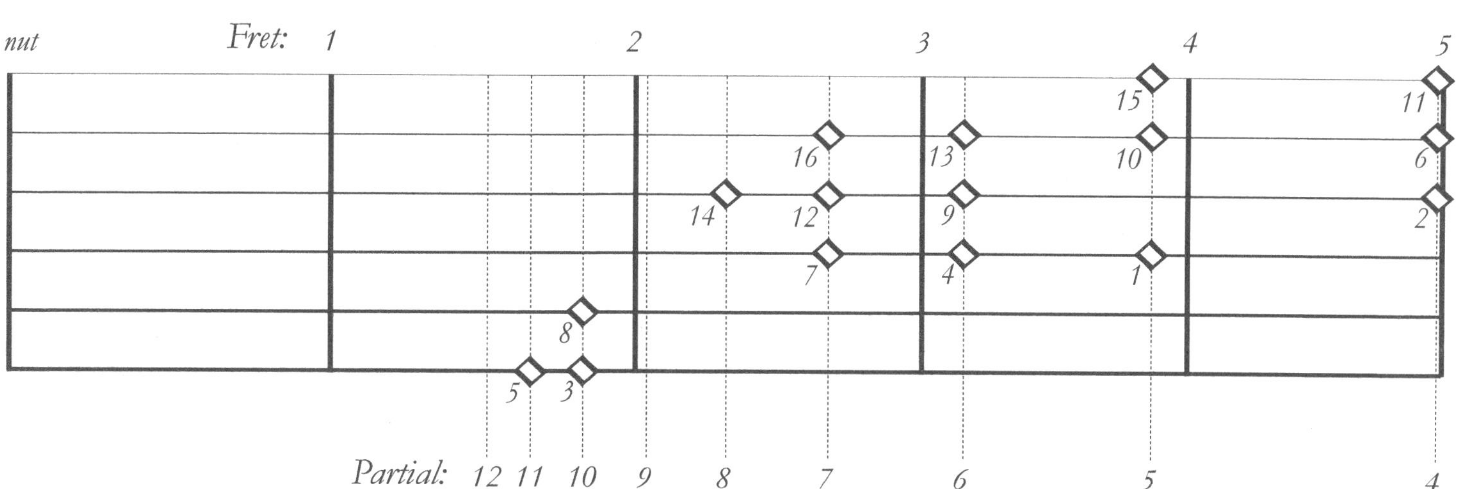

Concept

STOPPED PITCHES

Natural harmonics are induced by lightly touching a string that has its full length in motion. When the fretting hand fully depresses the string at some point along the neck of the guitar, it divides the string into two sections - a stopped part between the finger and the nut, and a vibrating part between the finger and the bridge. This vibrating part is essentially a new, shorter string with a higher pitch than the fundamental. The relationship between the *frequency* of the pitch and the length of the string can be expressed this way:

frequency of new pitch = (frequency of fundamental) x (inverse of string ratio)

The string ratio can be thought of as the fraction of the string that is in motion. For example, take the A string of the guitar, which is usually tuned to a frequency of 110 Hz. If we stop the string halfway from the bridge, the string ratio is 1/2 (one half of the entire string is in motion, producing a pitch). The inverse of 1/2 is 2/1. So, the frequency of the new pitch is:

$$(110\ Hz) \times (2/1) = 220\ Hz$$

This is the octave, A 220. If we stop the string 2/3 of the distance from the bridge, the calculation becomes:

$$(110\ Hz) \times (3/2) = 165\ Hz$$

This is a perfect fifth in *just intonation,* E 165. This pitch is slightly different (about 2 *cents* sharper) than the E from *equal temperament* that we hear on a fretted guitar.

In just intonation, pitches are derived from whole number relationships. Even if these numbers are very large (such as 99/70, a close approximation of the equal tempered tritone), they are still in the realm of just intonation, because they are a ratio of whole numbers.

In the most common type of equal temperament (the one that divides the octave into 12 tones), pitches are derived from a logarithmic system with semitones separated by equal distances determined by the 12th root of 2. In order to get an equal tempered tritone, we would multiply the fundamental frequency by the square root of 2. The result is an irrational number, meaning it cannot be expressed as a ratio of whole numbers.

Even though the guitar uses equal temperament for the placement of the frets, we are taking a look at just intonation here in order to understand the nature of the string and its basic physical properties. The following page visualizes some string ratios on an unfretted instrument and their corresponding just intonation pitches.

Illustration

STRING LENGTH AND FREQUENCY

Showing:

The relationship between pitch and the location of a stop on a string tuned to A 110 Hz (open 5th string on a fretless guitar). Pictured are the common name of the pitch in relation to the fundamental, string visualization with vibrating fraction of string labeled, frequency, derivation of the frequency from the fundamental, closest equal tempered pitch in staff notation, and correction in cents of the equal tempered tuning to match the actual pitch of the stopped note. Numbers are rounded to 5 significant digits and strings are drawn to scale.

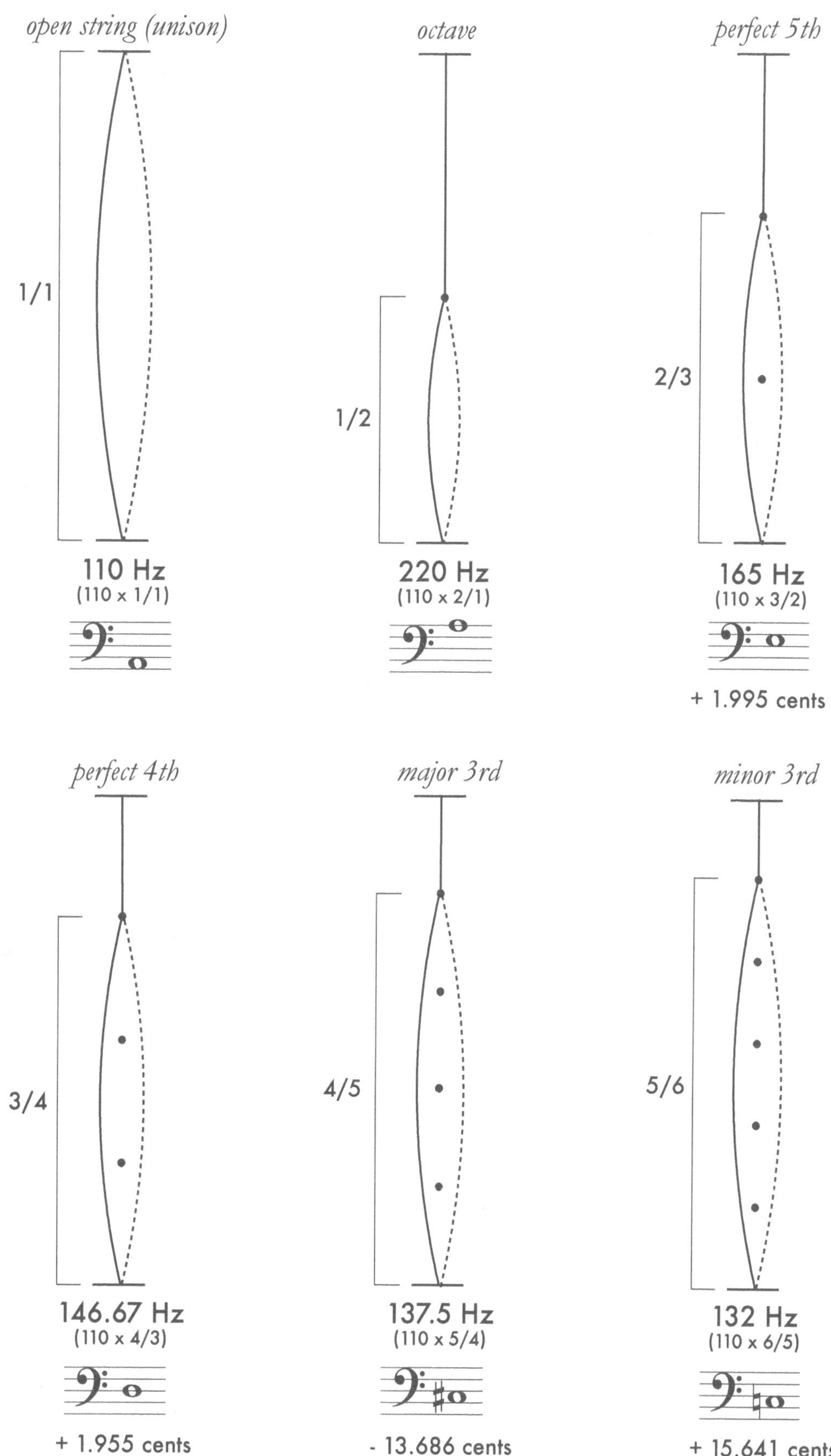

Concept BUILDING A CHROMATIC SCALE IN JUST INTONATION

The first partial is the fundamental open string, and the second partial is the octave. The third partial gives us the first essential building block of tonality, the perfect 5th (3/2). Connecting 12 consecutive perfect fifths in just intonation creates a kind of chromatic scale:

C	G	D	A	E	B	F♯	C♯	G♯	D♯	A♯	E♯	B♯
1/1	3/2	9/8	27/16	81/64	243/128	729/512	2187/2048	6561/4096	19683/16384	59049/32768	177147/131072	531441/524288
0	701.96	203.91	905.87	407.82	1109.78	611.73	113.69	815.64	317.60	1019.55	521.51	23.46

A chain of 13 perfect fifths in just intonation, showing pitch names, harmonic ratios, and tuning in cents (rounded to two decimal places). Ratios are adjusted to bring all pitches within an octave - for example, the third pitch 9/1 is lowered three octaves to 9/8.

The harmonic ratios show how this system quickly gets into very large numbers, and the measurements in cents show how each consecutive pitch is increasingly sharp until the B#, which is nearly a quarter tone above the original C.

The fourth partial is another octave, and the fifth partial gives us another new building block, the major 3rd (5/4). This interval is numerically simpler than the major 3rd of four stacked perfect 5ths (81/64), and smaller by about 21.5 cents. With a combination of perfect 5ths and major 3rds we can build a compact 12-tone lattice in two dimensions centered around the perfect fifth from C to G. Add perfect fifths above G and below C, then add major thirds above and below the F-C-G-D chain:

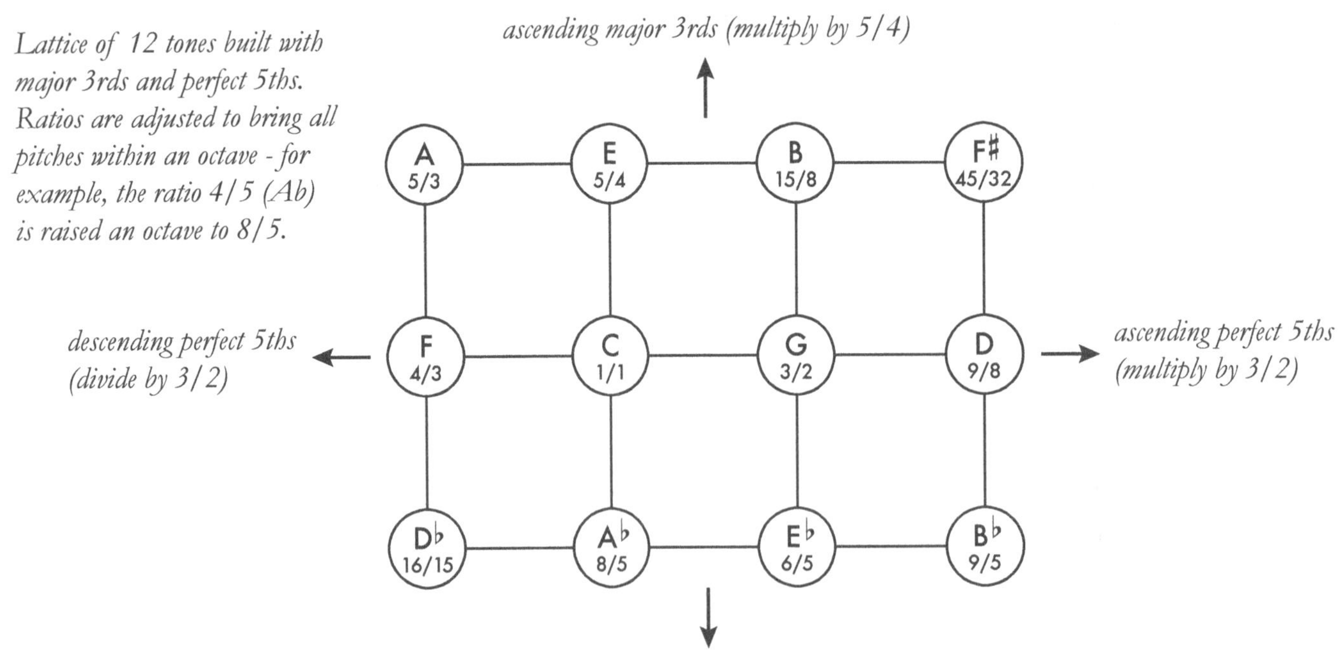

Lattice of 12 tones built with major 3rds and perfect 5ths. Ratios are adjusted to bring all pitches within an octave - for example, the ratio 4/5 (Ab) is raised an octave to 8/5.

This setup uses simpler harmonic ratios than a continuous chain of 5ths and is symmetrical around the root/5th foundation. The harmonic ratios could be inverted into string length fractions for the placement of frets to make an instrument that uses this tuning. For example, if the fundamental of the string is C, place the fret for the pitch A at a location 3/5 of the way from the bridge to the nut. The following page visualizes frets for all 12 tones in comparison to standard equal tempered frets.

Illustration

Showing:

FRETS IN EQUAL TEMPERAMENT AND 5 LIMIT JUST INTONATION

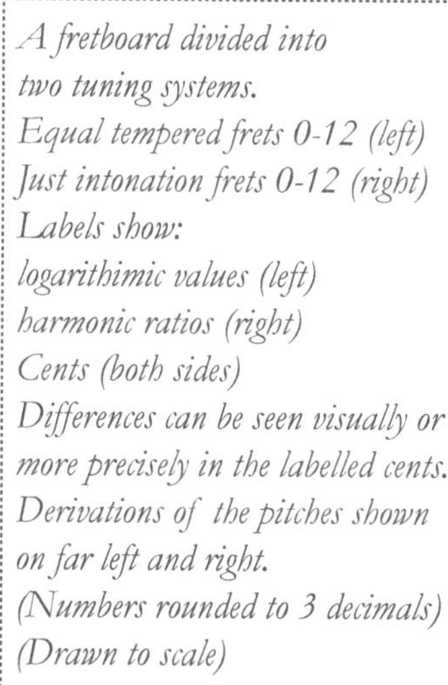

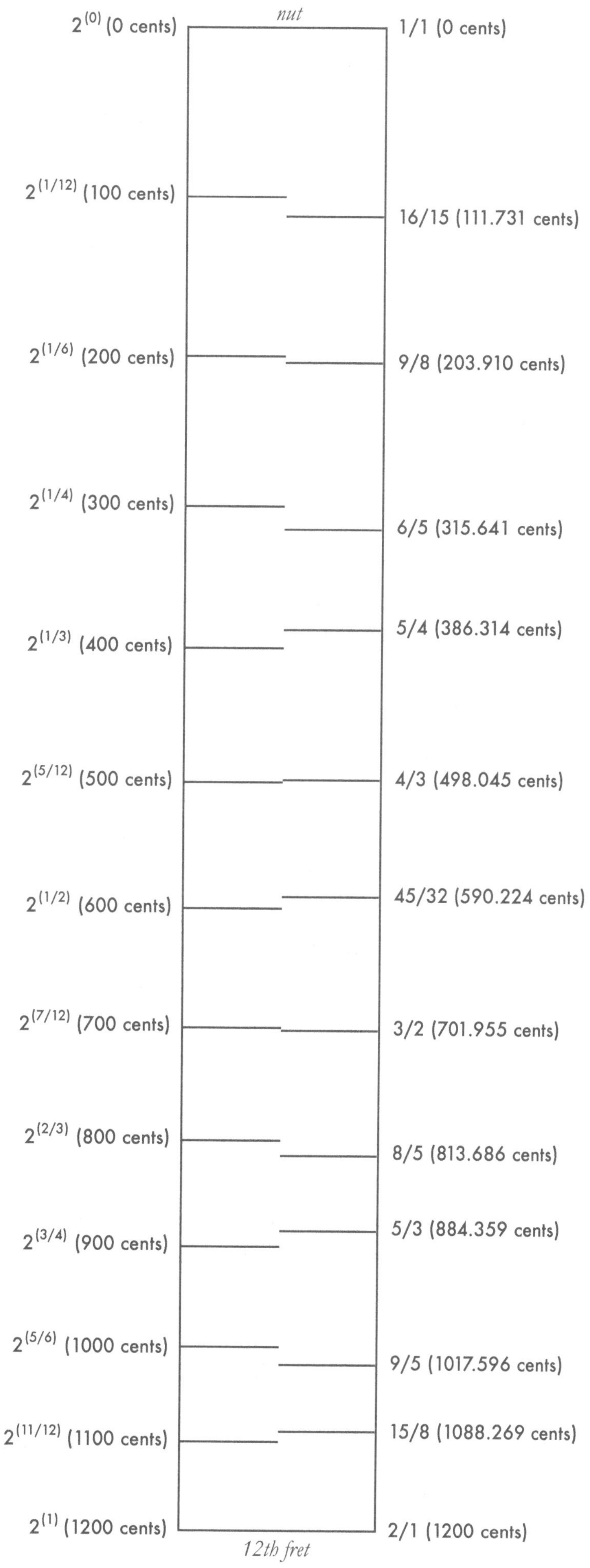

A fretboard divided into two tuning systems.
Equal tempered frets 0-12 (left)
Just intonation frets 0-12 (right)
Labels show:
logarithimic values (left)
harmonic ratios (right)
Cents (both sides)
Differences can be seen visually or more precisely in the labelled cents.
Derivations of the pitches shown on far left and right.
(Numbers rounded to 3 decimals)
(Drawn to scale)

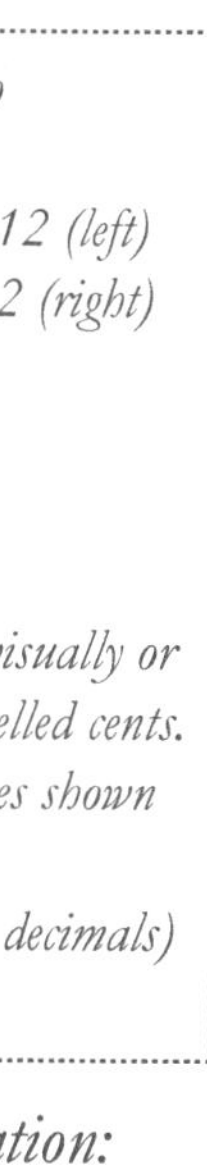

Logarithmic Derivation:

(left fretboard)

$2^{(x/12)}$

Where x *is the number of semitones above the fundamental. Frets are placed at a distance from the nut that is the inverse of this number multiplied by the string length.*

For example:
Equal Tempered 5th = 7 semitones

$2^{(7/12)} \approx 1.4983$

Inverse ≈ 0.67742
If the string length is 24.75 *inches, the fret will be placed a distance of* (0.67742)(24.75) = 16.519 *inches from the bridge, and* 8.481 *inches from the nut.*

Harmonic Derivation:

(right fretboard)

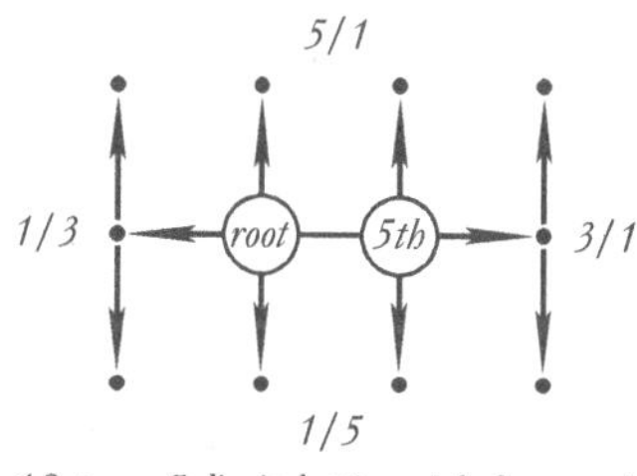

12 tone, 5 limit lattice with frequencies derived as symmetrical extensions of the root and 5th through 3rd or 5th partials (details on far right).

For example:
Just Intonation 5th = 3/2
Inverse = 2/3
If the string length is 24.75 *inches, the fret will be placed a distance of* (2/3)(99/4) = 16.5 *inches from the bridge, and* 8.5 *inches from the nut.*

Equal temperament (left)	Fret	Just intonation (right)	Derivation
$2^{(0)}$ (0 cents)	*nut*	1/1 (0 cents)	*Fundamental (1/1)*
$2^{(1/12)}$ (100 cents)		16/15 (111.731 cents)	*5th partial below 3rd partial below Fundamental (1/1) (1/3) (1/5) = 1/15 raised 4 octaves = 16/15*
$2^{(1/6)}$ (200 cents)		9/8 (203.910 cents)	*3rd partial above 3rd partial above Fundamental (1/1) (3/1) (3/1) = 9/1 lowered 3 octaves = 9/8*
$2^{(1/4)}$ (300 cents)		6/5 (315.641 cents)	*5th partial below 3rd partial above Fundamental (1/1) (3/1) (1/5) = 3/5 raised 1 octave = 6/5*
$2^{(1/3)}$ (400 cents)		5/4 (386.314 cents)	*5th partial above Fundamental (1/1) (5/1) = 5/1 lowered 2 octaves = 5/4*
$2^{(5/12)}$ (500 cents)		4/3 (498.045 cents)	*3rd partial below Fundamental (1/1) (1/3) = 1/3 raised 2 octaves = 4/3*
$2^{(1/2)}$ (600 cents)		45/32 (590.224 cents)	*5th partial above 3rd partial above 3rd partial above Fundamental (1/1) (3/1) (3/1) (5/1) = 45/1 lowered 5 octaves = 45/32*
$2^{(7/12)}$ (700 cents)		3/2 (701.955 cents)	*3rd partial above Fundamental (1/1) (3/1) = 3/1 lowered 1 octave = 3/2*
$2^{(2/3)}$ (800 cents)		8/5 (813.686 cents)	*5th partial below Fundamental (1/1) (1/5) = 1/5 raised 3 octaves = 8/5*
$2^{(3/4)}$ (900 cents)		5/3 (884.359 cents)	*5th partial above 3rd partial below Fundamental (1/1) (1/3) (5/1) = 5/3*
$2^{(5/6)}$ (1000 cents)		9/5 (1017.596 cents)	*5th partial below 3rd partial above 3rd partial above Fundamental (1/1) (3/1) (3/1) (1/5) = 9/5*
$2^{(11/12)}$ (1100 cents)		15/8 (1088.269 cents)	*5th partial above 3rd partial above Fundamental (1/1) (3/1) (5/1) = 15/1 lowered 3 octaves = 15/8*
$2^{(1)}$ (1200 cents)	*12th fret*	2/1 (1200 cents)	*Octave*

Concept

RECONCILING THE ANCIENT AND MODERN

The point of this study of intonation is to understand something fundamental about the guitar. The open strings of the guitar are the same pitches as a pentatonic scale, which can be built from a chain of five perfect 5ths, and is perhaps the most universal expression of tonality:

G major pentatonic scale, as a chain of five 5ths.

Instruments of the violin family are tuned in a series of four 5ths, and retain some ambiguity because of their symmetry. But with a chain of five 5ths we reach the major third, which completes the pentatonic formation and pulls the ear in a very specific direction. On the guitar, the ordering of the strings themselves further reinforces this directionality. The 5ths are inverted into 4ths and the major 3rd is brought together on adjacent strings. In this tuning, the top three strings form a minor triad, and the next three form its relative major:

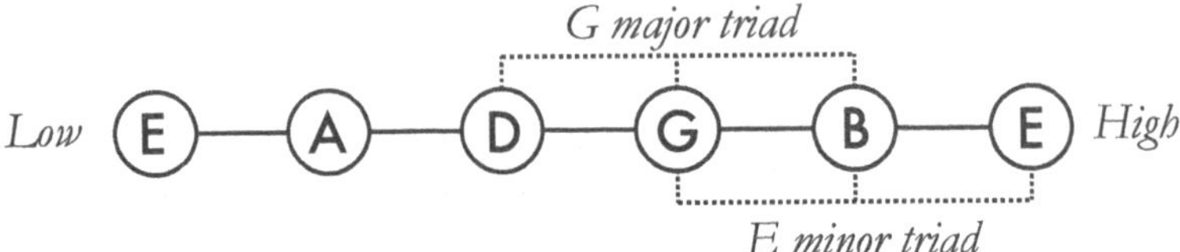

Every guitarist who tunes by ear has had difficulty with the G and B strings. It's likely that this happens because these pitches are at opposite ends of the pentatonic chain of 5ths, but are on adjacent strings on the instrument. Especially when tuning with harmonics, the ear naturally leans toward perfect 5ths in just intonation, which leaves the G and B strings nearly a quarter tone out of tune with each other. This is described in detail on the following page.

In standard tuning, the guitar gravitates toward the area of G major / E minor, but it has frets that allow for transposition. This can be seen as a mixture of ancient (just intonation) and modern (equal temperament) tuning systems, and small adjustments have to be made to reconcile the two. Just intonation has a purity to the ear but does not create a uniform chromatic scale. The semitones from the previous page vary in size, in a series of ratios that yield the octave when multiplied:

$$(16/15)(135/128)(16/15)(25/24)(16/15)(135/128)(16/15)(16/15)(25/24)(27/25)(25/24)(16/15) = 2$$

Equal temperament has a purity in its uniform logarithmic division of the octave, but requires a slight compromise of pure intervals. This is most noticeable with equal tempered major thirds, which deviate from the 5th partial by about 14 cents. The 12 semitones of the equal tempered chromatic scale are all exactly the same size, each larger than the previous by a factor of the 12th root of 2. Multiplying the 12th root of 2 by itself 12 times also yields an octave:

$$(2^{(1/12)})(2^{(1/12)})(2^{(1/12)})(2^{(1/12)})(2^{(1/12)})(2^{(1/12)})(2^{(1/12)})(2^{(1/12)})(2^{(1/12)})(2^{(1/12)})(2^{(1/12)})(2^{(1/12)}) = 2$$

With these two systems pulling at one another, the guitar can be seen to have a kind of harmonic duality, a blend of the rational and the irrational. The following page explores the tuning of the guitar with this concept in mind.

Exercise

TUNING THE GUITAR

- Detune all strings. To match pitches, slowly raise the tuning while listening for the beats between the two notes to slow down and disappear.
- Tune the open A string to a tuning fork or some other source (4th partial = A 440).
- Tune the 3rd partial of the D string to match the 4th partial of the A string.
- Tune the 3rd partial of the G string to match the 4th partial of the D string.
- Tune the 4th partial of the low E string to match the 3rd partial of the A string.
- Tune the open B string to match the 3rd partial of the low E string.
- Tune the open high E string to match the 3rd partial of the A string.

The guitar is now tuned in just intonation, with the A string as the fundamental.
- Compare the 4th partial of the B string with the 5th partial of the G string.
- The pitch produced by the B string should be noticeably higher.
- Play octaves or triads in different keys, and notice where things sound "out of tune."

-Detune all strings, tune the open A string to a tuning fork or some other source.
- Do as before, with these adjustments:
- When tuning the D string to the A string, push it slighty sharp (about 2 cents)
- Do the same when tuning the G string to the D string.
- When tuning the low E string to the A string, pull it slighty flat (about 2 cents)
- Do the same when tuning the B string to the low E string, and tuning the high E string to the A string.

The guitar has now been "tempered" by ear.
- Compare the 5th partial of the B string with the 4th partial of the G string.
The difference between the two pitches should be less noticeable.
- Play octaves or triads in different keys, and see if things sound more "in tune."

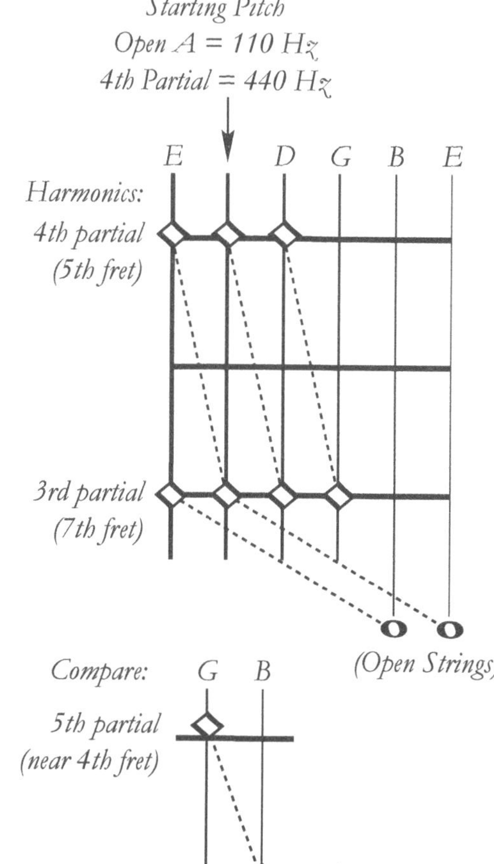

Illustration

Showing:

The numerical results of tuning in just intonation.
A 110 is used as the fundamental.
Pitches are built from A to the left and right using perfect 5ths.
The difference between the two ends of the chain is shown with dotted lines as a comparison between the 5th partial of the G string and the 4th partial of the B string, in terms of:

1) The Harmonic Ratio (the 81/80 comma)
2) Cents (the percentage of a semitone)
3) Hertz (the frequency in cycles per second)

(values in cents and Hz are rounded to the nearest whole number)

This is equivalent to the first part of the exercise above.

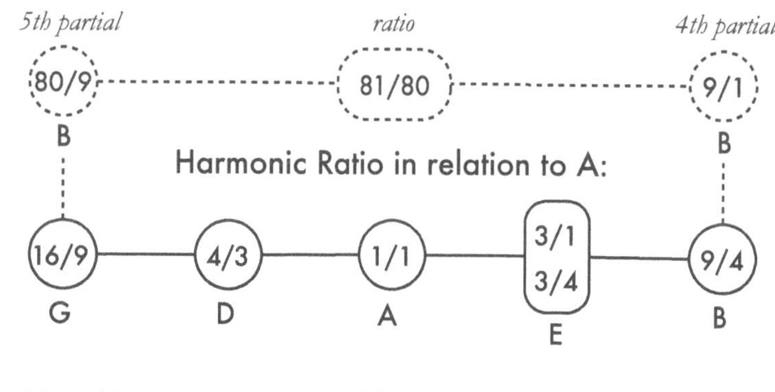

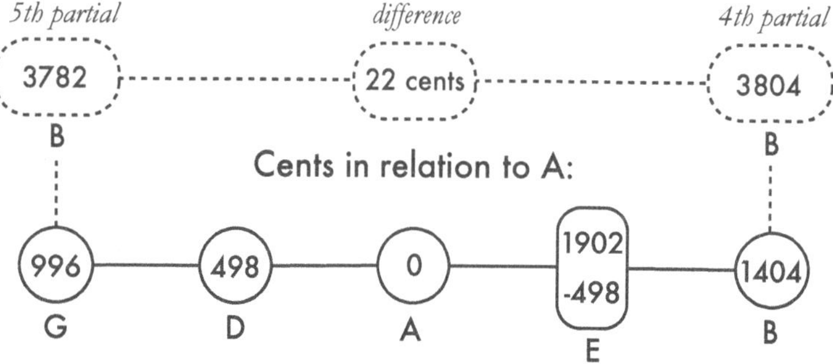

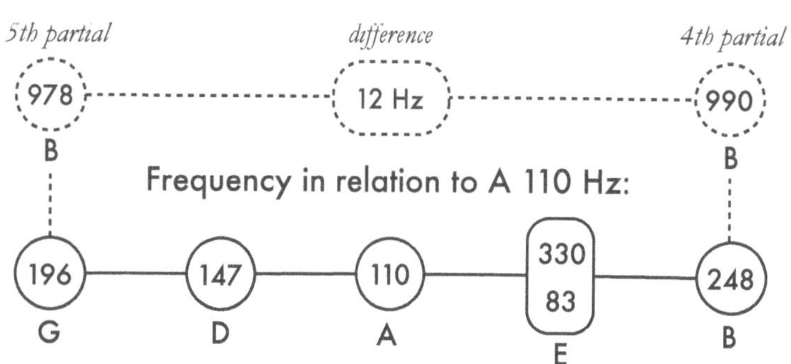

Illustration

THE HARMONIST

Design for a guitar based on the harmonic proportions of the string. Scale length: 25", Instrument length: 37.5"
Labels show diameters of harmonic circles (fundamental = 25", 2nd partial = 12.5", 4th partial = 6.25")

Fret Locations (distance from nut):

1) 1.403"
2) 2.728"
3) 3.978"
4) 5.157"
5) 6.271"
6) 7.322"
7) 8.315"
8) 9.251"
9) 10.135"
10) 10.969"
11) 11.757"
12) 12.500"
13) 13.202"
14) 13.864"
15) 14.489"
16) 15.079"
17) 15.636"
18) 16.161"
19) 16.657"
20) 17.125"
21) 17.567"
22) 17.985"
23) 18.378"
24) 18.750"

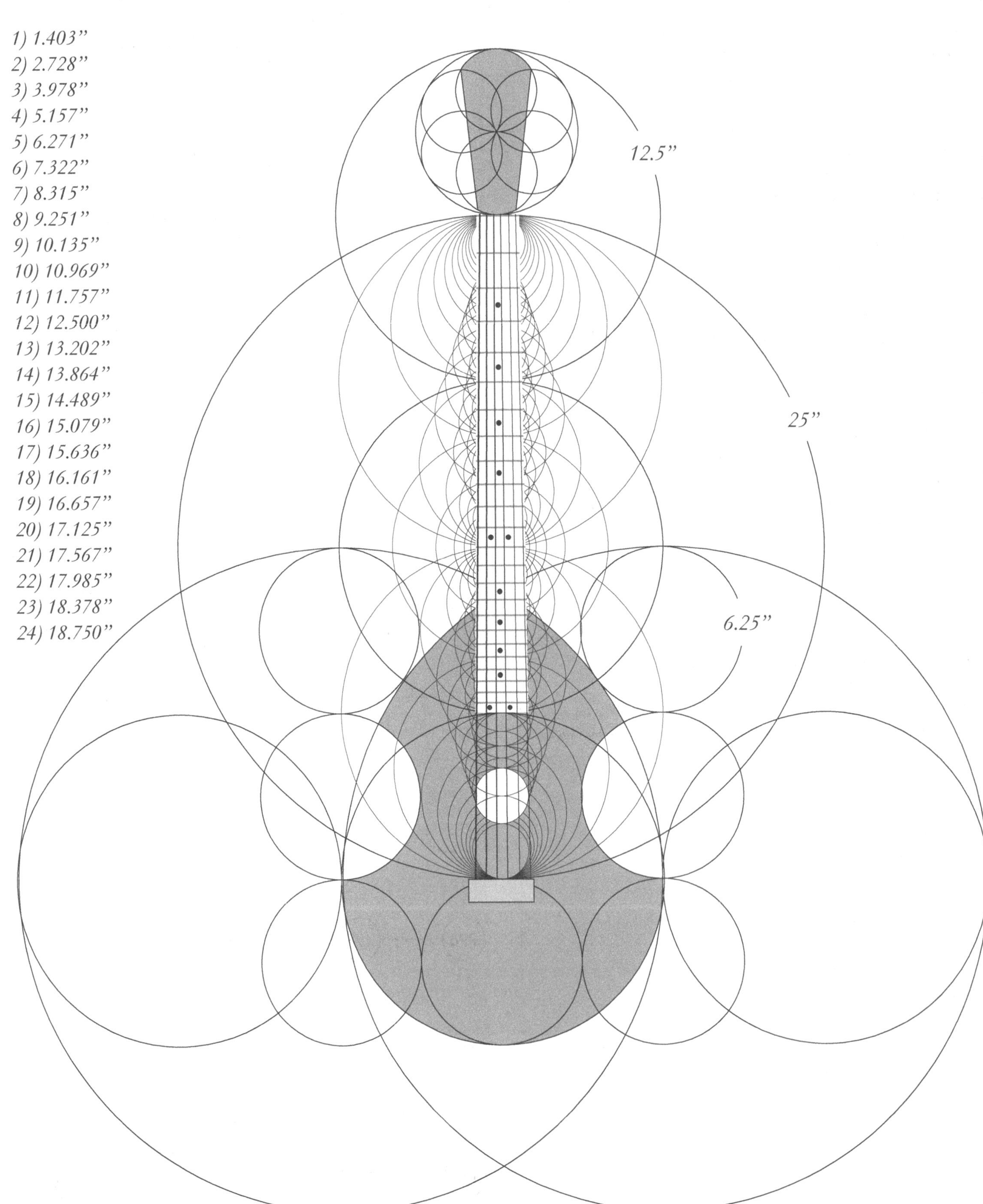

Notes *Idea: Use these pictures of the guitar neck to record the locations of interesting combinations of natural harmonics.*

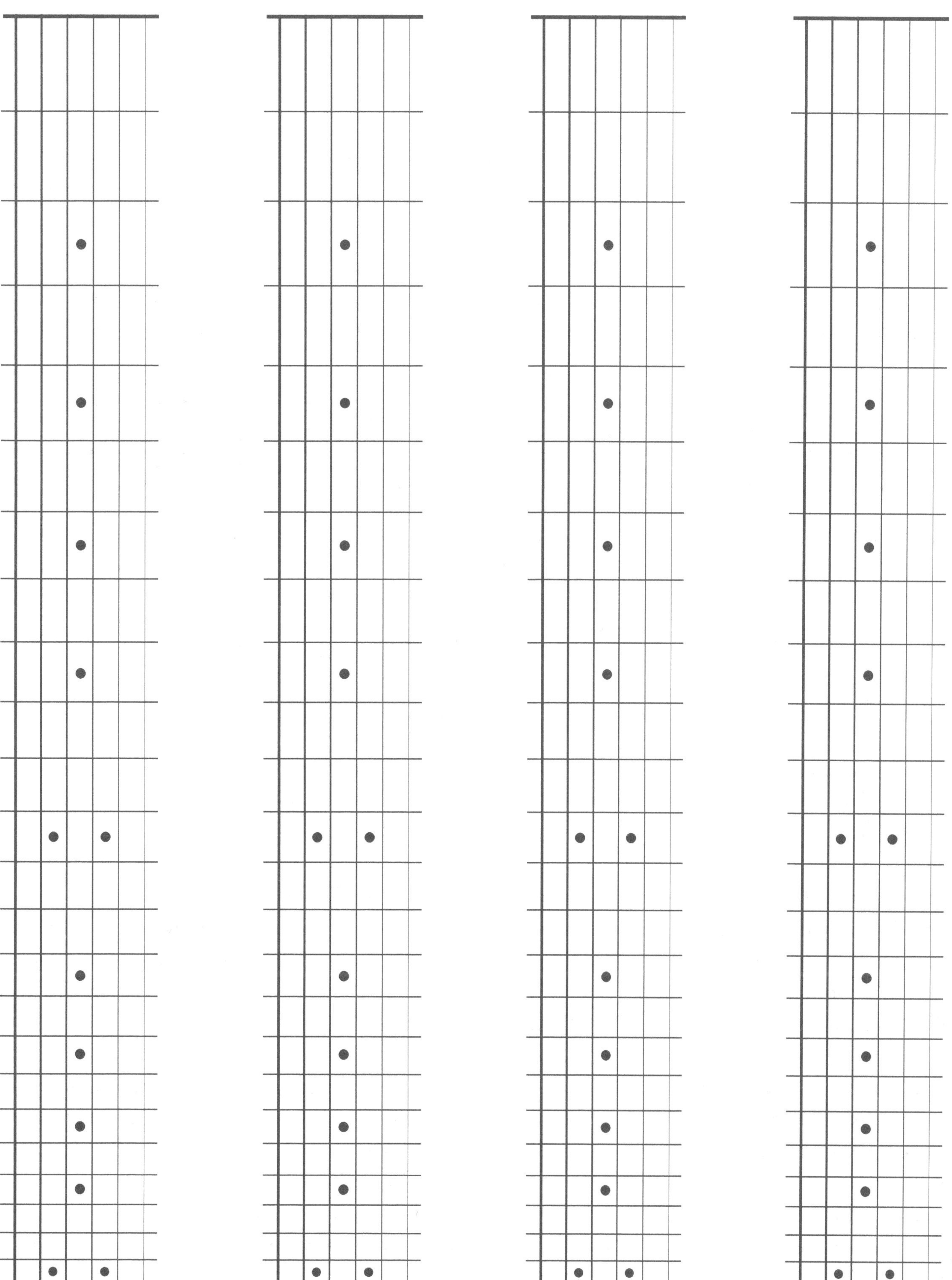

Concept

THE MONAD
(SINGLE PITCH)

Here are the strings and neck of a typical guitar:

On this 24-fret guitar, there are 144 possible stopped pitch locations and 6 open strings. Here is the fretboard only, showing possible finger placements as black nodes and open strings as white circles:

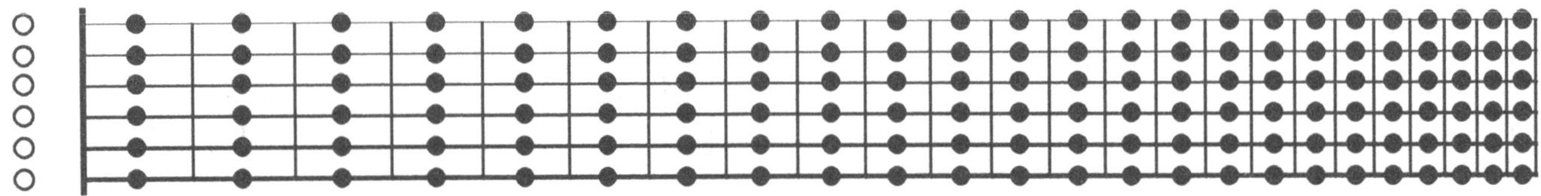

About 2/3 of these pitches are duplicates. In this case, there are 49 unique pitches out of 150 possibilities. The location of each unique pitch closest to the nut would look like this:

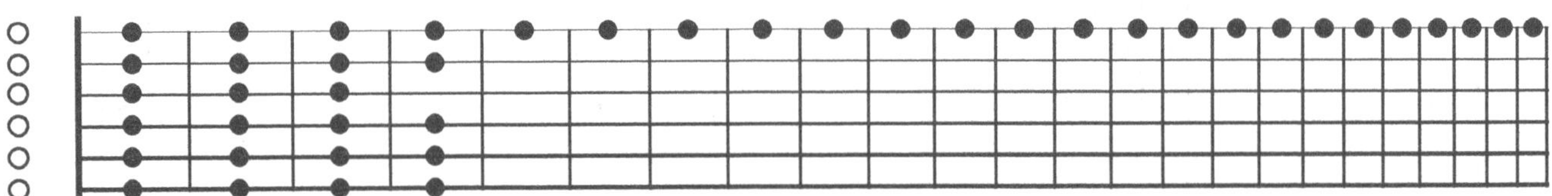

All other locations are alternate versions of these unique pitches, which differ in timbre because of the varying sonic qualities of each string. Negotiating this range of options is a fundamental challenge for the guitarist.

To understand this better, consider the guitar fretboard as a two dimensional grid, with the strings in one direction and the frets in another, where any pitch location can be described by two coordinates (x, y) that correspond to string and fret. We can compare this to the linear model of the piano, where only one coordinate is needed. For example, middle C on the piano has one location, but middle C on the guitar can be found at: (2,1), (3,5), (4,10), (5,15), and (6,20).

The illustration on the following page visualizes this concept for the entire guitar. Each string of the guitar is mapped onto a section of the piano. Lines connecting the keys of the piano to an exploded view of the six strings show how many possible fingerings there are for any given pitch. The strings are then reassembled on the fretboard grid, retaining the coloring of the piano keyboard. This piano/guitar comparison is essentially a mapping from one to two dimensions, where one dimension on the guitar (lengthwise, down the neck) is chromatic, and the other (laterally, across the neck) is pentatonic.

Illustration

MAPPING BETWEEN PIANO AND GUITAR

Showing: *Four Octave Piano Keyboard, Exploded Guitar, Normal Guitar (24 frets).*
Lines from piano keys to exploded guitar show number of possible fingerings on guitar for any given pitch.
Colors on normal guitar show correlation to black and white keys on the piano. Middle C in grey. (Drawn to Scale)

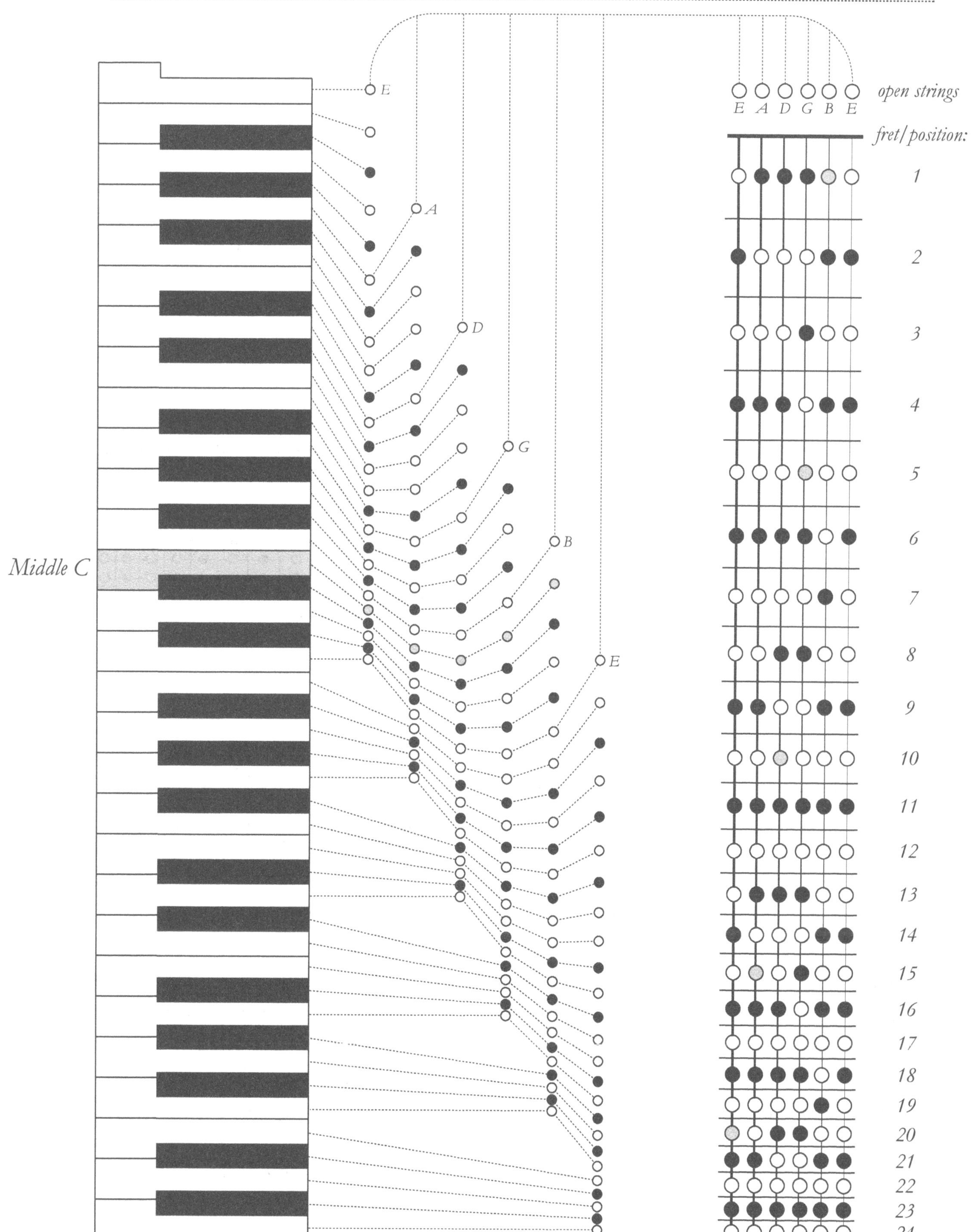

Concept

THE PENTATONIC SKELETON

Take a chromatic scale, and select seven pitches to form a diatonic scale in any key. The remaining five pitches will form a pentatonic scale in a key a tritone away. This is seen clearly on the piano, where the white keys are a diatonic scale in C, and the black keys are a pentatonic scale in Gb. The diatonic and pentatonic are complementary, meaning that the positive space of one is the negative space of the other, and together they make all 12 tones. We could visualize this on a chromatic line:

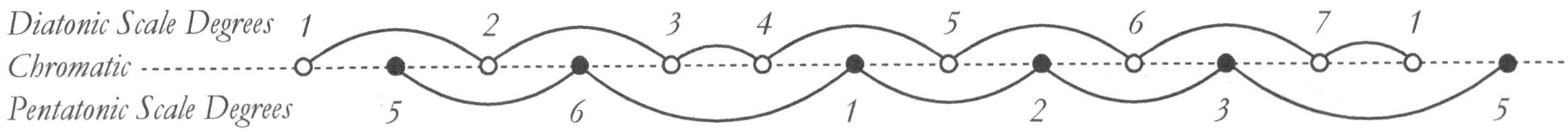

The pattern is cyclical, so it could also be bent into a circle:

Circle: Chromatic
Exterior: Diatonic
Interior: Pentatonic

The piano-derived guitar diagram on the previous page showed the pitches of Gb major pentatonic in black. Here is a closely related image, with the pitches of G major pentatonic in black. This corresponds to the pitches of the open strings, and every other location of those pitches on the instrument.

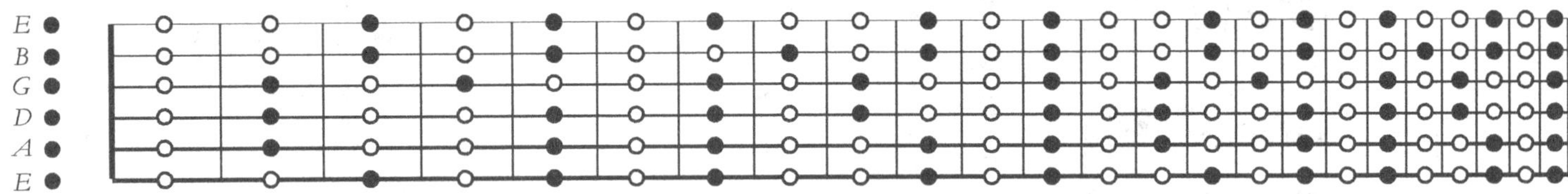

Removing the negative space (the Db diatonic scale) exposes the fundamental tonal architecture of the guitar, a repeating pentatonic skeleton that divides the space into five regions:

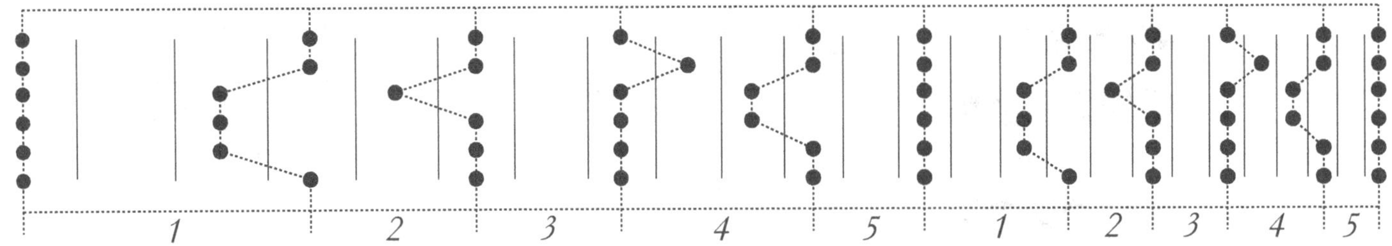

This formation is the template that determines the shape of things on the guitar. It's hard to overstate the importance of understanding this concept. These pentatonic regions are the containers that hold all tonal information on the guitar, which must flow into their asymmetrical shape. Transposition is equivalent to moving these shapes up or down the length of the neck, but the template itself does not change - it is built into the standard tuning of the instrument. Like trying to draw a straight line on a sphere, playing the guitar always involves motion on an irregular surface that distorts the material to fit its contours. For guitarists who desire a uniform, pattern-based system, this can be a continual source of frustration, and easy solutions (such as tuning in pure fourths) are available. But there is another way to see it, which is to recognize the guitar's roots in pentatonics and create structures that take advantage of the beauty of this natural harmonic foundation. The broken symmetry of the pentatonic skeleton can be seen as a reflection of nature - based on fundamental principles, but mysterious and unquantifiable in the multitude of forms that it can make.

THE FIVE REGIONS

Each of the five regions defined by the pentatonic scale has its own sonic shape and character. Practicing and internalizing them individually and connecting one to another can gradually lead to an ability to see the entire template as one fluid structure. The figure below shows the pentatonic skeleton broken into five parts. Below each region are descriptions in terms of scale degrees from two perspectives:

1) Global - scale degrees refer to the major pentatonic that governs the entire structure.
2) Local - scale degrees refer to the internal structure of the region, with the first pitch as the root.

White circles are locations of the root of the major key.

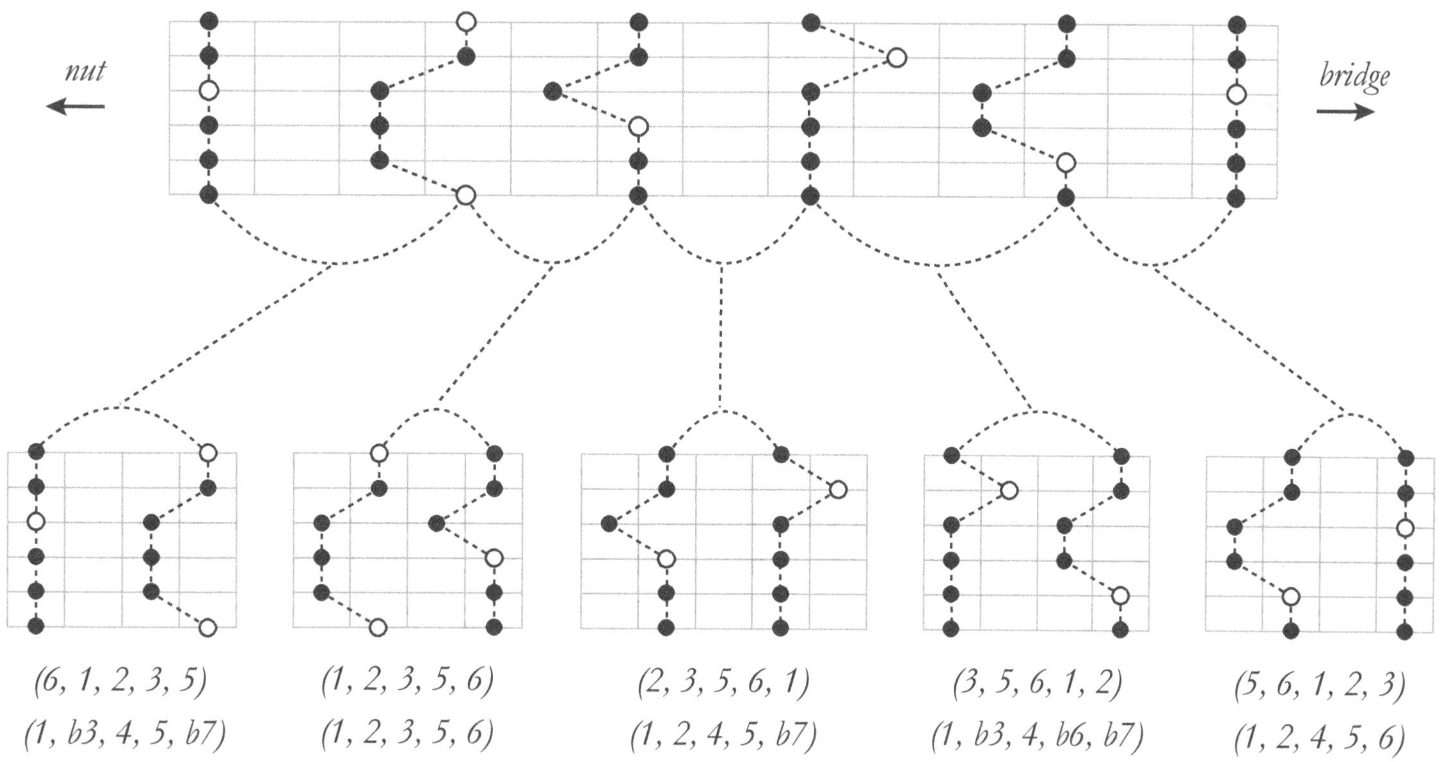

Scale degrees in terms of: 1) The root of the global key
2) The beginning of the local mode

These shapes all have two notes per string, which works well with a binary picking pattern (alternating up and down with a pick, or between two fingers without a pick). The formations also fall naturally under the hand, never requiring a stretch beyond four frets.

In the course of practicing, try these two approaches:
1) Series - all regions in one key, up and down the neck
2) Parallel - all keys in one area of the neck

A strong feel for these foundational structures will help with every other area of study on the guitar. The exercise on the following page can help make this topic more interesting and practical by using improvisation as a tool for internalization.

Exercise

THE MODULATION GAME

for two musicians (or one musician and a recording)

Musician 1:
- Play a perfect 5th in any key, in any tempo, with any kind of groove, rhythmic figure, or time cycle.
- Change to a new key at regular intervals of time (e.g. every 8 bars).

Musician 2:
- Staying in one position, improvise using the pentatonic scale that corresponds to the key being played by Musician 1.
- Use the ear only (don't look at the fingers of the other musician).

- After a while, trade roles.
(to practice without a partner, make a recorded loop that is too long to memorize, and play along with it)

Variations:
1) Improvise a continuous melody through the point of modulation, making as few mistakes as possible
2) Play a single pitch from the previous key at the exact point of modulation. Figure out how this pitch relates to the new key, and move into the new key accordingly.
3) Do the same as (2), with the added requirement that the first note in the new key has to be the root.
4) Create and memorize a melody in one key. After the modulation, repeat this melody in the new key, in the same area of the guitar (this is good for musicians with perfect pitch, since this skill will not be very useful in this context).
5) Change the relationship of the perfect 5th to the scale being used. For example, instead of playing in the major key, use the perfect fifth in reference to one of the other four pentatonic "modes." Start by using the "minor pentatonic" mode (1, b3, 4, 5, b7) as the home key for each modulation cycle.
6) Return to this exercise with other types of scales and modes that are found in later sections of the book.

The pentatonic regions corresponding to all twelve keys can be played in any six fret span of the guitar. Here are the formations for a complete trip through the circle of fifths spanning frets 5 - 10. The position is labeled on the upper left of each fretboard, and the major and relative minor key is given. Consider beginning the exercise above with this set of fingerings, which are in a comfortable location in the middle range of the instrument.

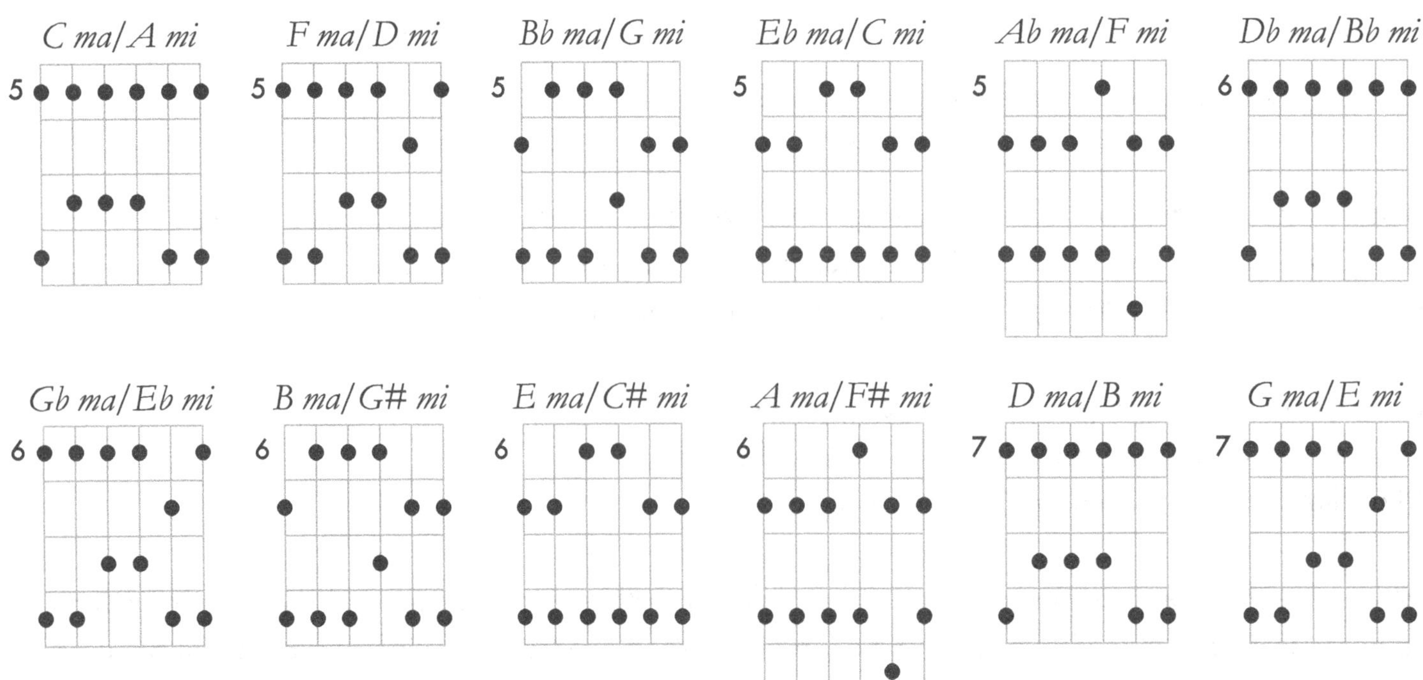

CREATING THE DIATONIC MODES

Showing:

The five regions of the fretboard defined by the Pentatonic Scale.
The addition of a chain of tritones to create the Diatonic Scale.
The division of the Diatonic template into five modes.
All diagrams show Pentatonic regions with dotted lines.

○ = *root of key center*

● = *other pitches*

Pentatonic + Tritones = Diatonic

Individual Modes:
(with common name)

Aeolian

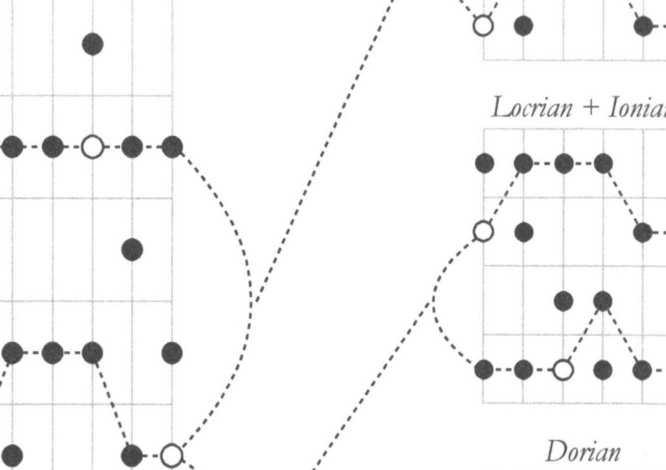

Locrian + Ionian

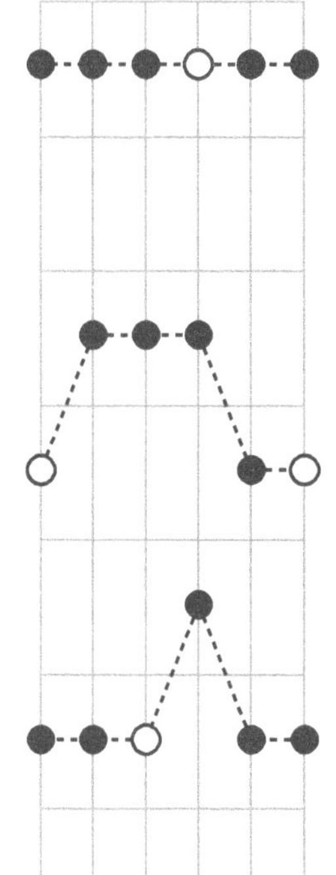

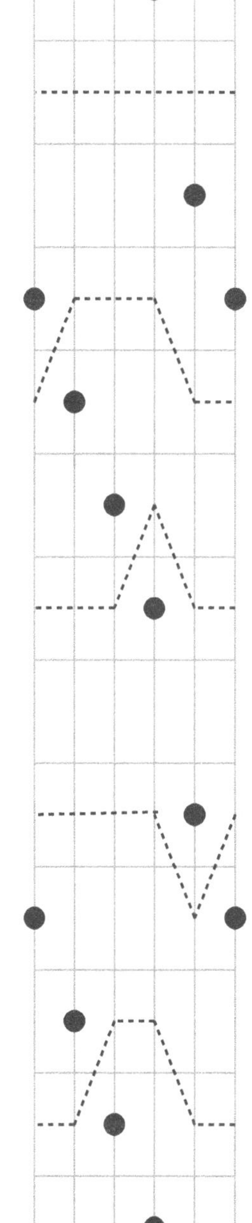

Dorian

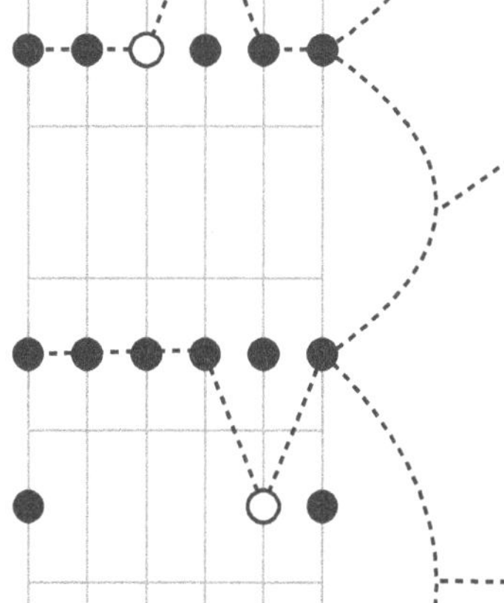

Phrygian + Lydian

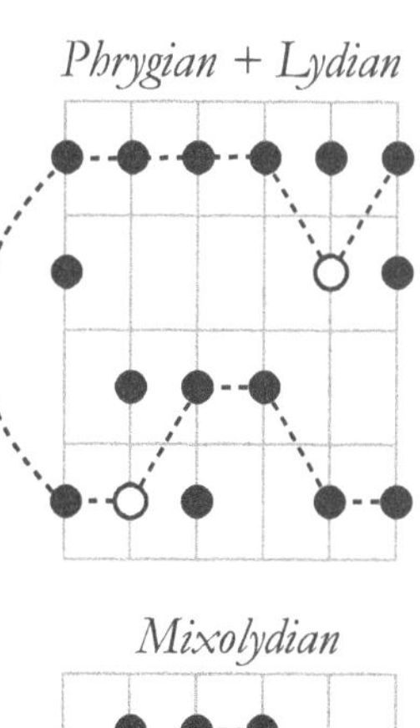

Mixolydian

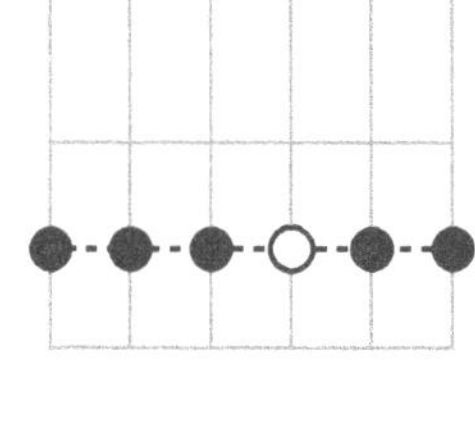

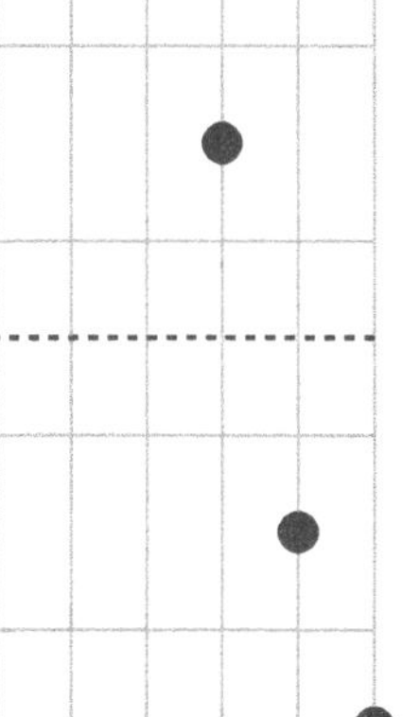

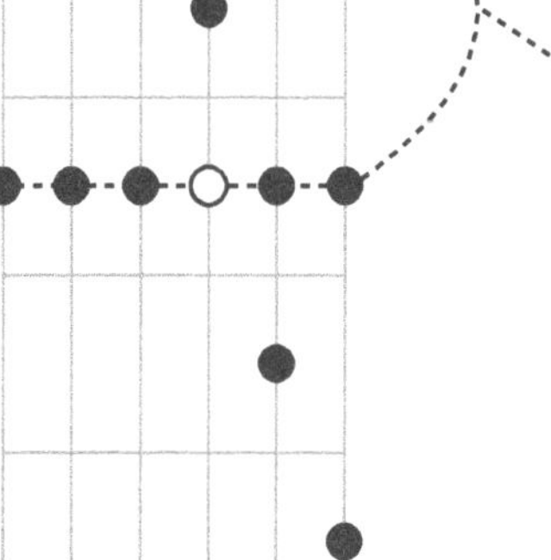

Exercise

DIATONIC MODES IN SERIES

One Key, Five Positions.
○ = *root of key center, and* ● = *other pitches*
Shown with fretboard diagram and staff notation (with guitar transposition) in G major.
See Part II of this book for versions of these modes using Symmetrical Picking and Legato articulation.

- Memorize and Internalize these five modes in all keys until they are automatic.
- Practice all five modes while singing a pedal tone on the tonic (or another pitch)

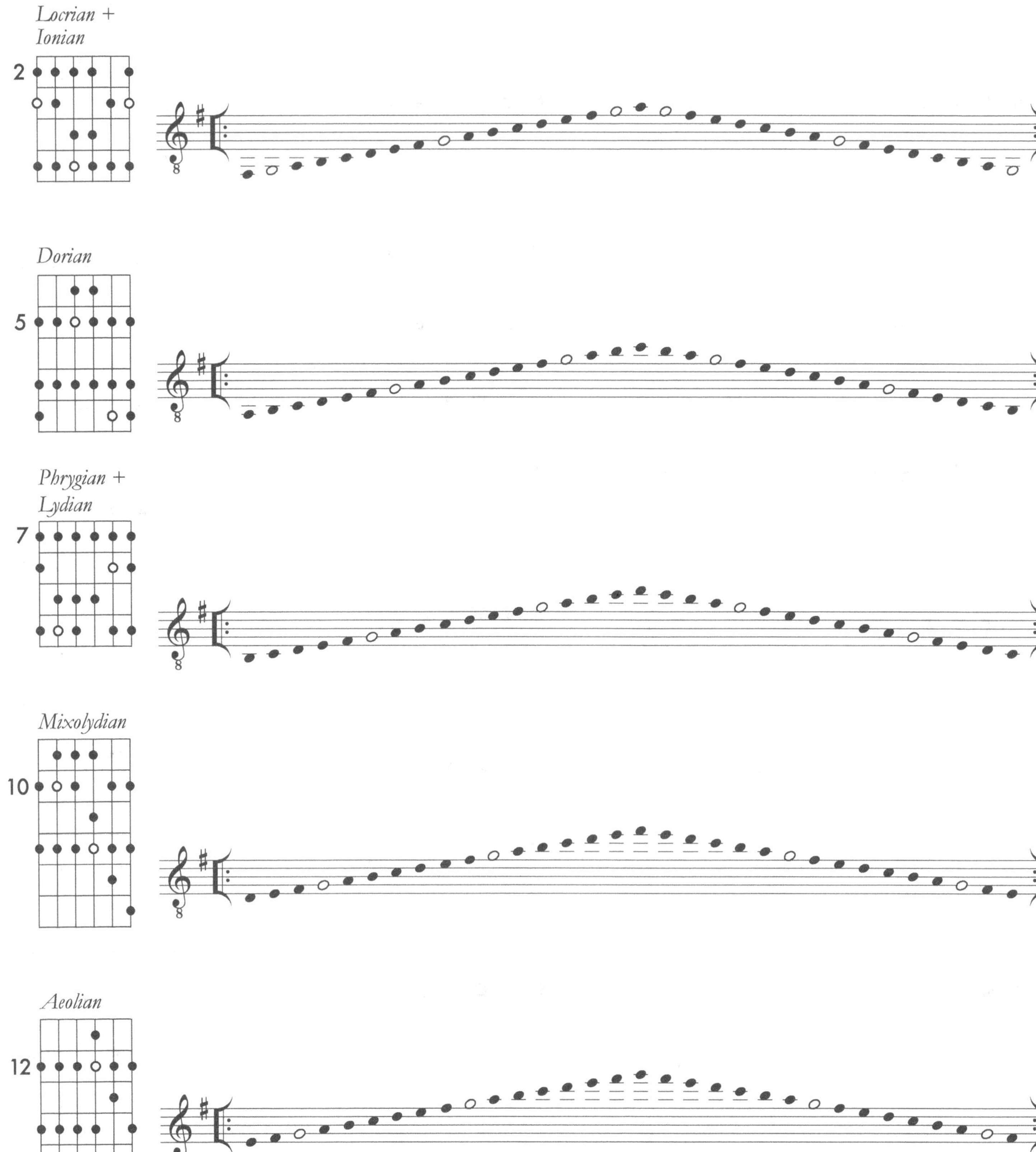

Exercise

DIATONIC MODES IN PARALLEL

One Position, Five Keys
○ = root of key center, and ● = other pitches
Shown with fretboard diagram and staff notation (with guitar transposition) with changing key signatures.
See Part II of this book for versions of this page with Symmetrical Picking and Legato articulation.

- *Practice the modes in sequence while singing a pedal tone on the tonic. The pedal tone will move through the Circle of Fifths.*
- *After five keys, move the entire pattern up a semitone to continue. Ascend through 12 positions to play all modes in all keys.*
- *Reverse the sequence, descending on the fretboard while singing the pedal tone in the opposite direction.*

Mixolydian

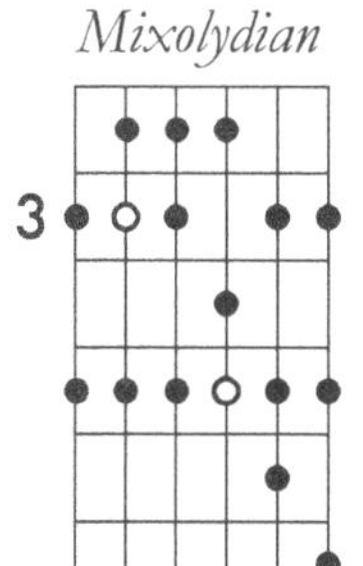

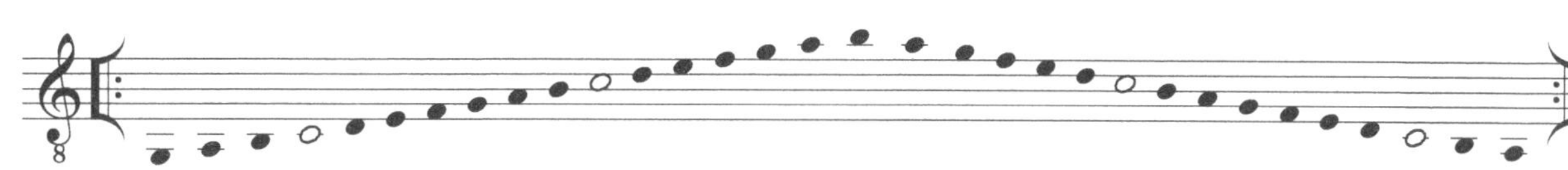

Dorian

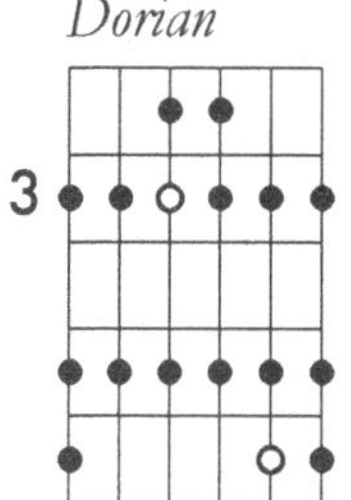

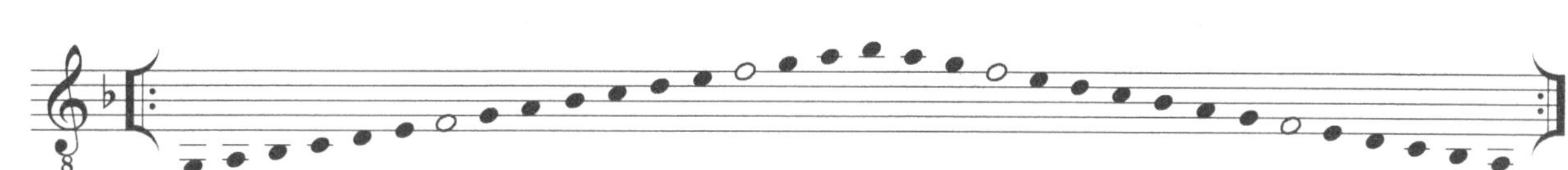

Aeolian

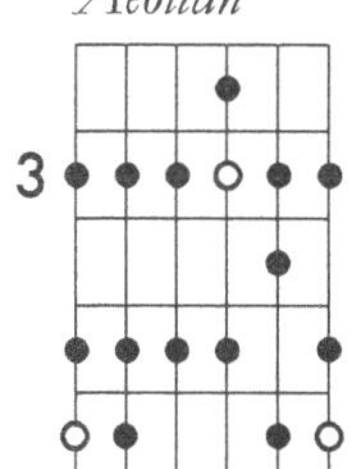

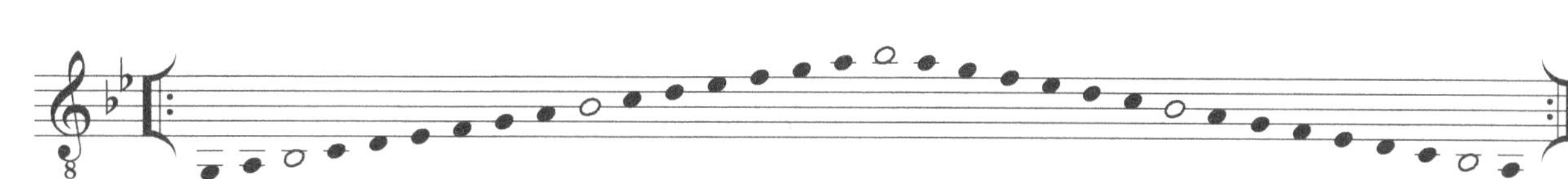

Phrygian + Lydian

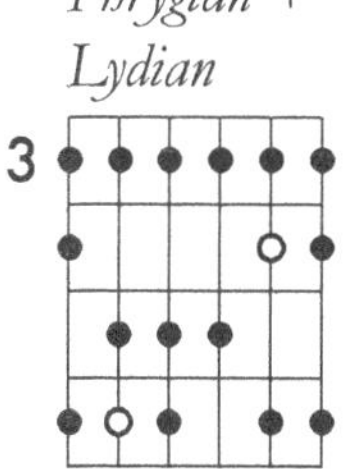

Locrian + Ionian

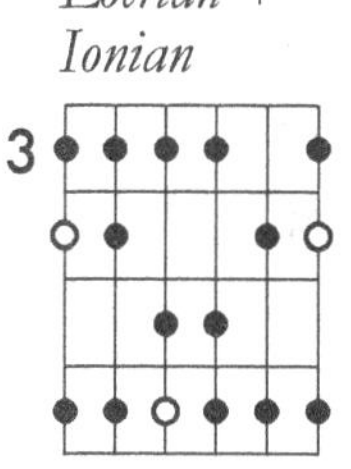

Concept

THE CASE FOR AND AGAINST PATTERNS

A pentatonic scale can be created from a chain of five perfect 5ths:

Extending this chain to seven perfect 5ths creates a diatonic scale:

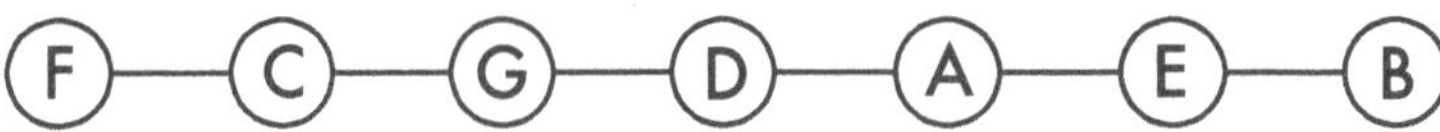

The far ends of this chain are a *tritone* apart. The diatonic can be thought of as an expanded version of the pentatonic, with added 4th and 7th scale degrees that form this tritone. Here is the same comparison on pitch circles, which can be transposed to any key:

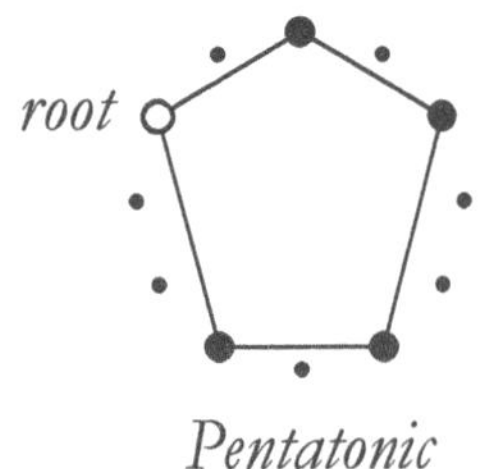

Pentatonic

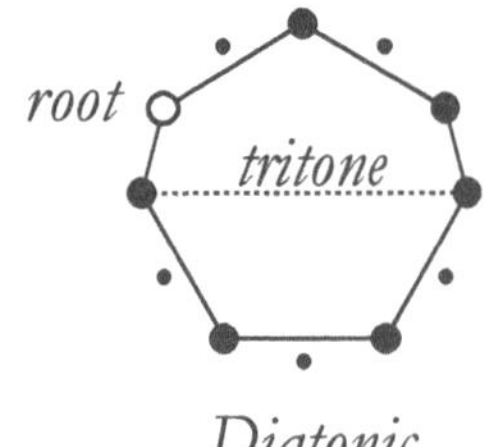

Diatonic

One of twelve possible chromatic pitch circles (right): On this circle, the two shapes to the left would be the Bb pentatonic and diatonic scales.

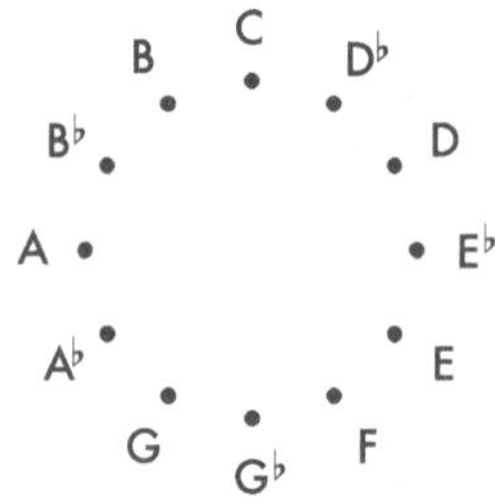

The greater density of the diatonic scale greatly increases the intervallic content between the pitches. Within the pentatonic scale, there are 10 possible ways to move from one pitch to another, and 4 different interval types. Within the diatonic scale, there are 21 possible ways to move from one pitch to another, and 6 different interval types.

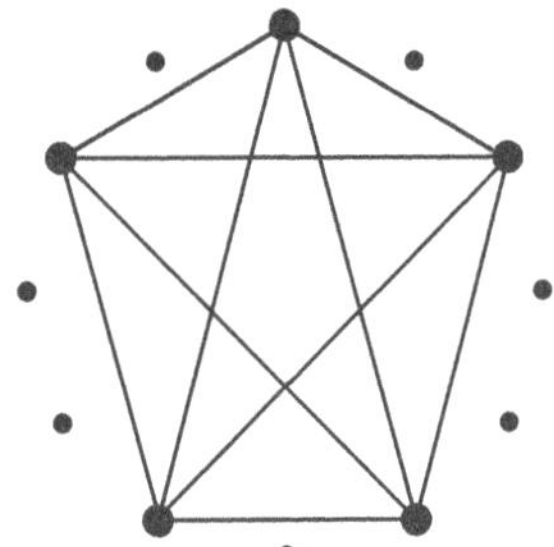

1 version of 4/8 semitones
2 versions of 3/9 semitones
3 versions of 2/10 semitones
4 versions of 5/7 semitones

1 version of 6 semitones
2 versions of 1/11 semitones
3 versions of 4/8 semitones
4 versions of 3/9 semitones
5 versions of 2/10 semitones
6 versions of 5/7 semitones

Note that intervals are shown as complementary pairs. For example, the presence of a perfect 4th (5 semitones) implies a perfect 5th (7 semitones) as well, because moving up by one and down by the other will arrive at the same pitch.

Notice that the diatonic scale contains a different number of every type of interval. This implies that a regimen of training with the diatonic scale will also include a full survey all possible intervallic movements. Hard-wired, instantaneous access to these movements can be a huge benefit to a musician, and thorough study can be made with patterns, which are useful for building muscle memory, dexterity, endurance, and other motor skills.

Unfortunately, patterns can also be tedious and creatively empty. One way to maximize the physical benefit of patterns is to eliminate redundancies by practicing only unique movements. The table on the following page shows that there are only 12 unique movements using two-note cells of an octave or smaller, ascending or descending through the scale. Redundant patterns are grouped together. This is a good place to start. It is followed by a similar, much longer study of three-note cells. A motivated guitarist will find that a short calisthenic warmup with a few of these shapes can lead to rapid physical progress and serve as good preparation for the muscles and mind to do creative work.

Exercise

12 TWO-NOTE DIATONIC PATTERNS

Use these patterns in conjunction with any of the five diatonic modes, in any key (examples here are in C major), Two ways of naming the same movement in terms of a two note cell are given in each box. The graph shows the pattern's shape. The cell is described with numbers, where (13) is an ascending third, (41) is a descending fourth, etc.
- While playing, think about the pattern in terms of either of the two cells, and make a note of which one makes the most sense.

Ascending by Diatonic Steps

(13) ... etc
or
(21) ... etc

(14) ... etc
or
(31) ... etc

(15) ... etc
or
(41) ... etc

(16) ... etc
or
(51) ... etc

(17) ... etc
or
(61) ... etc

(18) ... etc
or
(71) ... etc

Descending by Diatonic Steps

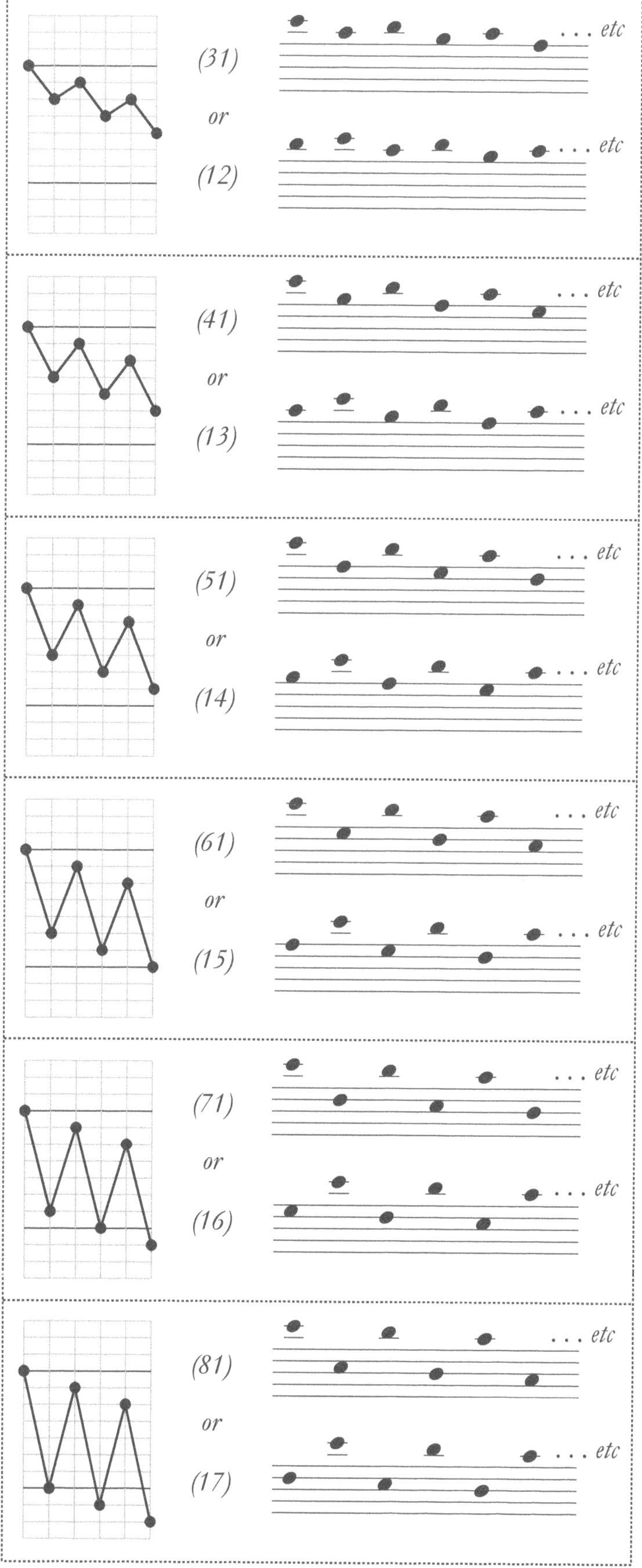

Exercise

62 THREE-NOTE DIATONIC PATTERNS

The 62 possible physical movements created by three note diatonic cells ascending or descending by diatonic steps.
Cells are limited to an octave span. Redundancies are shown in the three possible cells that can create each physical pattern.
- Practice the patterns in any key, any position.
- Think about the pattern in terms of each of the three cells, and make a note of which one makes the most sense.

Ascending by Diatonic Steps

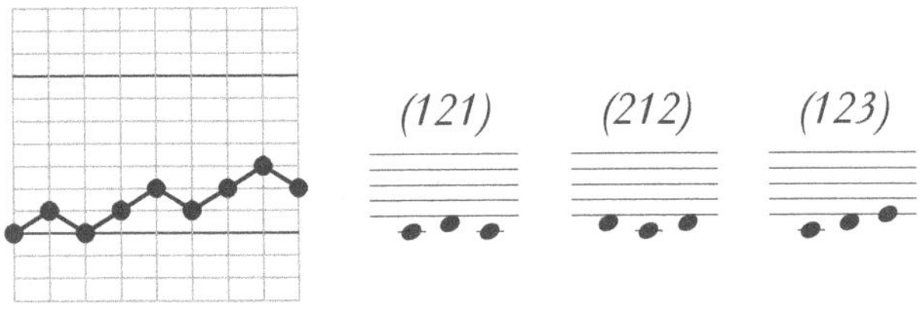

(121)
(212)
(123)

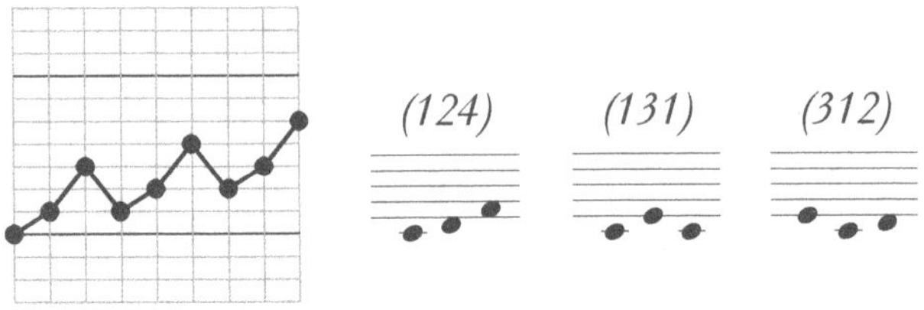

(124)
(131)
(312)

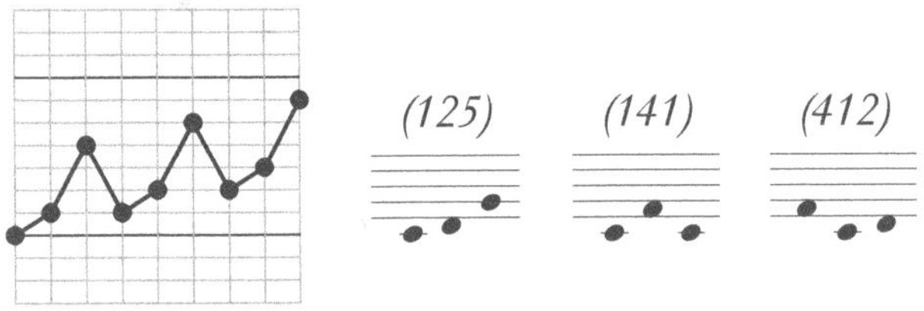

(125)
(141)
(412)

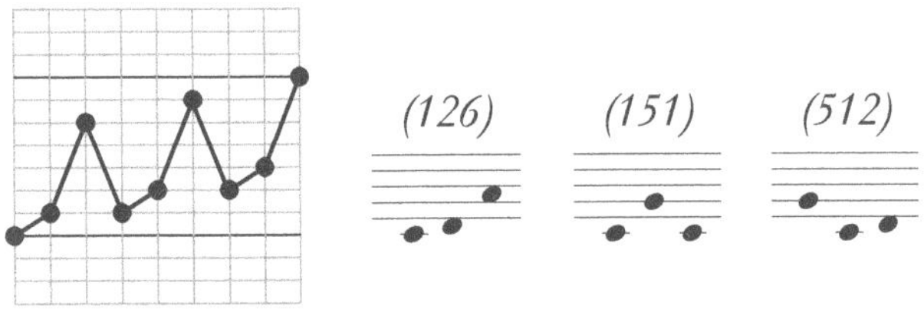

(126)
(151)
(512)

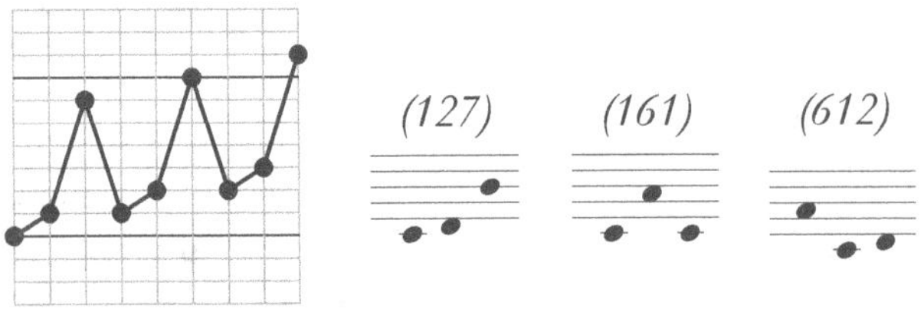

(127)
(161)
(612)

(128)
(171)
(712)

Descending by Diatonic Steps

(212)
(121)
(321)

(431)
(313)
(132)

(541)
(414)
(143)

(651)
(515)
(154)

(761)
(616)
(165)

(871)
(717)
(176)

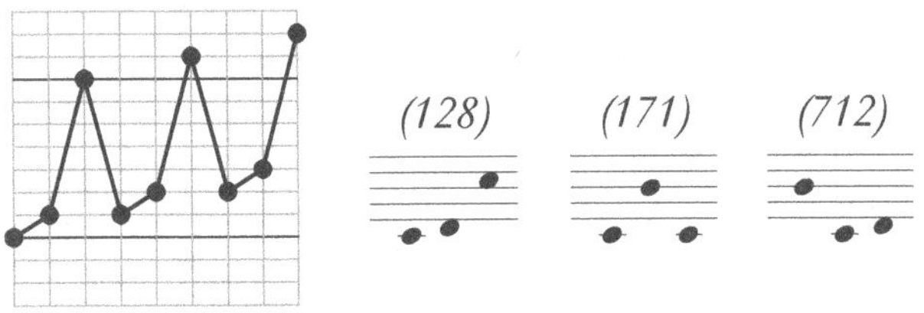

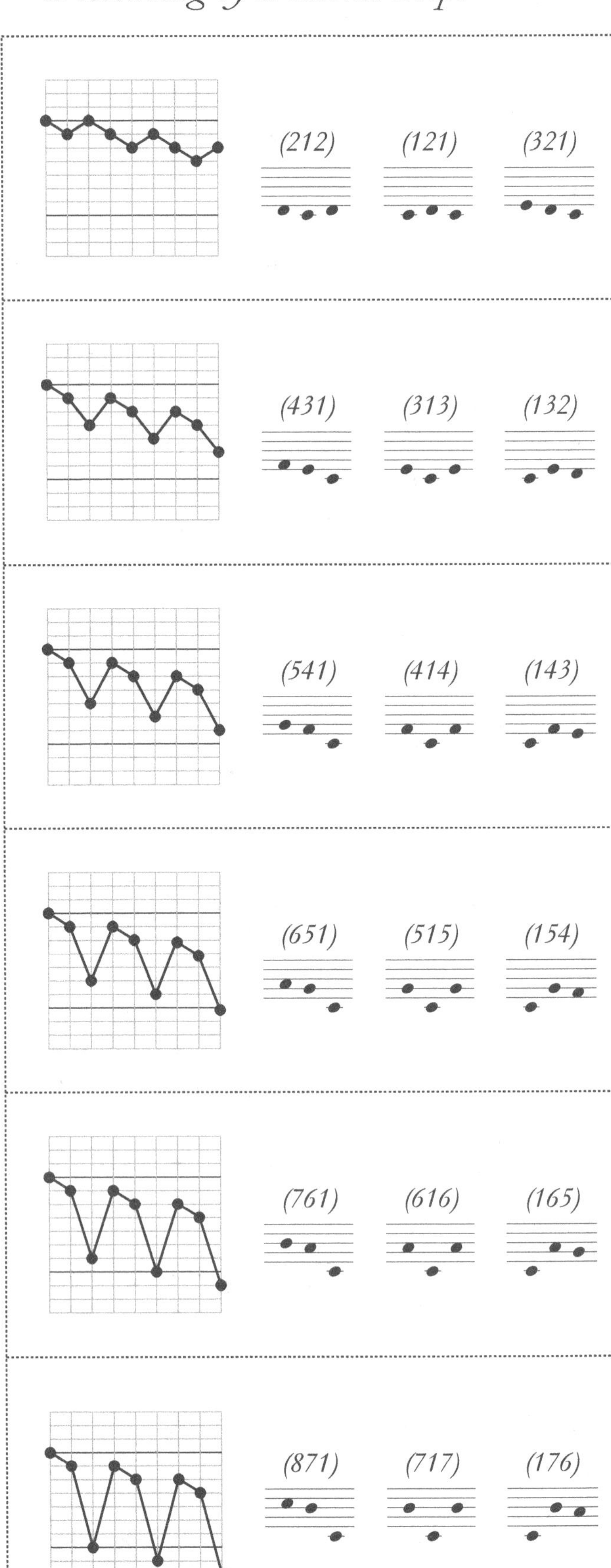

Exercise

Ascending by Diatonic Steps

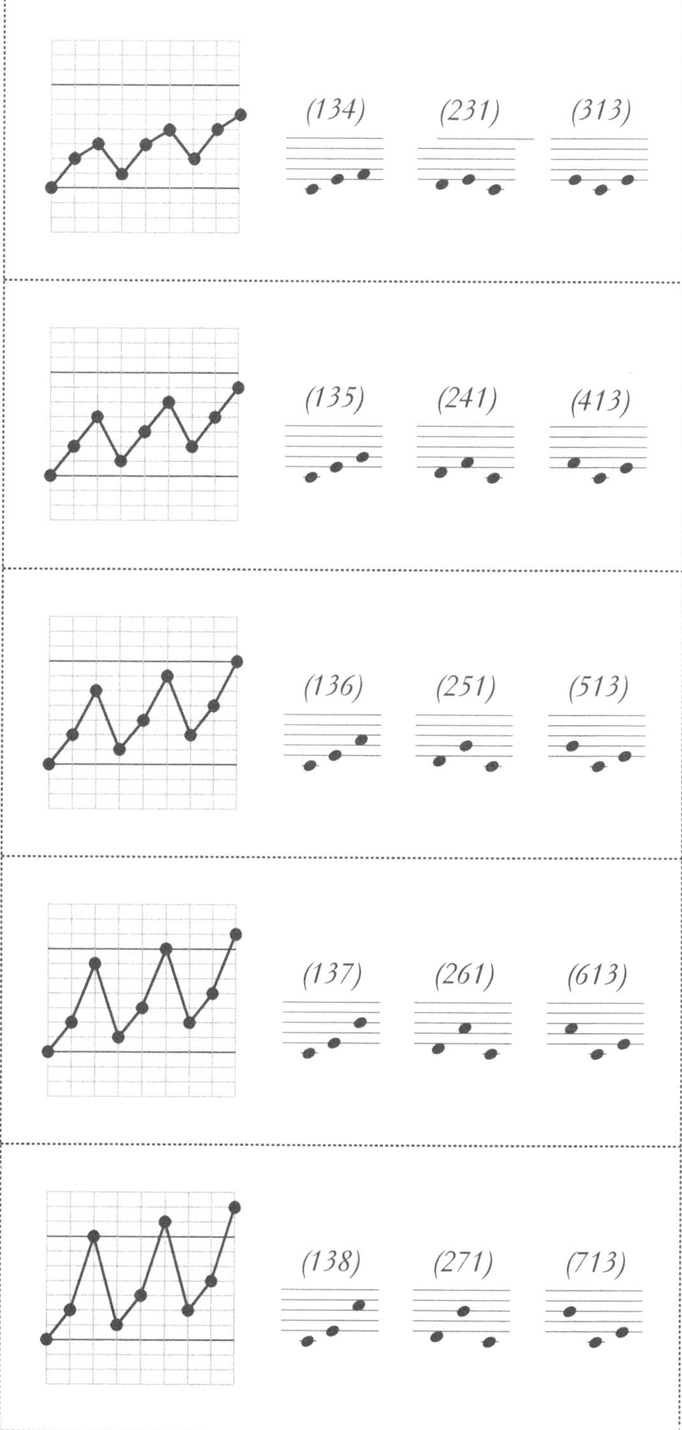

Descending by Diatonic Steps

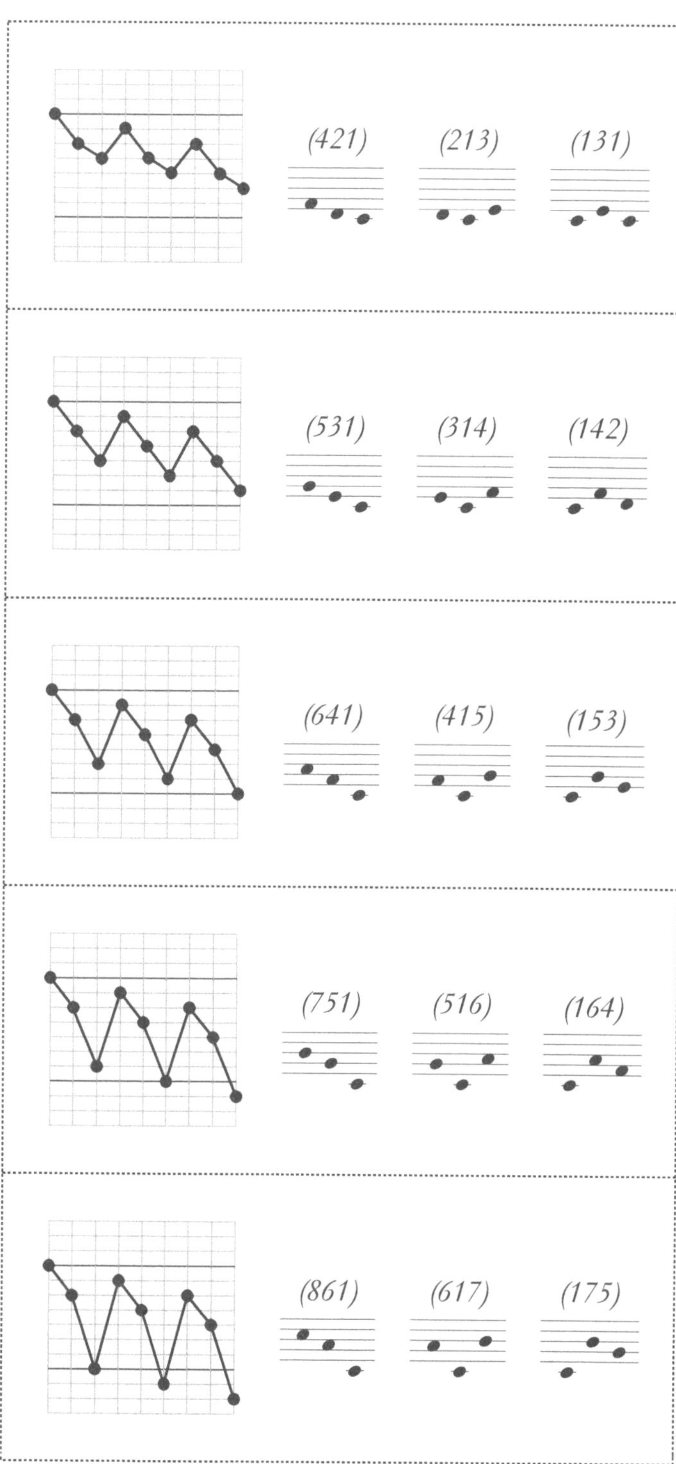

Exercise

Ascending by Diatonic Steps

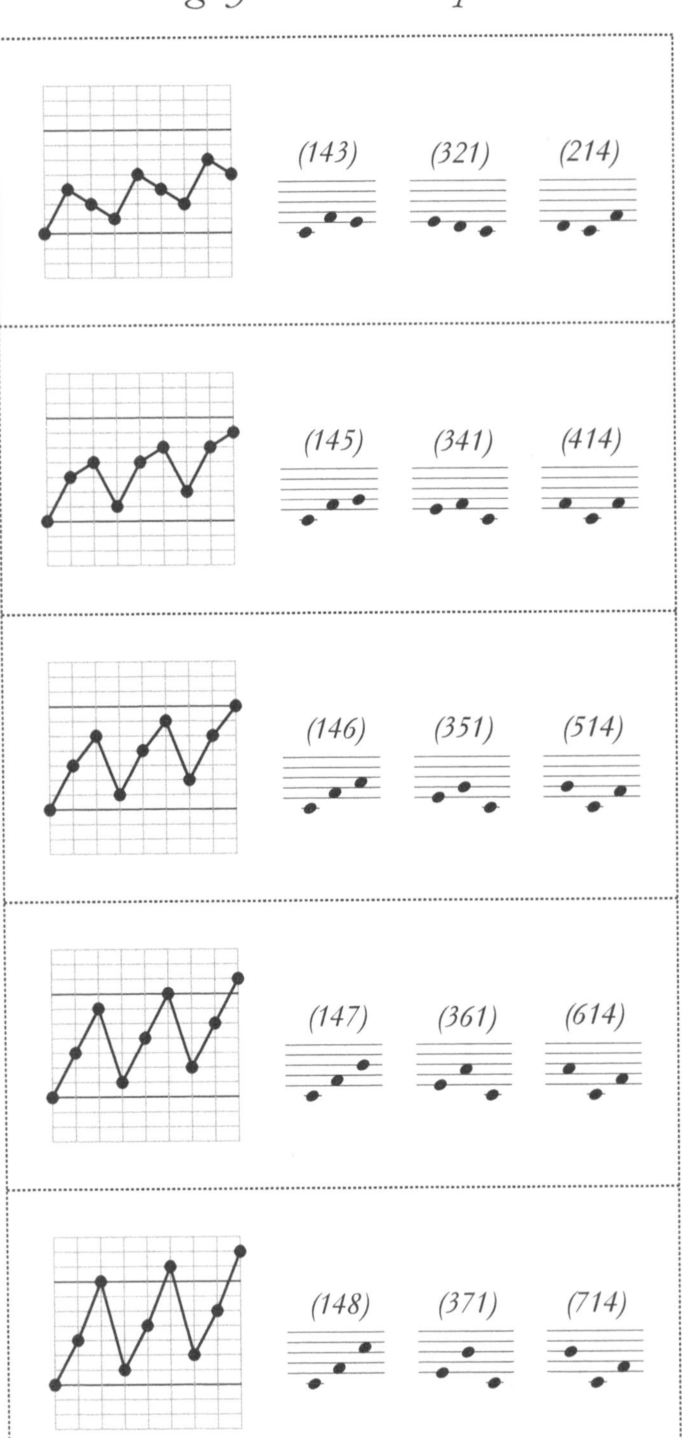

Descending by Diatonic Steps

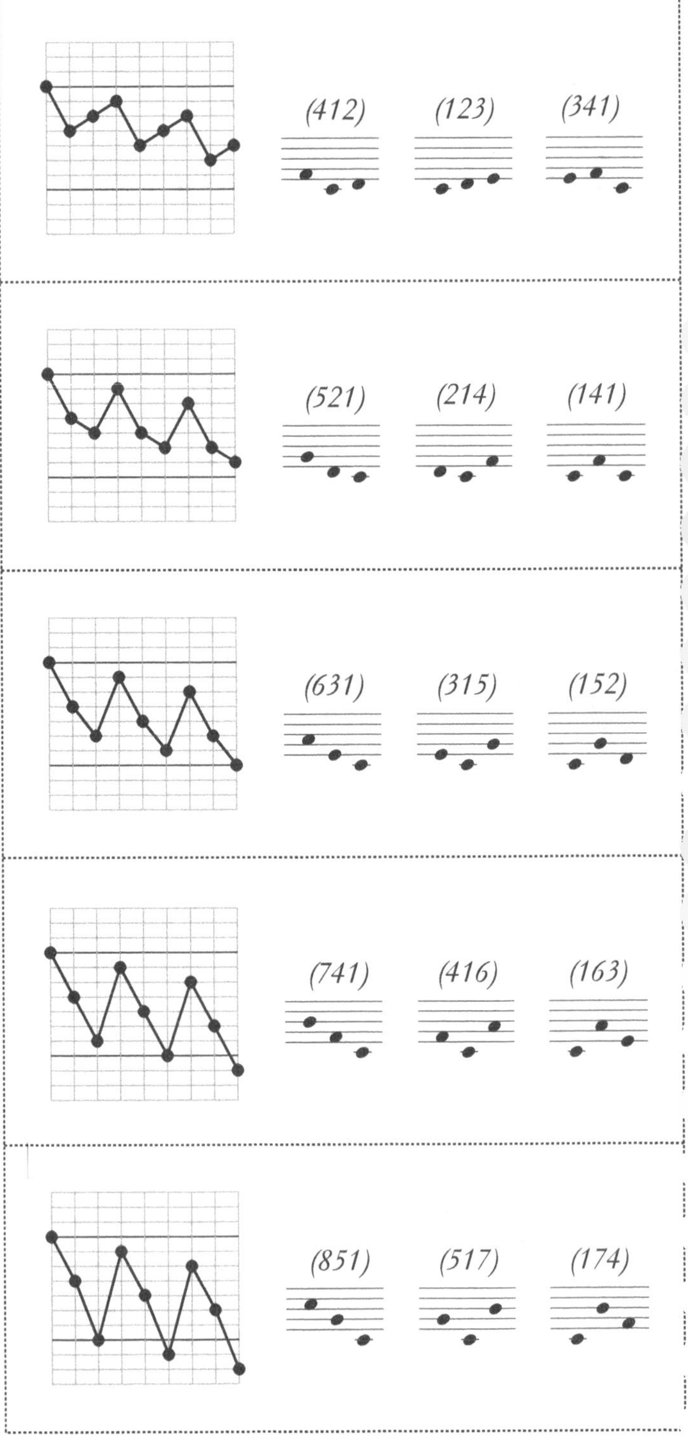

Exercise

Ascending by Diatonic Steps

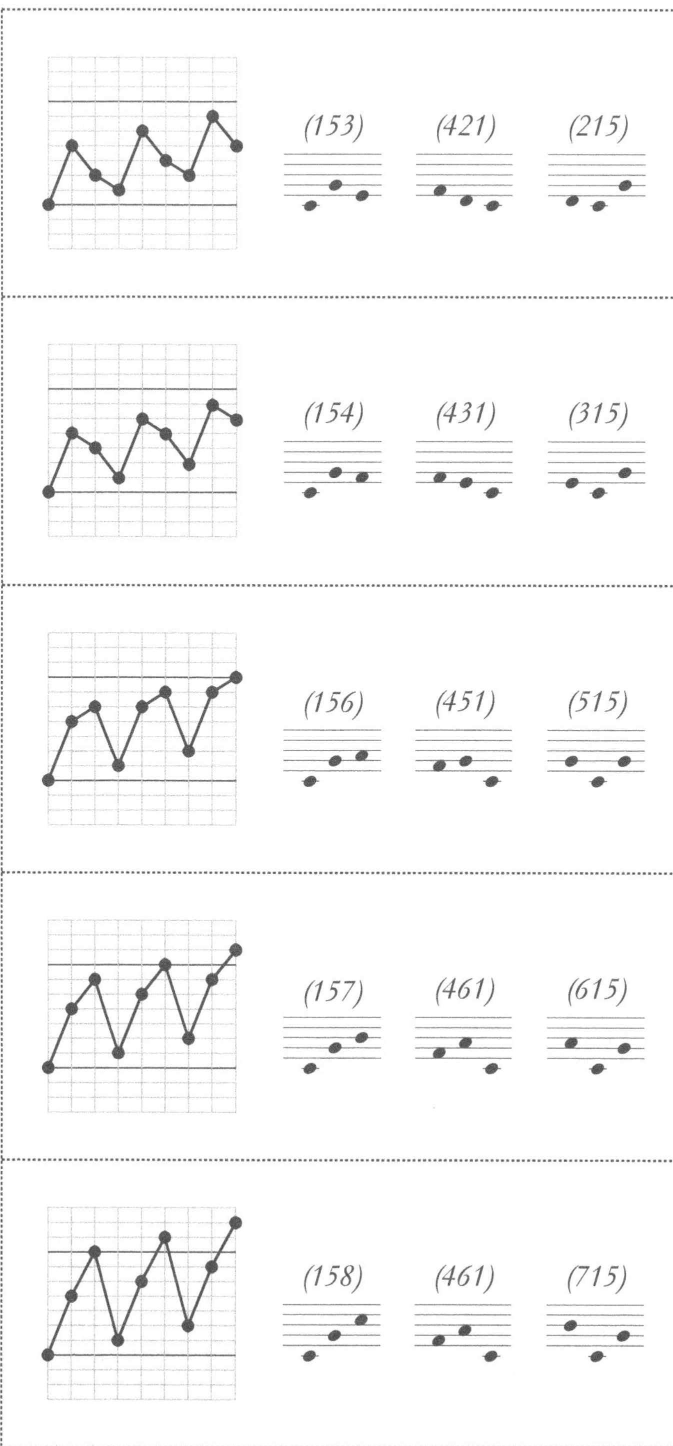

Descending by Diatonic Steps

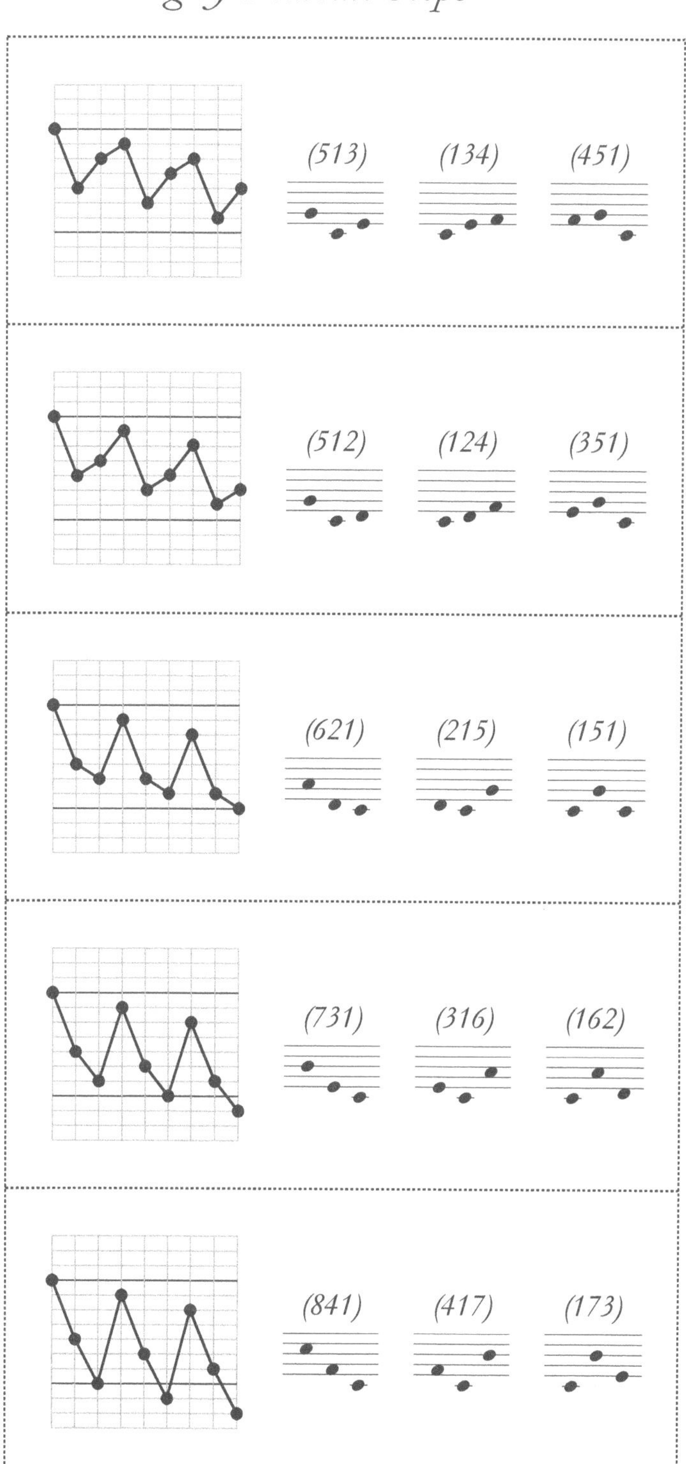

Exercise

Ascending by Diatonic Steps

(163) (521) (215)

(164) (531) (315)

(165) (541) (416)

(167) (561) (616)

(168) (571) (716)

Descending by Diatonic Steps

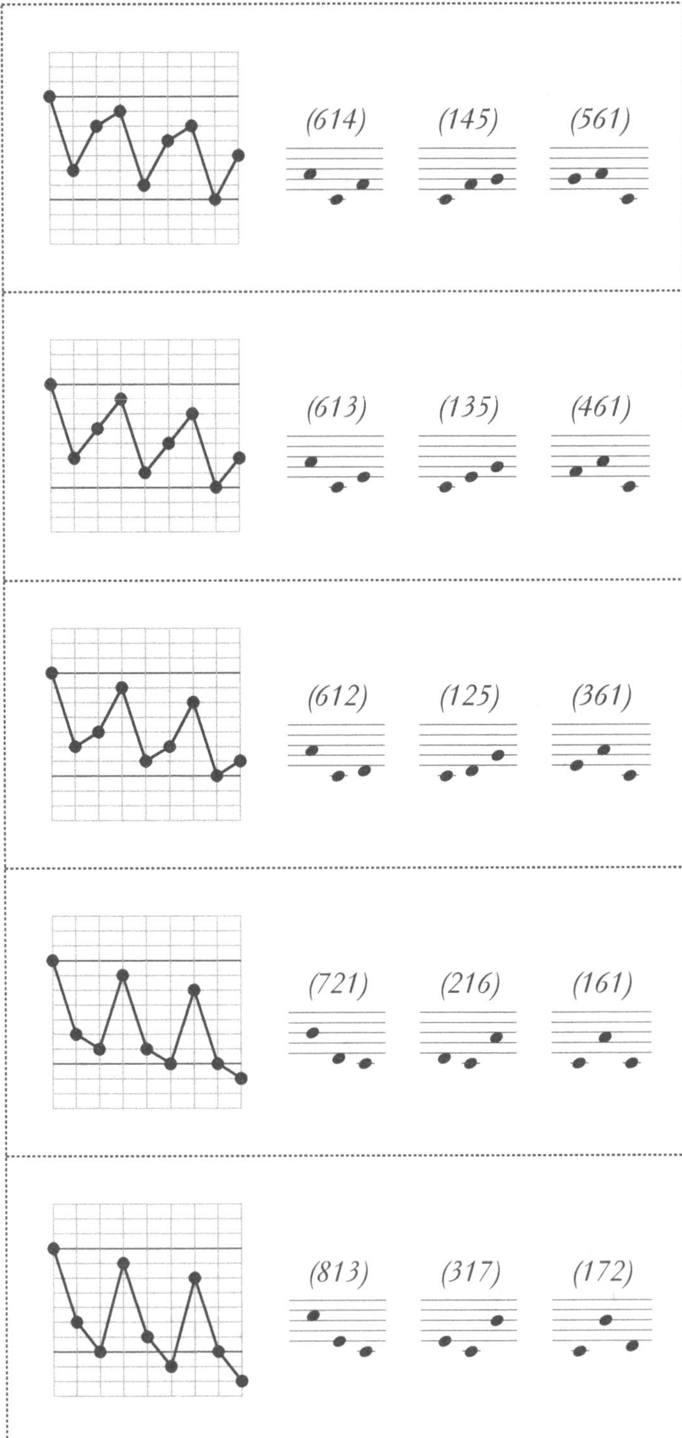

Exercise

Ascending by Diatonic Steps

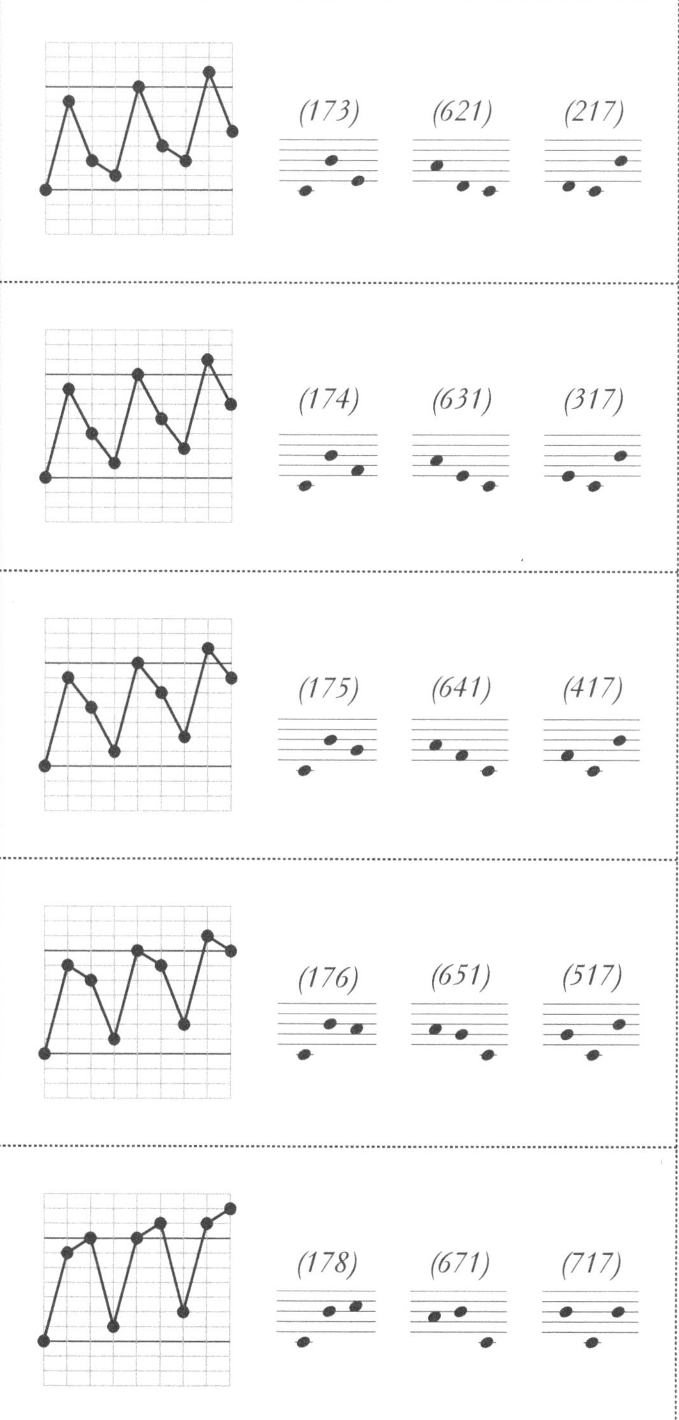

Descending by Diatonic Steps

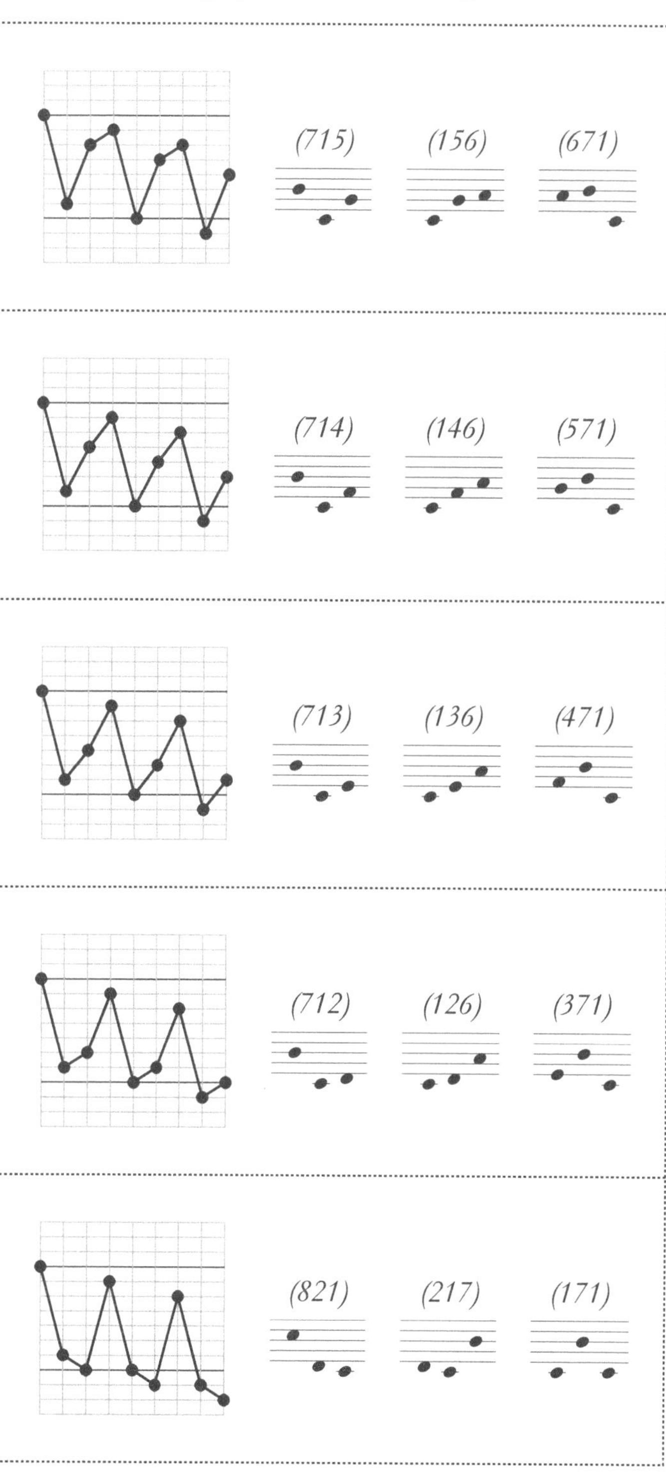

Notes *Idea: Use these diatonic grids to create different patterns. The dark lines are the roots.*

Notes *Idea: compose diatonic melodies that avoid anything that seems like a pattern.*

Illustration

Showing:

THE 62 DIATONIC FRAGMENTS

All subsets of the Diatonic, grouped by number of pitches. Shown on transposable chromatic pitch circles with possible key centers indicated by white dots.

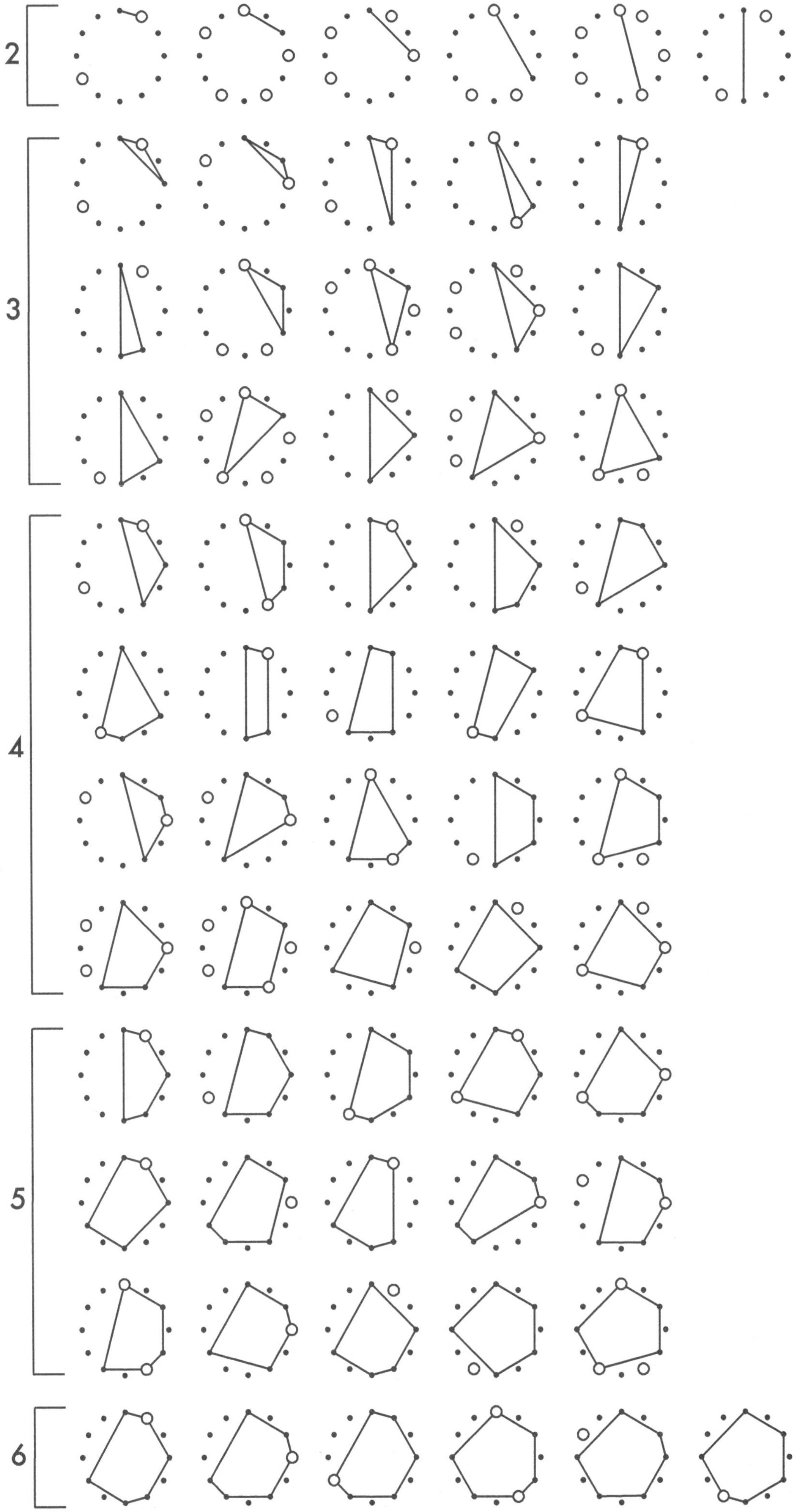

In the diatonic scale, there are:

- 6 different dyad types
- 15 different triad types
- 20 different tetradtypes
- 15 different pentad types
- 6 different hexad types

These are the 62 diatonic fragments.

It is more efficient to display these fragments on pitch circles than staff notation, which dictates specific pitches rather than shapes. For example, this is a diatonic scale in any key (white circle is the root):

If a fragment can be found in more than one key, the diagram will have more than one white circle. For example, if "C" is at "12:00" on this diagram,

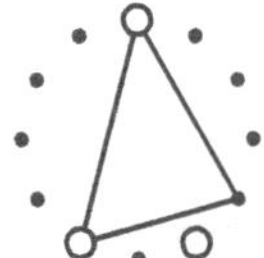

the pitches of the fragment will be (C, E, G), and the possible key centers (diatonic scales that contain these three pitches) will be C, F, and G. If "Ab" is at the top of the same diagram, the pitches will be (Ab, C, Eb) and the possible key centers will be Ab, Db, and Eb.

This can be checked with basic music theory - the shape above is a major triad, and any diatonic scale contains three major triads (I, IV and V), which means that any particular major triad can be found in three keys.

2

3

4

5

6

Exercise

DIATONIC GATEWAYS

To increase understanding of the Diatonic Scale through an exploration of its parts.
To develop fluency and internalization of any key in any position.
- Suggested Preparation: Diatonic Scales in Series and Parallel
- Play exercises in the same position, different key and same key, different position.

Improvise with the semitone/major 7th (B,C) using it to move between the Keys of C and G:

B C → C or G

Improvise with the tritone (B, F) using it to move between the Keys of C and Gb:

B F → C or G♭

Improvise with the major 3rd/minor 6th (C, E) using it to move between the Keys of C, F, and G:

C E → C or F or G

Improvise with the minor 3rd/major 6th (E, G) using it to move between the Keys of F, G, C and D:

E G → F G C D

Improvise with the whole tone/minor 7th (A, B) using it to move between the Keys of A, C, D, E, and G:

A B → A C D E G

Improvise with the perfect 4th/perfect 5th (E, A) using it to move between the Keys of E, F, G, A, C, and D:

E A → E F G

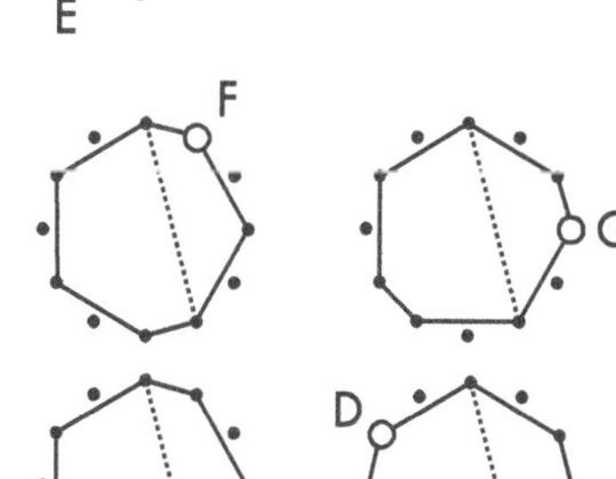

A

Further Study:
Transpose these examples to different keys.
Explore the transpositional possibilities of the 3, 4, 5, and 6 note Diatonic Fragments.
Find ways to move through all keys using these movements to create Diatonic "chains."

Exercise

DIATONIC MAGIC SQUARE

Each row and column of the square contains a melody with seven different pitches.
- Read any row or column, using each pitch as the start of a diatonic shape - (for example, play triads in one key off each pitch)
- Create a diatonic melody, or use a pre-existing melody, and transpose it to each pitch.
- Change the key signature or read the page upside-down to increase options.
- Work through several keys in one positions, and then one key in several positions.

Exercise

THE SCRAMBLER

A modulation exercise.

Each long row, long column, and small 3x4 rectangle (dotted lines) contain a complete set of 12 different pitches.

Suggested Preparation: Diatonic Scales in Series and Parallel.

- Staying in one area of the neck, improvise through a row, column, or rectangle, changing key centers according the pitch names.

- Begin by staying in each key for a comfortable amount of time, then move more rapidly.

- Change the mode (instead of the pitch name representing the root of the ionian mode, use it as the first pitch of a different mode).

- Compose a melody, and transpose it to each key in a row, column, or rectangle.

- Return to this exercise later, using other material that can be transposed (other scale types, chromatic melodies, chords, progressions, etc.)

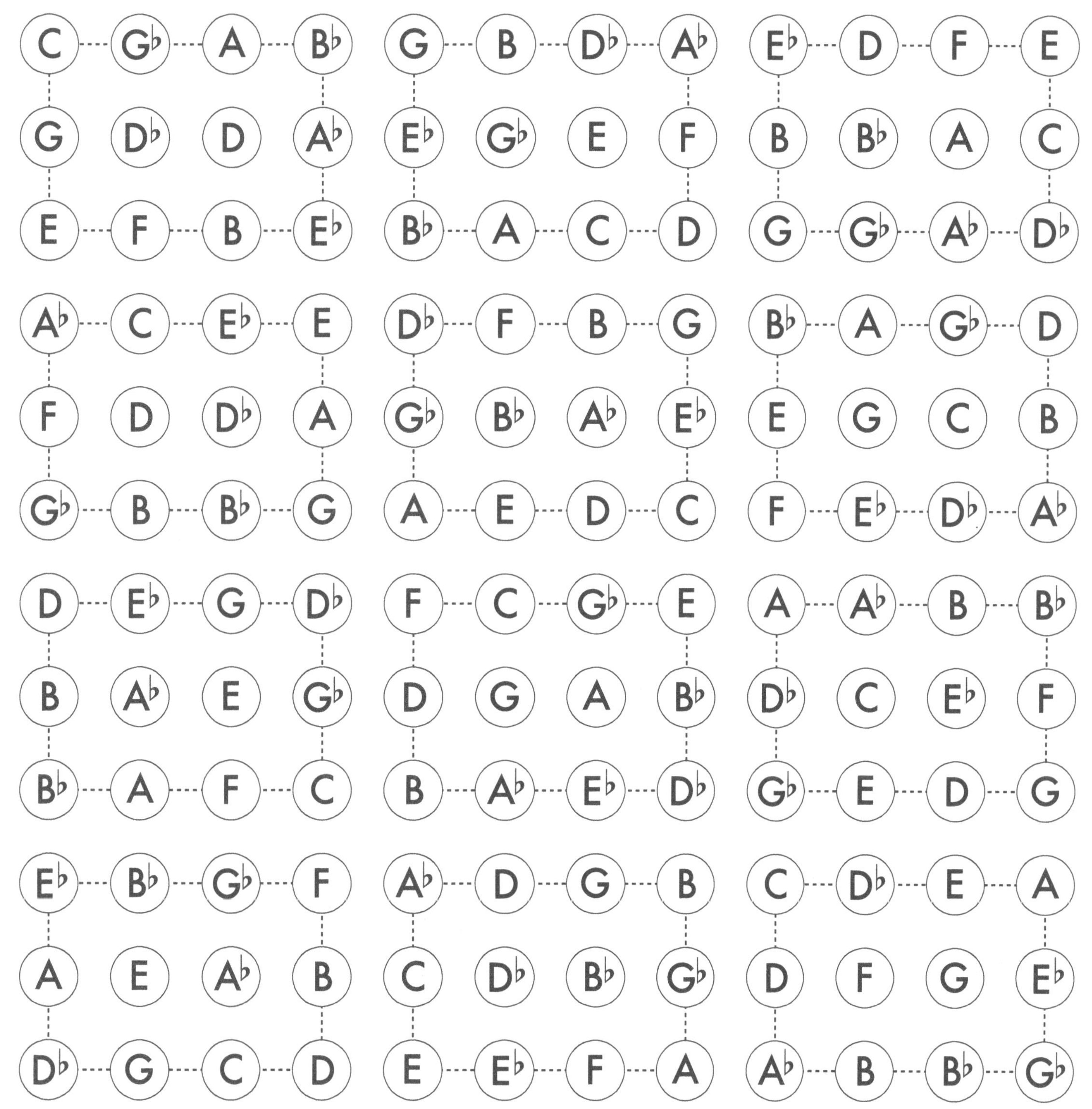

Illustration

TONAL CYCLOID

Showing:

A visualization of a chain of 5ths as cyclic movements around a pitch circle, with emphasis on three stages:
1) From the beginning to the pentatonic, the last structure before the formation of semitones.
2) From the pentatonic to the diatonic, the last structure before the formation of chromatic clusters.
3) From the diatonic to the chromatic, the final stage before the cycle repeats.

Concept

BEYOND THE DIATONIC

Consider the illustration on the previous page. The idea is that the pentatonic, diatonic, and chromatic are *terminal* structures, places that the ear gravitates to because they are the final points in the progression before an important transition. For example, the pentatonic is made of only minor 3rds and whole tones, and the next iteration introduces the semitone. The diatonic is made of only whole tones and semitones, and the next iteration introduces chromaticism (consecutive semitones).

Another way to put it would be this: take a certain number of pitches and distribute them as evenly as possible around a 12-point circle. 2, 3, 4, and 6 pitches can divide the circle into equal parts, commonly called the *tritone, augmented triad, diminished 7th,* and *whole tone scale*:

But with 5 or 7 pitches, some intervals will have to be larger than others. Maximum spacing between all pitches with 5 notes will lead to these three possibilities, the only 5-note shapes without semitones:

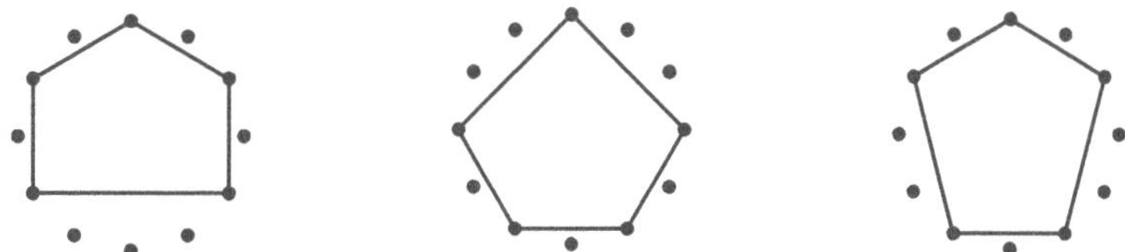

The first shape is closely related to a whole tone scale (missing one pitch), and the second is a subset of the diatonic, most likely sounding like *(1,2,3,5,b7)* or *(1,b3,4,5,6)*, depending on the context. The third is the pentatonic. To most eyes, the pentatonic looks the most even of the three in terms of pitch distribution, since the other two have whole tones in a continuous cluster. The whole tone scale is covered in the section on symmetry. The second shape is included in the 62 Diatonic Fragments, and the pentatonic is discussed in many places.

Maximum spacing between all pitches with 7 notes will lead to these six possibilities, the only 7-note shapes without consecutive semitones:

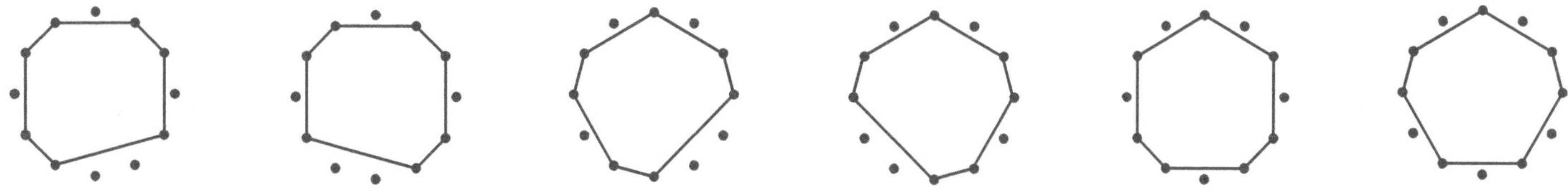

The first and second shapes are closely related to the *octatonic* scale (missing one pitch). The third and fourth shapes are commonly known as *harmonic minor* and *harmonic major*, respectively. The fifth shape is commonly known as *melodic minor,* and the sixth is the diatonic. To most eyes, the diatonic looks the most even in terms of pitch distribution, since the others either have the whole tones in a continuous cluster or a 3-semitone interval (minor third or augmented second).

The octatonic (alternating whole tones and semitones) is the only possible 8-note formation without consecutive semitones. 9 or more notes will always contain chromatic clusters. So this study ends with the heptatonic (7-note) scales above. The octatonic is covered in the discussion of symmetry.
The following pages show fingerings for the four remaining scales.

4 HEPTATONIC SCALES

Showing: *The Diatonic and the three scales that differ from it by one semitone movement, on a 12-fret template. Changing the 3rd, 5th, and 6th degree of the Diatonic creates the other three (shown with curved arrows). Lines of symmetry are shown within the scale (first two diagrams) and between scales (second two diagrams). Common names of scales are given, where:*

○ = root of key center, ◍ = different pitch from the Diatonic, and ● = other pitches

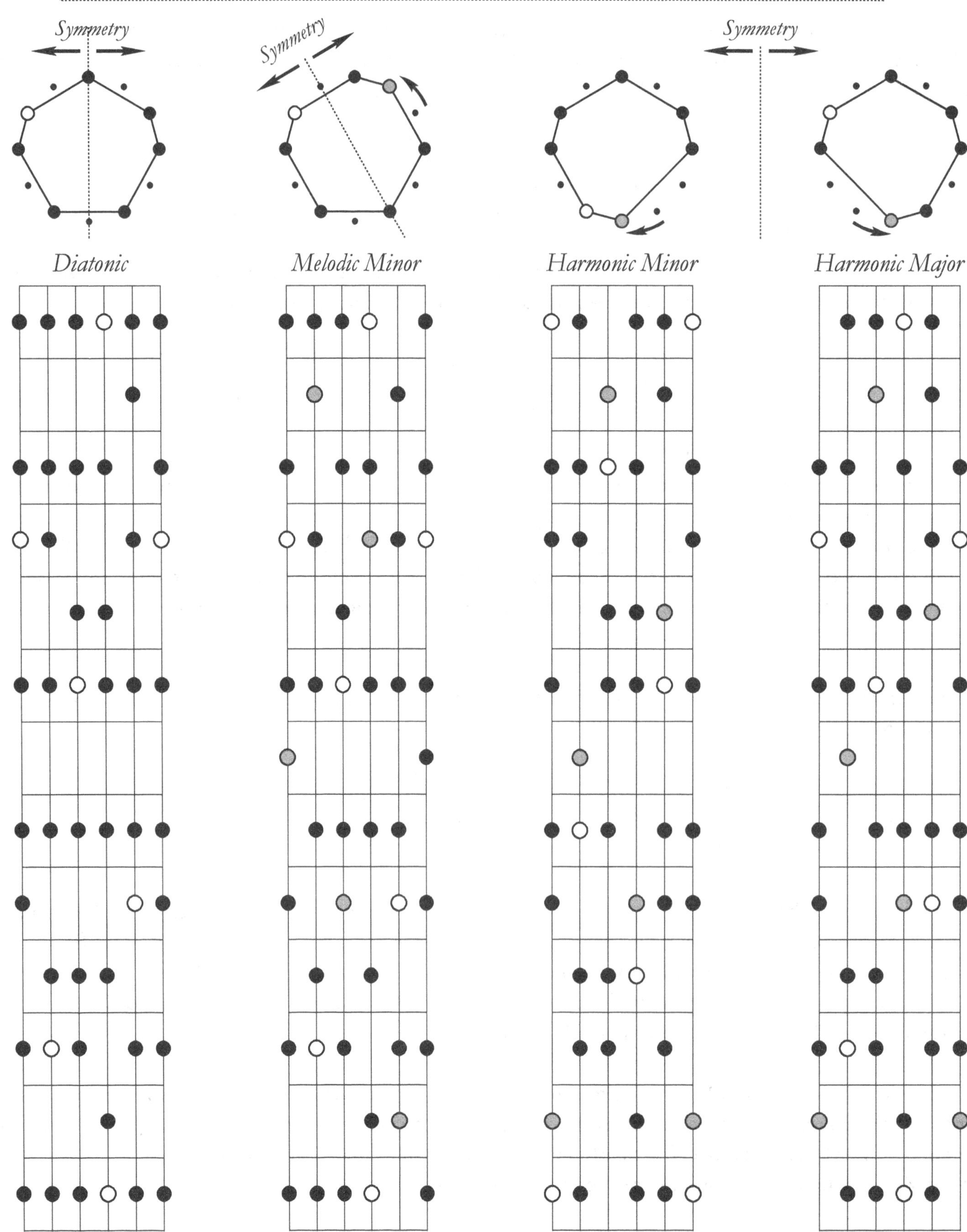

Exercise

20 HEPTATONIC MODES

The four heptatonic scales split into five regions. ○ = root of key center, and ● = other pitches.
- Play each mode ascending and descending as a 32-pitch loop. Mark in the fingerings that are most comfortable.
- Use these modes to memorize the larger templates (on the previous page) in sections.
- Compare each mode to its counterpart in the Diatonic (in the same row), and note that only one pitch is different.

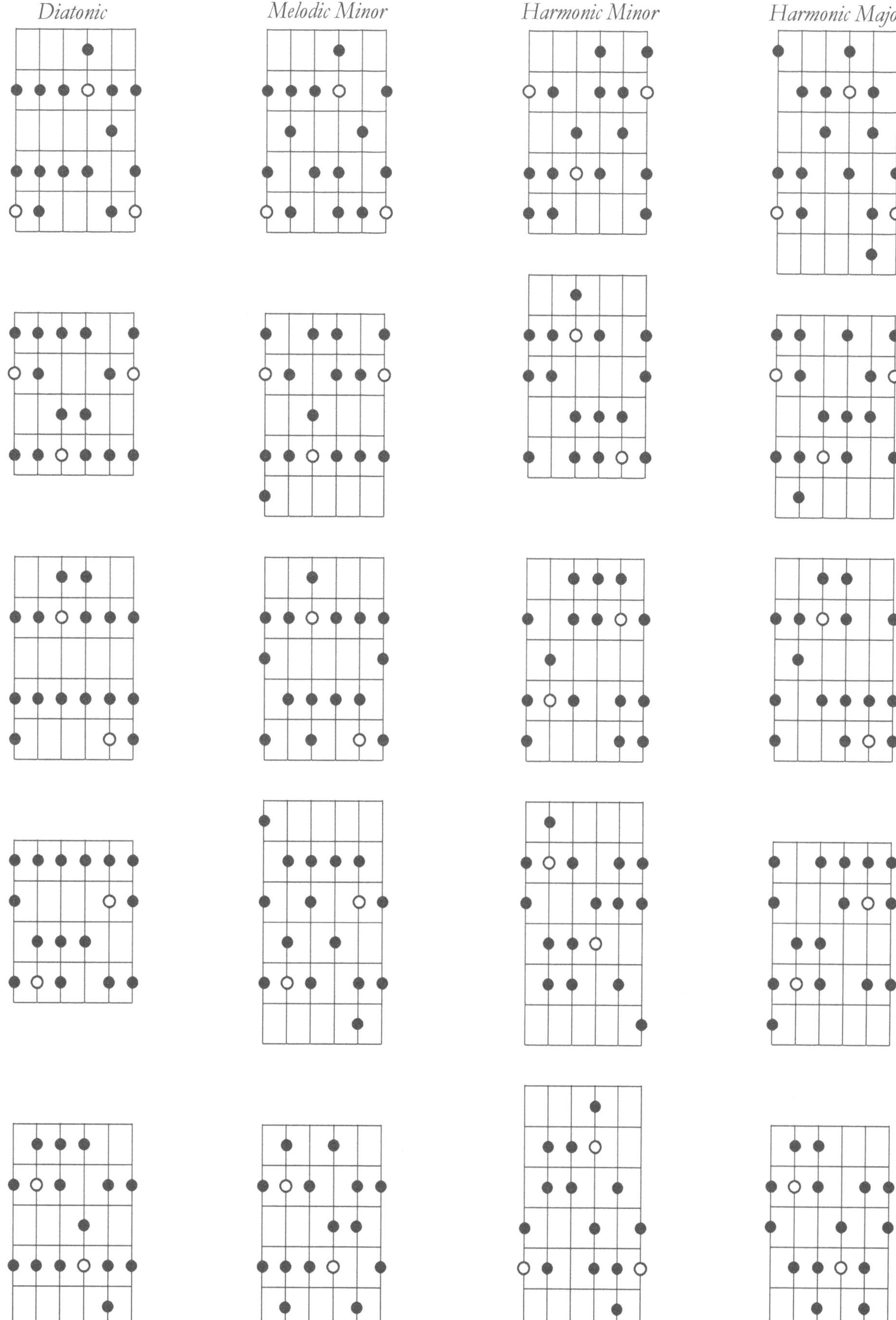

Illustration

16 SYMMETRICAL PITCH SHAPES

Showing: *The five ways to divide 12 pitches into smaller parts of equal size, and the possible ways to fill in these parts with pitches. Columns show division of the octave into 2, 3, 4, 6, and 12 parts. Rows show patterns that share a common shape. Divisions shown with dotted lines, empty pitches as white circles, and filled pitches with black circles. There are 16 rows, showing the 16 possible repeating patterns within an octave.*

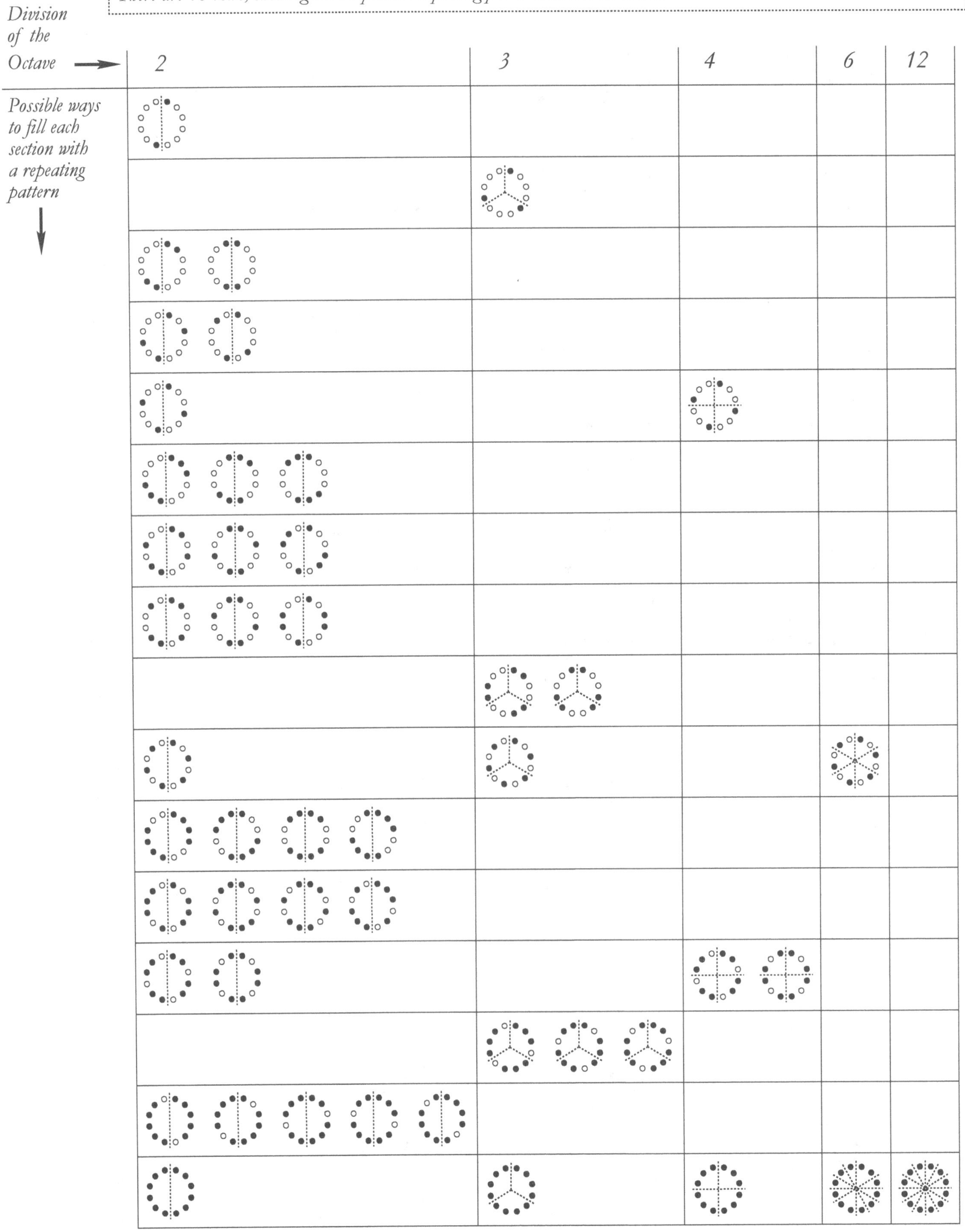

Division of the Octave →	*2*	*3*	*4*	*6*	*12*
Possible ways to fill each section with a repeating pattern ↓					

Concept

C, Gb

C, E, Ab

C, Db
Gb, G

C, D
Gb, Ab

C, Eb
Gb, A

C, Db, D
Gb, G, Ab

C, Db, Eb
Gb, G, A

C, D, Eb
Gb, Ab, A

C, Db
E, F
Ab, A

C, D, E
Gb, Ab, Bb

C, Db, D, Eb
Gb, G, Ab, A

C, Db, D, E
Gb, G, Ab, Bb

C, Db, Eb, E
Gb, G, A, Bb

C, Db, D
E, F, Gb
Ab, A, Bb

C, Db, D, Eb, E
Gb, G, Ab, A, Bb

Chromatic

SYMMETRY WITHIN AN OCTAVE

The table on the previous page is a study of possible symmetries within a 12-tone equal tempered octave. The process of finding all possible symmetries could also be described in words:

- *1) Take a 12-note chromatic scale and divide it into smaller parts of equal size. (2 groups of 6, 3 groups of 4, 4 groups of 3, 6 groups of 2, and 12 groups of 1)*
- *2) Within each section, fill the space in as many ways as possible, starting with the first pitch, and repeating this pattern in the other sections.*
- *3) Make a list to find out how many unique shapes there are, eliminating duplicates and transpositions.*

This will produce the 16 unique shapes shown on the left.
A pitch example is shown next to each shape, starting on C.

Looking at these shapes, it becomes clear that any of them can be made from some combination of the first two shapes, commonly known as a *Tritone* and *Augmented Triad*. These are the basic building blocks of binary and ternary tonal symmetry. There are 13 ways to layer tritones, and 5 ways to layer augmented triads, if we consider all rotations (transpositions) to be equivalent:

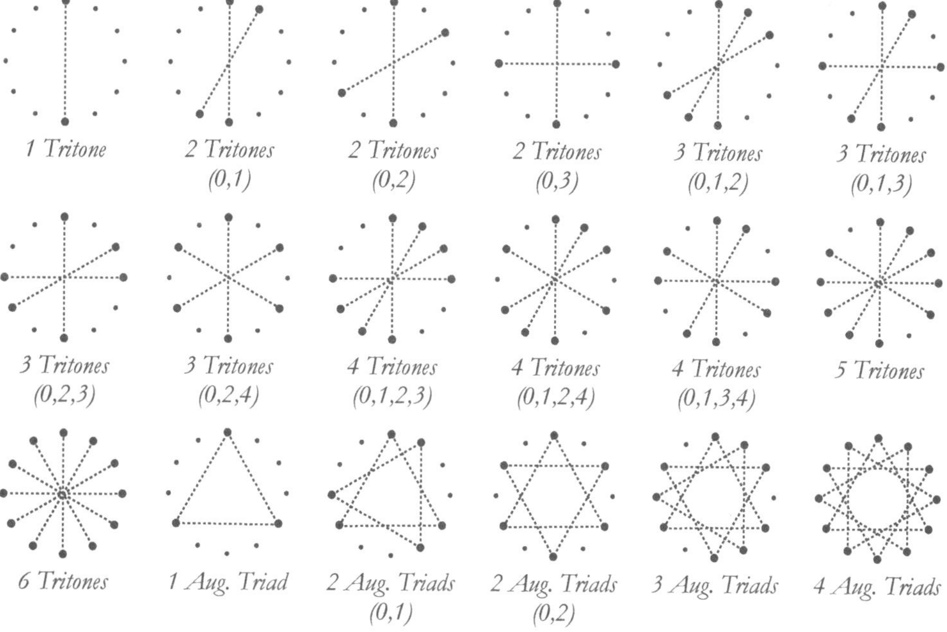

Labels indicate how many tritones or augmented triads are involved, and how they are spaced by semitones, starting at 0. Notice that there are two duplicates, since both tritones and augmented triads can produce the *whole tone* and *chromatic* scale:

3 Tritones (0,2,4) = *2 Aug. Triads (0,2)* and *6 Tritones* = *4 Aug. Triads*

This leaves 16 unique shapes, as shown before. The following pages show fingerings on the guitar for these 16 symmetrical shapes.

Exercise

16 SYMMETRICAL PITCH COLLECTIONS

Pitch circles, fretboard diagrams, and one octave of each scale starting on C are shown.
Dotted lines show how each shape is made of tritones or augmented triads (they do not indicate pitch order)
- Practice and find fingerings that feel comfortable. Mix different scales together. Transpose to all keys.

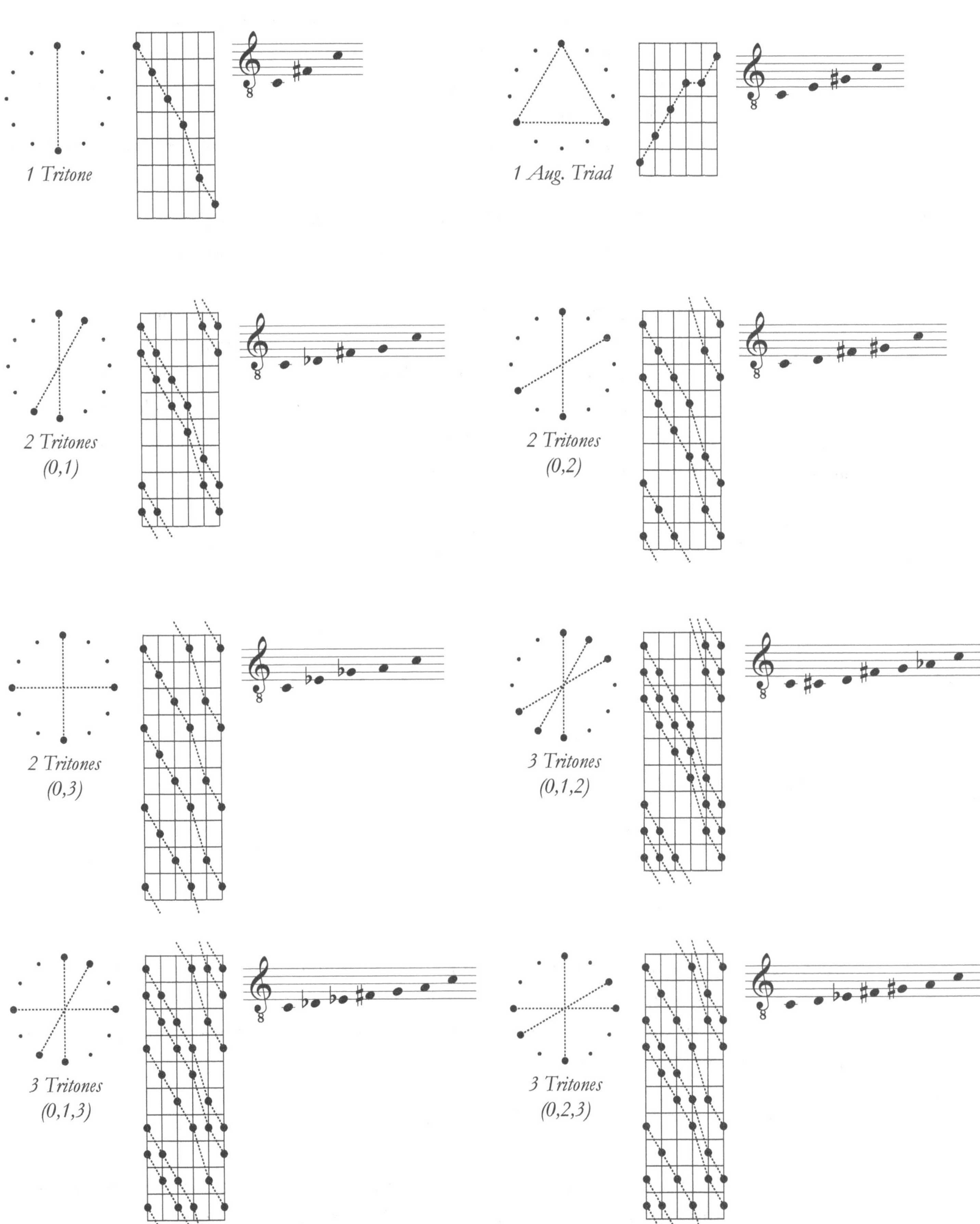

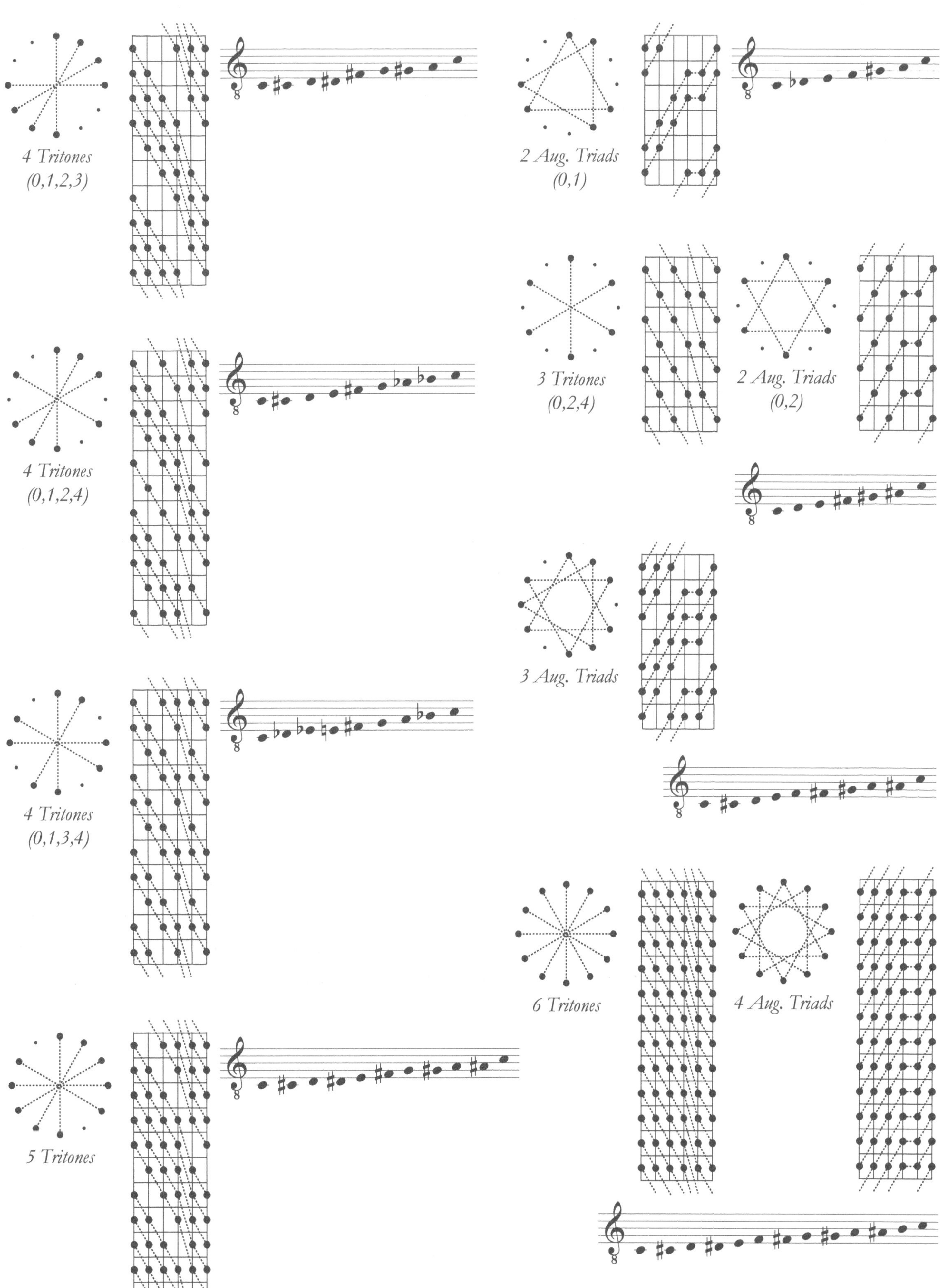
4 Tritones
(0,1,2,3)
4 Tritones
(0,1,2,4)
4 Tritones
(0,1,3,4)
5 Tritones
2 Aug. Triads
(0,1)
3 Tritones
(0,2,4)
2 Aug. Triads
(0,2)
3 Aug. Triads
6 Tritones
4 Aug. Triads

Concept

WHOLE TONE AND DIMINISHED SCALES

While studying the previous pages, it may become clear that there are only two symmetrical scales that are made of whole and half steps without consecutive semitones. These are commonly called the *whole tone* and *diminished* scales. They are extremely powerful tools, and a thorough study of them can open many musical doors. Either of them fits comfortably onto a five fret span of the neck - here they are in 5th position:

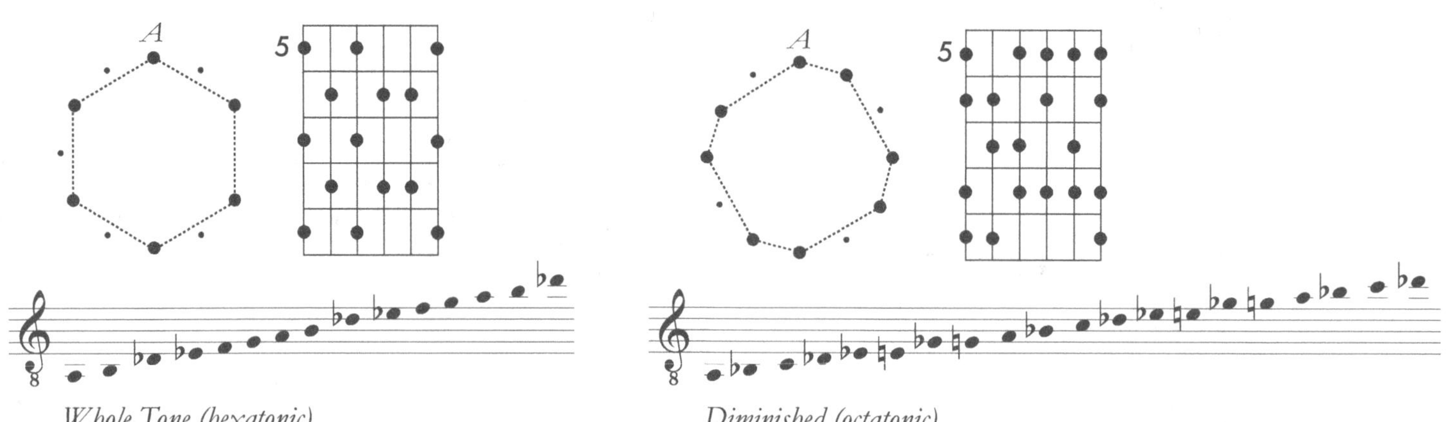

Whole Tone (hexatonic)

Diminished (octatonic)

It may also become clear that any diminished scale shares four pitches with any whole tone scale, and vice versa. For example, the two scales above share the pitches {*A, Db, Eb, G*}. This is a complex idea, but there is a way to visualize this with maximal simplicity - take a chromatic pitch circle, and distort it so that every other pitch is pushed to the interior:

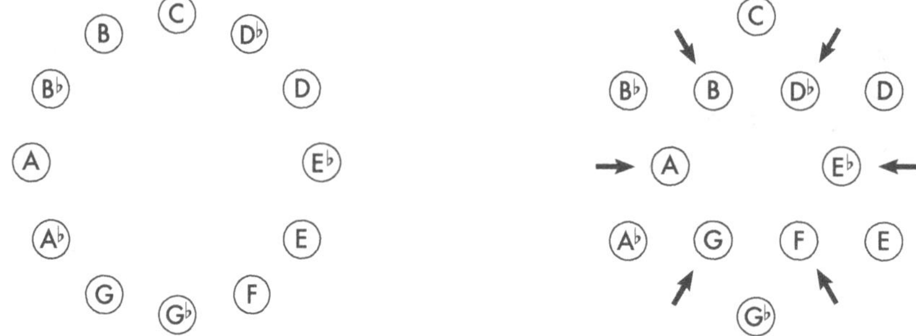

In this arrangement, the scales become simple geometric shapes. The outer hexagon is one whole tone scale, the inner hexagon is the other, and the three large rectangles in different rotations are the three diminished scales. Each whole tone scale has four common tones with any diminished scale, and each diminished scale has four common tones with a different diminished scale. Meditate on the elegance of this shape. Use the exercise on the following page to work it out on the instrument.

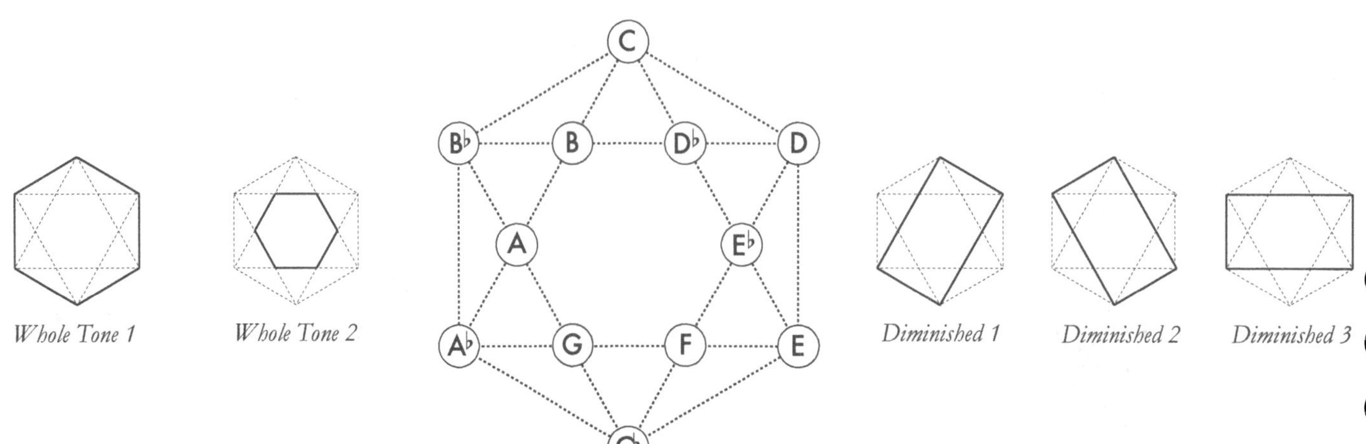

Exercise

SYMMETRICAL SHIFTING

For developing an ability to move between different symmetrical scales using common tones.
The two possible Whole Tone scales are shown above, and the three possible Diminished scales below, with a symbol to represent each.
Pathways for scale connection are shown with solid lines, with a symbol on the line showing the combined scales and 4 common tones.
Master pitch map shows how an aggregate of all 5 scales on one figure. For simplicity, only flats are used.
- Move between the two Whole Tone scales via each of the Diminished Scales.
- Move between any of the scales using the pathways, using one or more of the four common tones as a pivot points.

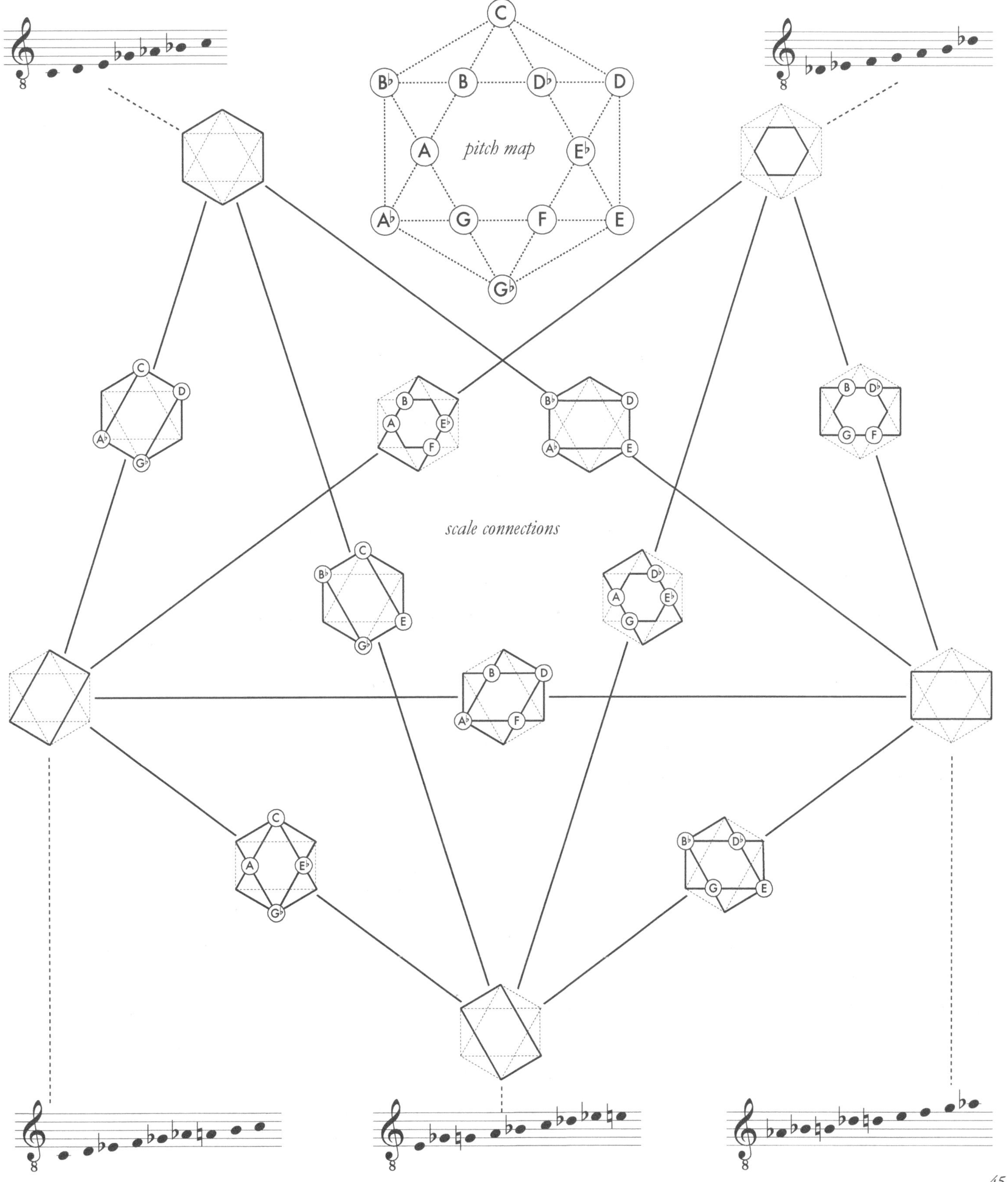

Concept

THE CHROMATIC SCALE

Chroma, or color, is one way to describe the feeling of different collections of pitches. The *Chromatic Scale* contains all pitches, and all colors. The chromatic scale and its smaller parts are a group of 351 pitch sets, each with a unique tonal character. They include:

- *1 monad (single pitch)*
- *6 dyads (2 pitches)*
- *19 triads (3 pitches)*
- *43 tetrads (4 pitches)*
- *66 pentads (5 pitches)*
- *80 hexads (6 pitches)*
- *66 heptads (7 pitches)*
- *43 octads (8 pitches)*
- *19 nonads (9 pitches)*
- *6 decads (10 pitches)*
- *1 undecad (11 pitches)*
- *1 dodecad (12 pitches, chromatic scale)*

Any shape made with the lines on this figure will be one of the 351 unique pitch structures:

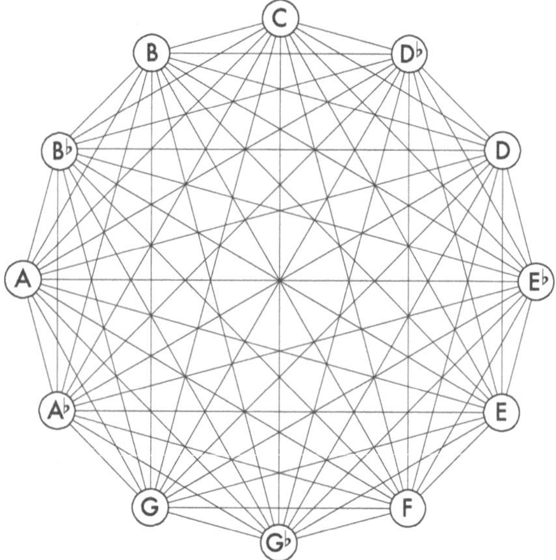

These are discussed in more detail in the chapters on multiple pitches.

The chromatic scale has a number of possible fingerings on the guitar. An easy solution would be:

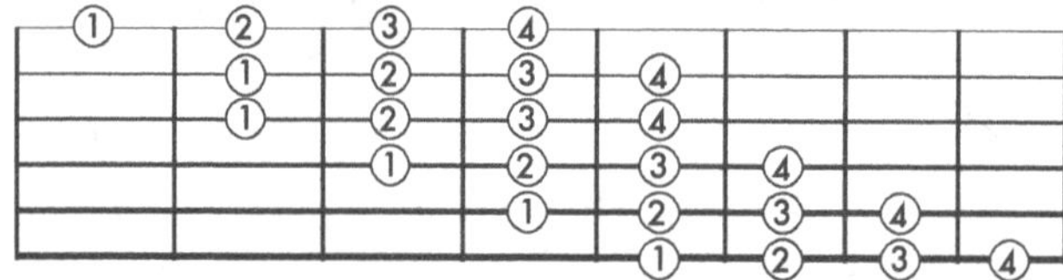

This is a logical shape where the four fingers play four chromatic pitches per string, and is well suited to a pattern-based approach. Drawbacks include the necessity to move across the length of the neck on an 8-fret span and the increased spacing between the frets on the higher notes - both of these lead to inconsistencies in the required hand position and reduced range of motion.

A solution that increases the range of the scale and decreases sideways motion is to stay in one position, using one of these fingerings:

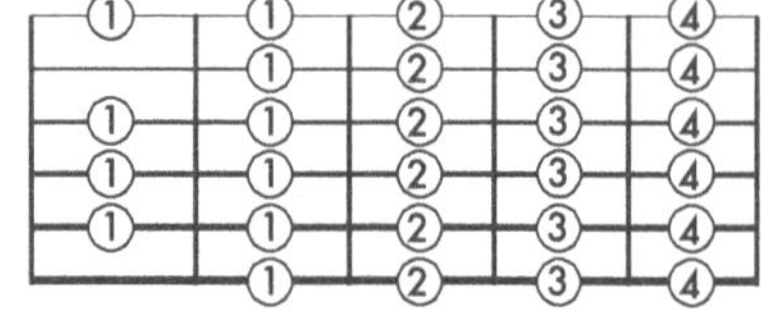

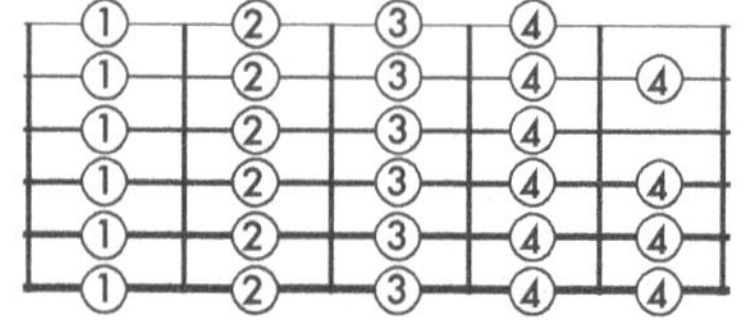

The obvious drawback is that in each case either the 1st or 4th finger must play two consecutive pitches. The awkwardness of this motion is minimized by using the fingering on the left when ascending and the fingering on the right when descending. This way, the motion of the doubling finger always contracts, pulling in toward the hand, which is stronger and more natural than stretching and pushing away. The exercise on the following page is designed to deal with this problem, training the doubling finger to move smoothly and independently. This is also good preparation for sight reading, which requires a full chromatic spectrum over a large range of pitches with a minimum of duplicates.

Exercise

CHROMATIC ROTATIONS

For working on control of the chromatic scale in a single position.
The fingering on the right avoids over-reliance on the 1st or 4th finger to play the pitches that fall on the string breaks (shown in 5th position).
- *Play the chromatic scale as smoothly as possible with no accents.*
- *Make all notes even, hiding string breaks and slides.*
- *Play with the given accents at the beginning of each six notes.*
- *After moving through all rotations, play the scale again without accents.*
- *Make note of any differences in the sound and feel.*
- *Try again in a different position.*

Symmetrical fingering for the Chromatic Scale in one position:

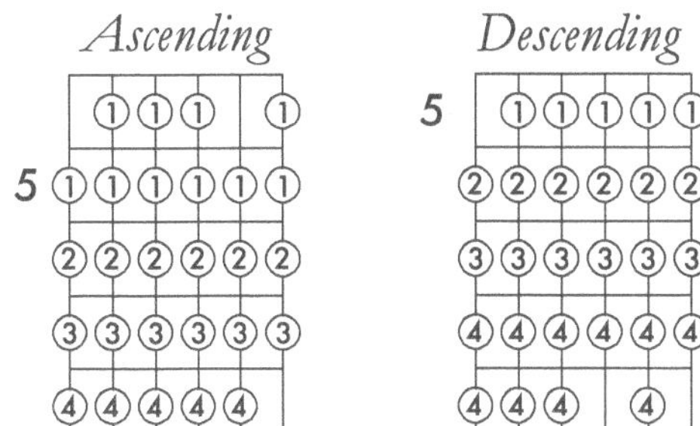

Notes *Idea: Find the shapes created by pentatonic, diatonic, melodic minor, whole tone, diminished, and chromatic scales. Look at how various shapes intersect and overlap. Think of possible musical applications.*

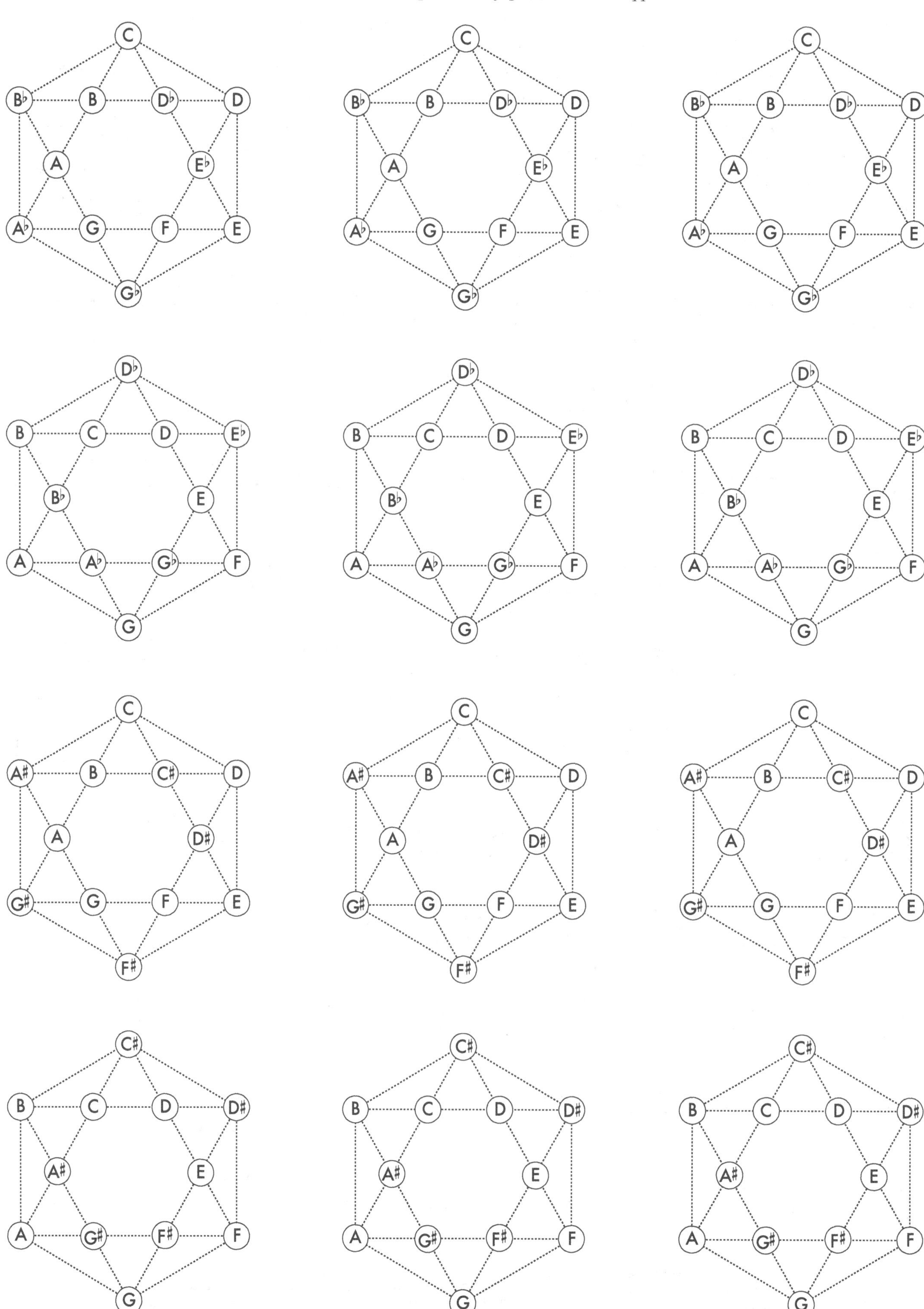

Concept

THE DYAD
(TWO PITCHES)

The 6 Dyads:

Take a circle of 12 points, connect any two points with a line, and you will get some rotation of one of the six shapes on the right. A line that divides the octave in half produces the tritone. Any other division will have a small and large part that combine to make an octave. This is the same as a list of six *intervals* and their *inversions*, in common terminology. The six dyads on the right are labeled in complementary pairs with their common names and a numerical description of the size of each interval in semitones, starting with zero. With the exception of the tritone, each shape can be described two ways, depending on which pitch you start with.

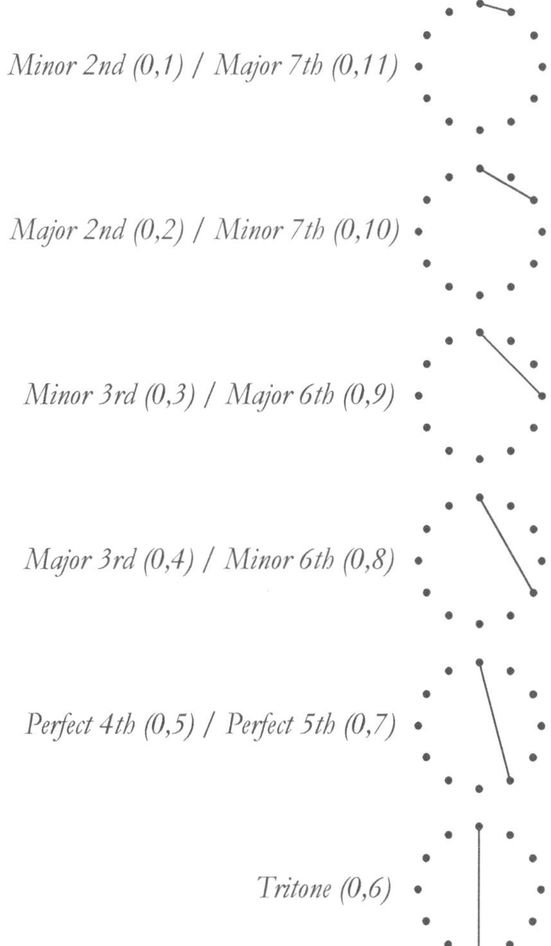

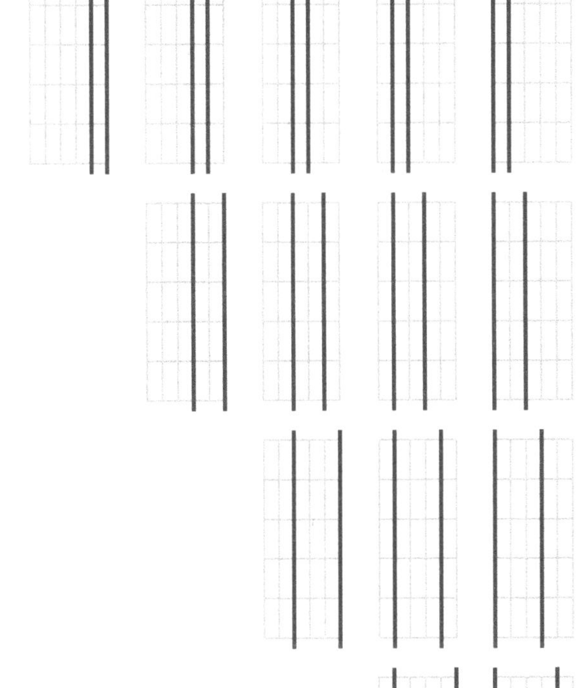

Play any two simultaneous notes on the guitar, and you will have to use one of the 15 pairs of strings shown on the left. The following pages show how each of the 6 dyads can be played on these string pairs, within a five fret span. Many guitarists can stretch beyond five frets, but these exercises are meant to stay in a comfortable range for a people with a variety of hand sizes.

The order of pitches from low to high determines their inversion (G above C is a perfect 5th, and G below C is a perfect 4th), and octave equivalency is used (major 10ths are listed with major 3rds). The array on the left is used as a visual template for all listings, and a blank space in the pattern indicates that it's not possible to play the given dyad on the given string set. For example, it's not possible within 5 frets to play a perfect fifth on the string pair {1,6}. All possible fingerings with these guidelines are given.

The 15 String Pairs:

{1,2} {2,3} {3,4} {4,5} {5,6}

{1,3} {2,4} {3,5} {4,6}

{1,4} {2,5} {3,6}

{1,5} {2,6}

{1,6}

Exercise

0 or 11

1 or 0

(0,1)

e.g. (C,D♭)

Common Name:

Semitone
Half Step
Minor 2nd/ 9th
Augmented Unison/ Octave

(0,11)

e.g. (C,B)

Common Name:

Major 7th/ 14th
Diminished Octave

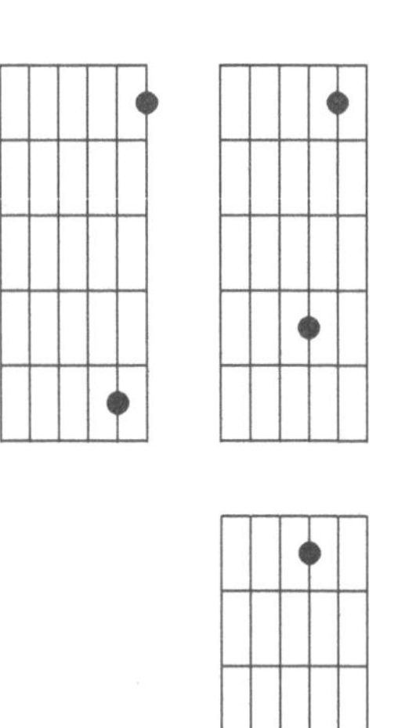
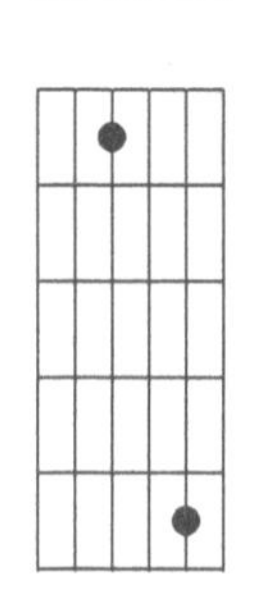
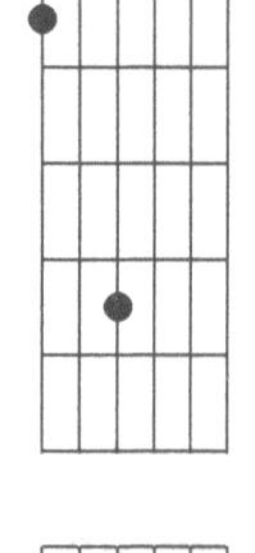
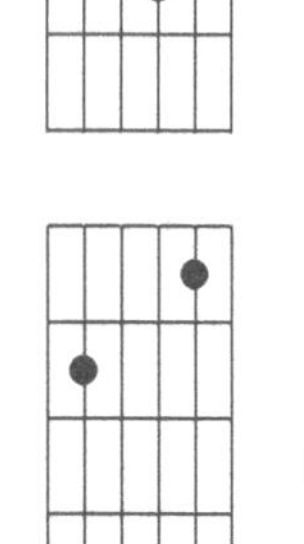
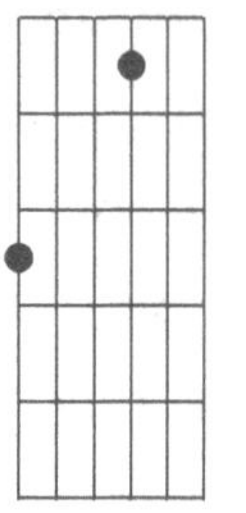
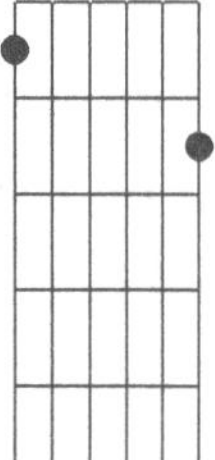
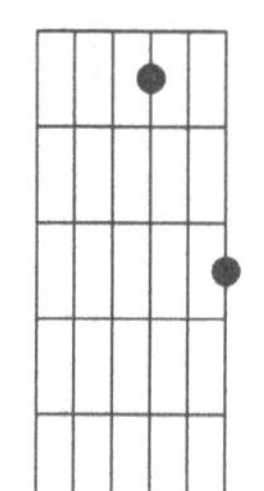
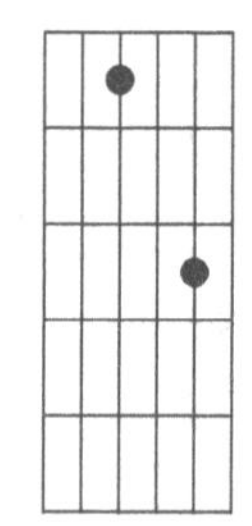
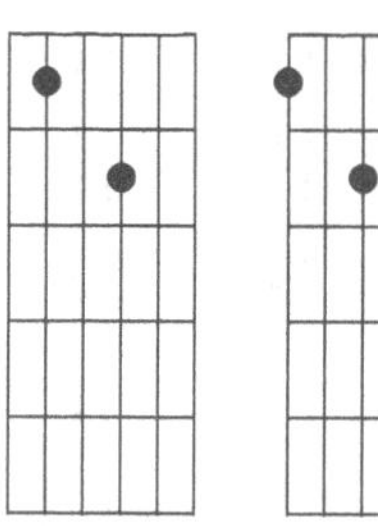
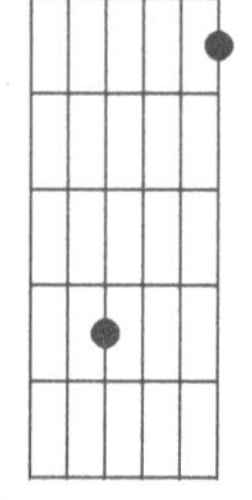
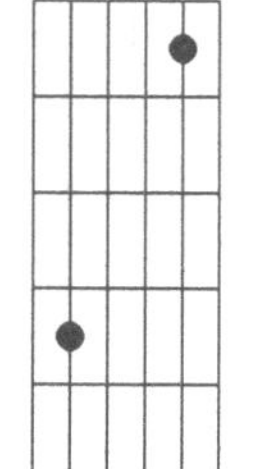
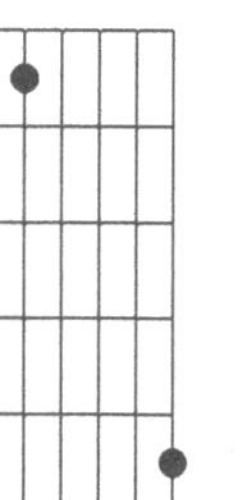
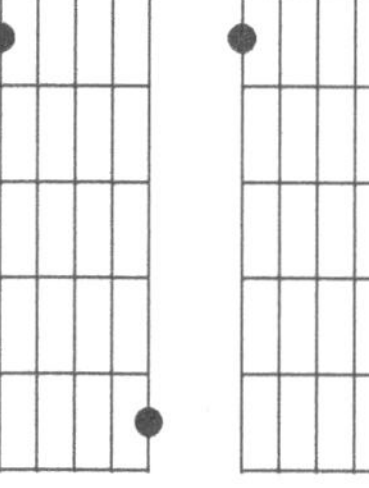
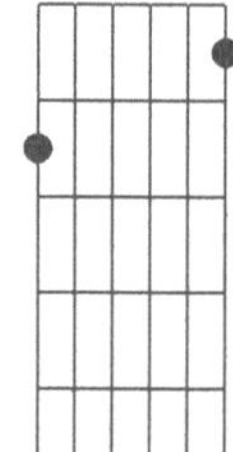

Exercise

(0,2)

e.g. (C,D)

Common Name:

Tone
Whole Step
Major 2nd/ 9th
Diminished 3rd/ 10th

(0,10)

e.g. (C,B♭)

Common Name:

Minor 7th/ 14th
Augmented 6th/ 13th

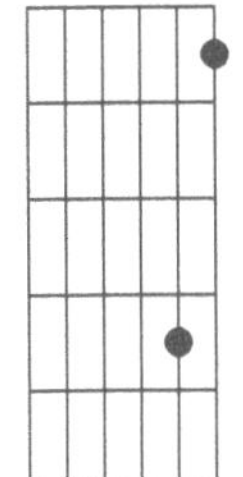
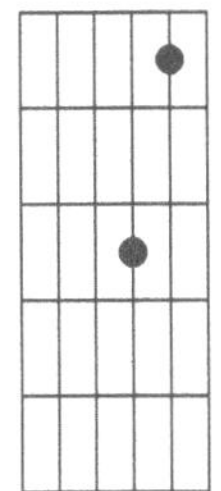
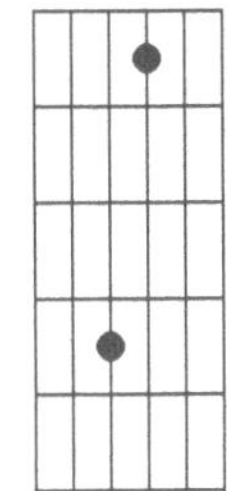
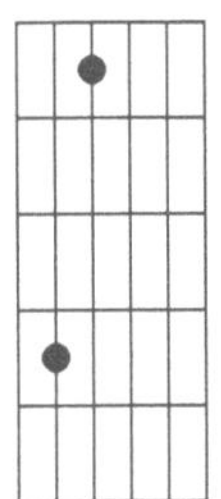
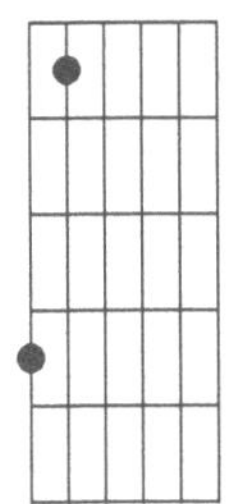
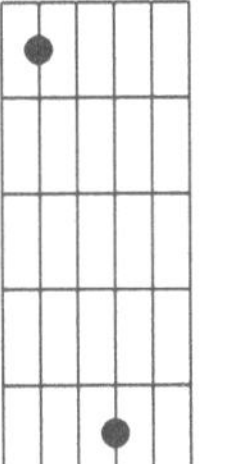
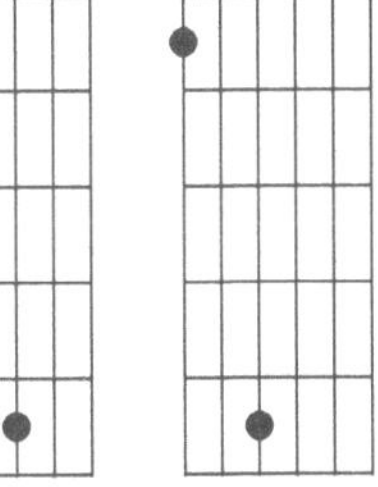
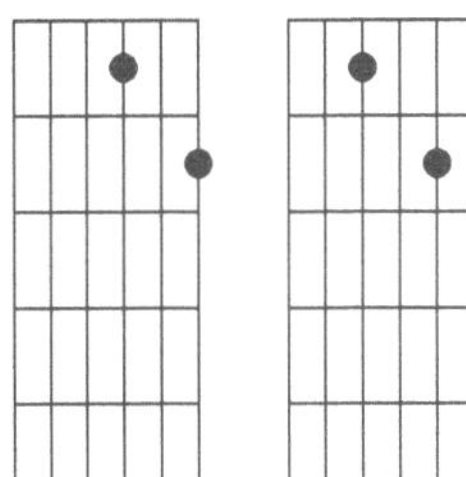
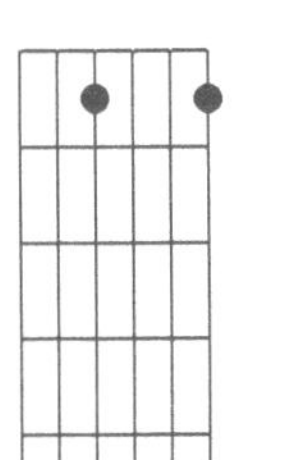
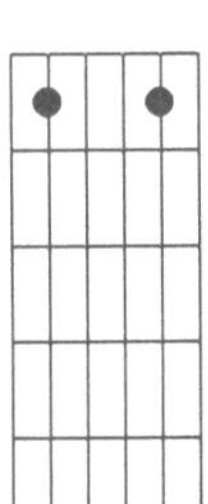
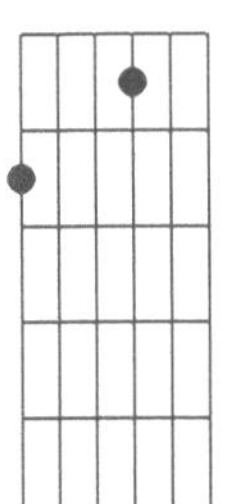
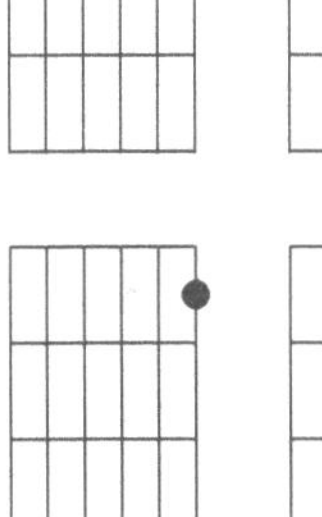
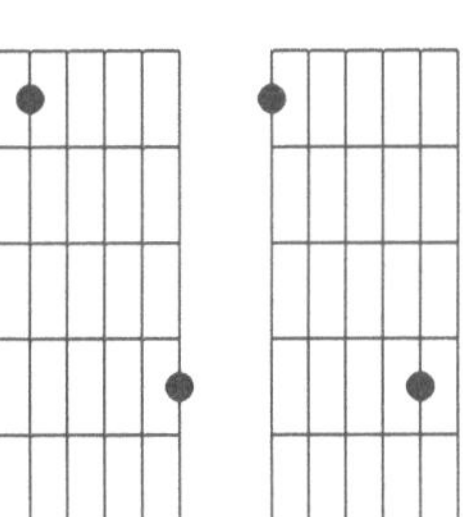
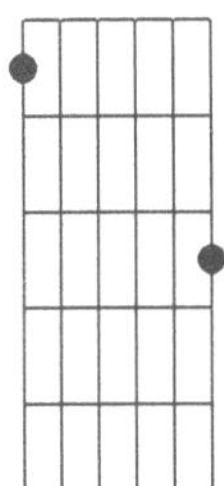
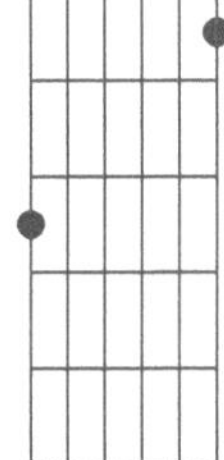

Exercise

0 or 9

3 or 0

(0,3)

e.g. (C,E$^{\flat}$)

Common Name:

Minor 3rd/ 10th
Augmented 2nd/ 9th

(0,9)

e.g. (C,A)

Common Name:

Major 6th/ 13th
Diminished 7th/ 14th

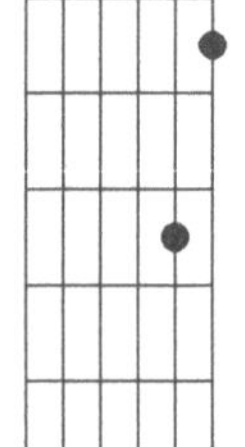
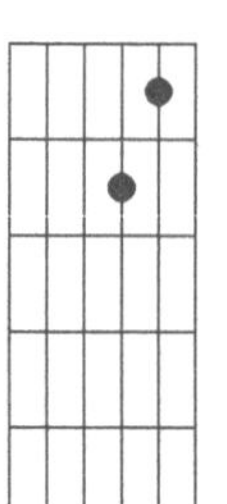
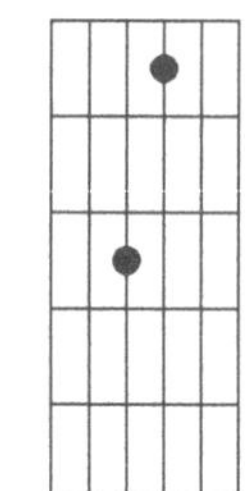
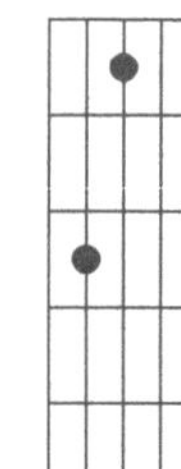
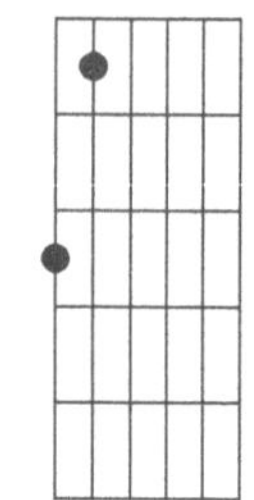
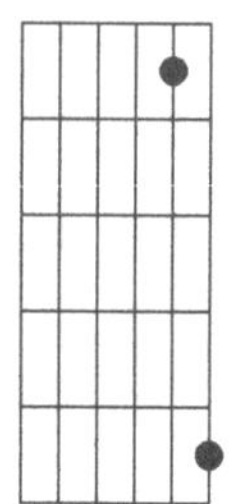
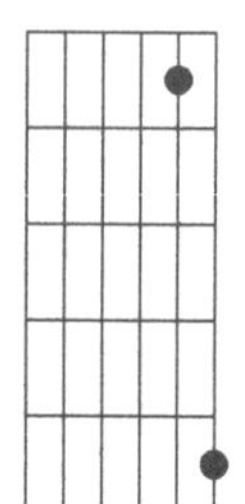

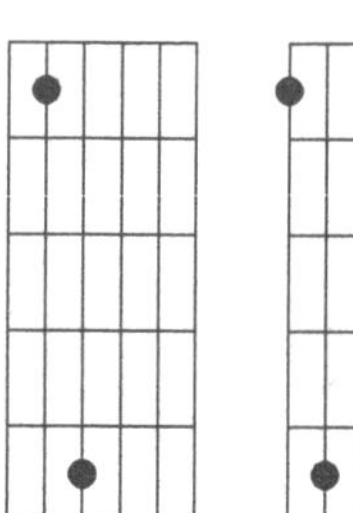
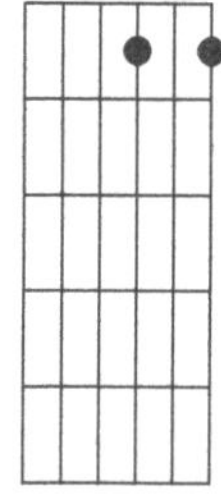
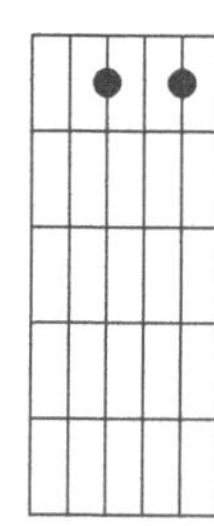
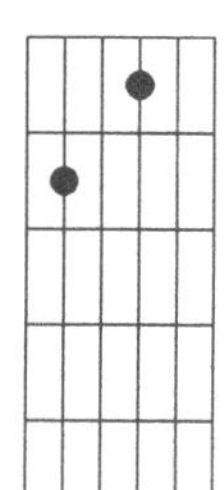
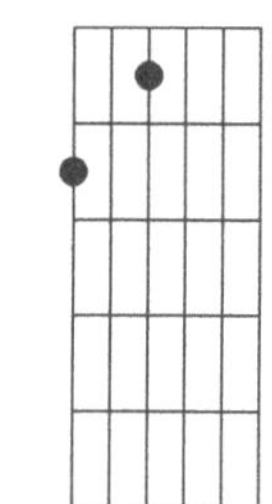
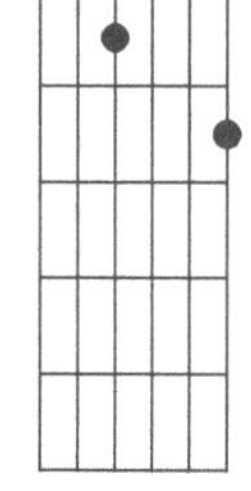
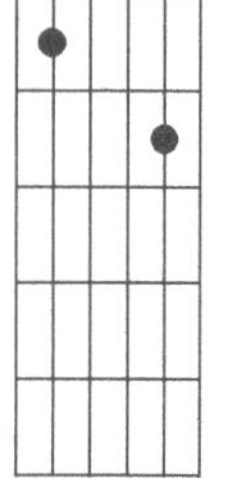
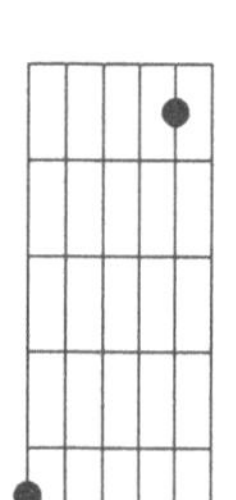
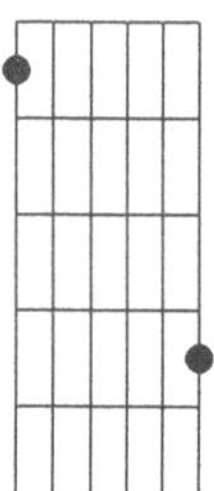
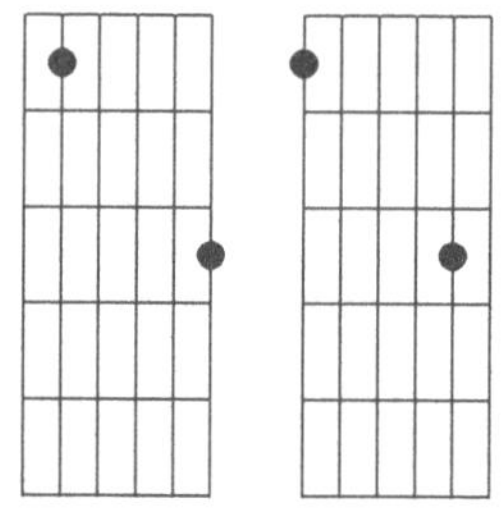
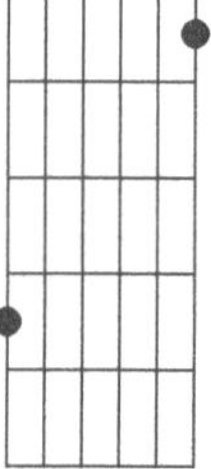

Exercise

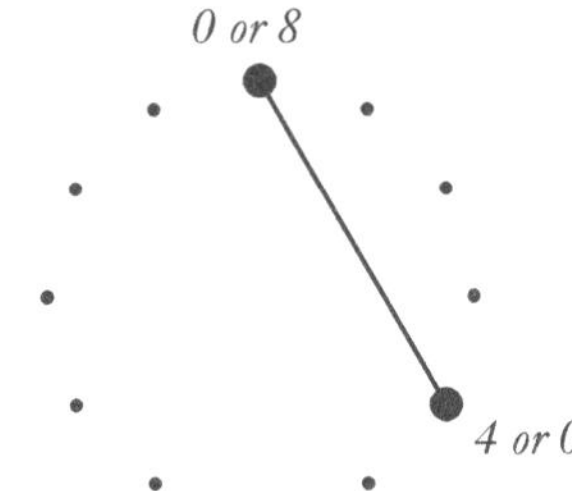

(0,4)

e.g. (C,E)

Common Name:

Major 3rd/ 10th
Diminished 4th/ 11th

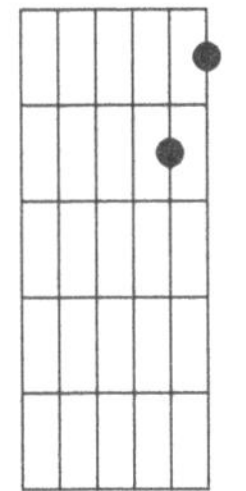
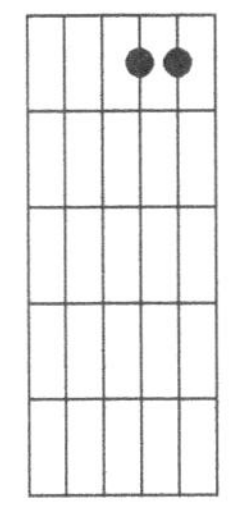
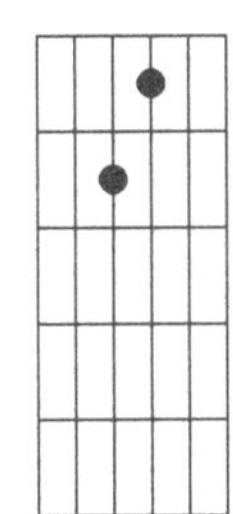
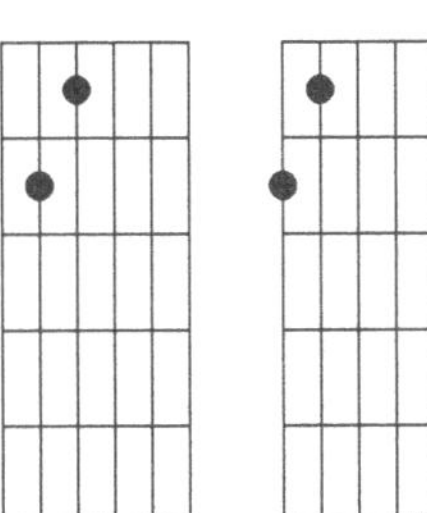
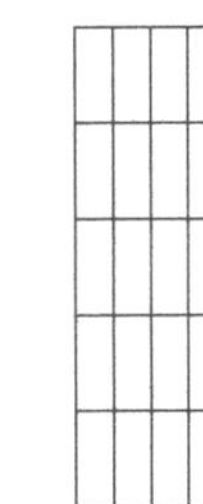
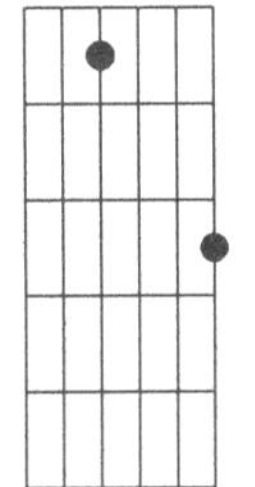
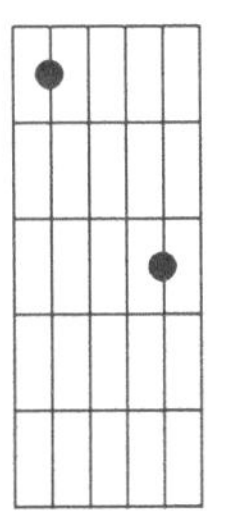
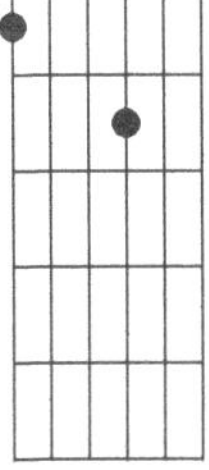
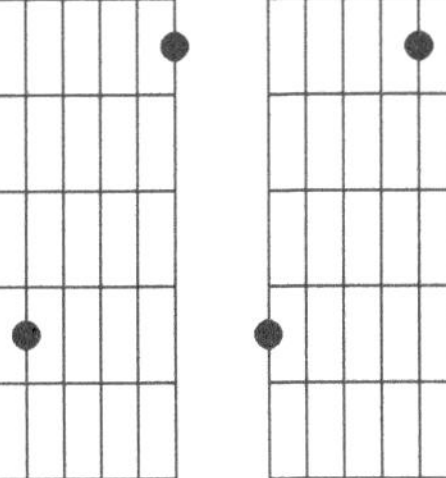
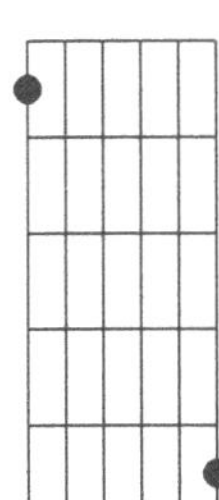

(0,8)

e.g. (C,A♭)

Common Name:

Minor 6th/ 13th
Augmented 5th/ 12th

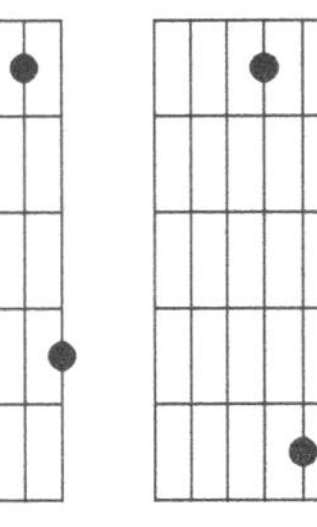
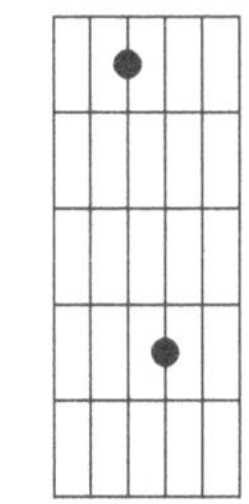
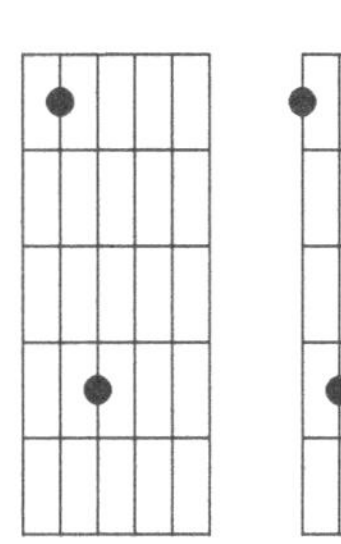
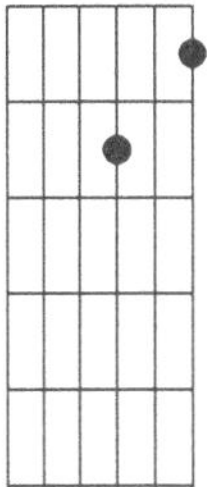

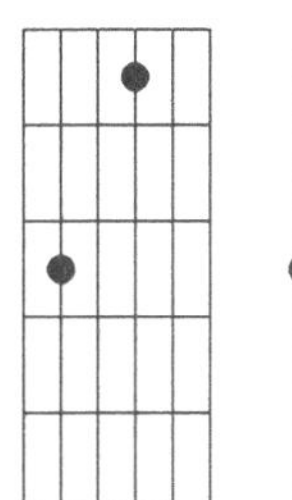
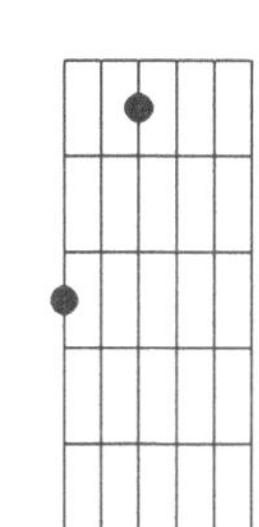
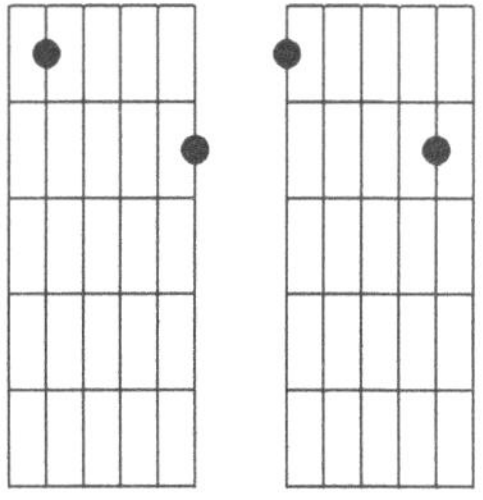
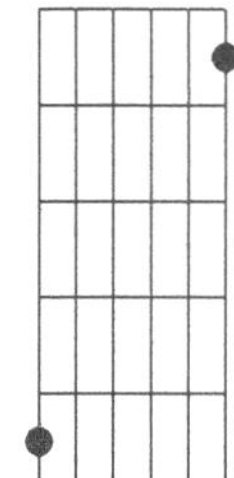

Exercise

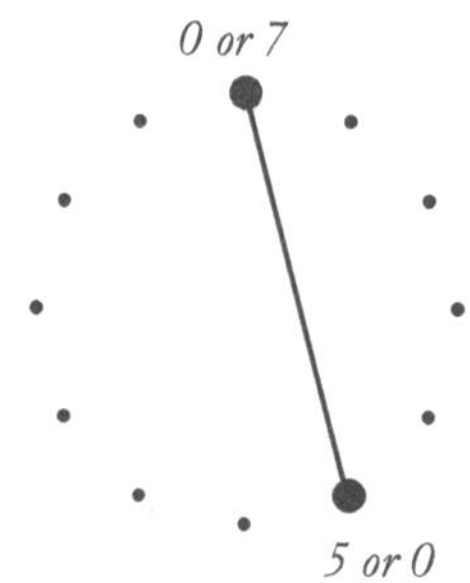

(0,5)

e.g. (C,F)

Common Name:

Perfect 4th/ 11th
Augmented 3rd/ 10th

(0,7)

e.g. (C,G)

Common Name:

Perfect 5th/ 12th
Diminished 6th/ 13th

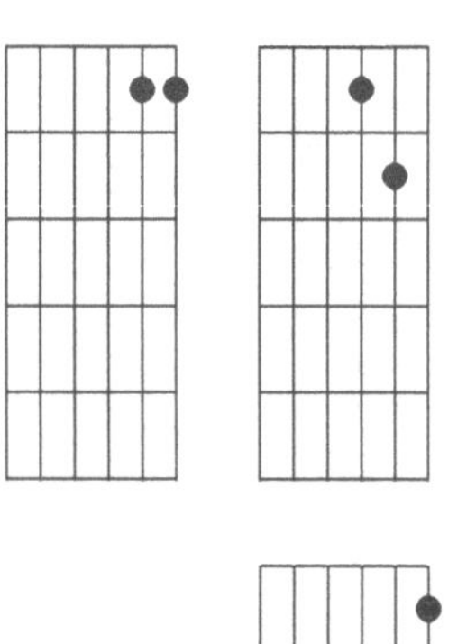

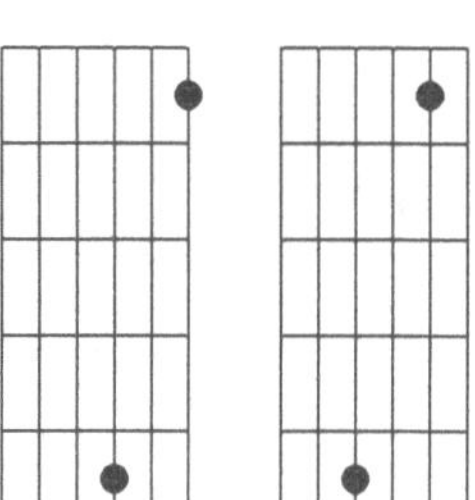

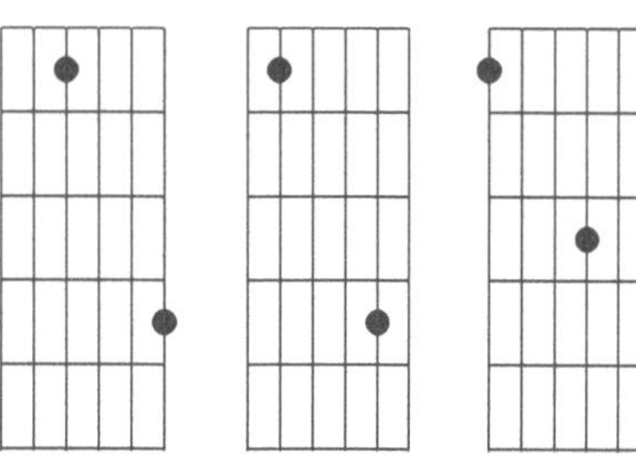

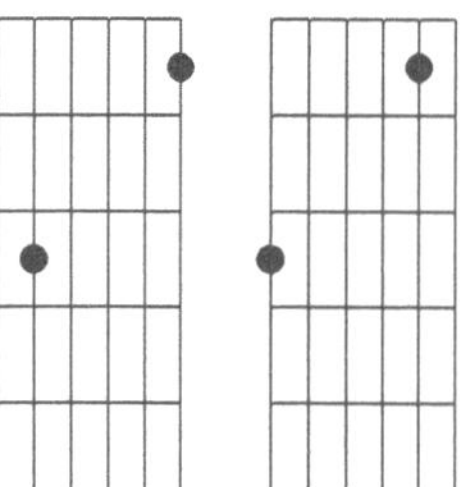

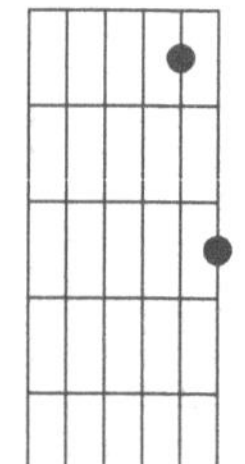

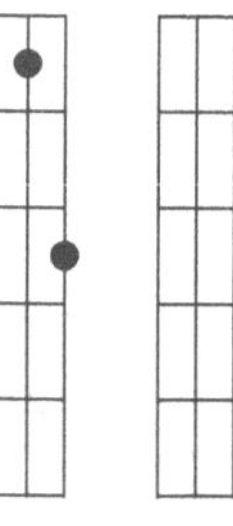

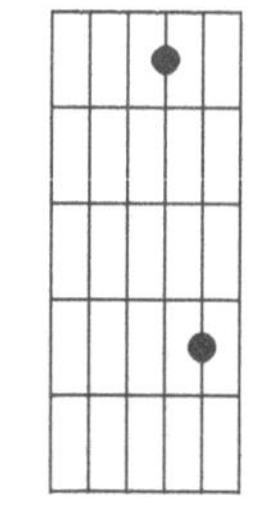

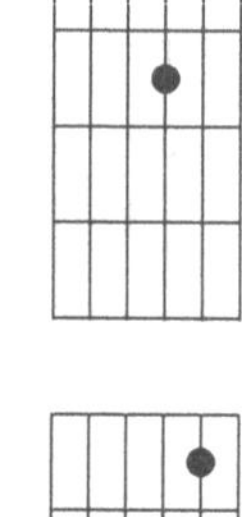

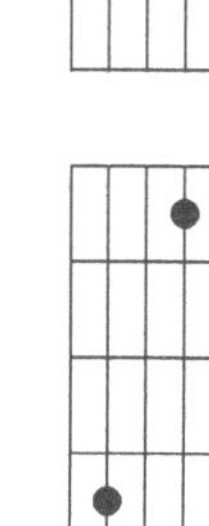

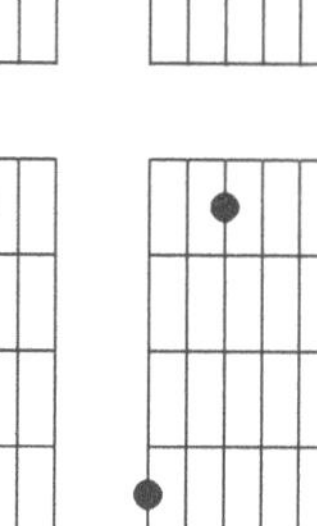

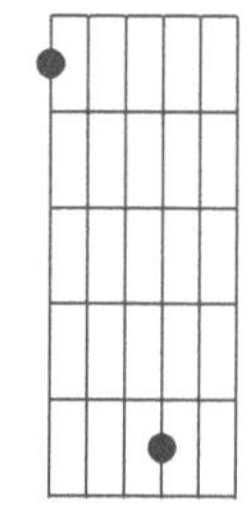

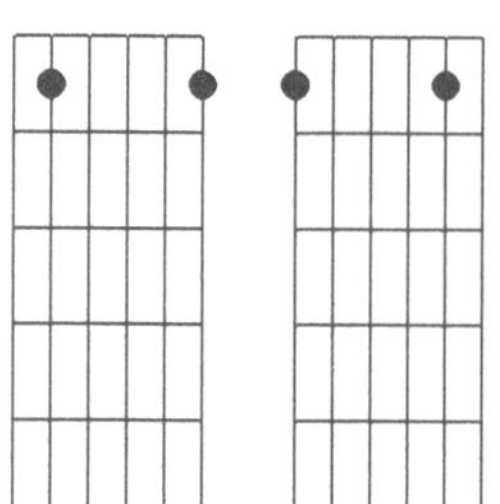

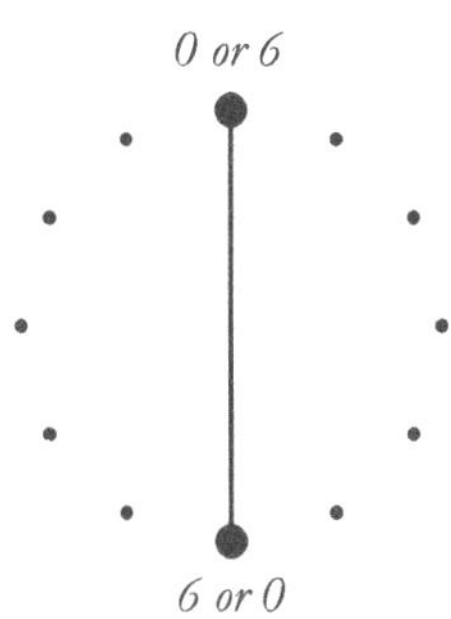

(0,6)

e.g. (C,G$^\flat$)

Common Name:

Tritone
Augmented 4th/11th
Diminished 5th/12th

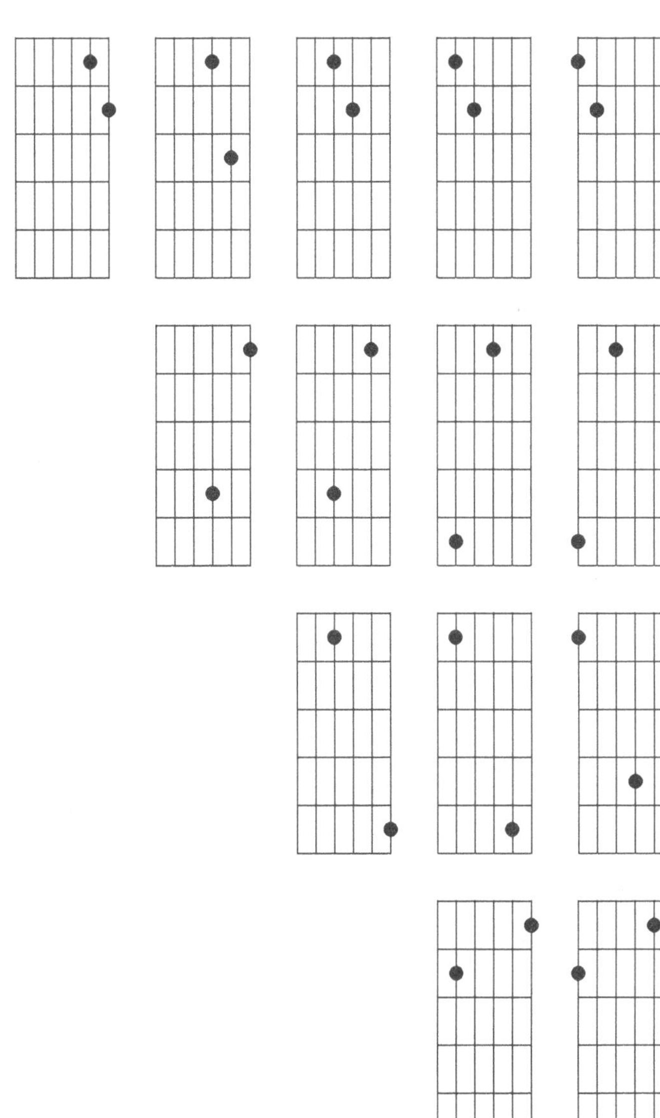

Exercise

127 DYAD FINGERINGS

This table shows the same information as the previous six pages, in 5th position (fingers do not move beyond frets 5-9).
Grouped staves show fingerings for interval pairs. Vertical lines show the type of string set being used.
- Play through these in 5th position. Read them in a different position, transposing by octaves when necessary.
- Make observations of commonalities in sounds on one staff, between a pair of staves, within one string set, and of dyads in general.

Exercise

INTERVAL TRAINER

The matrix below shows intervals in random order, where each row or column contains 11 different interval pairs.
Intervals are given in direction and number of semitones (for example, "+7, -5" means, "up a perfect 5th or down a perfect 4th").
Correspondences for all intervals are as follows:

1 = semitone, half step
2 = tone, whole step
3 = aug. 2nd, minor 3rd
4 = major third, dim. 4th
5 = perfect 4th
6 = tritone, aug. 4th, dim. 5th
7 = perfect 5th
8 = aug. 5th, minor 6th
9 = major 6th, diminished 7th
10 = aug. 6th, minor 7th
11 = major 7th, dim. octave

- *Without guitar: Starting on any pitch, sing through any row or column, picking the upward or downward interval to suit vocal range. After 11 intervals, the note should be a tritone away from the intital pitch. Sing two rows or columns to return to the original pitch.*
- *With guitar: Sing any comfortable, mid-range note. Play the same pitch on guitar, trying to match it on the first try. Read through any row or column, singing the interval first and then matching the pitch with the guitar.*

+7, -5	+2, -10	+6, -6	+9, -3	+5, -7	+10, -2	+8, -4	+11, -1	+4, -8	+1, -11	+3, -9
+6, -6	+8, -4	+1, -11	+2, -10	+11, -1	+4, -8	+9, -3	+3, -9	+10, -2	+5, -7	+7, -5
+3, -9	+10, -2	+2, -10	+5, -7	+6, -6	+9, -3	+7, -5	+8, -4	+1, -11	+11, -1	+4, -8
+9, -3	+11, -1	+8, -4	+10, -2	+7, -5	+2, -10	+5, -7	+6, -6	+3, -9	+4, -8	+1, -11
+8, -4	+1, -11	+10, -2	+11, -1	+4, -8	+5, -7	+3, -9	+7, -5	+6, -6	+9, -3	+2, -10
+4, -8	+6, -6	+3, -9	+1, -11	+10, -2	+8, -4	+11, -1	+9, -3	+2, -10	+7, -5	+5, -7
+10, -2	+9, -3	+5, -7	+4, -8	+2, -10	+7, -5	+6, -6	+1, -11	+11, -1	+3, -9	+8, -4
+5, -7	+7, -5	+9, -3	+3, -9	+1, -11	+6, -6	+10, -2	+4, -8	+8, -4	+2, -10	+11, -1
+2, -10	+3, -9	+4, -8	+7, -5	+9, -3	+11, -1	+1, -11	+10, -2	+5, -7	+8, -4	+6, -6
+1, -11	+5, -7	+11, -1	+6, -6	+8, -4	+3, -9	+4, -8	+2, -10	+7, -5	+10, -2	+9, -3
+11, -1	+4, -8	+7, -5	+8, -4	+3, -9	+1, -11	+2, -10	+5, -7	+9, -3	+6, -6	+10, -2

Notes *Idea: Without the guitar, compose a melody on the top staff. Write a counter melody on the next staff, and play both on guitar. Listen to the dyads. Write another melody on the third staff, and play 2nd and 3rd staves together. Continue.*

Concept

THE TRIAD
(THREE PITCHES)

The 19 Triads:

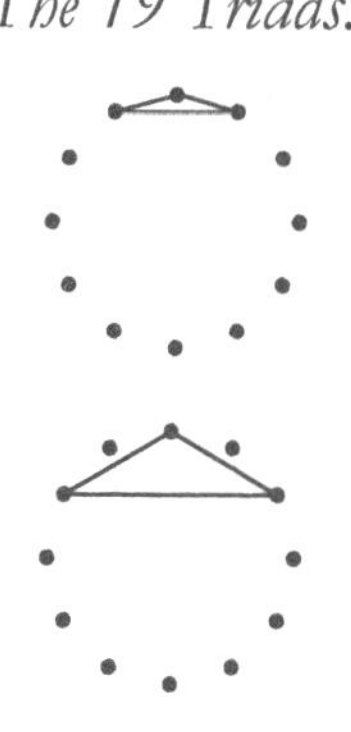

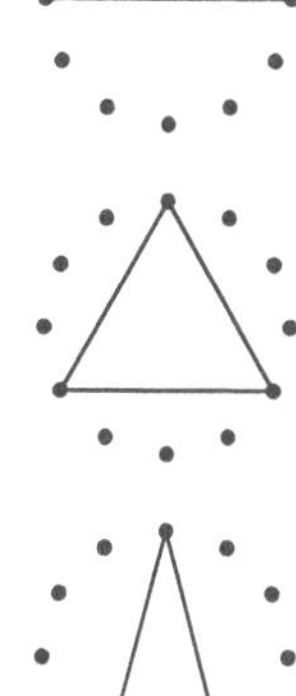

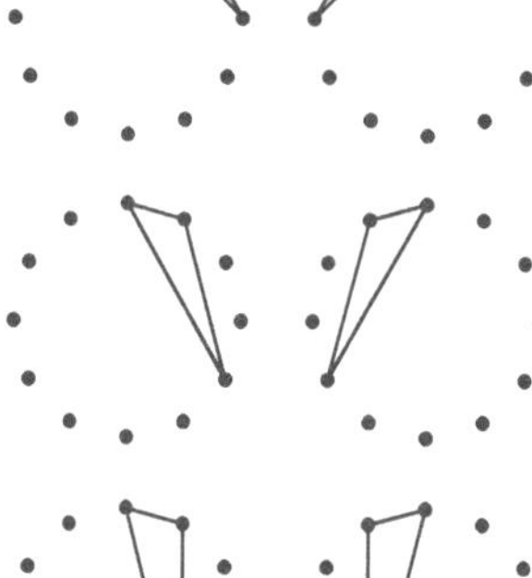

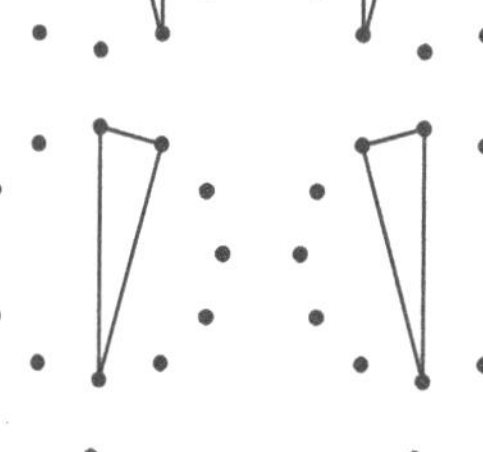

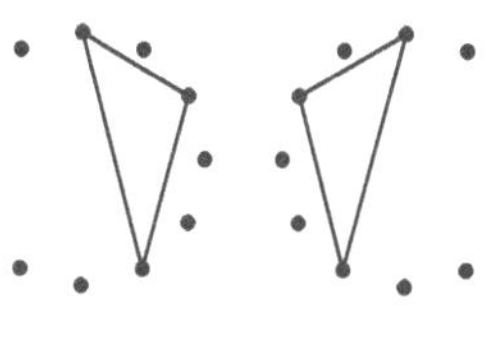

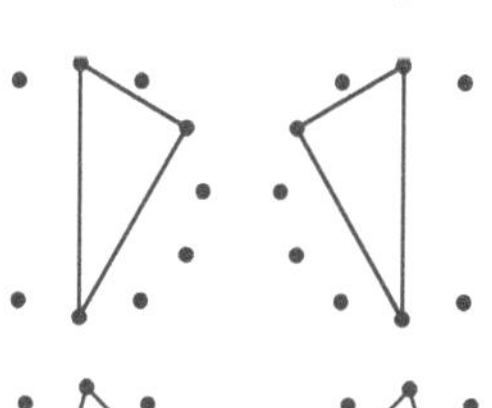

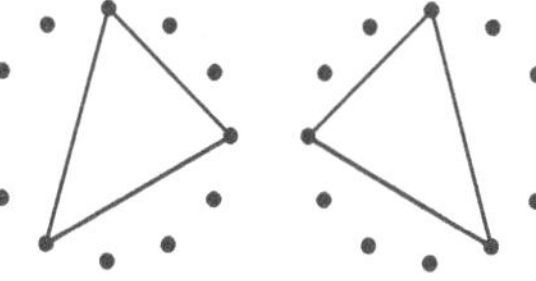

Take a circle of 12 points, connect any three points with a line, and you will get some rotation of one of the nineteen shapes on the right. The same 19 triads can also be made by taking any of the six dyads, adding one other pitch, and eliminating duplicates. Yet another, more methodical way to get this result is to see that there are only 12 ways to divide the octave into three parts:

1 + 1 + 10	*2 + 2 + 8*	*3 + 3 + 6*	*4 + 4 + 4*	*5 + 5 + 2*
1 + 2 + 9	*2 + 3 + 7*	*3 + 4 + 5*		
1 + 3 + 8	*2 + 4 + 6*			
1 + 4 + 7				
1 + 5 + 6				

There are five divisions that have two or more parts of equal size, shown on the top row. These triads will be symmetrical (the top five figures on the right), and changing the order of the intervals may transpose them, but does not change their fundamental quality. For example, the triad *(B, D, F)* has an interval structure of *(3 + 3 + 6)*. Changing the order to *(6 + 3 + 3)* will yield the triad *(B, F, Ab)*, which uses different pitches but is really just a transposition of the original structure by a tritone (from a B diminished triad to an F diminished triad). This is true of any of the five symmetrical triads.

The remaining 14 triads have intervals of three different sizes, and changing the order yields a structure that sounds fundamentally different. For example, the triad *(C, Eb, G)* has an interval structure of *(3 + 4 + 5)*. Changing the order to *(4 + 3 + 5)* will yield the triad *(C, E, G)*. These are the C minor and C major triads, two structures with the same intervallic content but different ordering and a different sonic impression. These 14 triads are shown on the right, in symmetrical pairs.

The following pages show, when possible, a fingering for each of the 3 inversions of each 19 triads for each 20 possible sets of three strings. The key on the following page describes this in detail. Fingerings are chosen with these guidelines:

1) If there are two or more options for a fingering, the one with the smaller fret span is chosen. For example, the first listing for the triad (0,1,6) has two possible fingerings. If we say the lowest note in each case is a "B", we get:

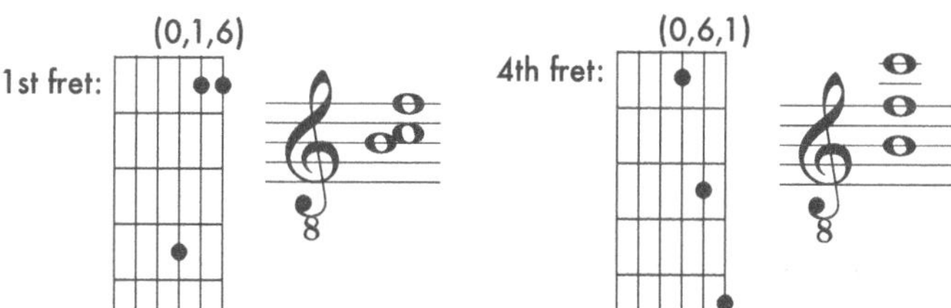

The same pitches are in each structure, but the first is listed because it is more physically compact.

If two possible fingerings have the same fret span, the one that is easier to physically grasp is chosen. For example, the second listing of the same triad has these possibilities, both with 5 fret spans:

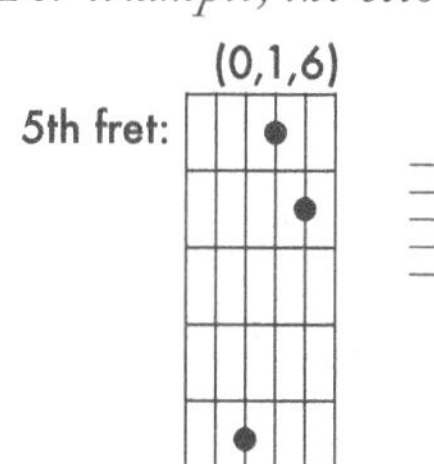

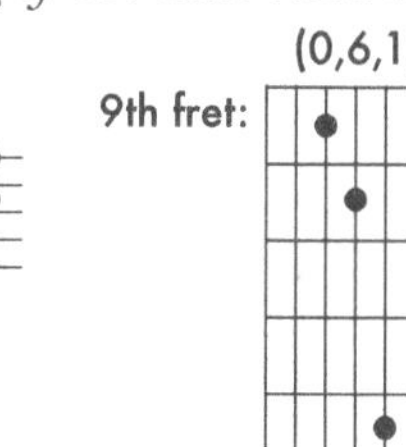

The second fingering is chosen because it is more physically natural.

Exercise

TABLE OF TRIADIC ELEMENTS

This is a key for the following pages.
There are 19 possible triads.
There are 3 possible inversions of each triad.
There are 20 possible combinations of 3 strings.
The 19 pages that folllow show all triads in all inversions on all string sets, omitting redundancies and instances where the fingering is impossible.
These are indicated by blank spaces.
Any three note shape within a span of five frets will be located somewhere in the table.

- Play through various fingerings on any page.
- Mark up the page, taking note of interesting shapes and sounds.

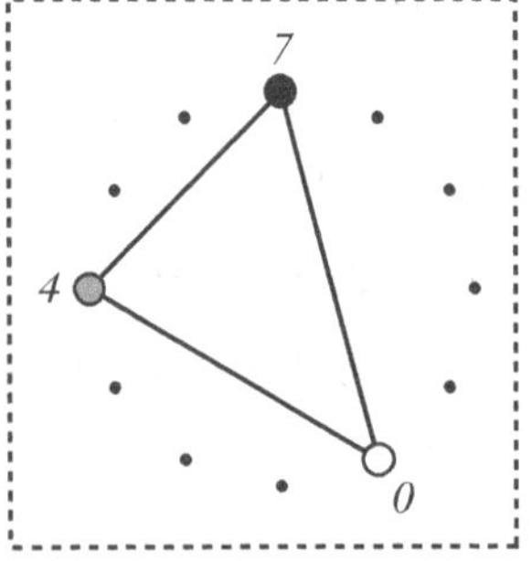

Upper Center:

Pitch set drawn on a chromatic circle, differentiated by color, labeled with numbers.

(0,4,7)
e.g. (C,E,G)

Upper Right Corner:

3 numbers describing the positions of pitches on the circle in clockwise order from the white circle.
Below this, an example in traditional pitch names, where ○ = 0 = C

String sets: *Fingerings follow this pattern of 20 sets of three strings. High E string = 1.*
Colors of circles in the fingerings correspond to the shape above.

Inversions:

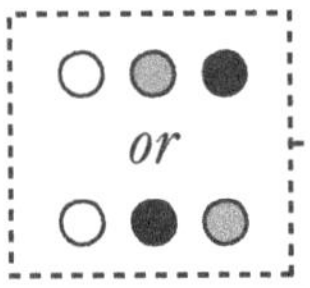

○ ◐ ● or ○ ● ◐
e.g. (C,E,G) or (C,G,E)

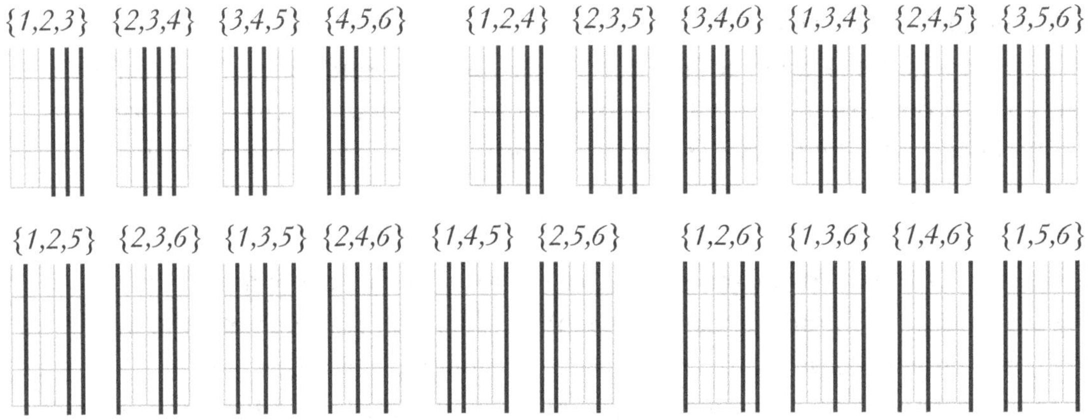

{1,2,3} {2,3,4} {3,4,5} {4,5,6} {1,2,4} {2,3,5} {3,4,6} {1,3,4} {2,4,5} {3,5,6}

{1,2,5} {2,3,6} {1,3,5} {2,4,6} {1,4,5} {2,5,6} {1,2,6} {1,3,6} {1,4,6} {1,5,6}

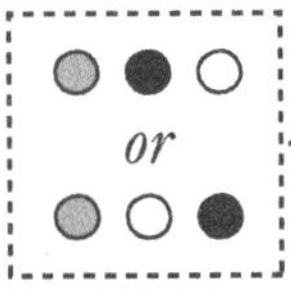

◐ ● ○ or ◐ ○ ●
e.g. (E,C,G) or (E,G,C)

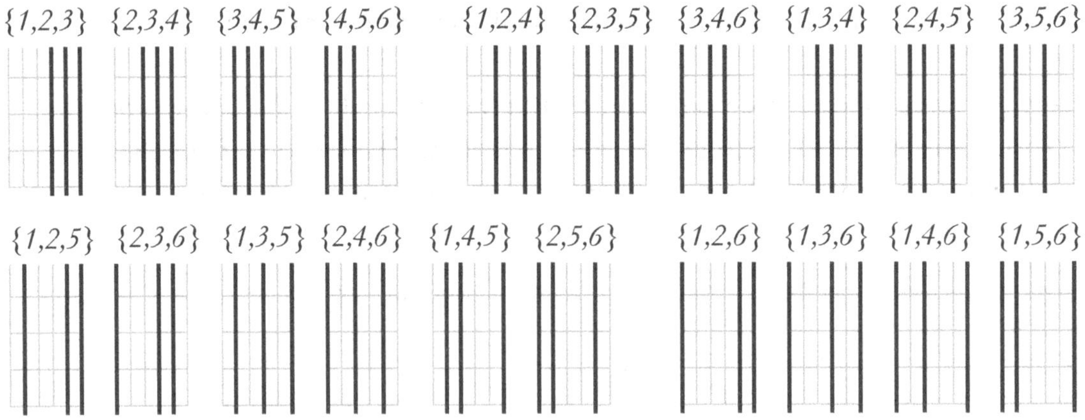

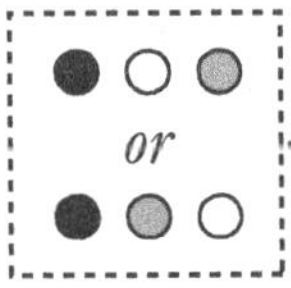

{1,2,3} {2,3,4} {3,4,5} {4,5,6} {1,2,4} {2,3,5} {3,4,6} {1,3,4} {2,4,5} {3,5,6}

{1,2,5} {2,3,6} {1,3,5} {2,4,6} {1,4,5} {2,5,6} {1,2,6} {1,3,6} {1,4,6} {1,5,6}

● ○ ◐ or ● ◐ ○
e.g. (G,C,E) or (G,E,C)

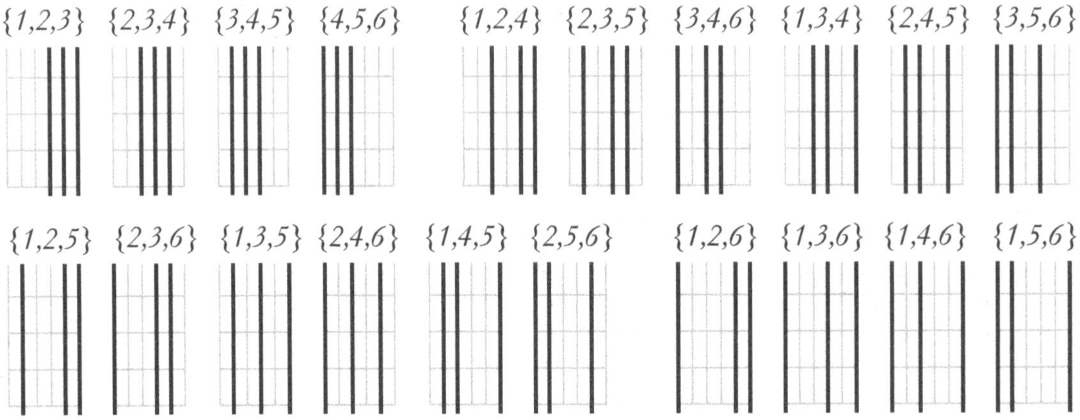

{1,2,3} {2,3,4} {3,4,5} {4,5,6} {1,2,4} {2,3,5} {3,4,6} {1,3,4} {2,4,5} {3,5,6}

{1,2,5} {2,3,6} {1,3,5} {2,4,6} {1,4,5} {2,5,6} {1,2,6} {1,3,6} {1,4,6} {1,5,6}

Exercise

(0,1,2)

e.g. (C,D♭,D)

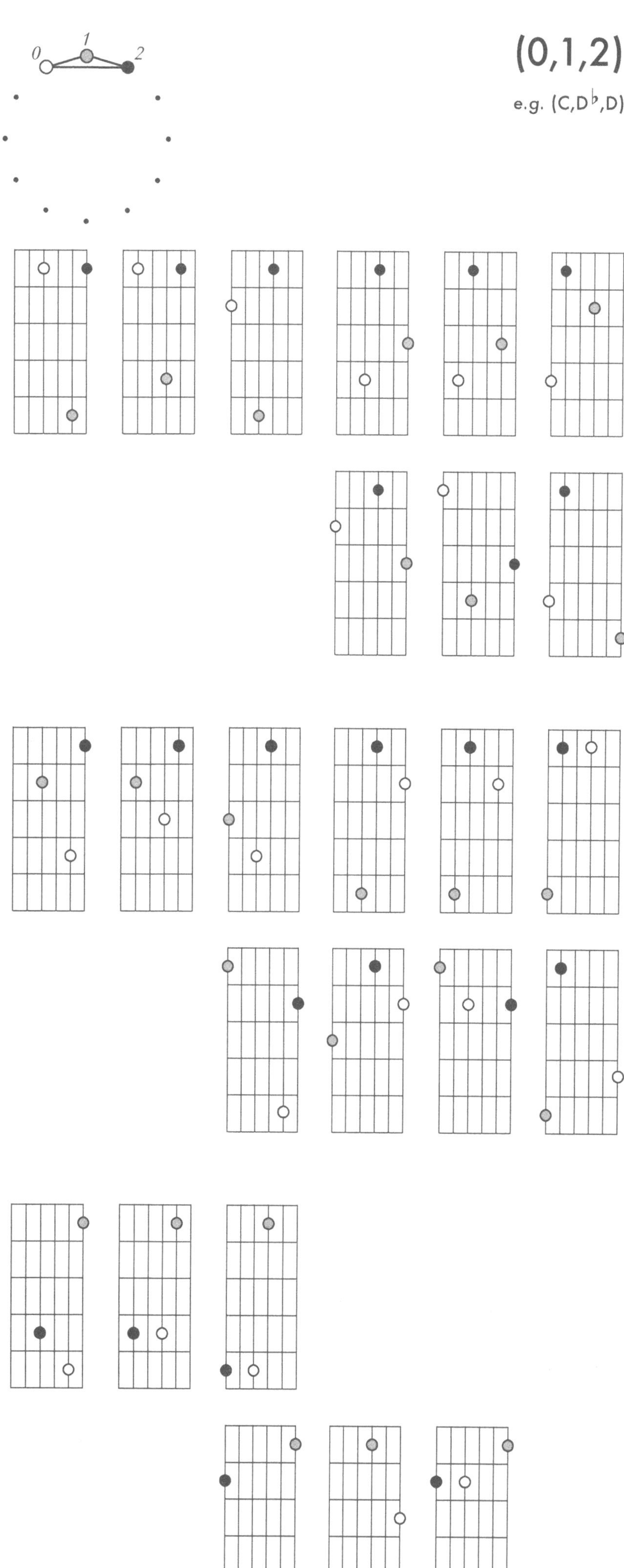

Exercise

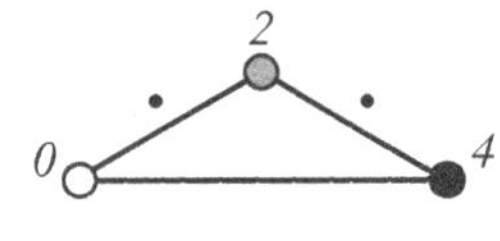

(0,2,4)

e.g. (C,D,E)

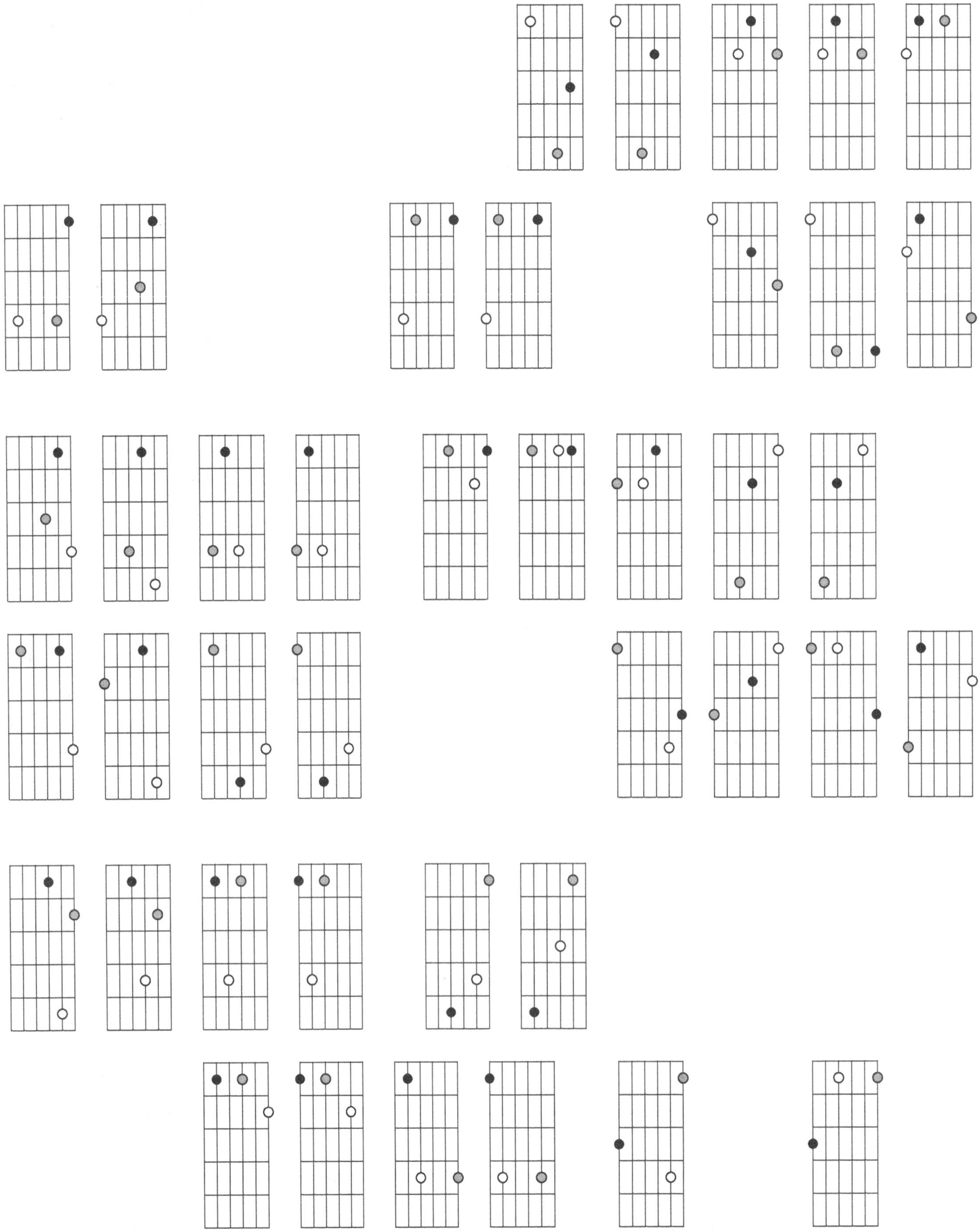

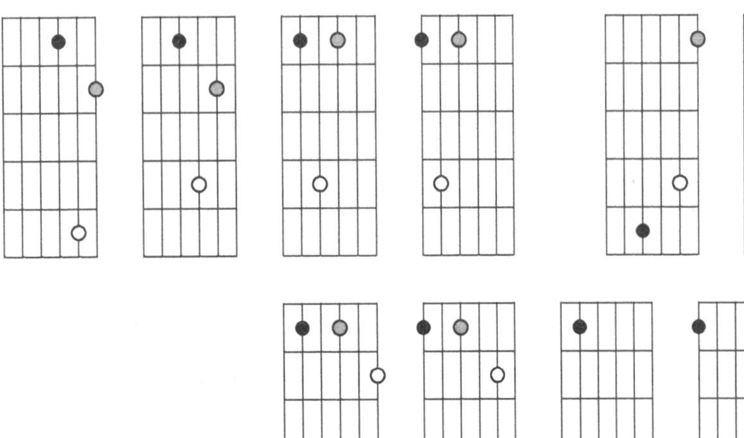

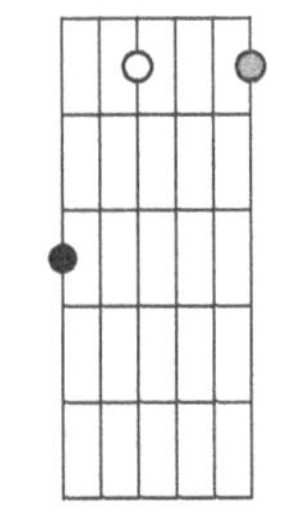

Exercise

(0,3,6)

e.g. (C,E$^{\flat}$,G$^{\flat}$)

Common Name: Diminished Triad

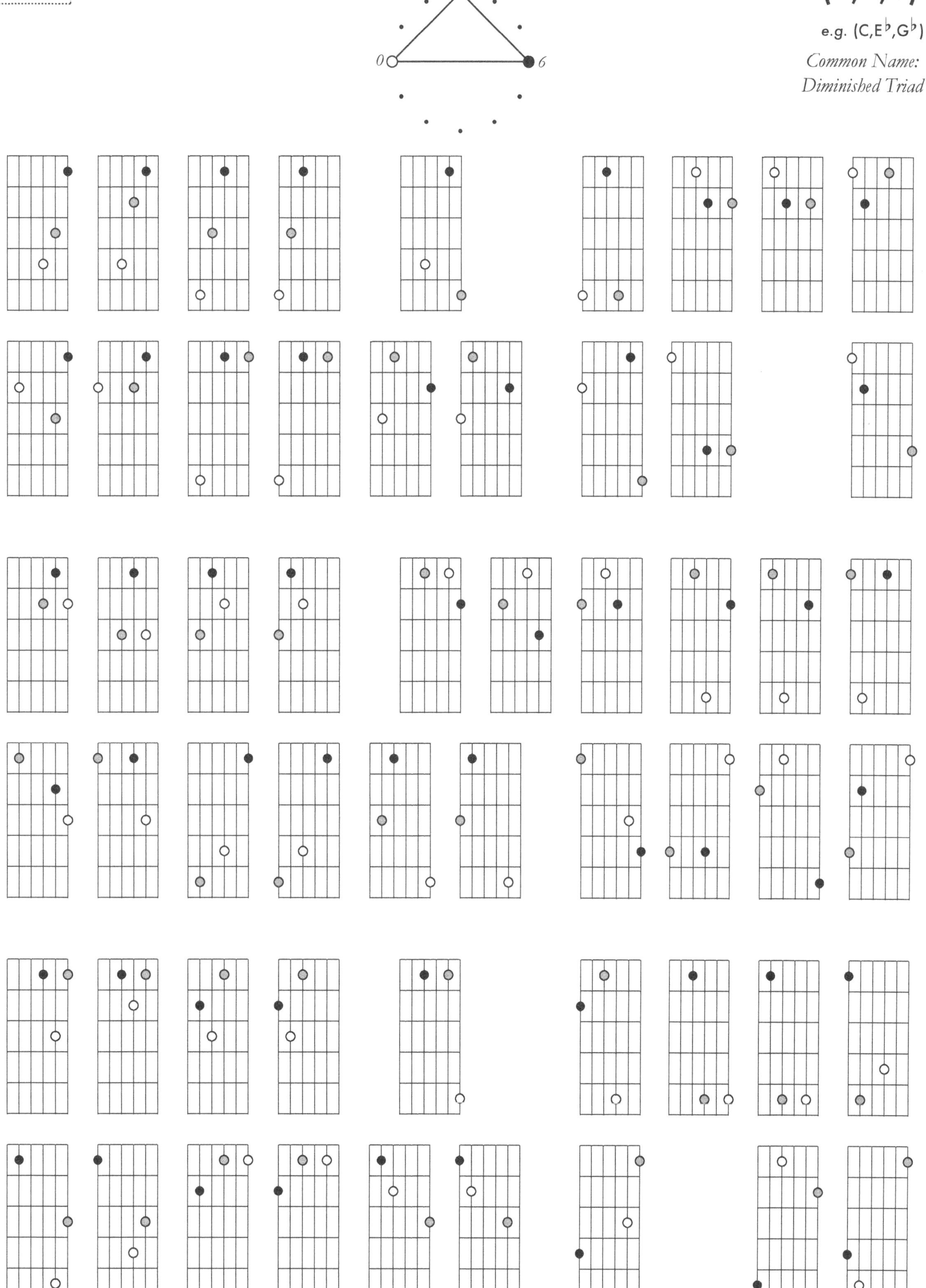

Exercise

Note:
Fingerings are all the same color on this page, because this triad has only one type of interval and all inversions are identical.

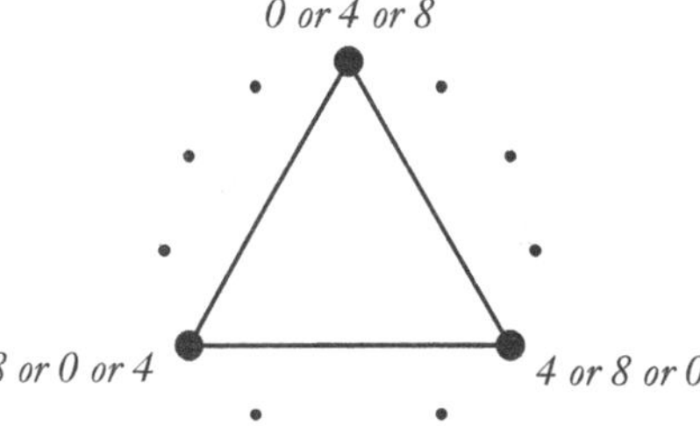

(0,4,8)

e.g. (C,E,A♭)

Common Name:
Augmented Triad

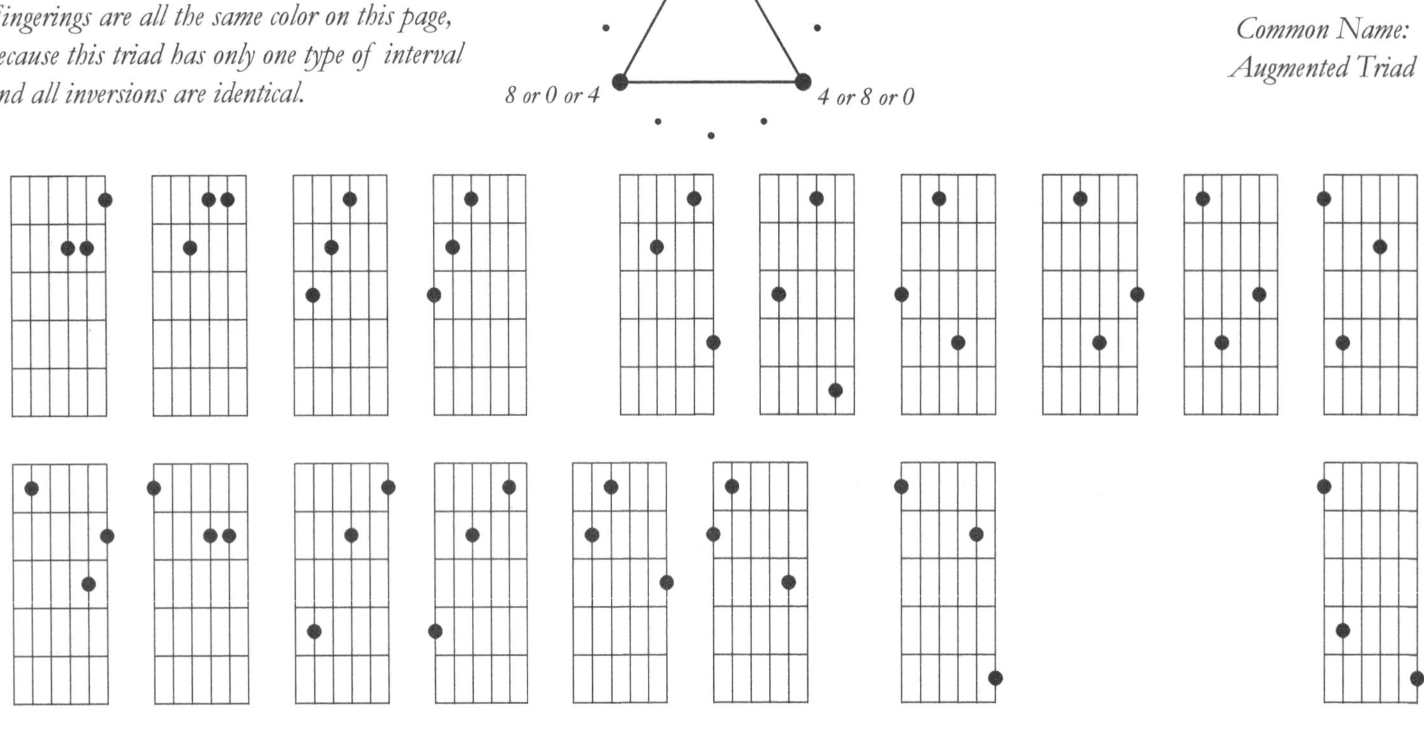

Exercise

(0,2,7)

e.g. (C,D,G)

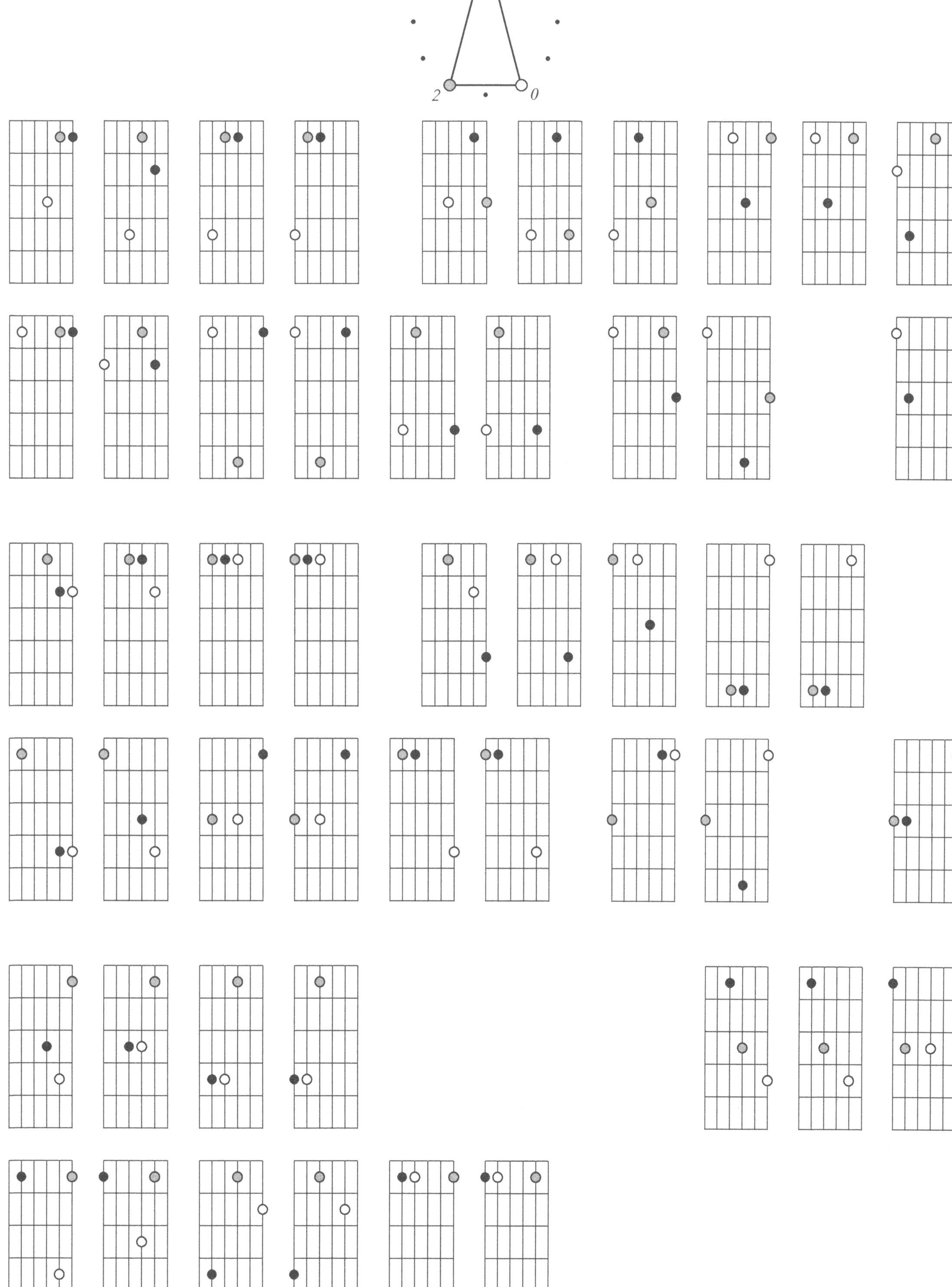

Exercise

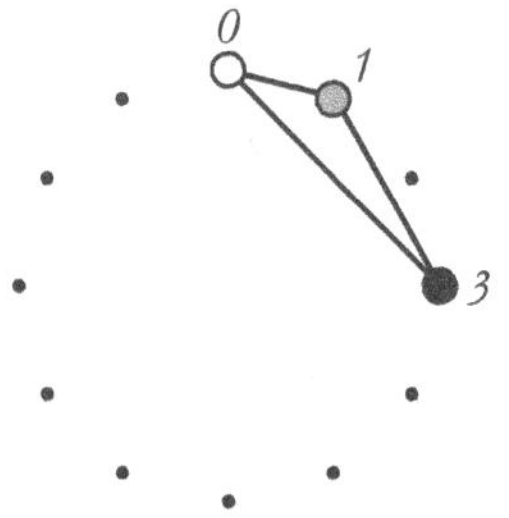

(0,1,3)

e.g. (C,D♭,E♭)

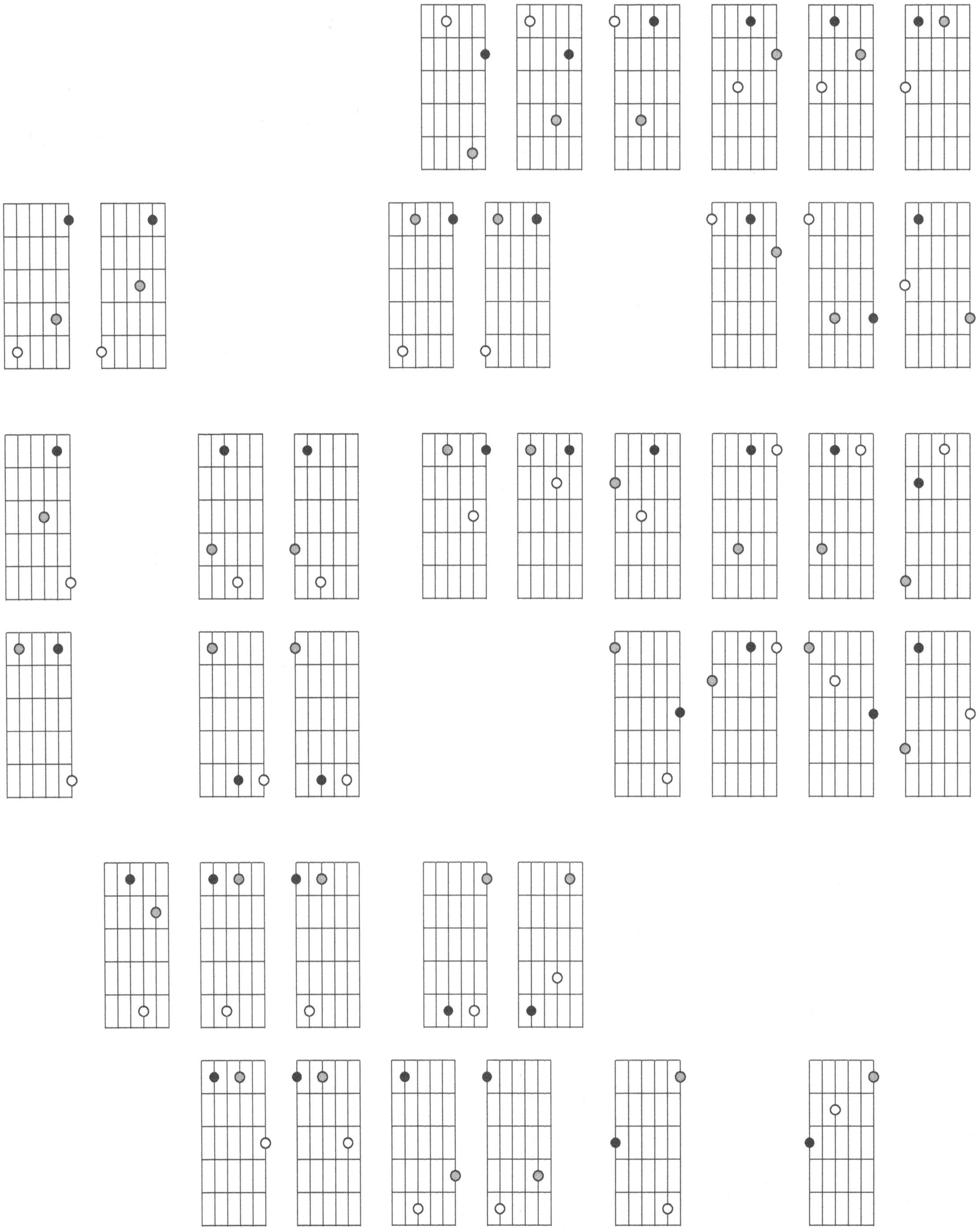

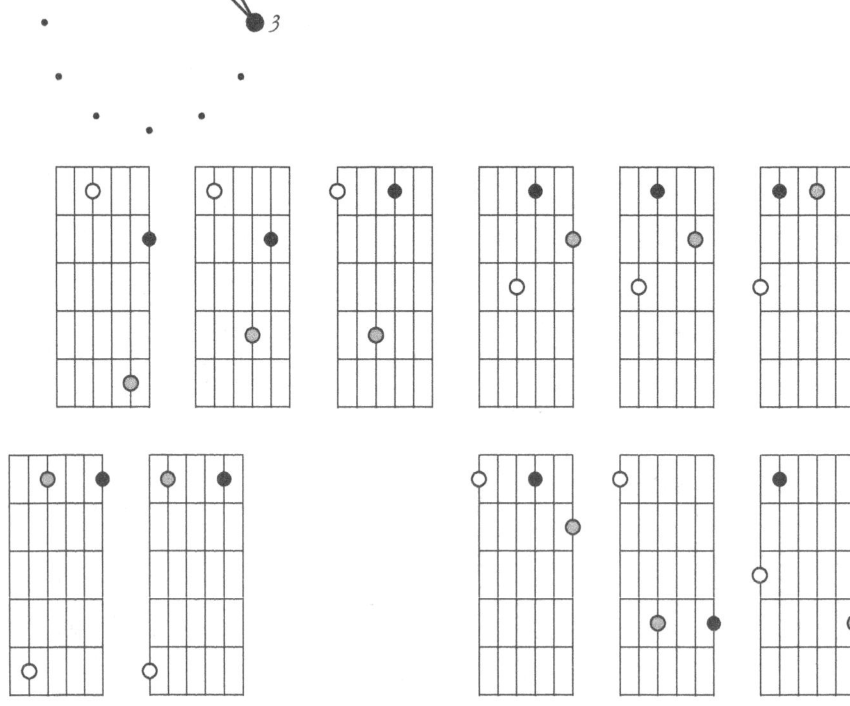

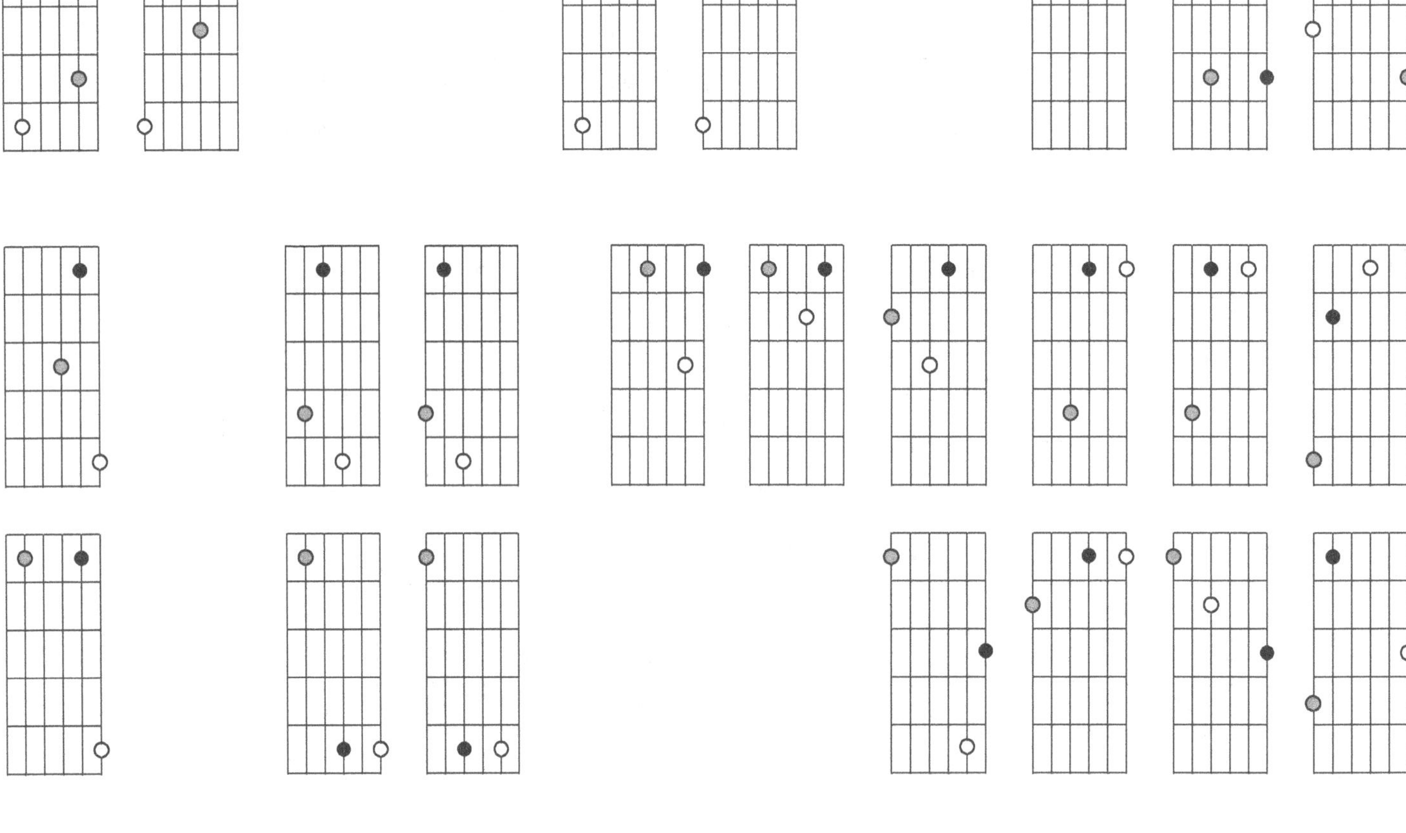

Exercise

(0,2,3)

e.g. (C,D,E$^{\flat}$)

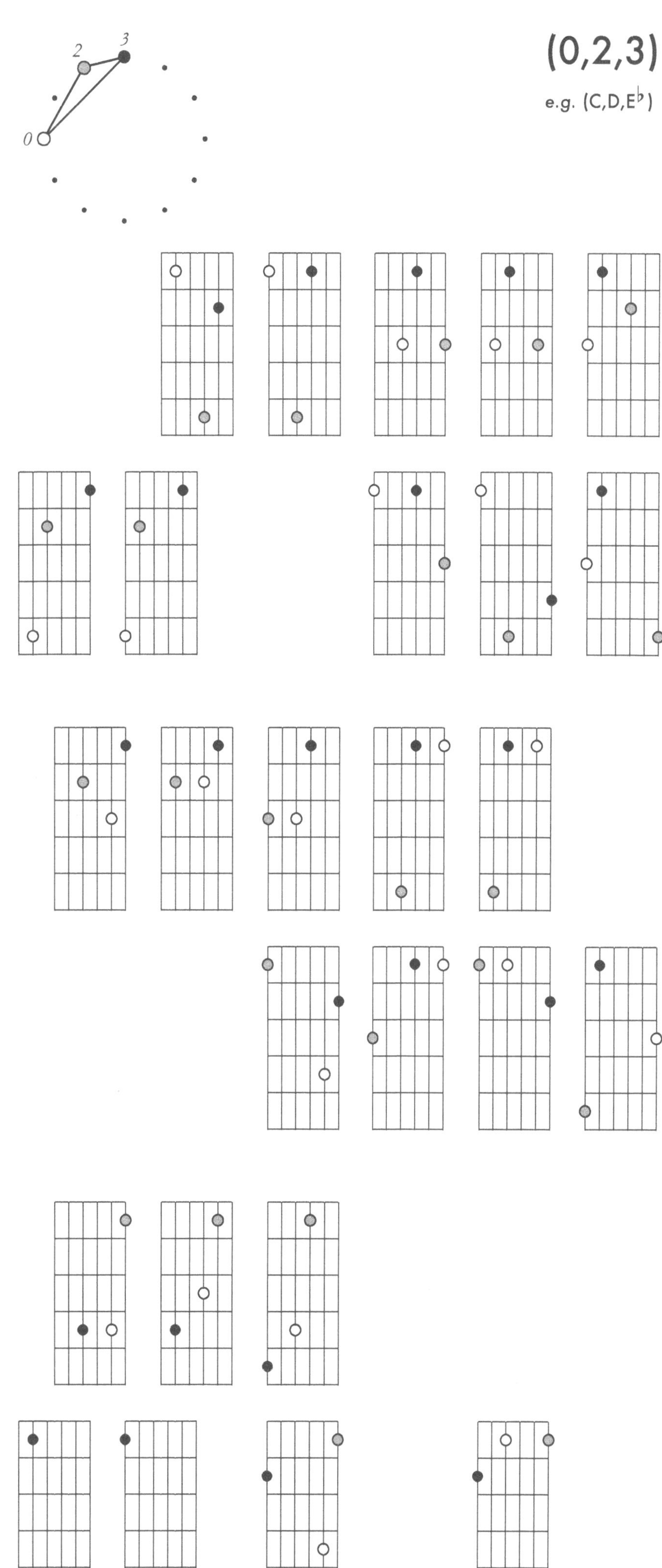

Exercise

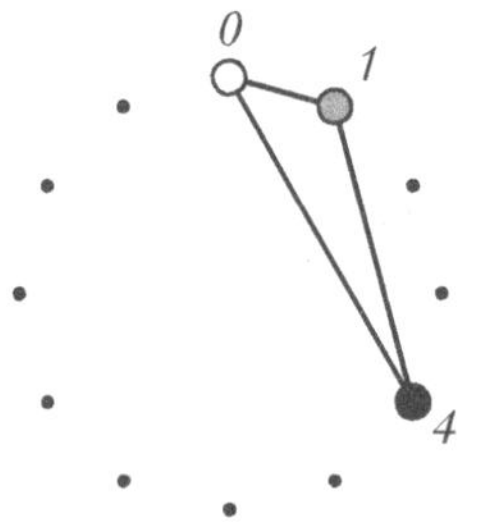

(0,1,4)

e.g. (C,D$^\flat$,E)

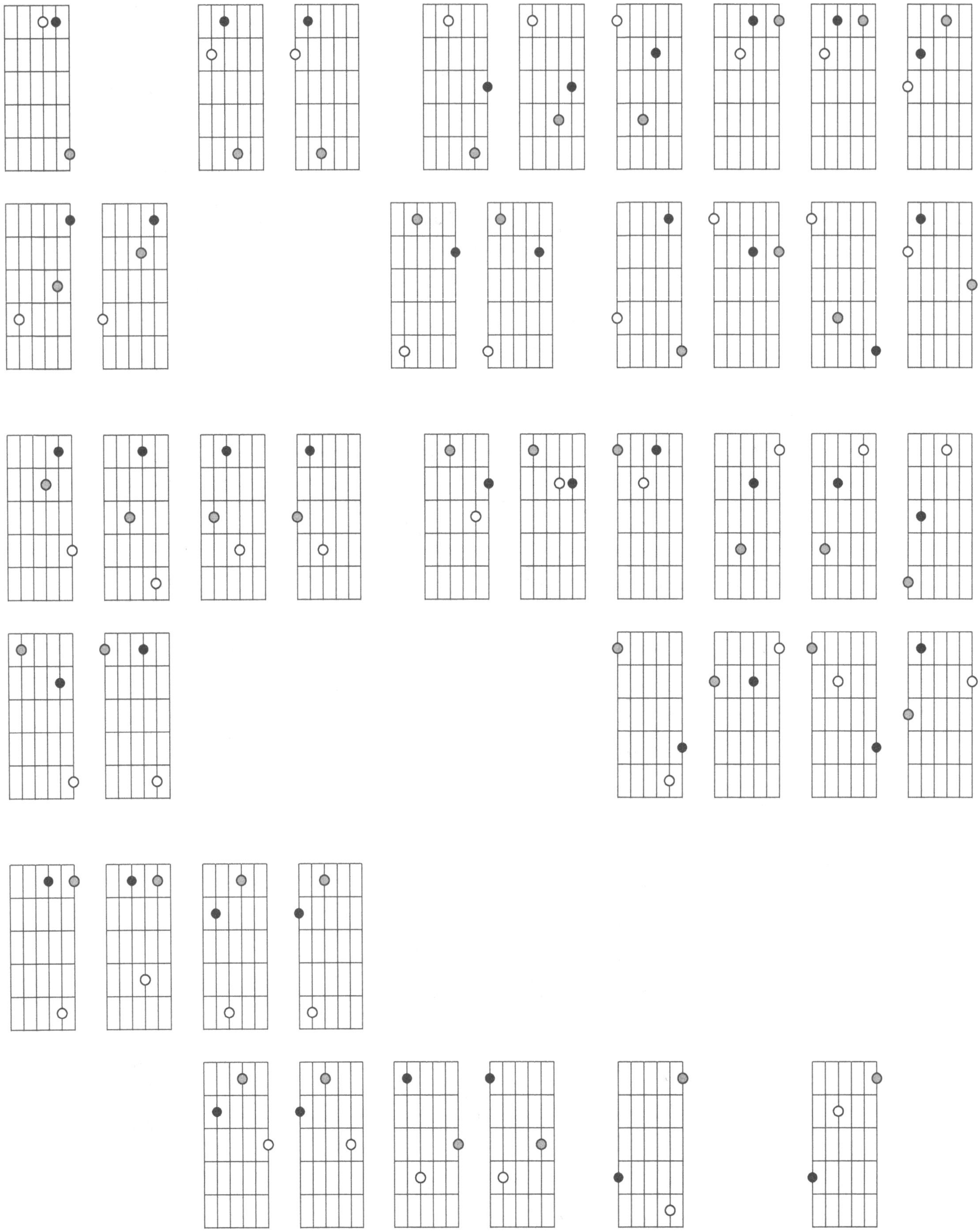

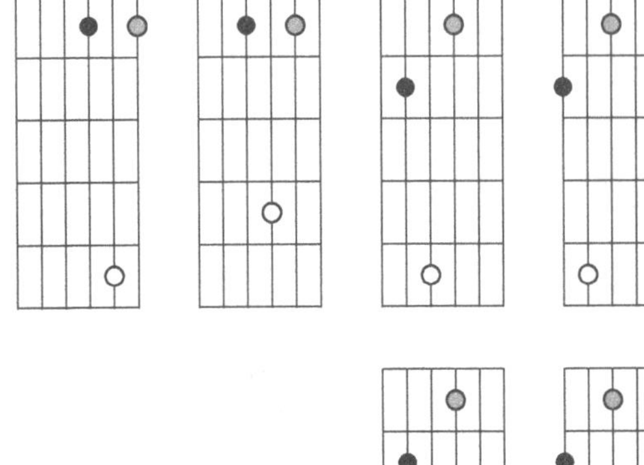

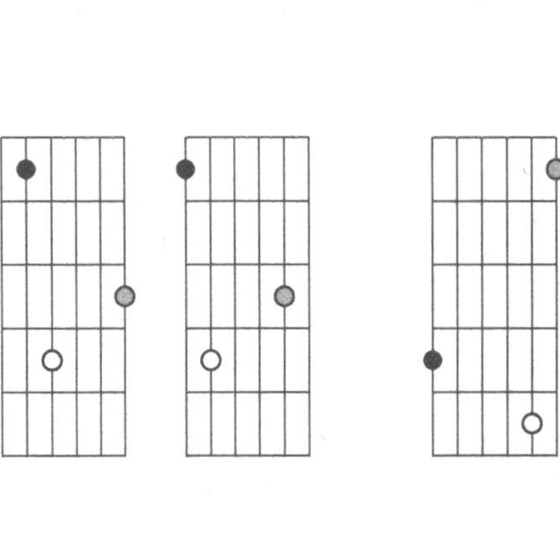

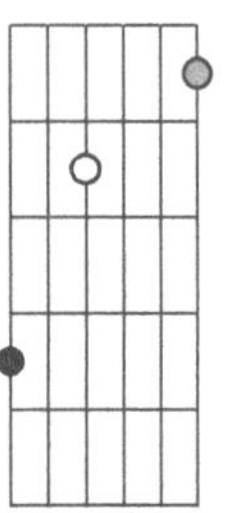

Exercise

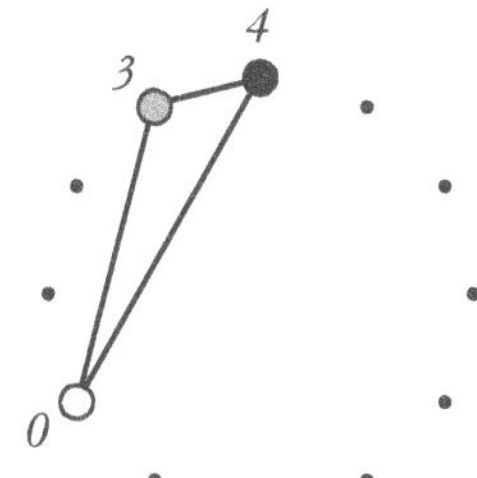

e.g. (C,D♯,E)

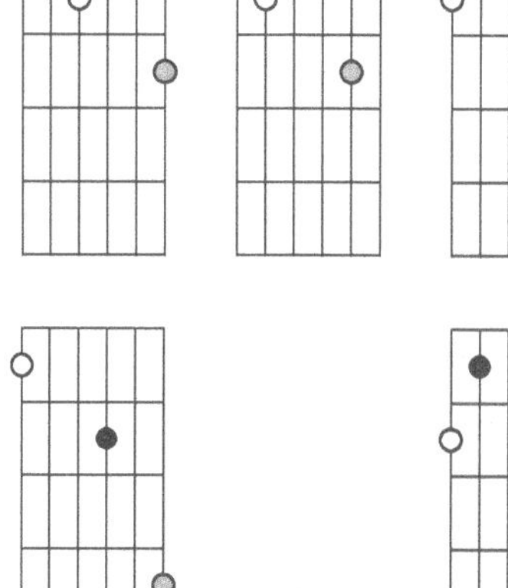

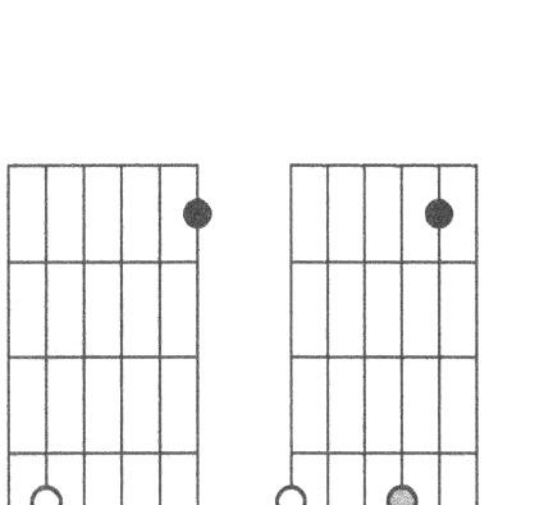

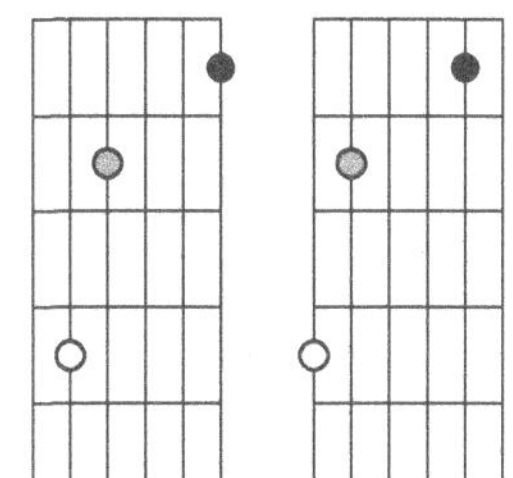

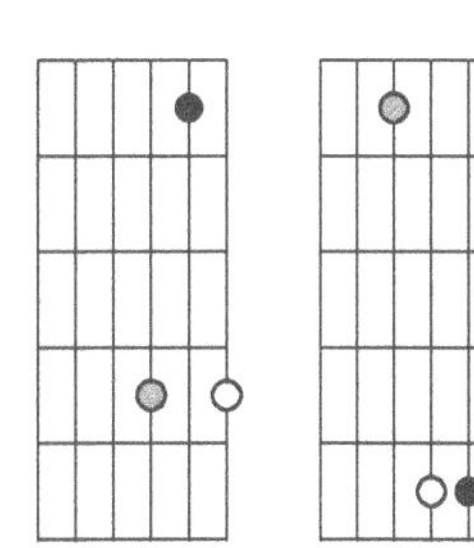

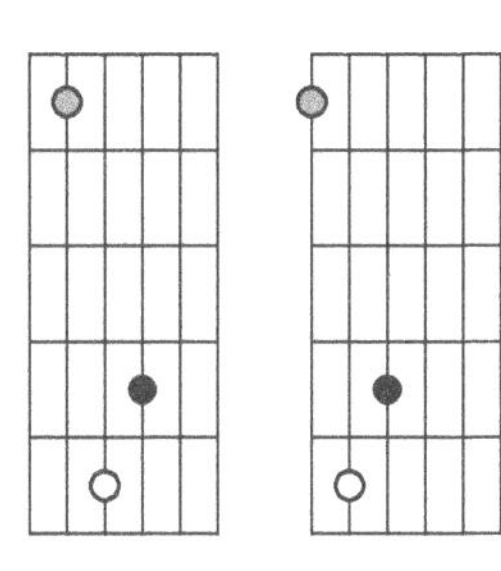

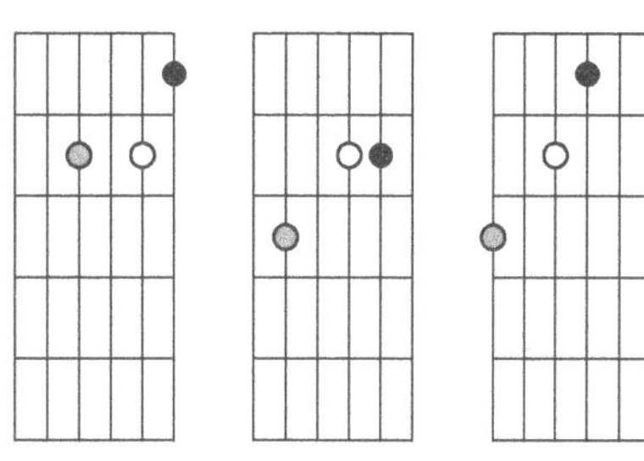

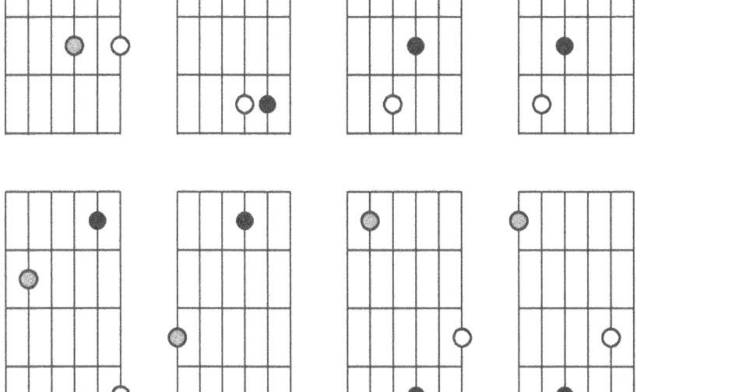

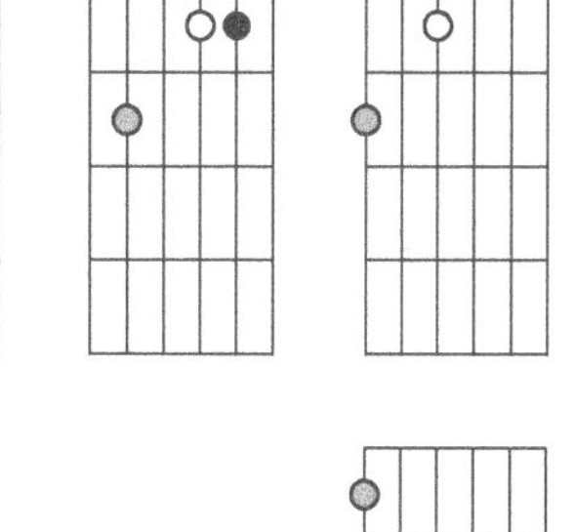

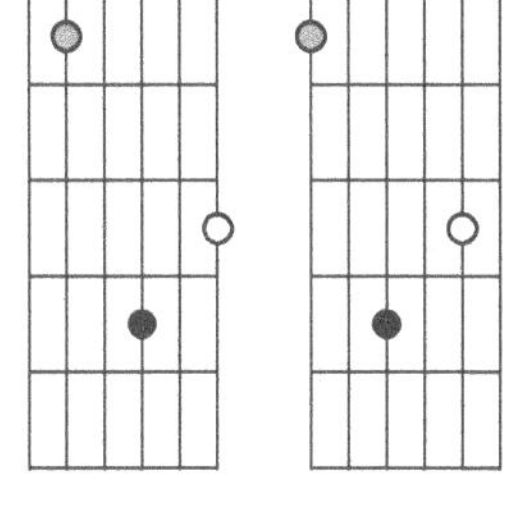

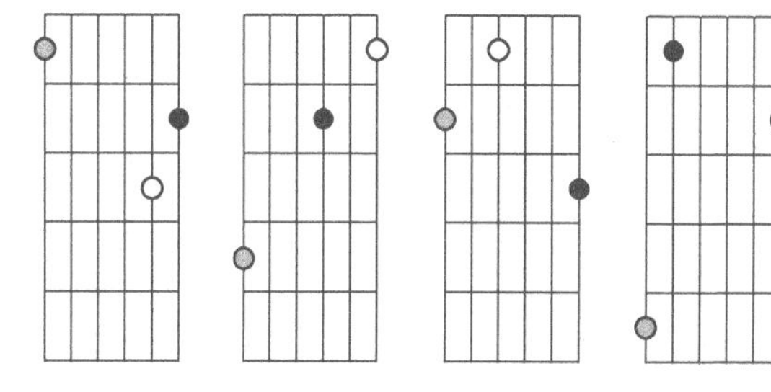

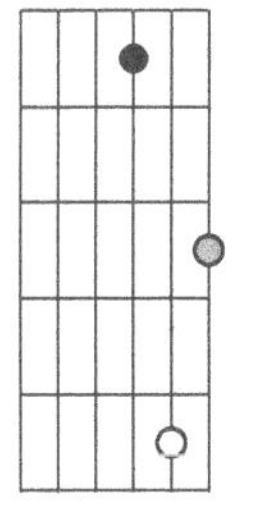

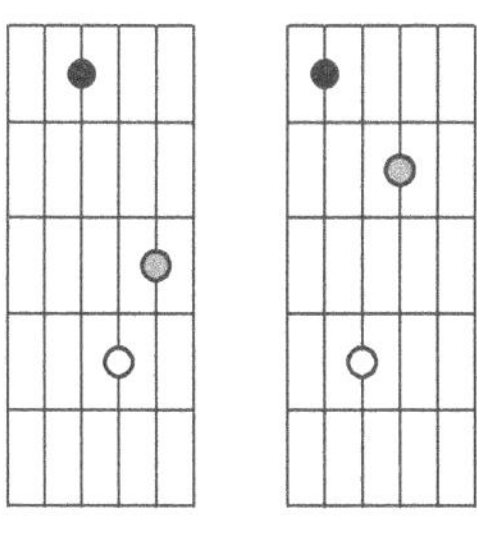

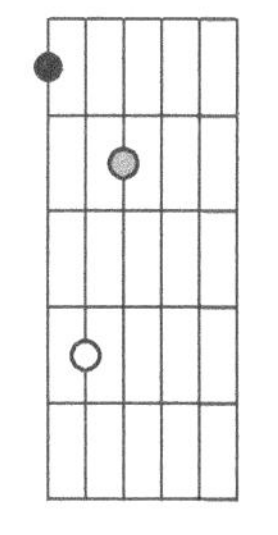

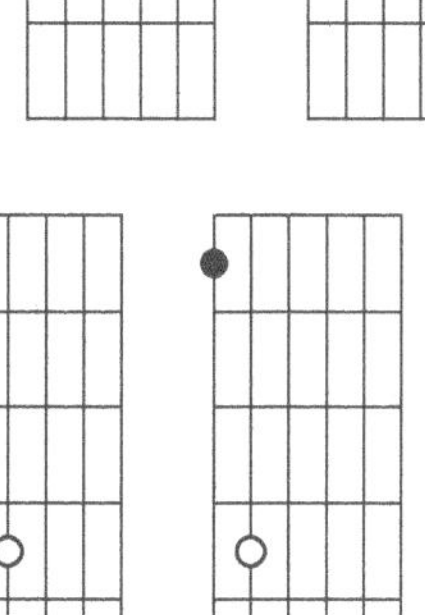

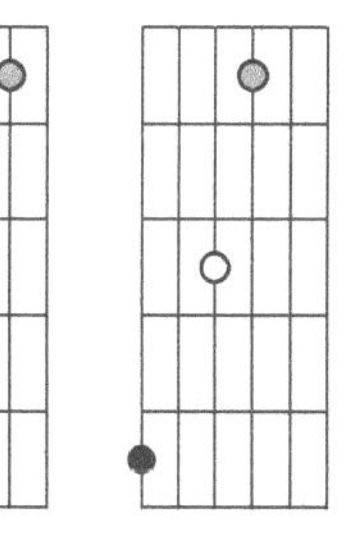

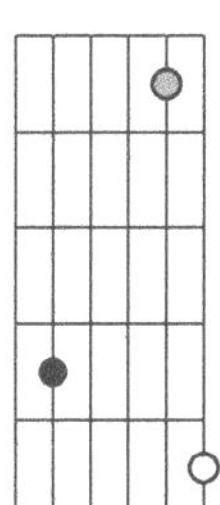

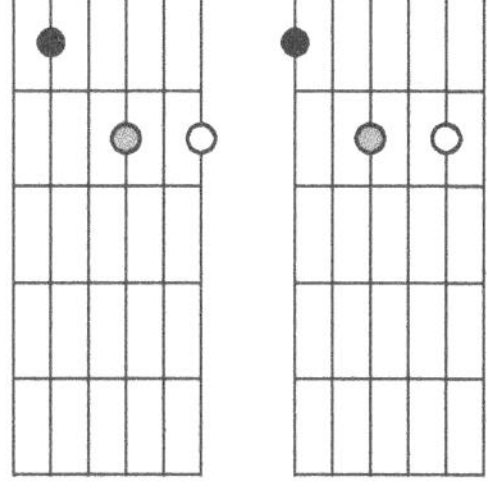

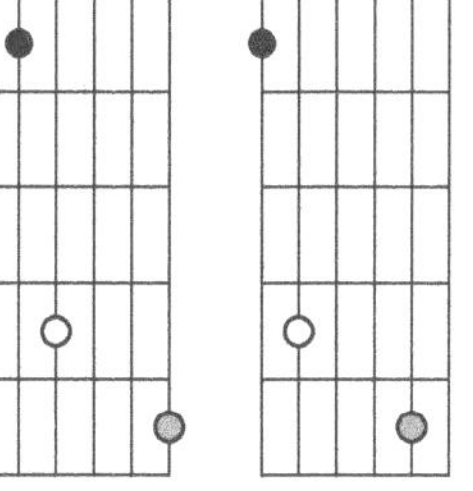

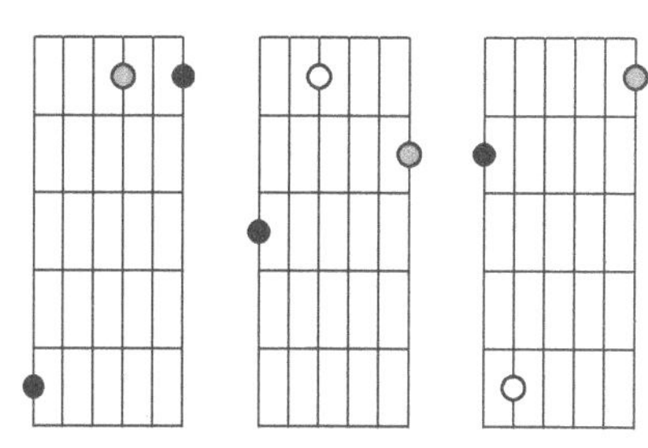

Exercise

(0,1,5)

e.g. (C,D♭,F)

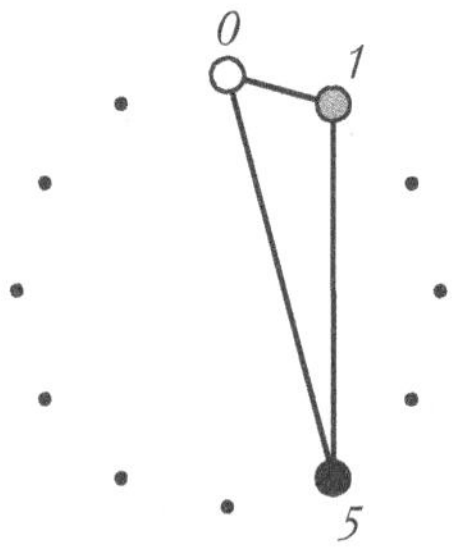

0 1 5

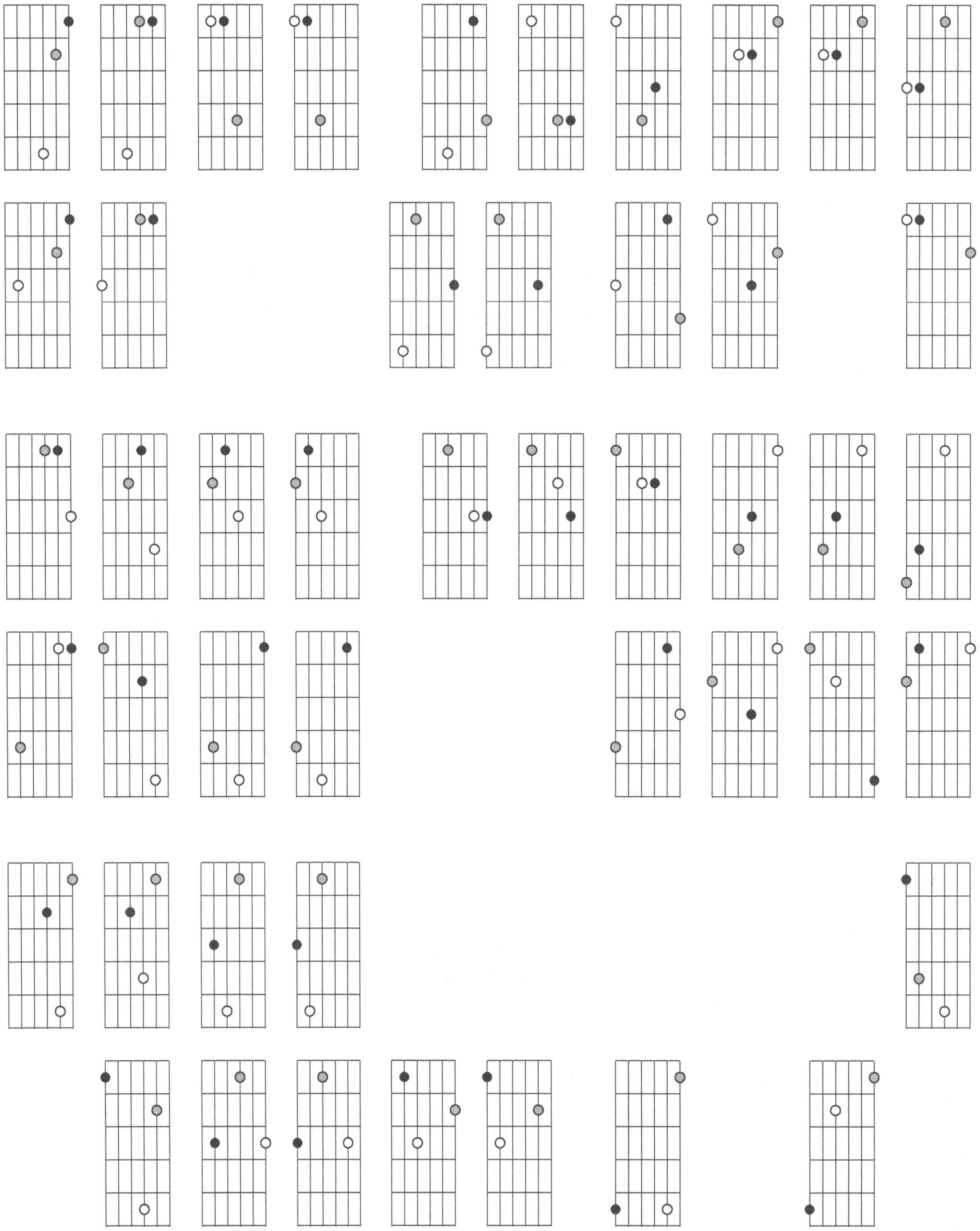

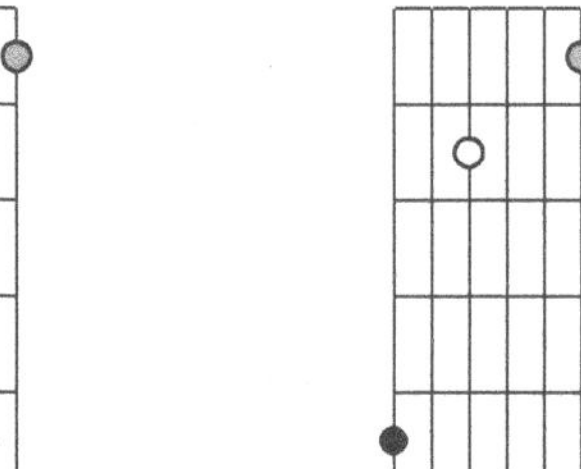

Exercise

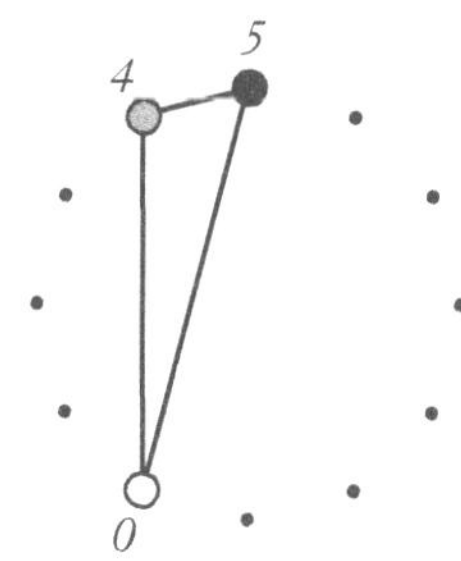

(0,4,5)

e.g. (C,E,F)

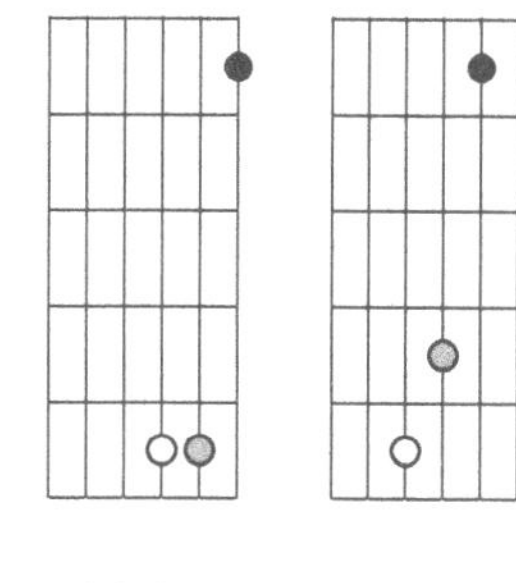

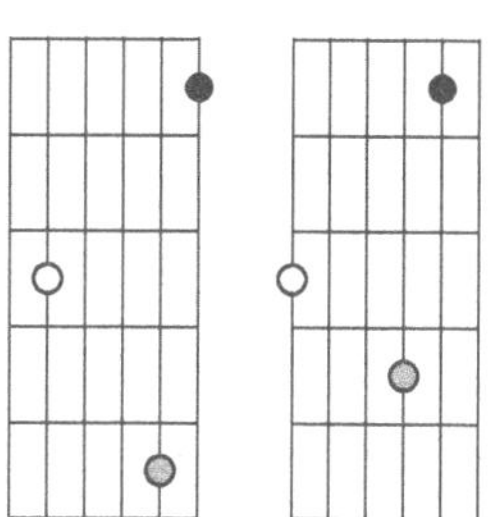

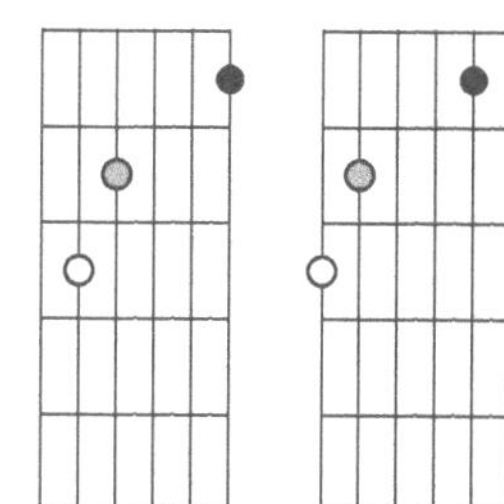

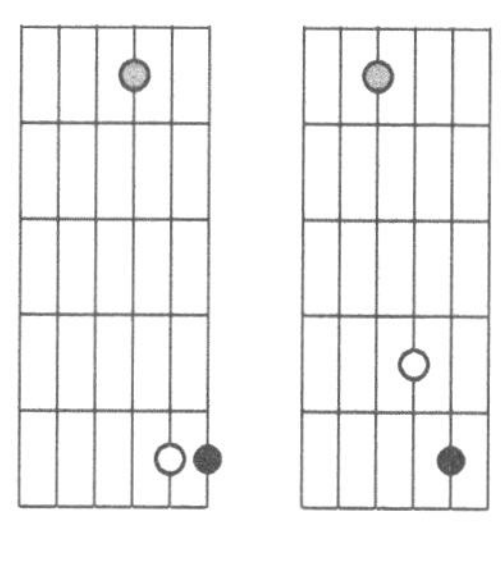

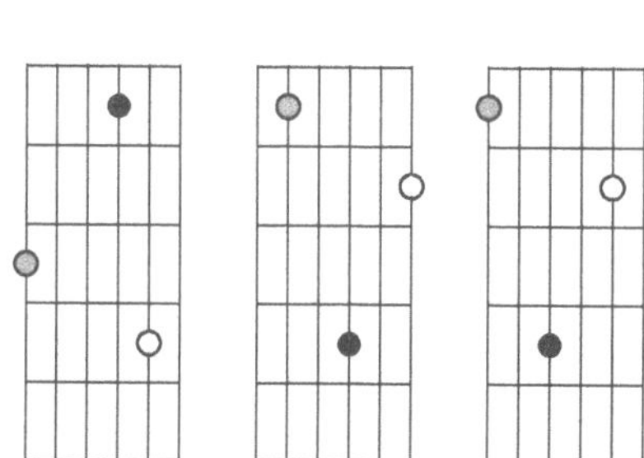

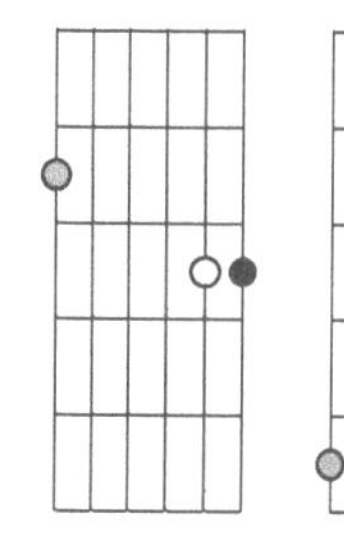

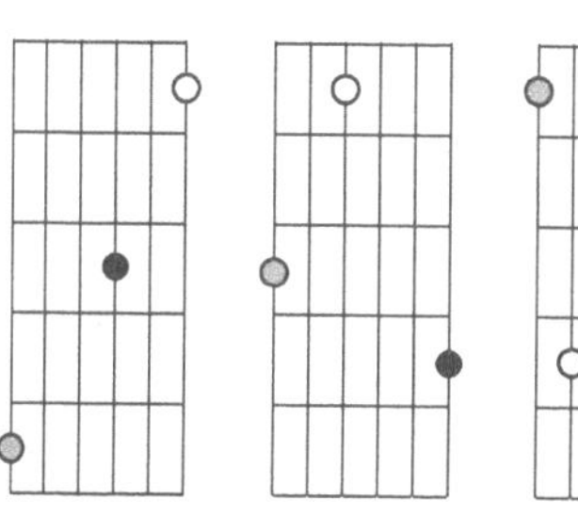

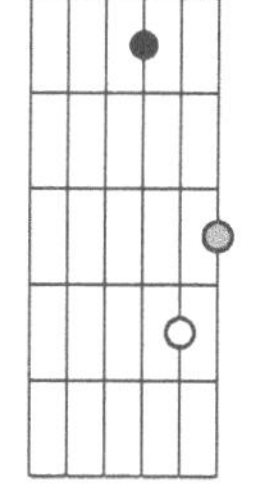

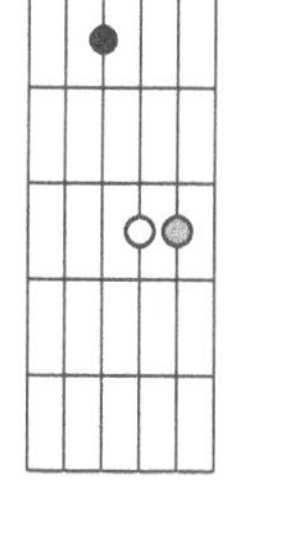

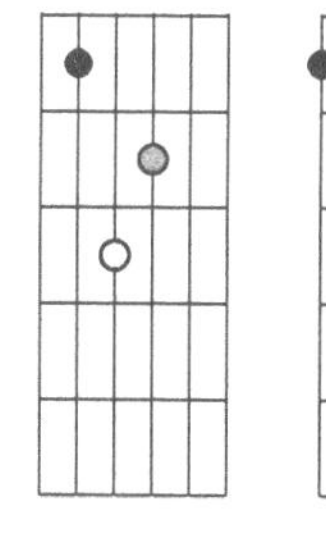

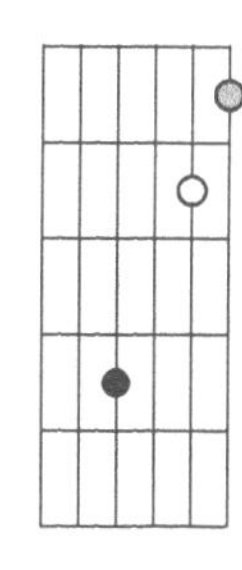

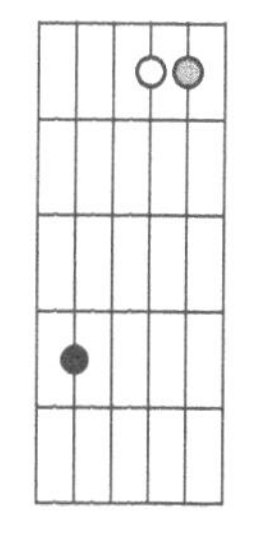

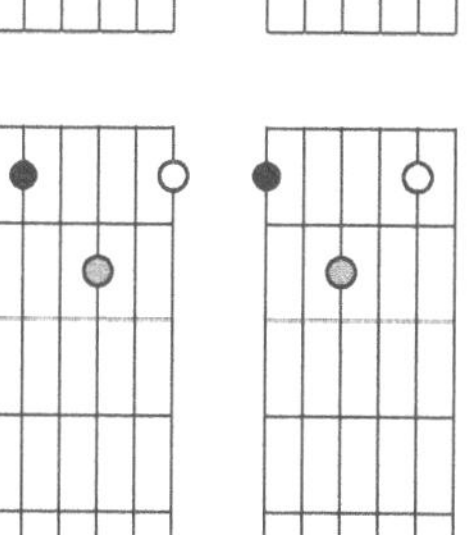

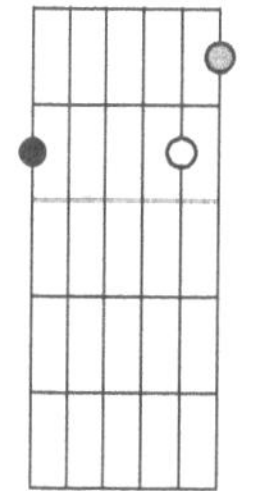

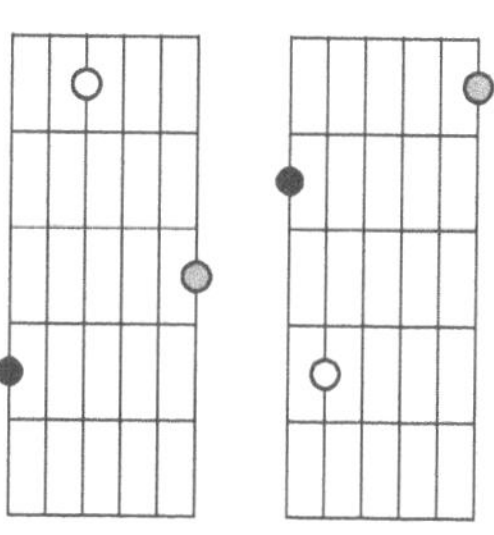

Exercise

(0,1,6)

e.g. (C,D$^\flat$,G$^\flat$)

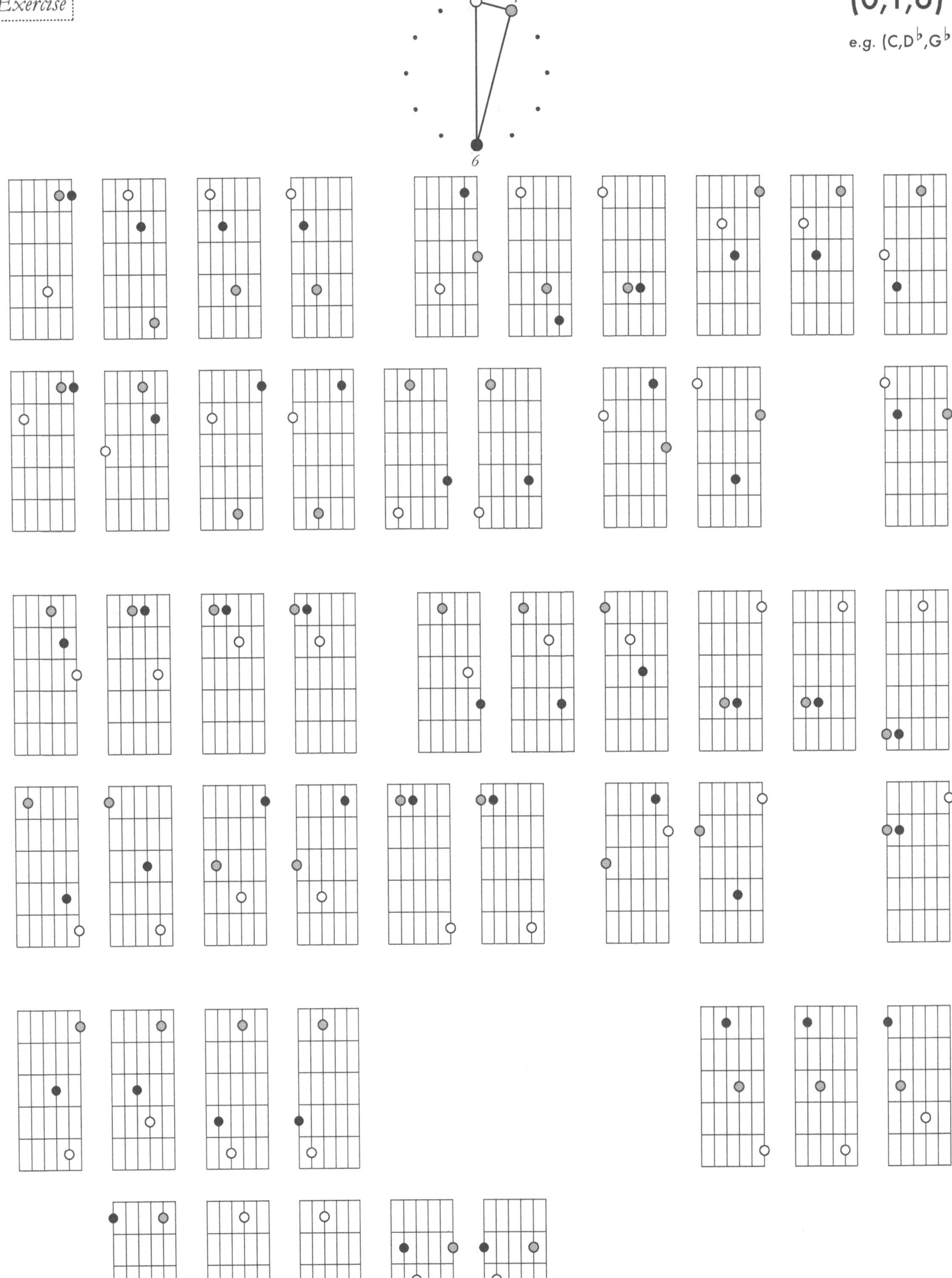

Exercise

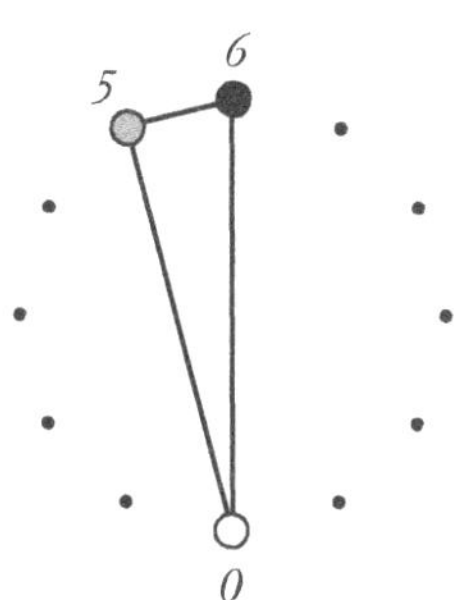

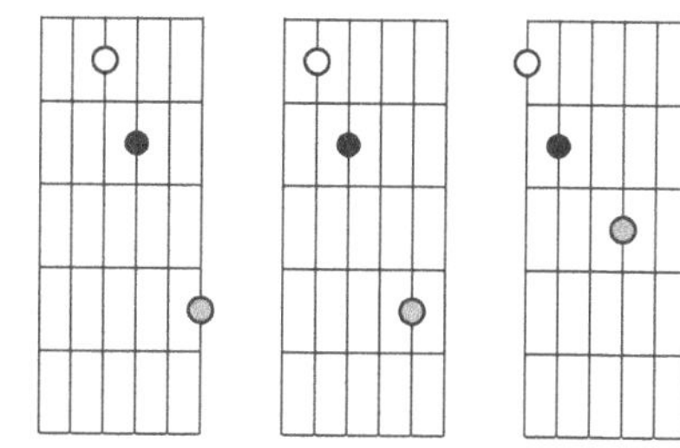

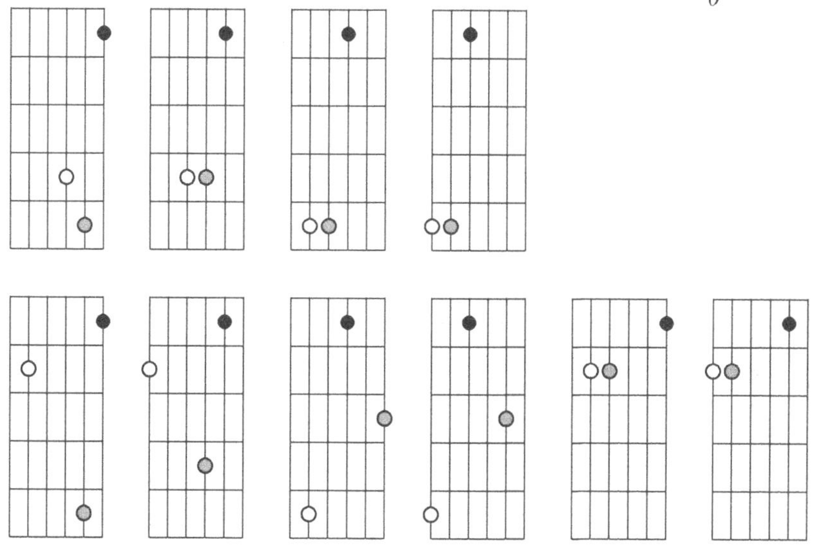

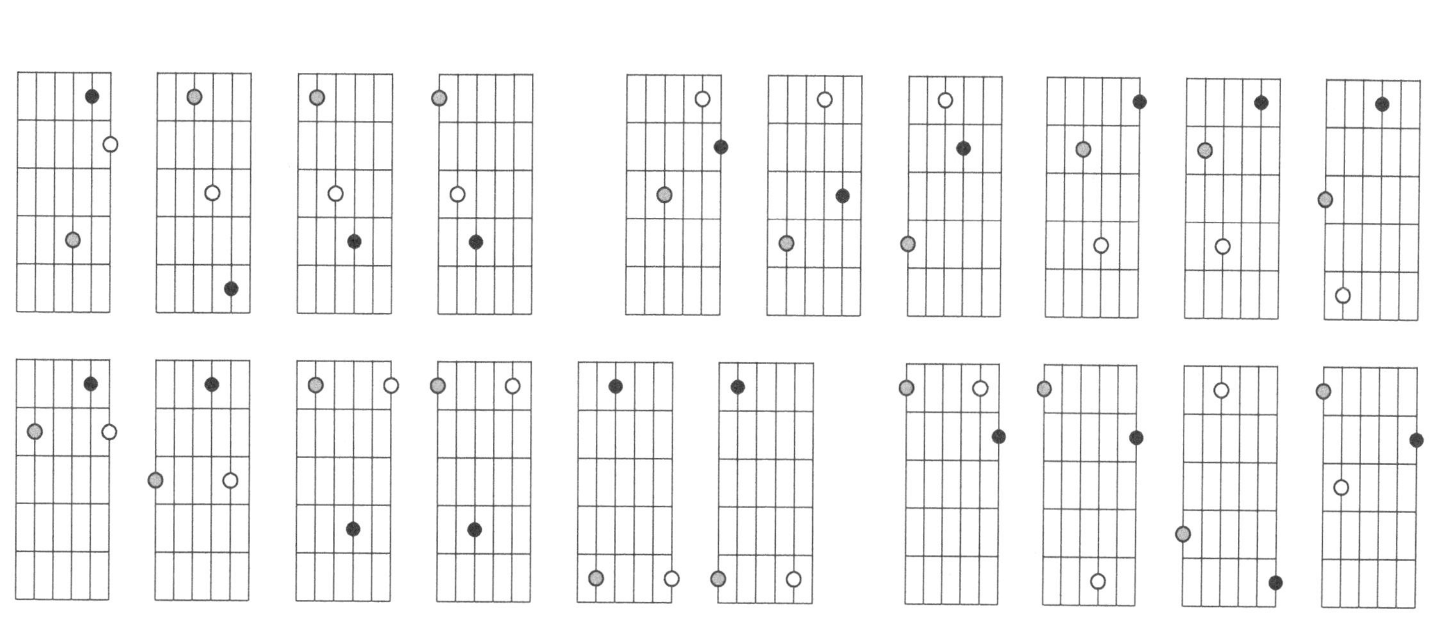

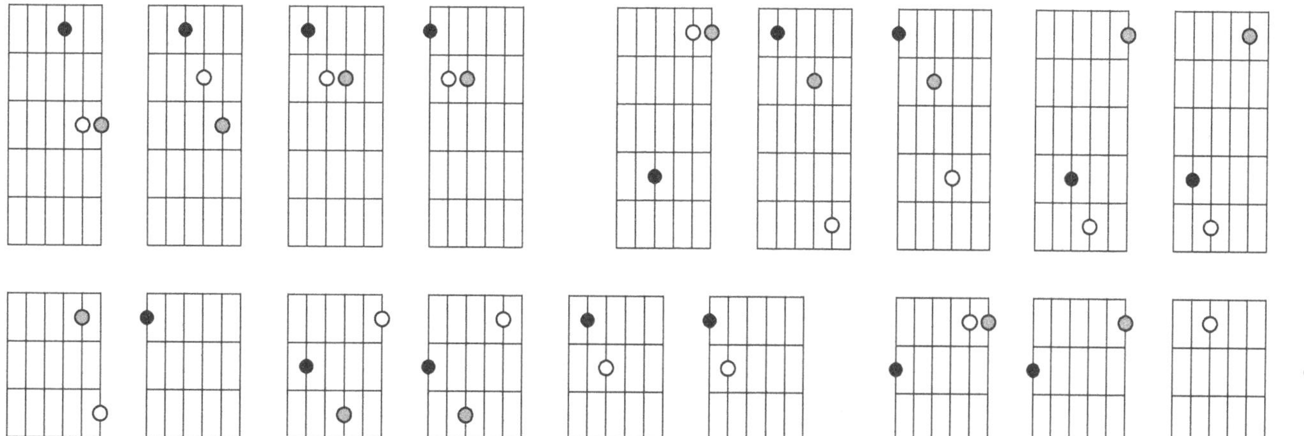

Exercise

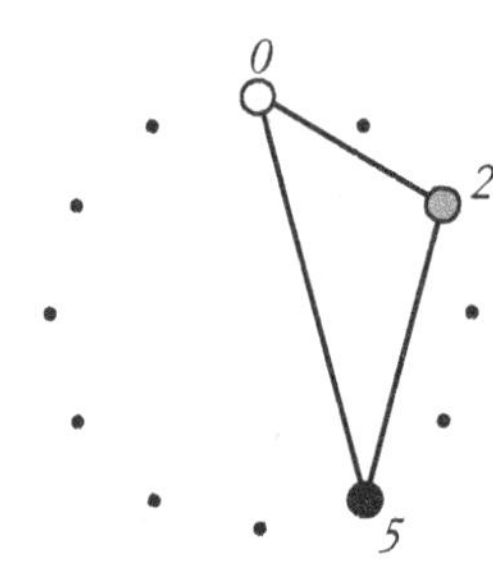

(0,2,5)

e.g. (C,D,F)

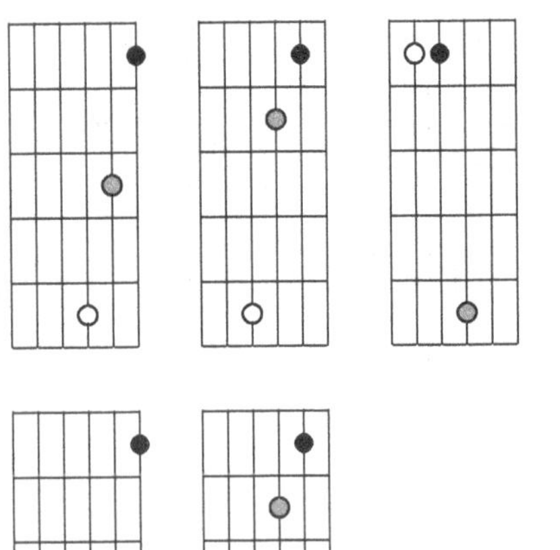

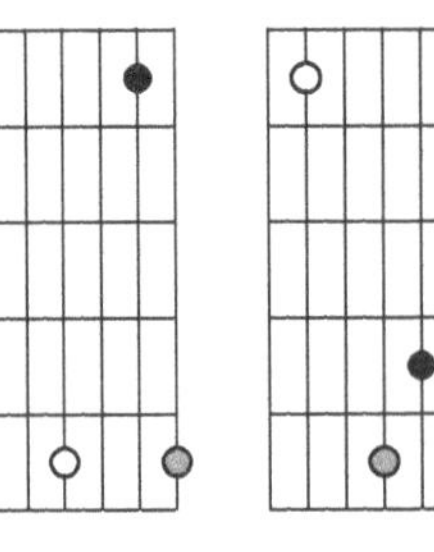
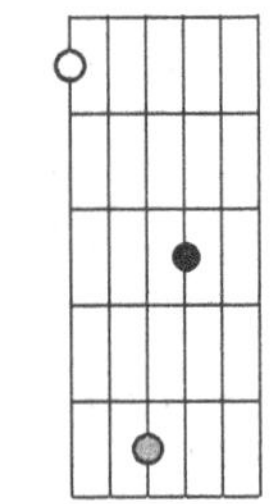
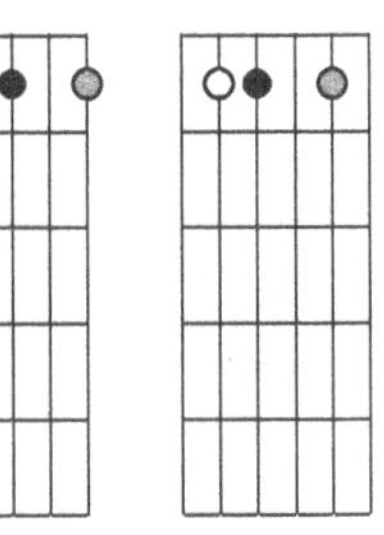
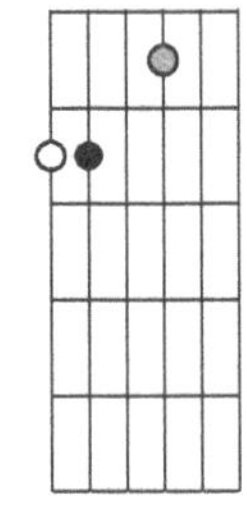
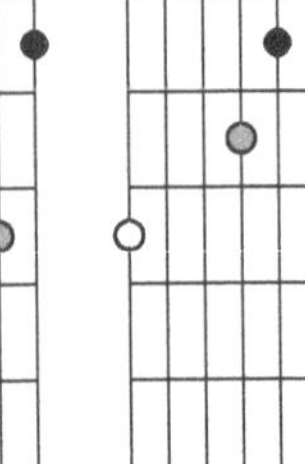
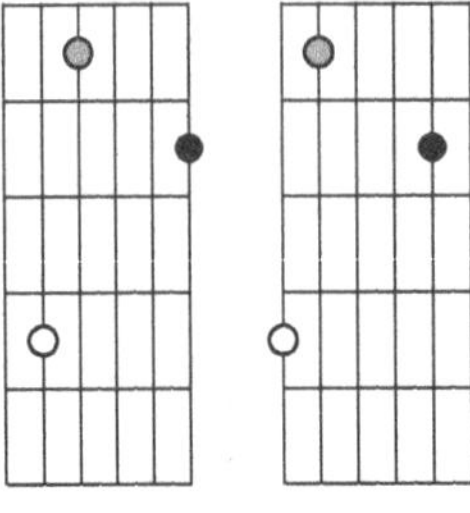
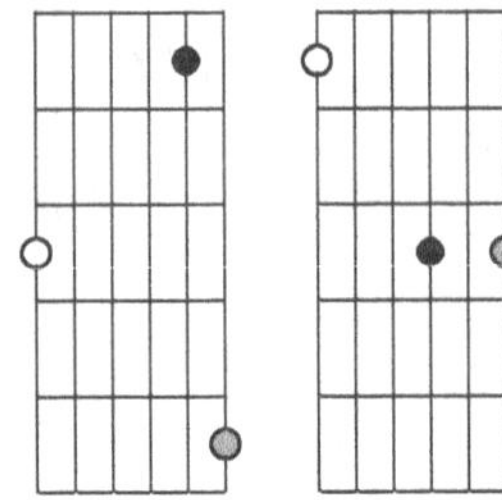
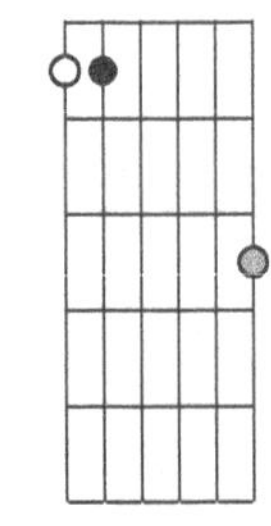
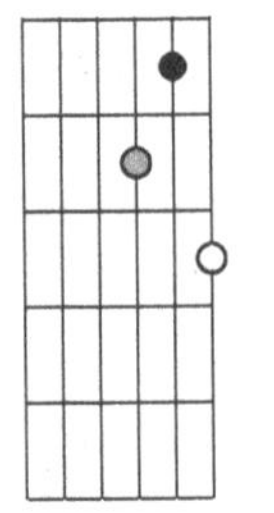

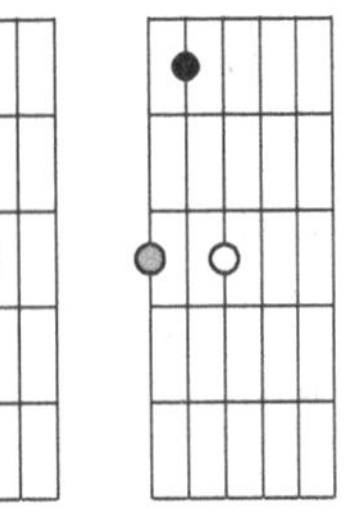
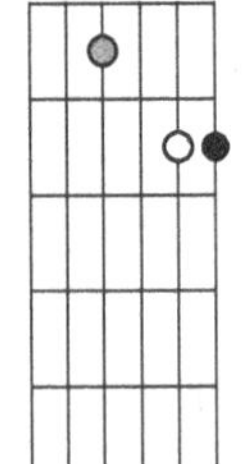
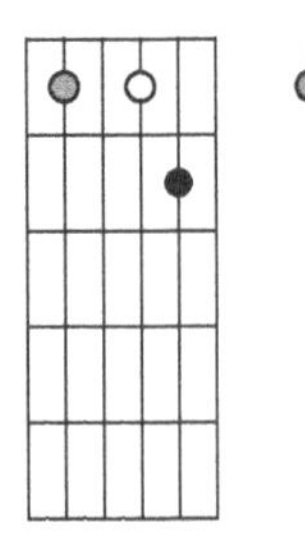
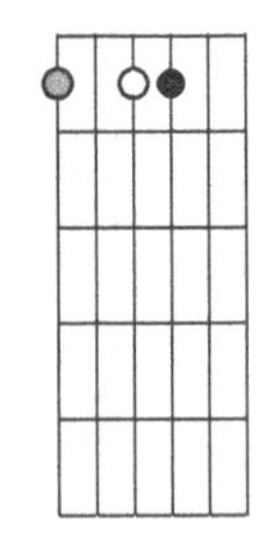
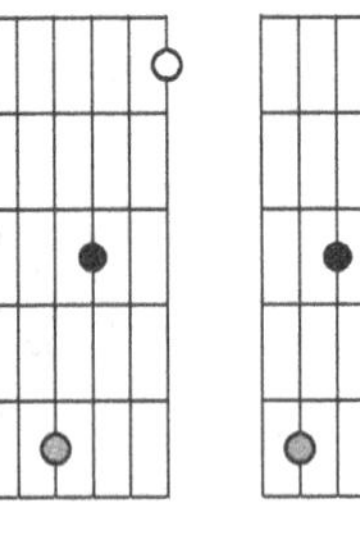
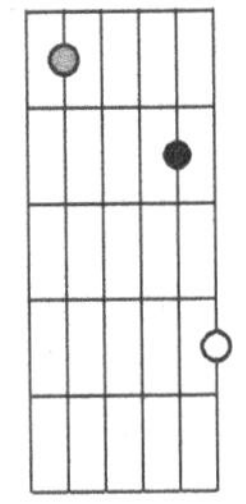
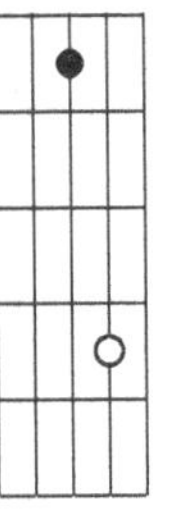
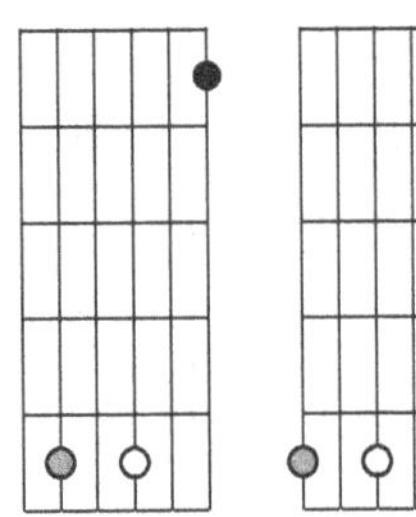

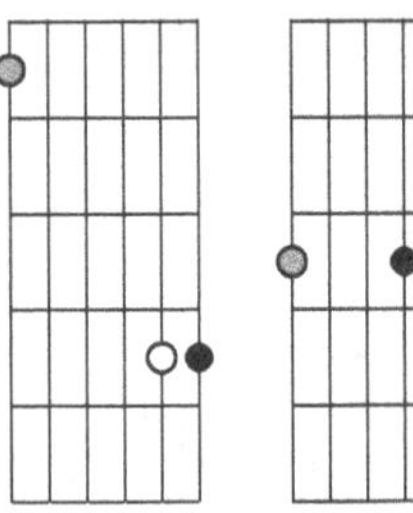
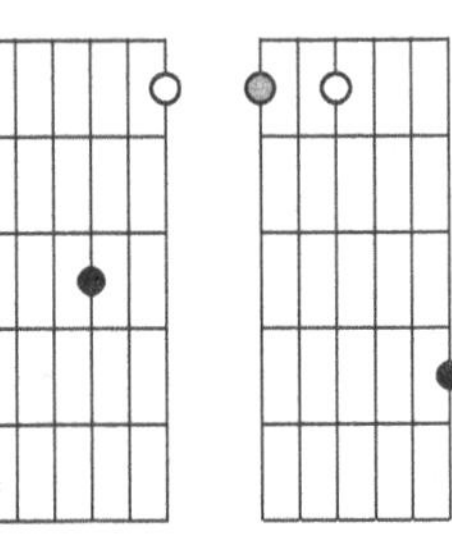
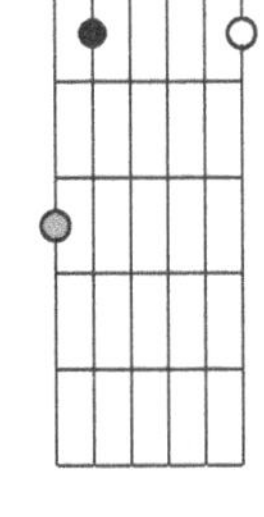
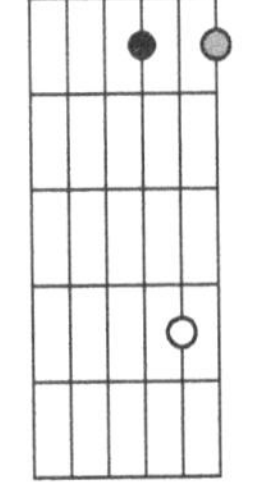
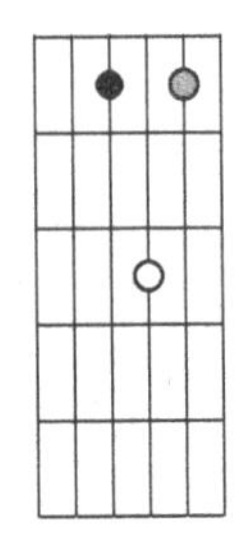
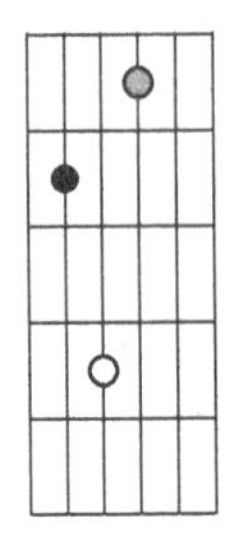
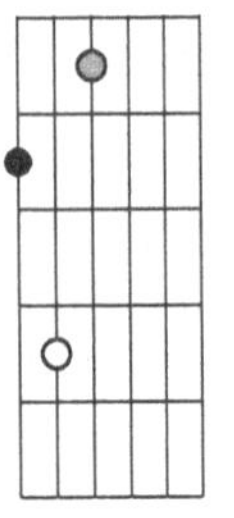
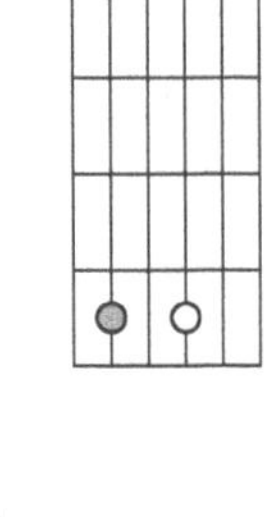
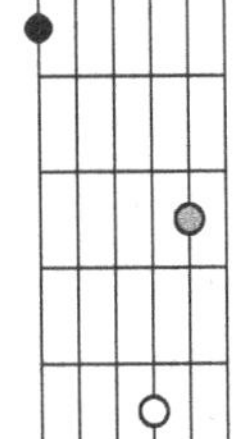
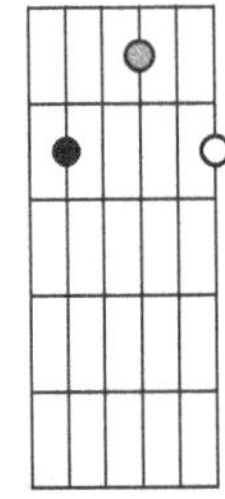
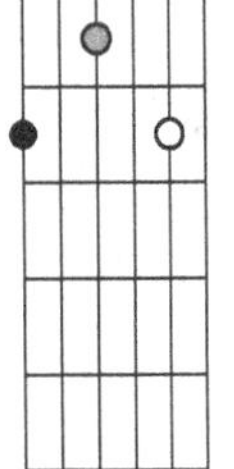
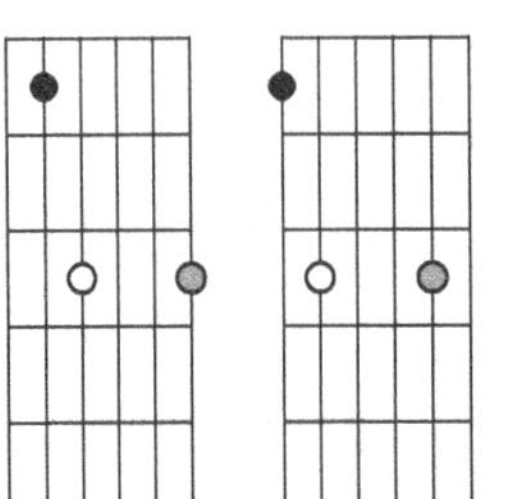
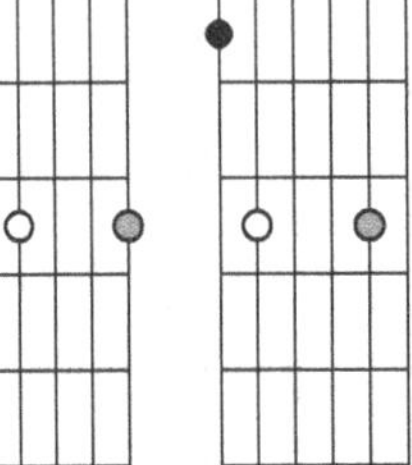
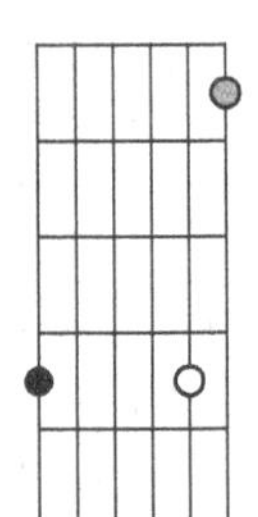
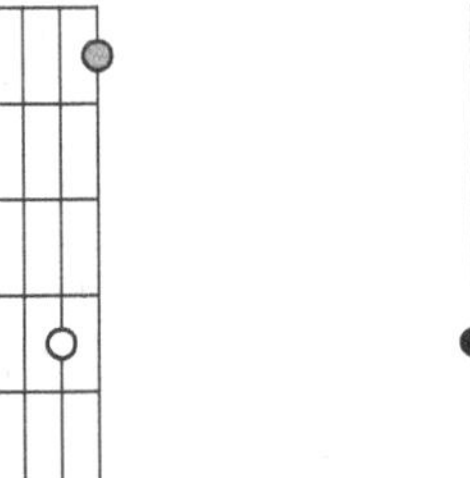

Exercise

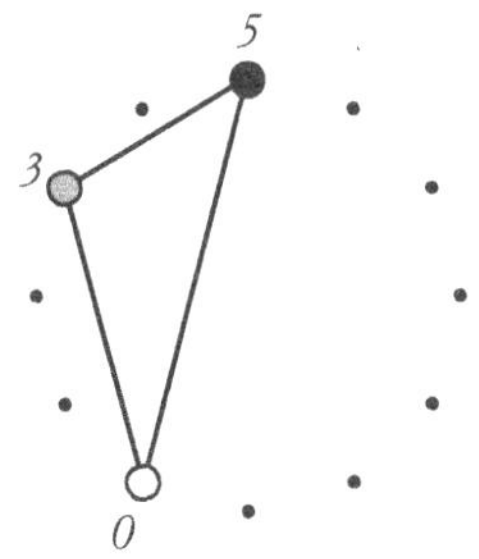

(0,3,5)

e.g. (C,E$^\flat$,F)

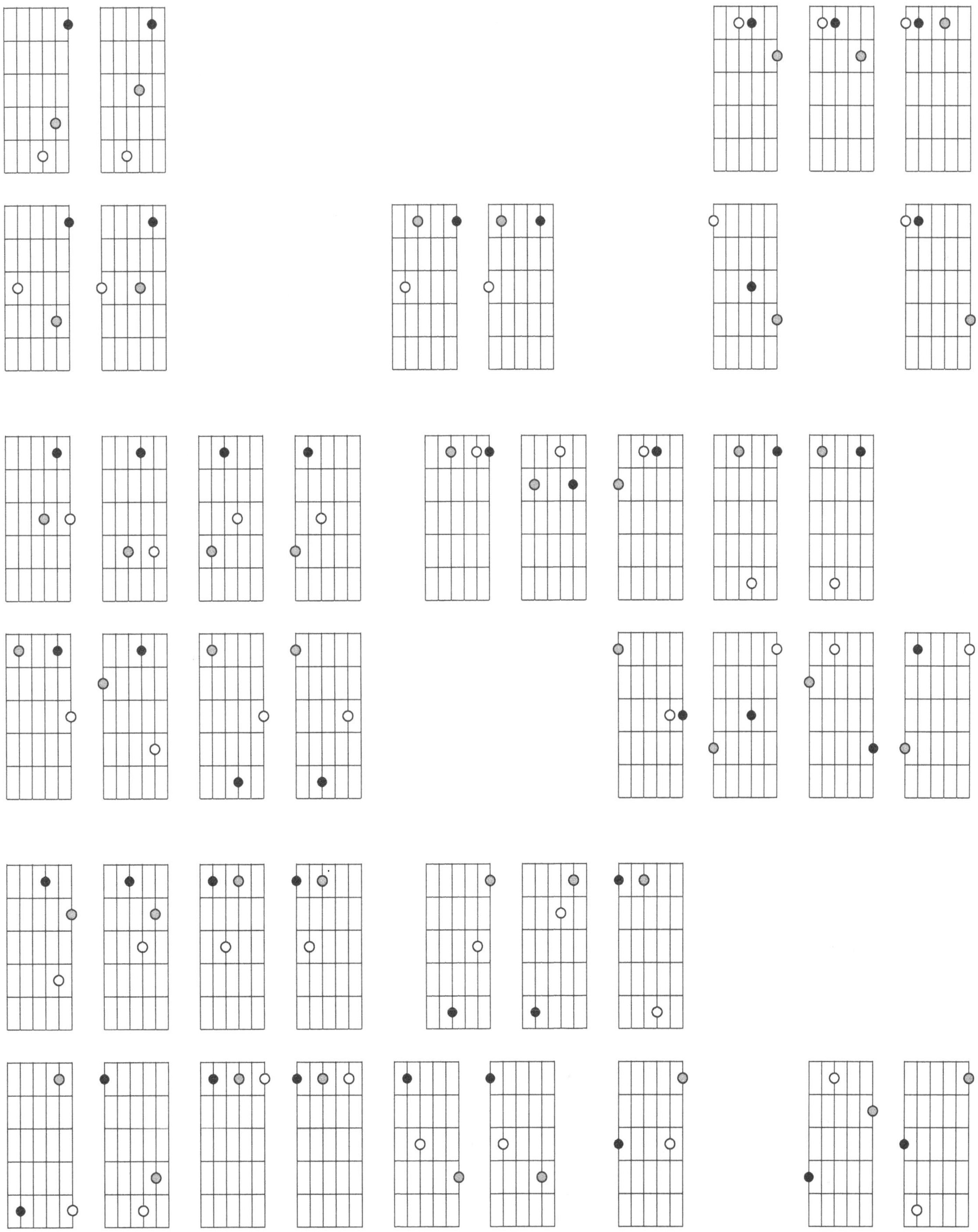

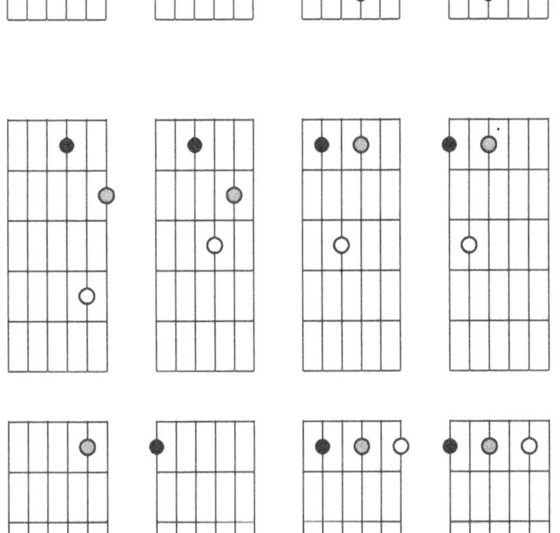

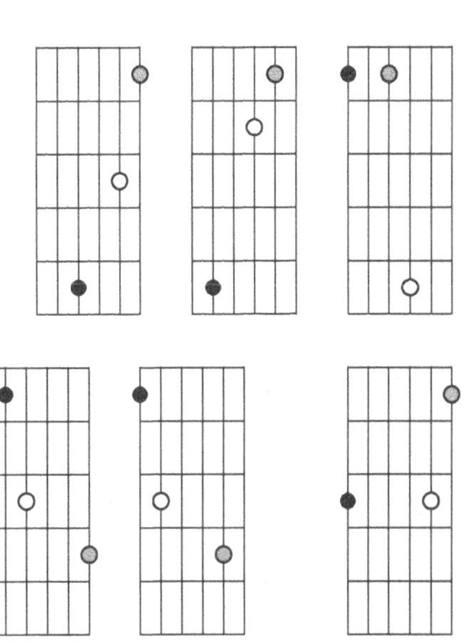

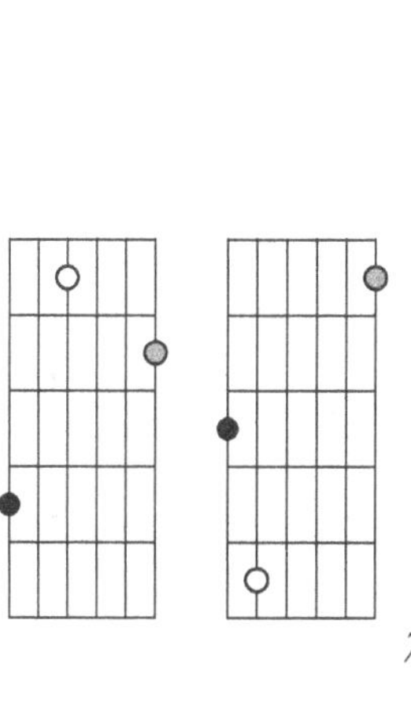

Exercise

(0,2,6)

e.g. (C,D,$G^\flat$)

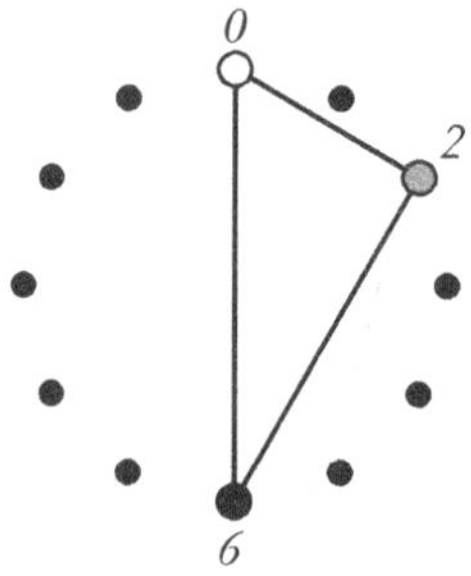

0

2

6

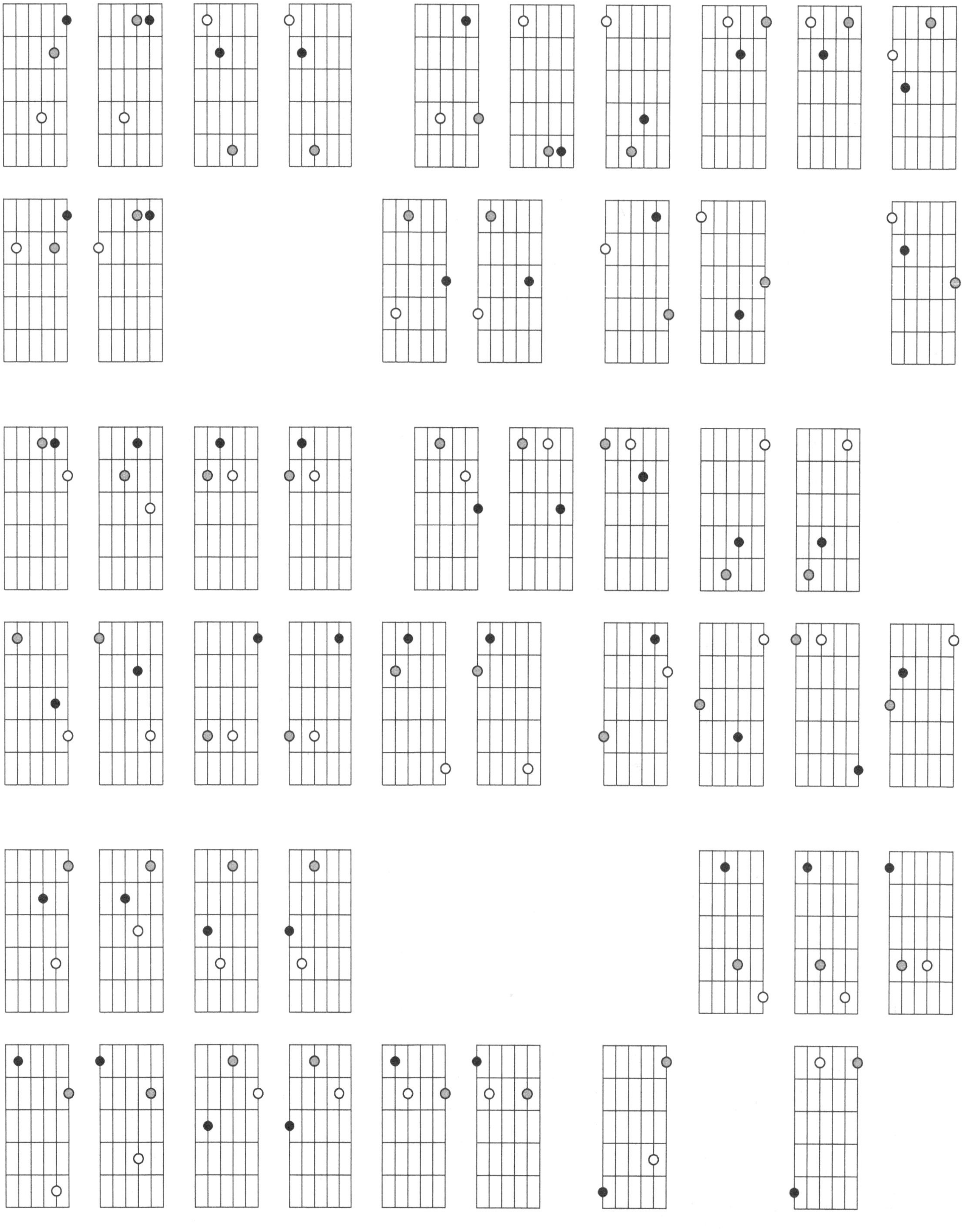

Exercise

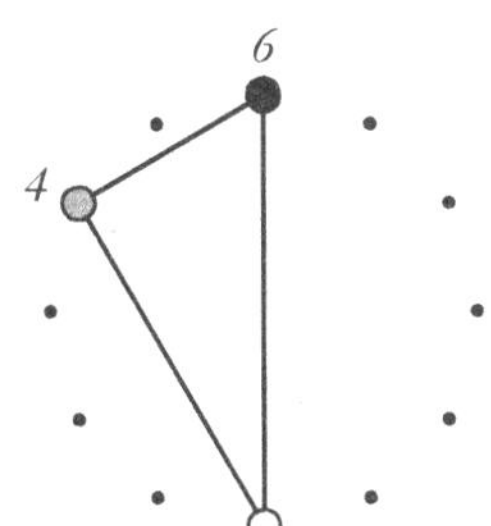

(0,4,6)

e.g. (C,E,G♭)

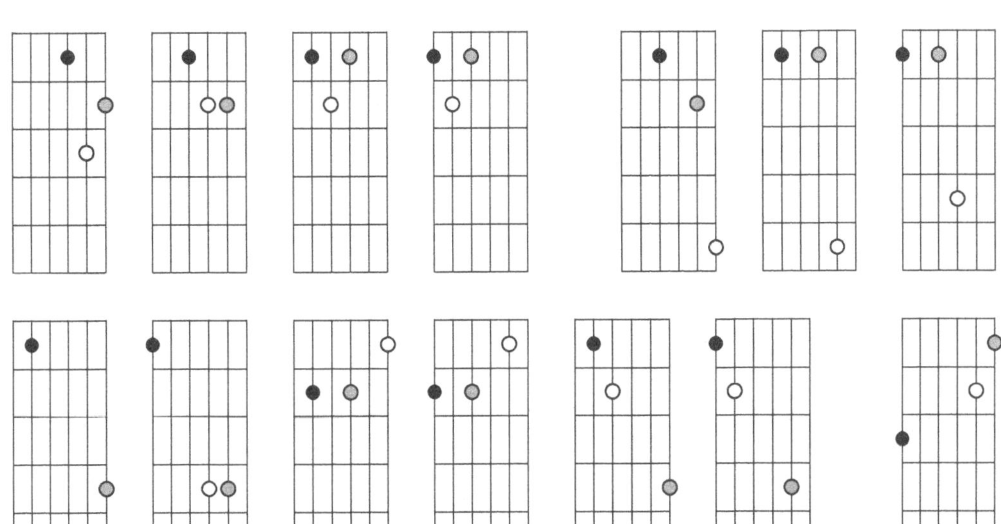

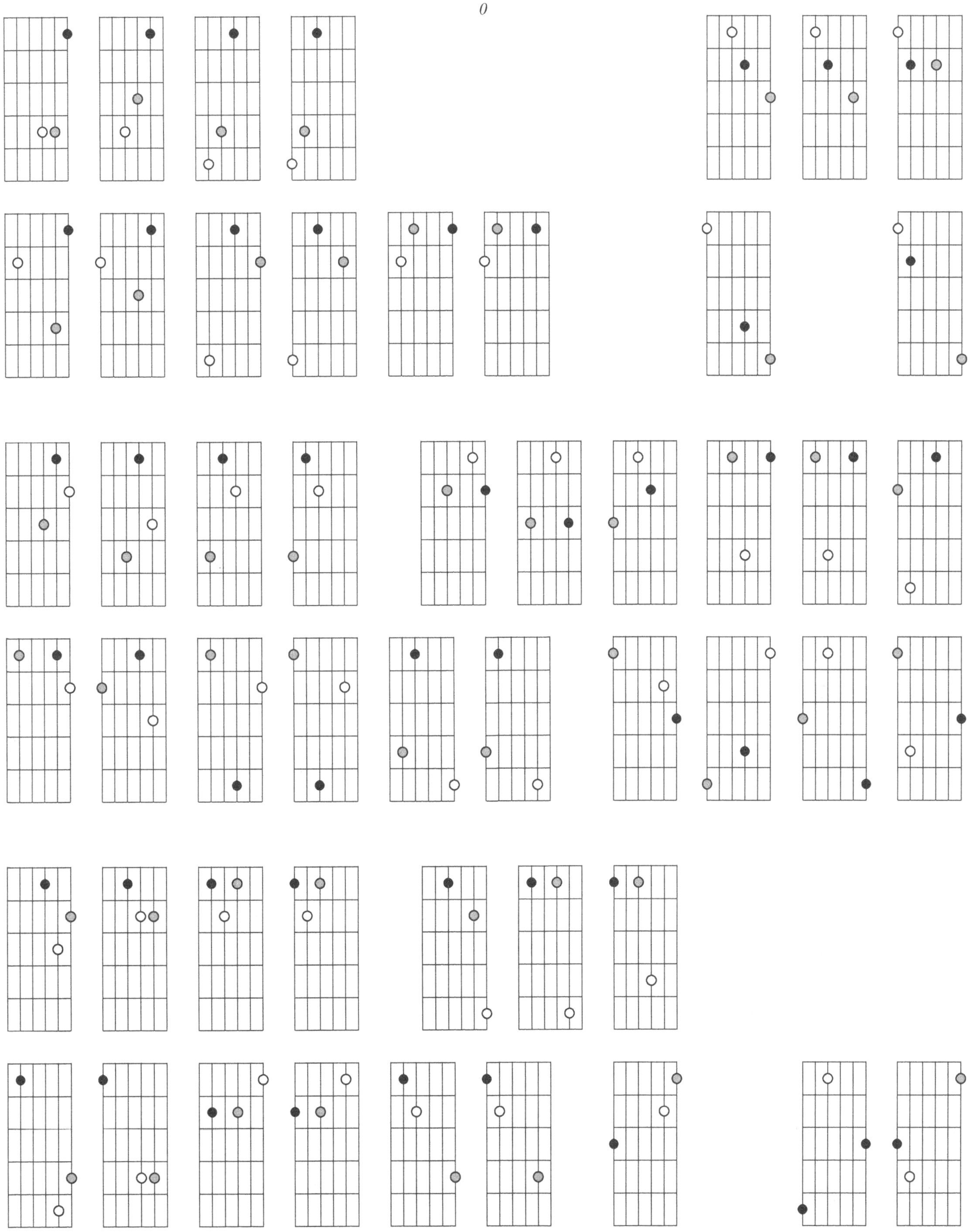

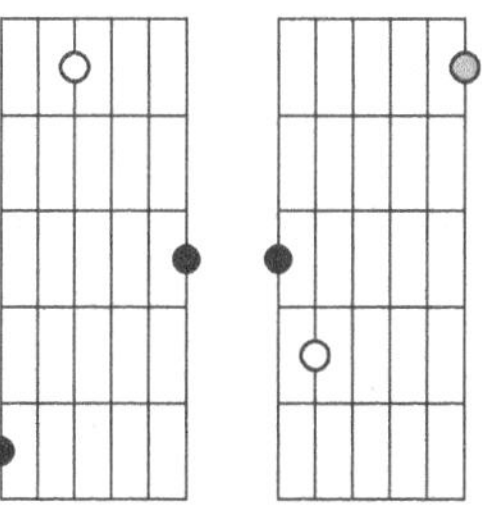

Exercise

(0,3,7)

e.g. (C,E♭,G)

Common Name: Minor Triad

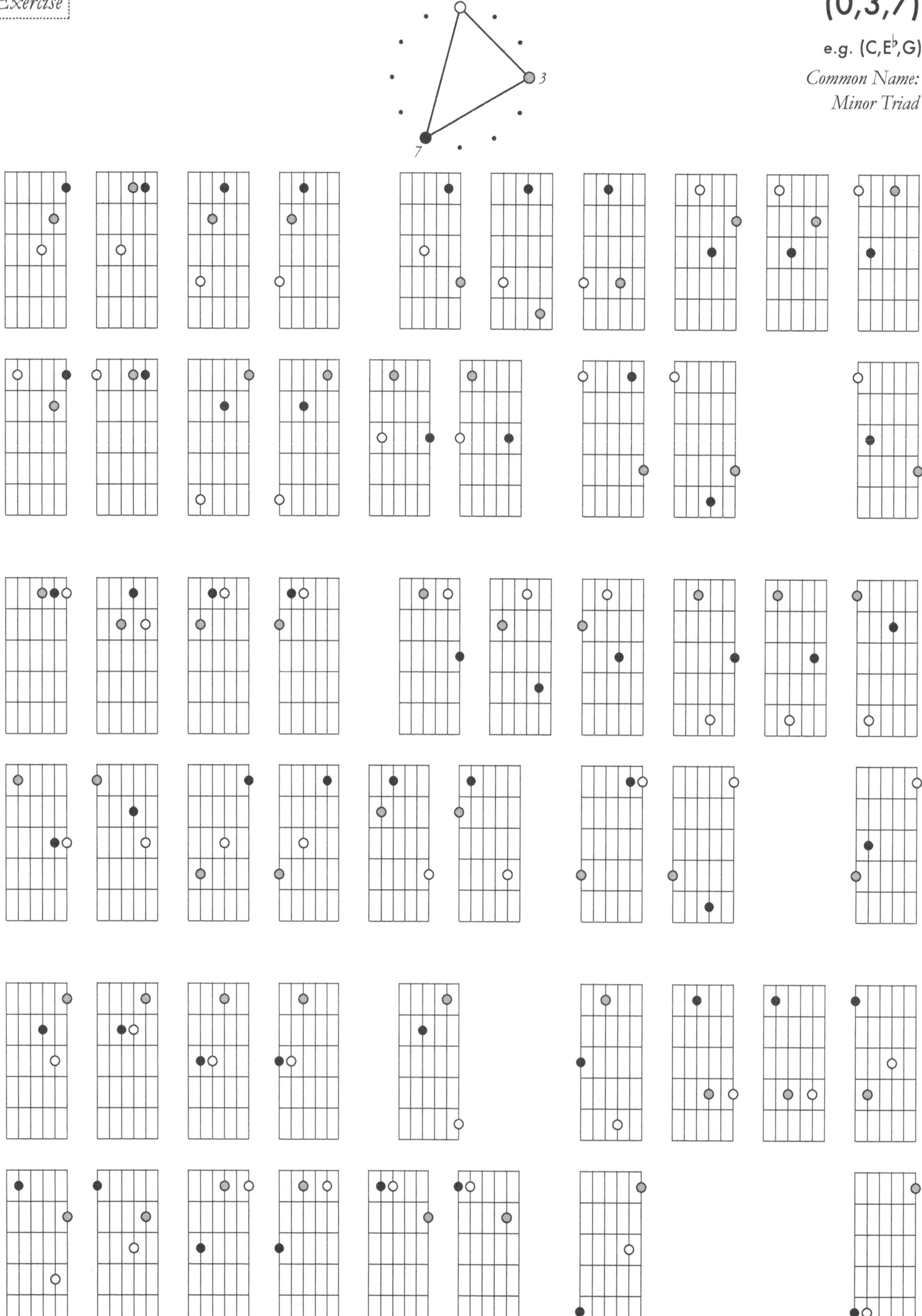

Exercise

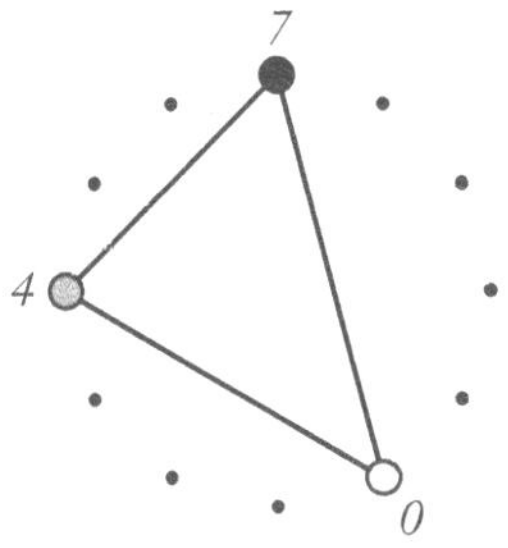

(0,4,7)

e.g. (C,E,G)

Common Name:
Major Triad

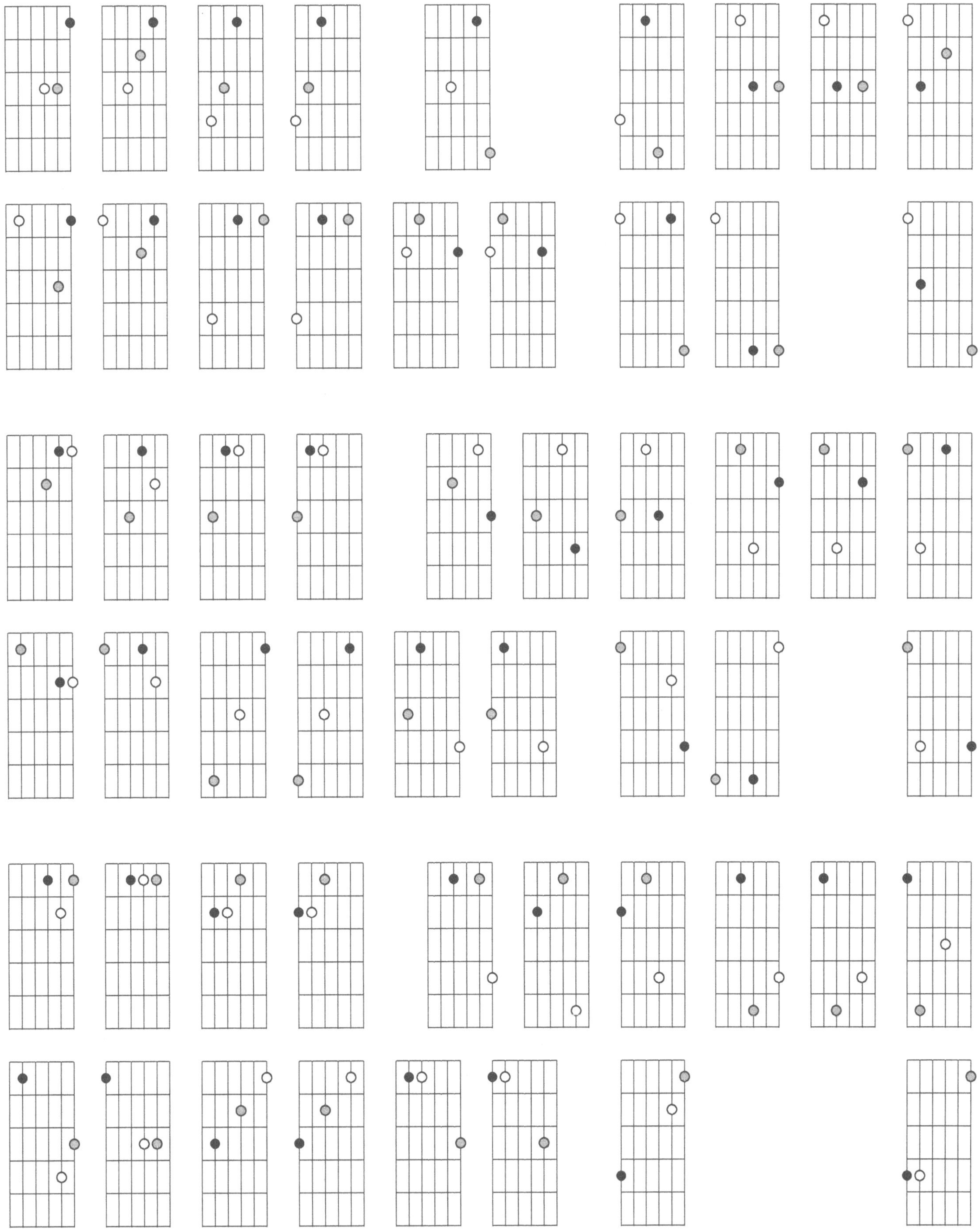

7

4

0

Exercise

TRIAD MANDALA

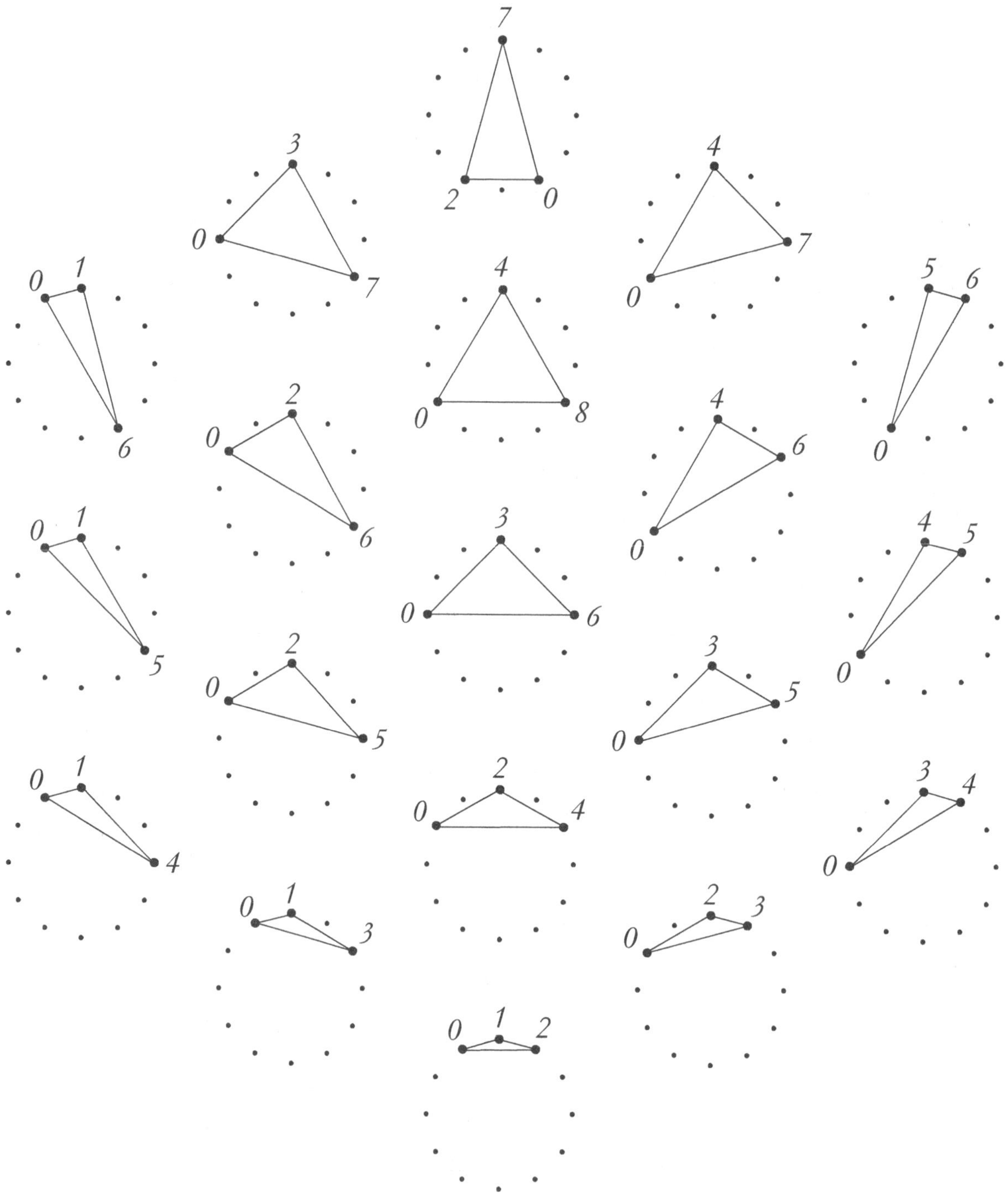

Above: the 19 triads in a symmetrical array, transposable to any key. Use as a reference to choose different triads.

Right: Various randomized 12 tone collections. Use as a reference for generating random pitch pathways.

-Choose a triad to work on.
-Read any pitch set on the right to play randomized sequences of the chosen triad (read in any direction, let the pitch be the triad's "root" {0} in each case).
-Use the smoothest possible voice leading, keeping the same string set if possible.
-Reflect or takes notes on the overall impression and character of the triad in various inversions and key centers.
-Create sequences with more than one type of triad. Make new pitch sets.
-This exercise can serve any level, depending on the choices of the musician.

E♭	B♭	G♭	F
A	E	A♭	B
D♭	G	C	D

C	F	A	G♯
A♯	D	F♯	E
D♯	G	C♯	B

E	C	G	A
C♯	B	D♯	D
F♯	F	A♯	G♯

F	C	G♭	E
D	G	A	B♭
B	A♭	E♭	D♭

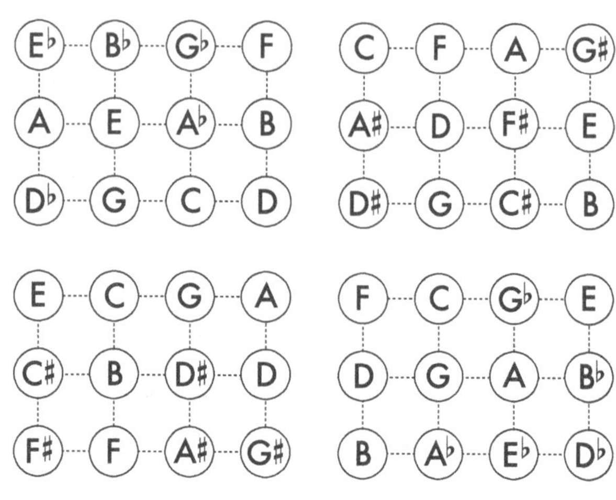

Four examples of the previous exercise, combining triads, string sets, and pitch collections.
Shown are:
Left: Triads used, String Set diagram, Pitch Set diagram, with reading direction.
Right: Staff notation, with roots and triad qualities above, and position and string set below.

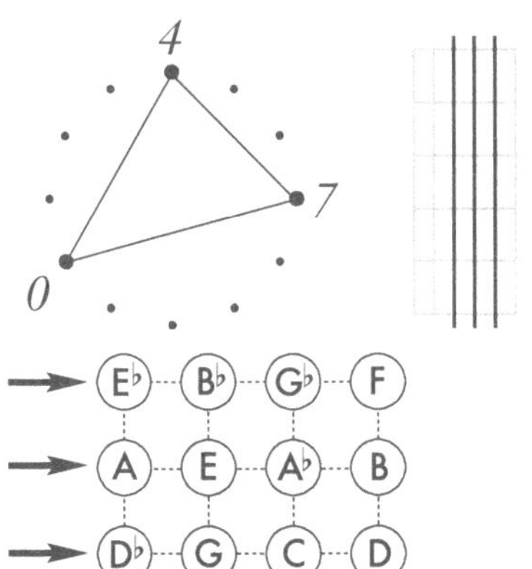

Triad (0,4,7) (Major Triad) only.
String set {2,3,4}.
Upper left pitch set, read in rows left to right.

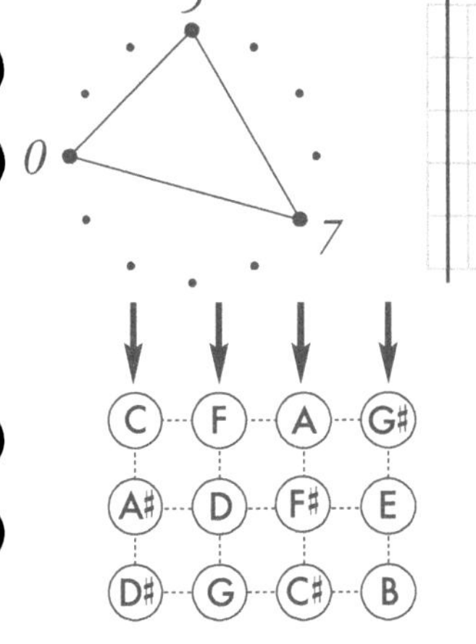

Triad (0,3,7) (Minor Triad) only.
String set {1,3,5}.
Upper right pitch set, read in columns top to bottom.
(this sequence has many 5-fret stretches)

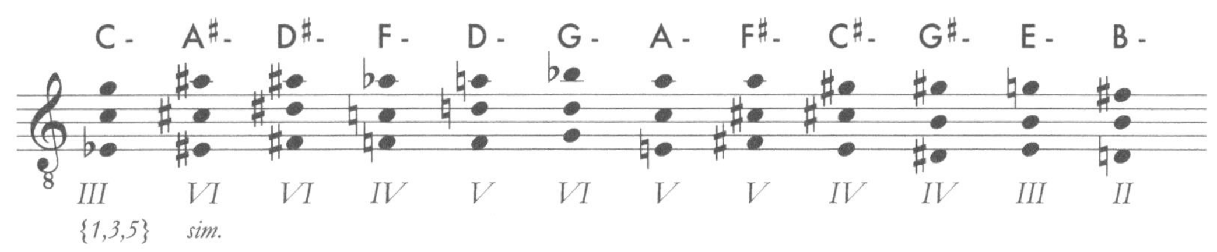

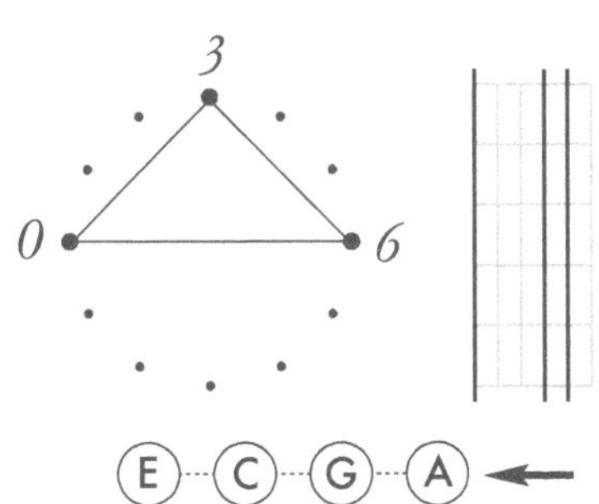

Triad (0,3,6) (Diminished Triad) only.
String set {2,3,6}.
Lower left pitch set, read in rows right to left.

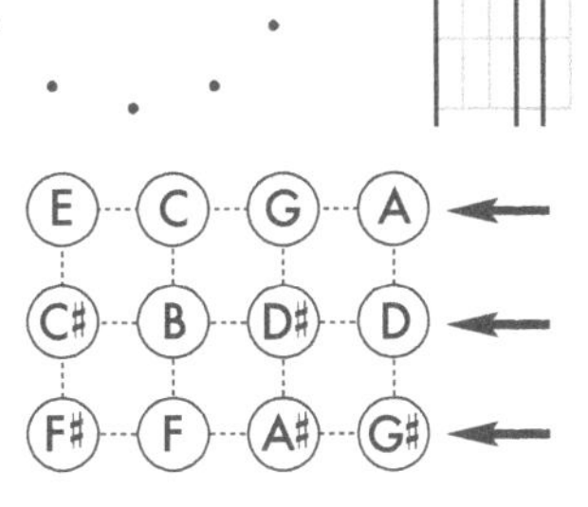

Mixed Triads (0,4,7),(0,3,7),(0,3,6) (Major, Minor, Diminished).
Initial string set {2,4,5}.
Lower right pitch set, read in columns bottom to top.
(this sequence changes string sets when necessary)

(0,4,7), (0,3,7), (0,3,6)

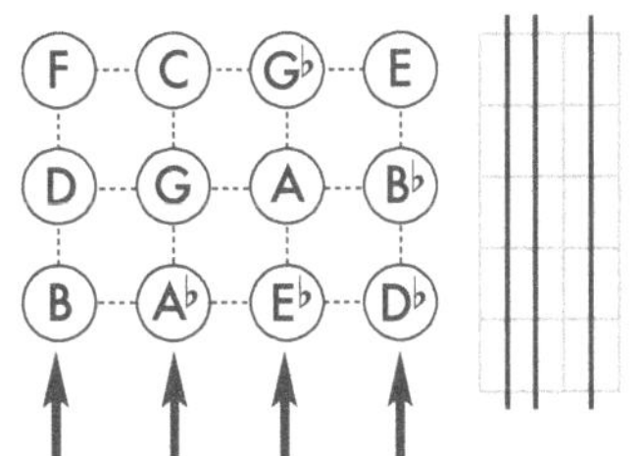

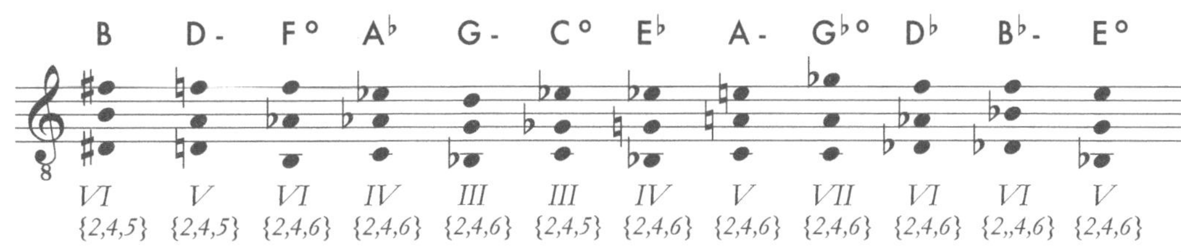

Exercise

TRIADIC MUTATION PATHWAYS

The 19 triads. Dotted lines show connect any triads that differ in shape by a single semitone movement (rotation may be necessary).
Triad rotations shown here emphasize the symmetry of the system, where pitches are placed on either side of the "12:00" point.
White circles show the location of (0).
- Begin by alternating between any (0,3,7) and (0,4,7). This equivalent to moving between a major and minor triad with the same root.
- Add in the diminished triad, which can be used to modulate the pattern by semitones: (e.g. Bmi, Bma, Cdim, Cmi, Cma, C#dim, etc).
- Add the augmented, which can be used to modulate by major thirds:
(e.g. Cma, C#dim, C#mi, C/E/Ab aug, Ema, Fdim, Fmi, E/Ab/C aug, Abma, Adim, Ami, Ab/C/E aug, Cma, etc.)
- Try to get to any key using these four triads.
- Make excursions to more distant triads, exploring the entire structure.
- Notice the special properties of triad (0,2,7), which can be used to travel very long distances.

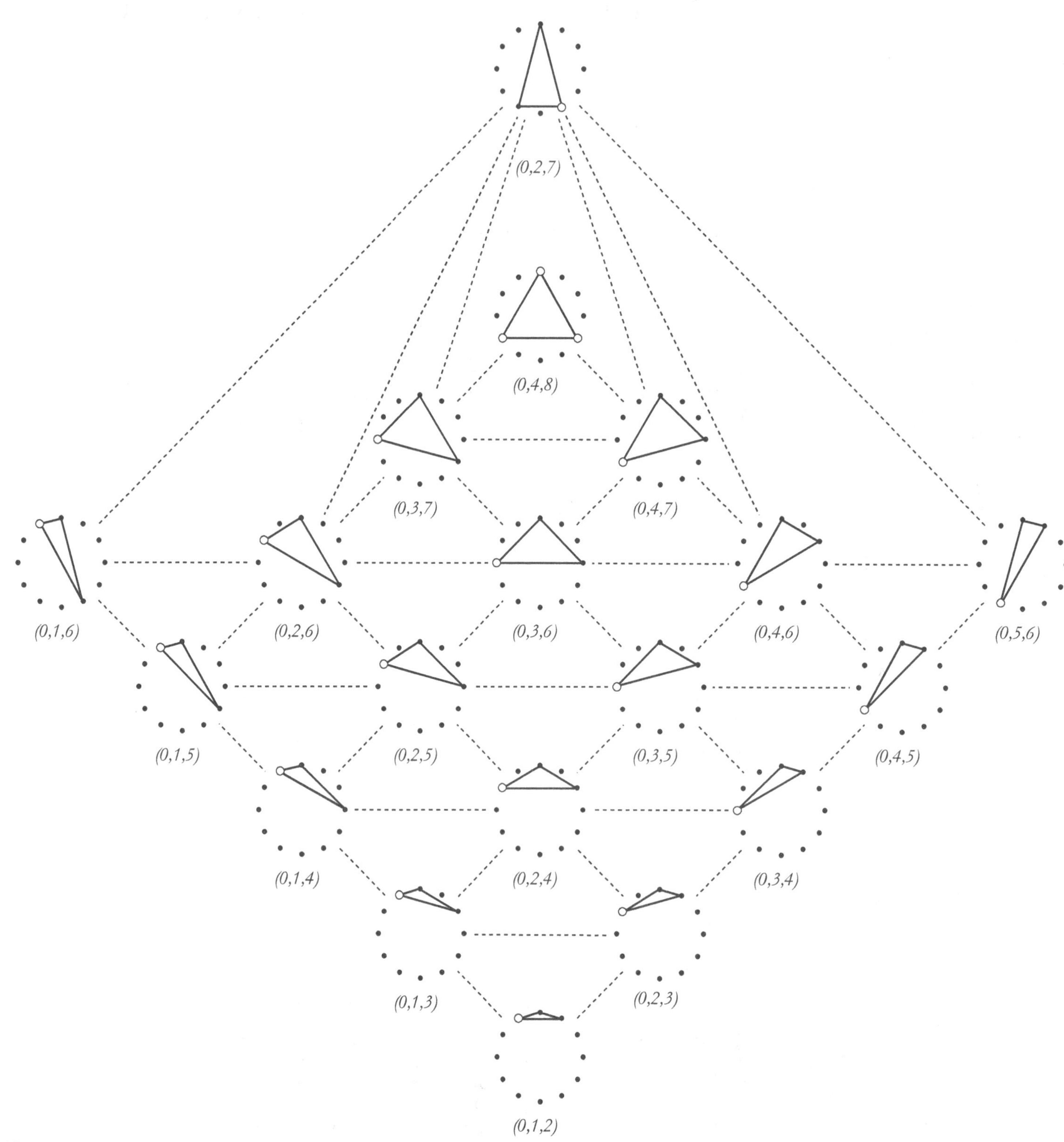

Four examples of the previous exercise, showing semitone triad mutations as visualizations and on staff notation.

Moving between a major and minor triad:

Moving between major, minor, and diminished triad, with modulations by a semitone every third chord:

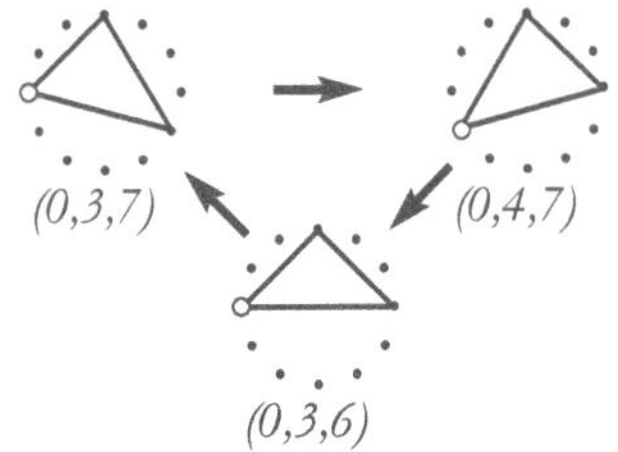

(start in 5th position)

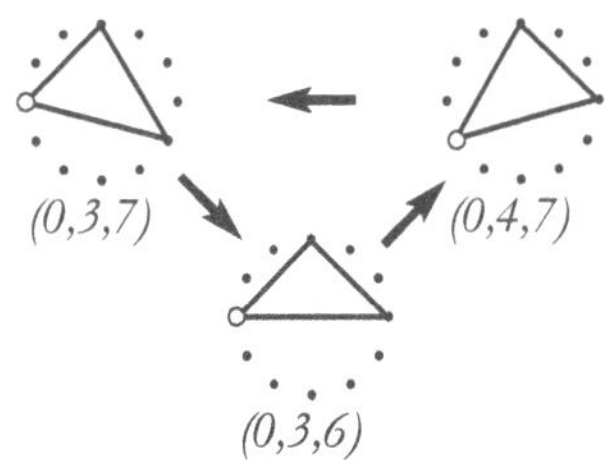

(start in 4th position)

A long sequence moving between major, minor, diminished, and augmented triads.
The augmented triad is used to modulate by major thirds:

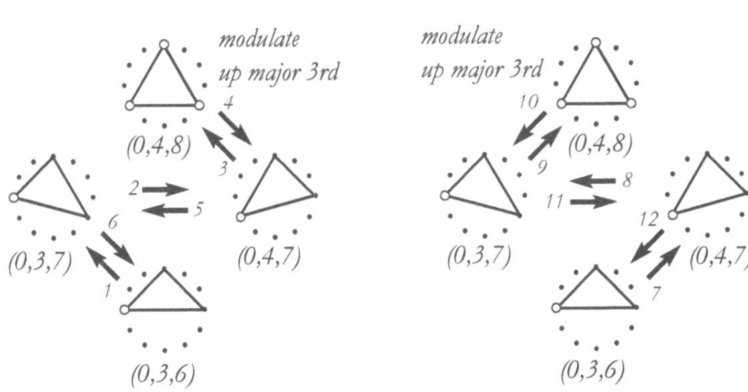

Numbered arrows show a 12 step mutation pattern. Each system of the staff notation below shows the same 12 step pattern, which passes through three modulations before returning to the original triad.

(start in 4th position) (for a stretching exercise, play only on string set {3,4,6}.

These examples use only four triads. Explore the other fifteen - give them names if they seem to indicate a tonality or familiar chord. Start with different strings sets in different positions, improvise the movements.

Exercise

CIRCULATION

A symmetrical exploration of the 19 triads. Played in first position, except triads (0,3,4) and (0,2,3), which are in 3rd position.
- Play up through the symmetrical triads, inhale. Play down through the asymmetrical triads, exhale.
- Alternate moving tdown the right and left sides. Play rhythmically freely, matching the harmonic cycle to breathing cycle.
- Observe any interesting effects.

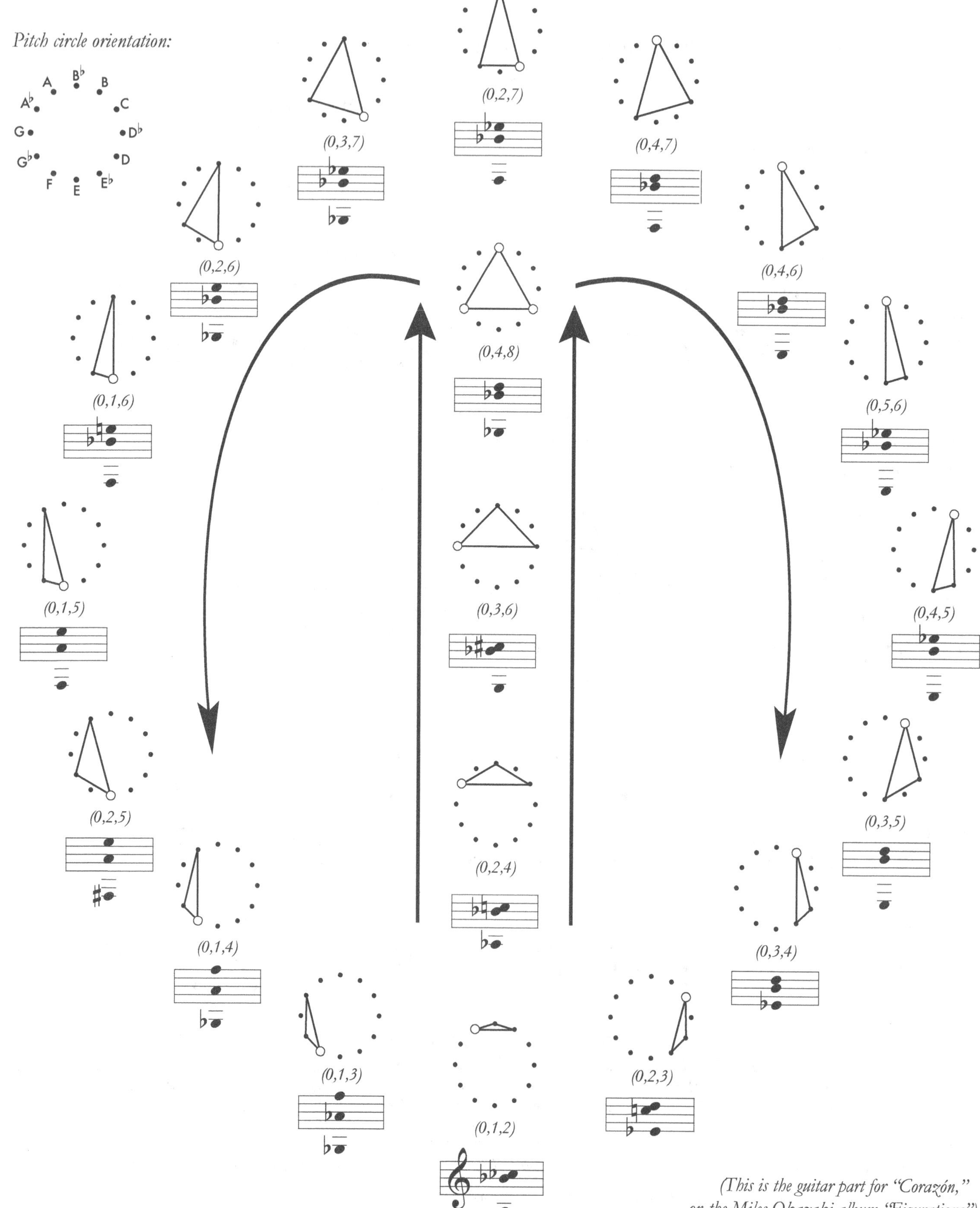

(This is the guitar part for "Corazón," on the Miles Okazaki album "Figurations")

TRIADIC WEAVING

Showing:

Right: The four types of triads built from a pair of stacked major and minor thirds, visualized as shapes on pitch circles and fretboards. Pitches are shown with different shapes in order to identify the triad type:

white circle = major
black circle = minor
black triangle = diminished
white triangle = augmented

Below:
Four ways that these four triads can be combined to fill all chromatic space. This is visualized as weaving threads on the fretboard grid, where the interlocking shapes form a complete tapestry.

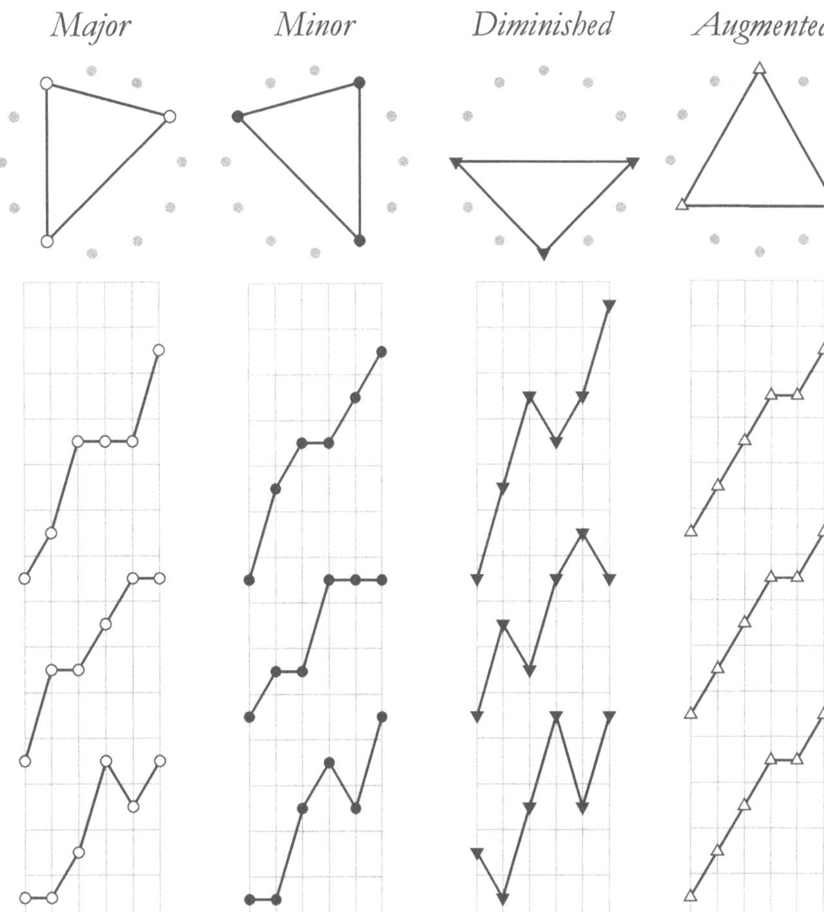

Two major and two minor triads (first possibility)

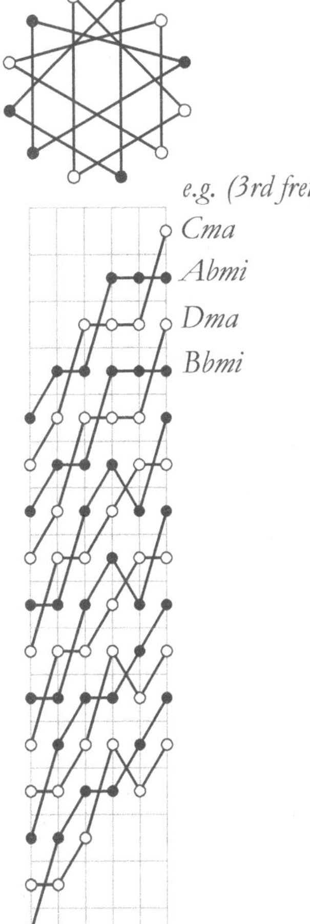

Two major and two minor triads (second possibility)

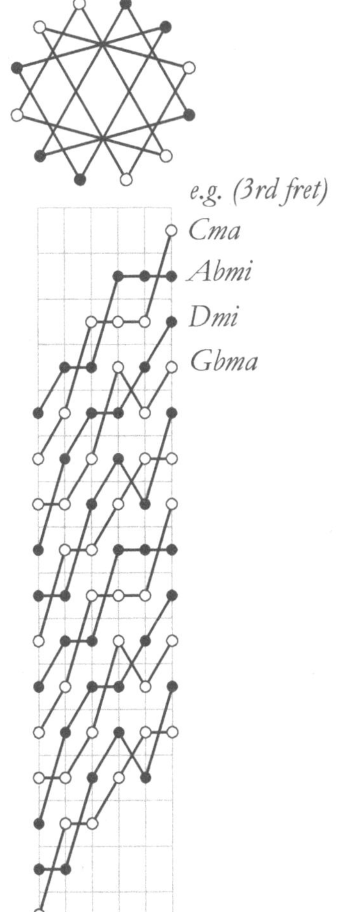

Three diminished and one augmented trichord

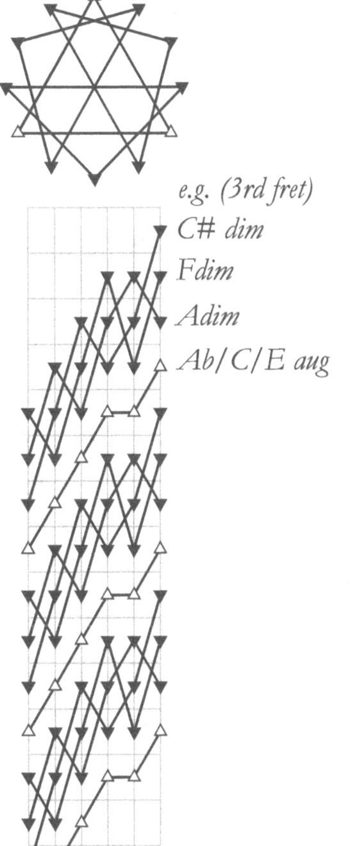

All four triads (only possibility)

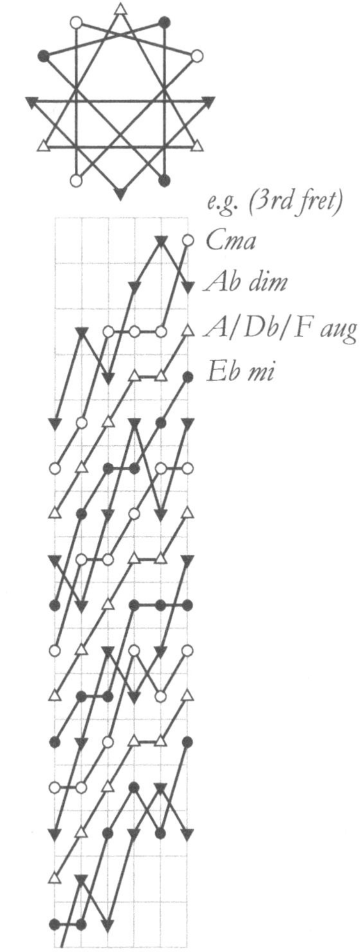

Concept

TRIADIC CHROMATICISM

A major triad can be paired with a minor triad whose root is a major third lower to make a symmetrical pitch set. This same pitch set can be made from transpositions of this triad pair by major thirds. Any of these pairs transposed by a tritone will create another symmetrical pitch set that is the negative space of the first one. Combine both pitch sets to get all 12 chromatic tones:

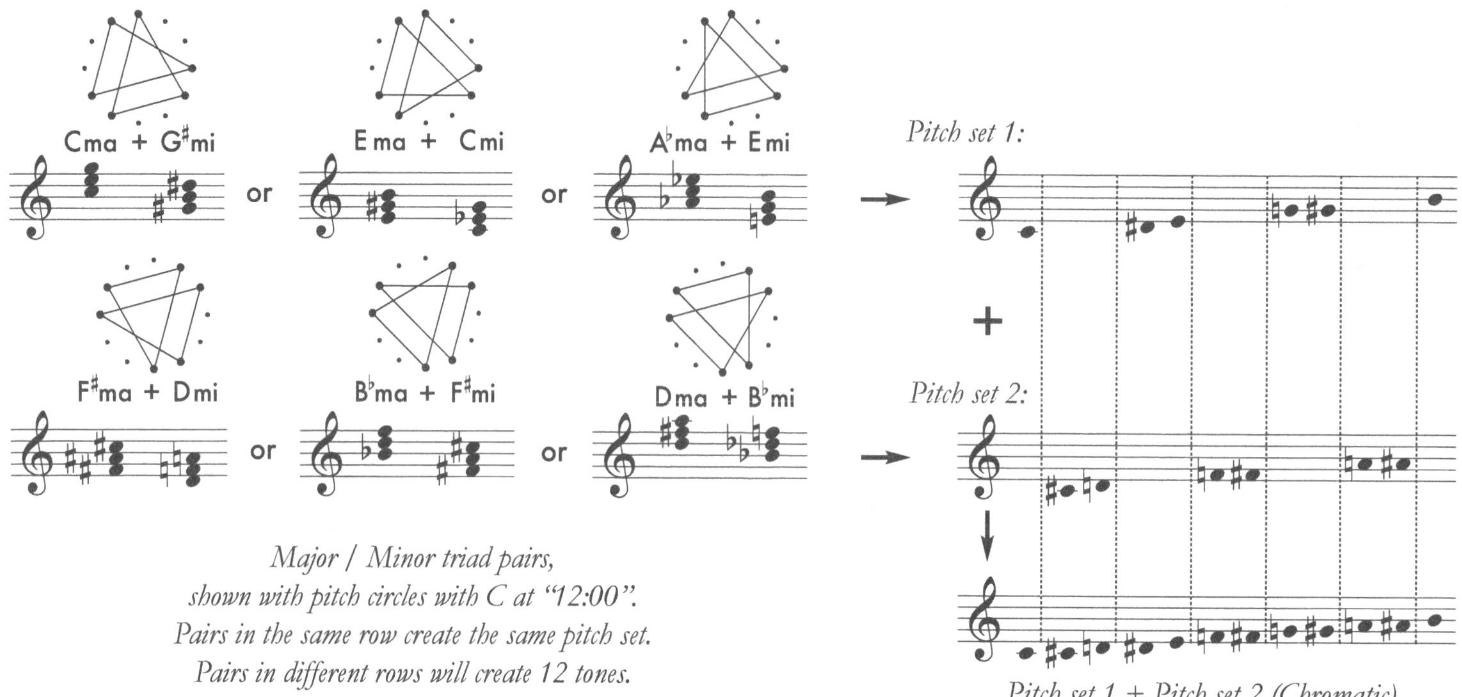

Major / Minor triad pairs, shown with pitch circles with C at "12:00". Pairs in the same row create the same pitch set. Pairs in different rows will create 12 tones.

This is a description of how to fill chromatic space with two major and two minor triads. It's convenient to visualize this idea as interlocking shapes on the two-dimensional space of the guitar fretboard. The illustration on the previous page shows combinations of major, minor, diminished, and augmented triads as tiling patterns.

This study can be extended to all 19 triads, with endless varieties. Notice that the earlier "Table of Triadic Elements" begins with the five symmetrical triads. Four of these can fill all 12 tones using transposition. For example, augmented triads *(0,4,8)* built off of four consecutive semitones will produce the chromatic aggregate. The diminished triad *(0,3,6)* cannot fill all 12-tones through transposition - three combined diminished triads will require one other triad type to complete the gamut. The other 14 asymmetrical triads are displayed in pairs on facing pages. These triads do not have internal symmetry, but show symmetry within each reflective pair. Two triads from each of these pairs can be combined to make 12 tones. This is shown in the example above, with the symmetrical pair of major and minor triads.

A study of these relationships can build insight into the partitioning of chromatic space into smaller functional parts. The triads cover 19 of the 350 pitch shapes. If the chromatic is a combination of all colors, then triadic tiling is a study of the possible ways to divide the chromatic into four colors. A full listing of these possibilities is beyond the scope of this book, but the exercise on the following page is provides a starting point. It uses the fretboard to visualize examples of triadic chromaticism using one, two and four triad types.

Exercise

TRIADIC TILING

Pitch tiling maps, showing triads filling the 2 dimensional space of the fretboard.
At the top of each map, an explanation of how the four triads are differentiated by color and shape.
The first shows a tiling of four transpositions of the triad (0,2,7).
The second shows a tiling of 2 major and 2 minor triads a tritone apart.
The third shows a tiling of a major, minor, diminished, and augmented triad.
- Before playing, look at the images and notice the formations made by each different element.
- Use the images as a guide, studying individual and combined triads (suggested study order to the right).
- Move through a variety of keys. Switch quickly between triads to increase ambiguity and chromaticism.
- Figure out other possible tilings for other triads, improvise.

Nine Studies:

○
●
△
▲
○ + ●
△ + ▲
○ + △
● + ▲
○ + ● + △ + ▲

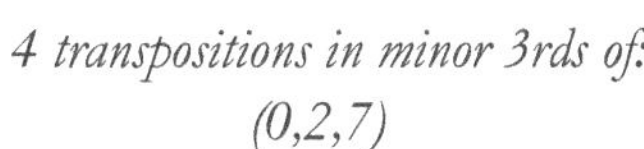

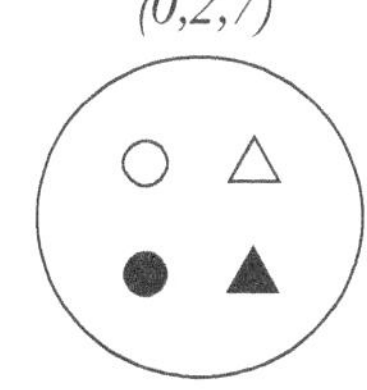

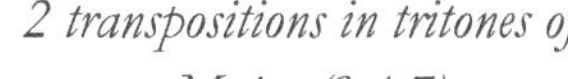

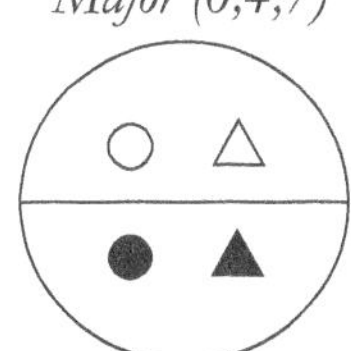

Minor (0,3,7)

1 version of each:

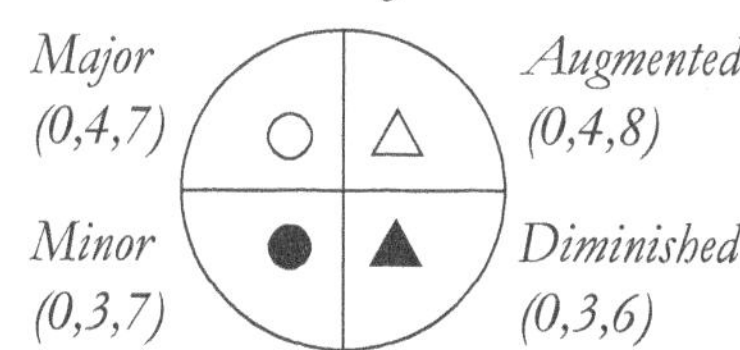

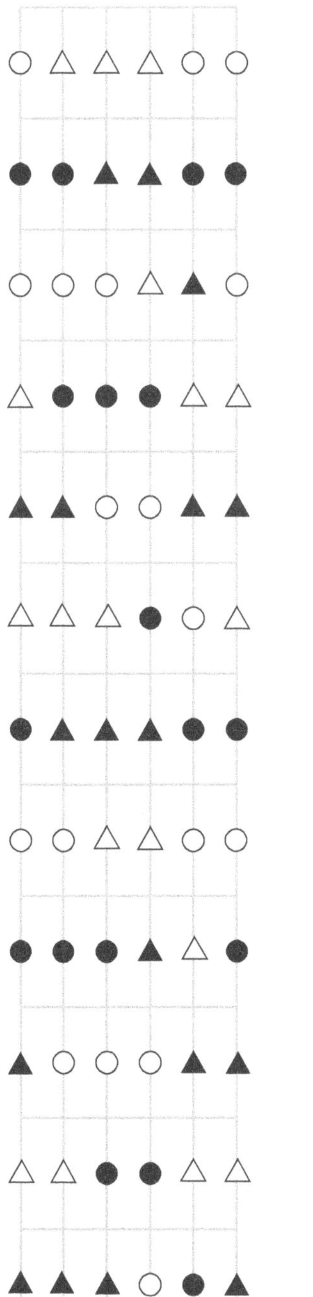

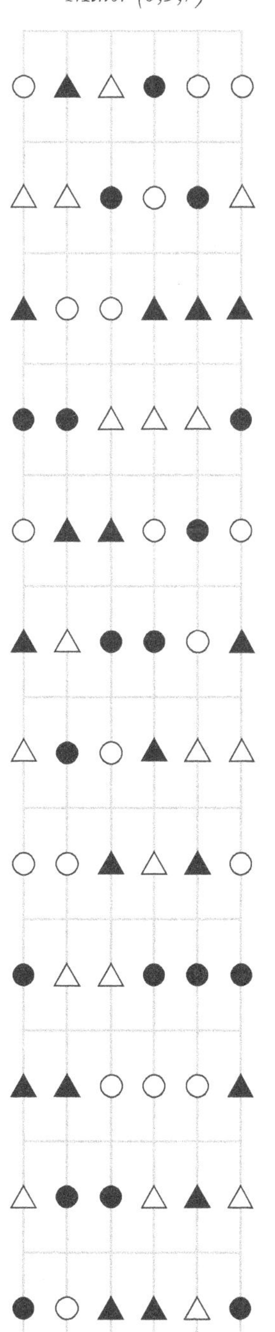

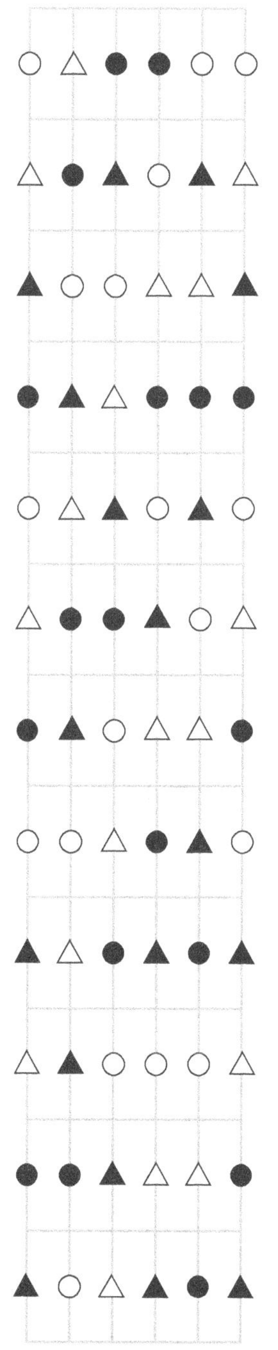

Notes

Idea: Compose a series of three-note sounds by ear on the guitar. Record it here, and label each triad. Take note of which of the 19 triads appear most frequently, less frequently, or not at all.

Concept

THE TETRAD
(FOUR PITCHES)

The 43 Tetrads:

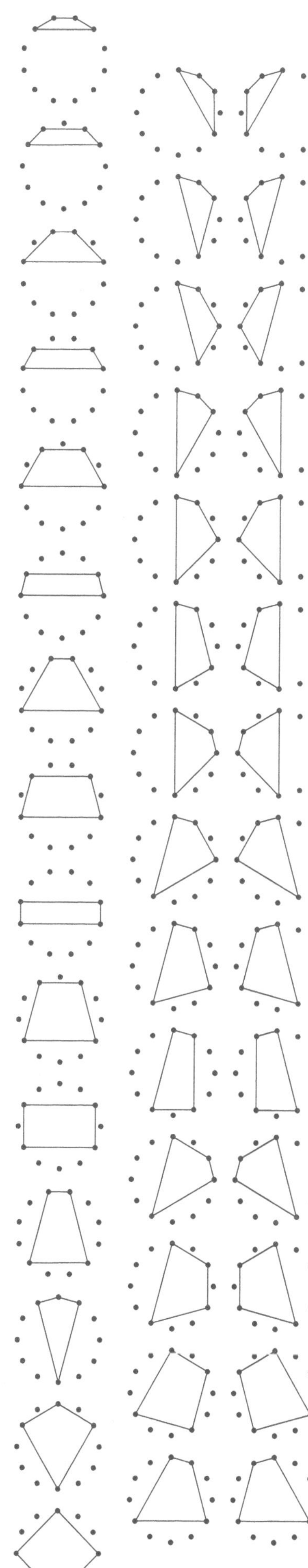

Take a circle of 12 points, connect any four points with a line, and you will get some rotation of one of the 43 shapes on the right. The same 43 tetrads can also be made by taking any of the 19 triads, adding one other pitch, and eliminating duplicates. Of the 43 tetrads, 15 are symmetrical, meaning that reflecting the interval structure does not change the fundamental quality, aside from transposition. For example, the tetrad *(C, E, G, B)* has an interval structure of *(4 + 3 + 4 + 1)*. Reflecting the intervals to *(1 + 4 + 3 + 4)* and starting on the same pitch will yield the tetrad *(C, Db, F, Ab)*, which uses different pitches but is clearly just a transposition of the original structure. These two tetrads are commonly called C major7 and Db major7.

It may be easiest to see the symmetry by looking at the 15 tetrads in the first column to the right. A visual way to describe them would be:
A four sided shape that is unchanged when reflected in a mirror.

The remaining 28 triads can have four different sized intervals *(e.g. 1 + 2 + 4 + 5)* or three different sized intervals, where the two similar intervals are adjacent *(e.g. 1 + 3 + 4 + 4)*. The asymmetry of these structures causes them to sound fundamentally different upon reflection. For example, the tetrad *(G, B, D, F)* has an interval structure of *(4 + 3 + 3 + 2)*. Reflecting the intervals to *(2 + 3 + 3 + 4)* and starting on the same pitch will yield the tetrad *(G, A , C, Eb)*. These are tetrads commonly called G7 and Cmi6, two structures with the same intervallic content but different ordering and a different sonic impression. All 28 asymmetrical tetrads are shown on two columns to the far right, in symmetrical pairs.

It's not possible within the space of this book to list all possible fingerings of each of these structures. A table similar to the one made for triads would require 4 inversions of 43 tetrads on 15 possible string sets (2,580 entries). It could be more efficient to just think of these as possible colorations of the 19 triads. For example, there are three tetrads that can be thought of as variations on an augmented triad:

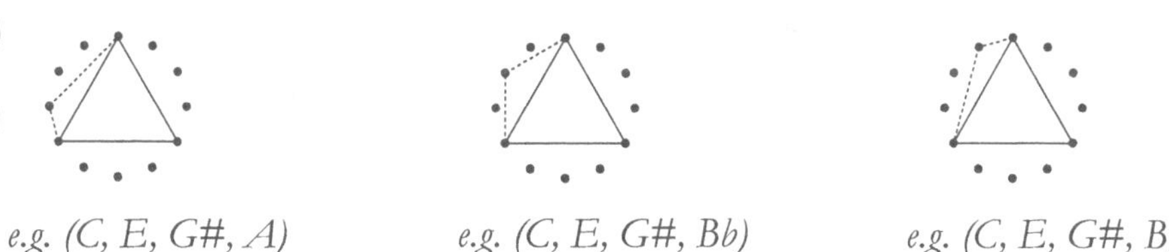

e.g. (C, E, G#, A) *e.g. (C, E, G#, Bb)* *e.g. (C, E, G#, B)*

Another perspective would be imagine a tetrad as two triads joined together by two common tones. This can be done two ways in any tetrad. For example,

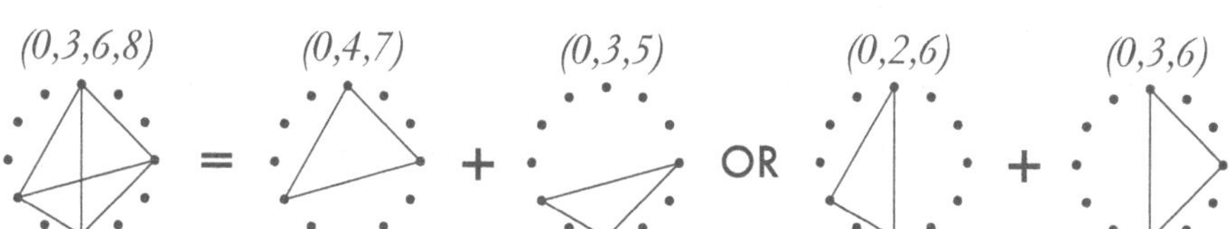

Concept

MAJOR 7th and MINOR 7th

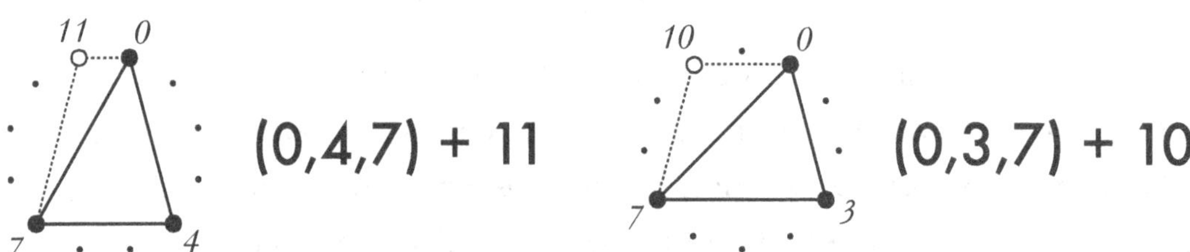

A good place to start with the study of tetrads are the four-note chords built from stacked thirds in various type of scales. In the four *heptatonic* scales, there are seven different combinations of major and minor thirds, shown here as types of thirds ascending from a root, with common names.

minor	*minor*	*minor*	*major*	*minor*	*major*	*major*
minor	*minor*	*major*	*minor*	*major*	*minor*	*major*
minor	*major*	*minor*	*minor*	*major*	*major*	*minor*
(Diminished 7th)	*(Dominant 7th)*	*(Minor 7th)*	*(Minor 7 b5)*	*(Major 7 #5)*	*(Major 7th)*	*(Minor Major 7th)*

The *Major 7th* (ma7) chord can be found in the diatonic (from 1st and 4th degree), in the harmonic minor (from the 6th degree) and in the harmonic major (from the 1st degree).
The *Minor 7th* (mi7) chord can be found in the diatonic (from the 2nd, 3rd, and 6th degree), the melodic minor (from the 2nd degree), the harmonic minor (from the 4th degree) and in the harmonic major (from the 3rd degree). Here is the distribution of ma7 and mi7 chord types in the four heptatonic scales:

These tetrachords have many fingerings. In order to reduce memorization, consider these tetrads as triads with an additional pitch. The major 7th and minor 7th tetrads can be thought of as colorations of the major and minor triads. We could return to the page for the major triad *(0,4,7)* and minor triad *(0,3,7)* and find every possible fingering ma7 and mi7 chords by adding a single pitch to each diagram, but this will produce many impractical voicings with awkward stretches. The following page shows all possible voicings for ma7 and mi7 that are within a three-fret span, which includes the most comfortable and practical fingerings.

Exercise

MAJOR AND MINOR EXTENDED

Compact fingerings for ma7 and mi7 chords. (3 or fewer frets)

Pitch circles show how a pitch is added to a triad to make the chord, with the traid in black and the added pitch in white.

Chords are grouped in rows, in the order that they are found in the Table of Triadic Elements, with common inversions in the same row.

-Play triad first, then add the major or minor 7th.

-For larger stretches, begin with any other triad fingering.

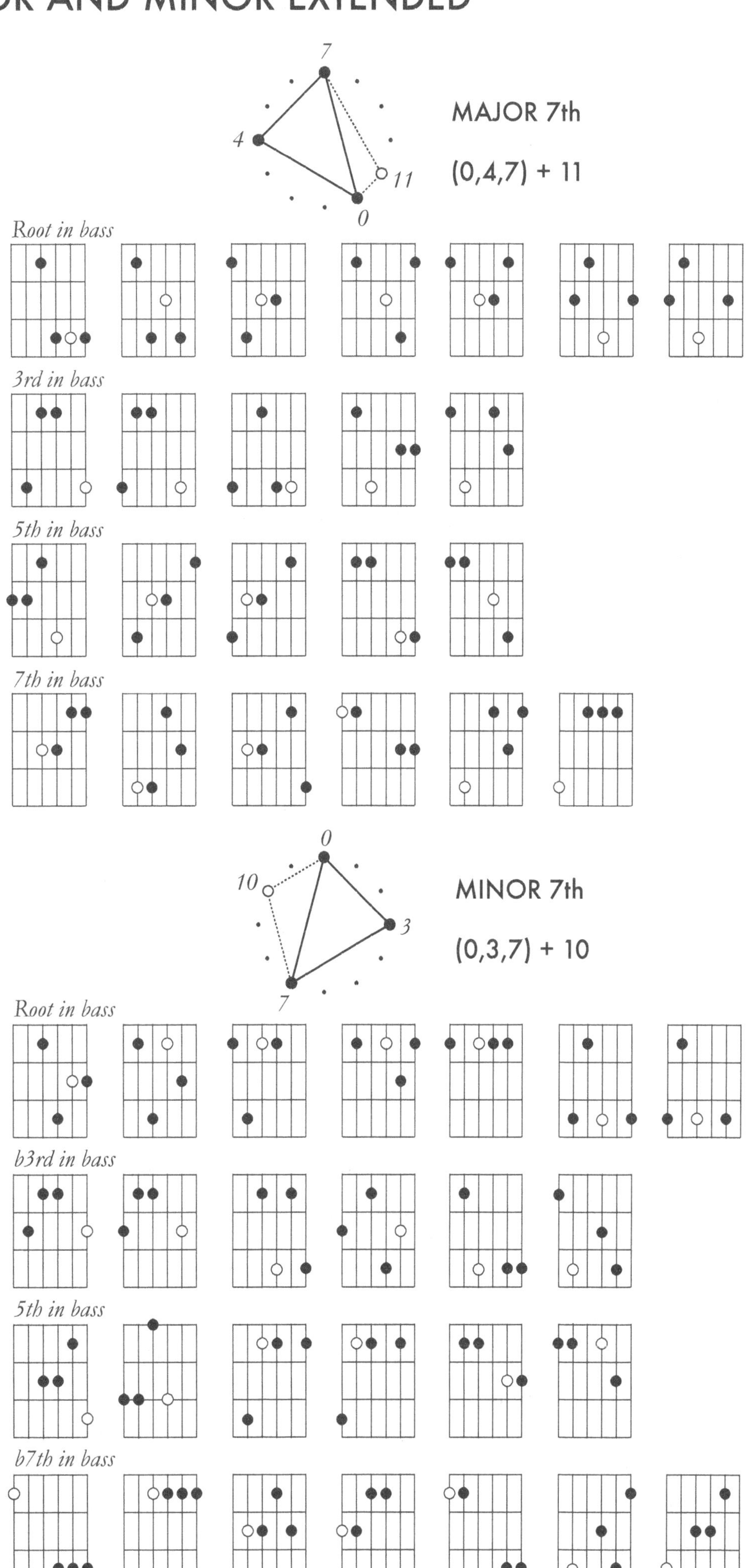

Concept

MINOR MAJOR 7th and MAJOR 7th #5

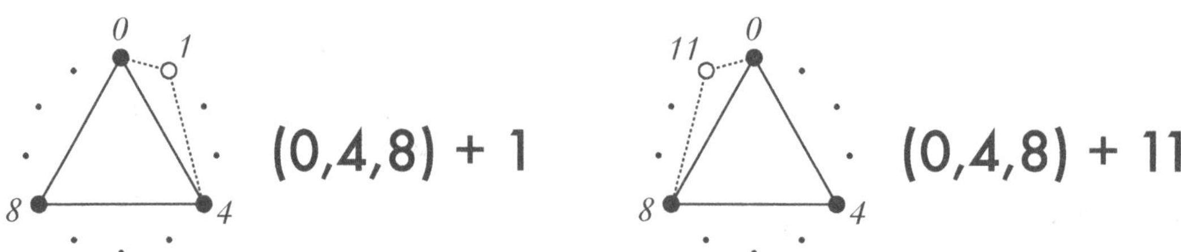

These chords contain an augmented triad, and could be thought of as colorations of this symmetrical sound. Adding any pitch to an augmented triad breaks the symmetry of the structure and changes the sonic impression.

Adding the pitch a semitone above (or a major 7th below, minor 9th above) one of the tones in the augmented triad produces the sound commonly called *Minor Major 7th* (- ma7, mi(ma7)), which can be found in the melodic minor and harmonic minor (from the 1st degree) and the harmonic major (from the 4th degree). Adding the pitch a semitone below (or a major 7th above, minor 9th below) one of the tones in the augmented triad produces the sound commonly called *Major 7th #5* (ma7#5), which can be found in the melodic minor and harmonic minor (from the 3rd degree) and the harmonic major (from the 6th degree). Here is the distribution of mi(ma7) and ma7#5 chord types in these three heptatonic scales (they don't exist in the diatonic, which has no augmented triad):

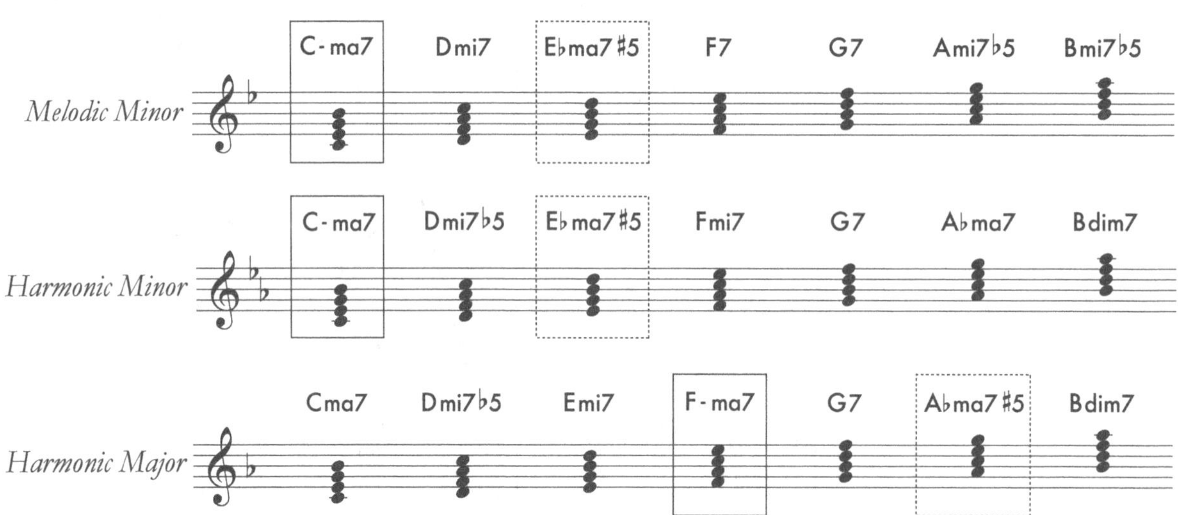

When making ma7 and mi7 chords from major and minor triads, the added pitch in both cases is the 7th (a major 7th and minor 7th above the root, respectively). In the case of the chords above, the added pitch is the 7th of ma7#5, but is the root of the mi(ma7). The reason for this is that this study references the convention of building chords from stacked thirds, which names them from the bottom note in closed position. The point of the study is to look at chords from one perspective (common nomenclature, ma7, mi7 etc) and think about what their fundamental sonic character is based on. In the case of ma7 and mi7, the sonic character is based on the underlying major and minor triads. With mi(ma7) and ma7#5, the sound is largely determined by the augmented triad, which is located in different places in each chord (from the b3rd and root, respectively). The following page shows all possible voicings for mi(ma7)and ma7#5 that are within a three-fret span, which includes the most comfortable and practical fingerings.

Exercise

AUGMENTED EXTENDED

Compact fingerings for mi(ma7) and ma7#5 chords (3 or fewer frets).

Pitch circles show how a pitch is added to a triad to make the chord, with the traid in black and the added pitch in white.

Note that for mi(ma7), the added pitch is the root, but with ma7#5, the added pitch is major 7th.

Chords are grouped in rows, in the order that they are found in the Table of Triadic Elements, with common inversions in the same row.

-Play triad first, then add the extra pitch.

-Notice that adding a pitch a semitone above or below any note in augmented triad makes mi(ma7) and ma7#5, respectively.

-For larger stretches, begin with any other triad fingering.

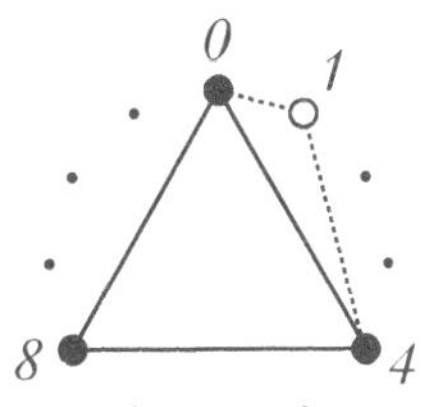

MINOR MAJOR 7th

(0,4,8) + 1 (root = 1)

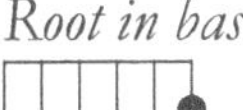

Root in bass

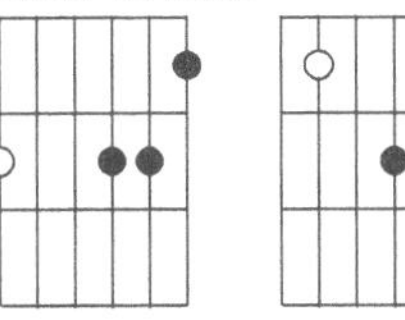
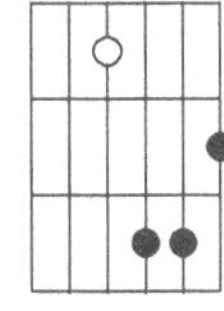
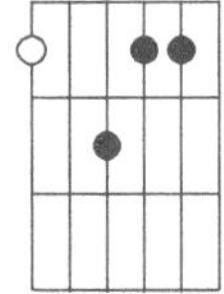
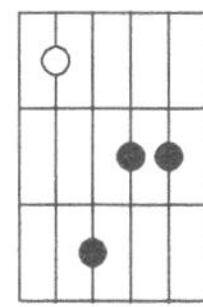
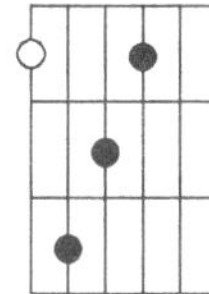
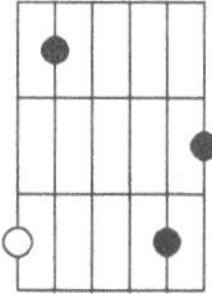

b3rd in bass

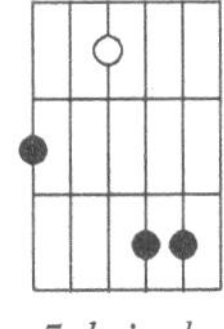
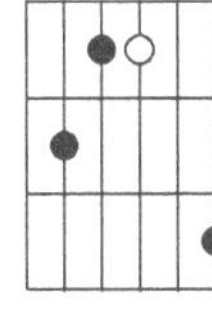
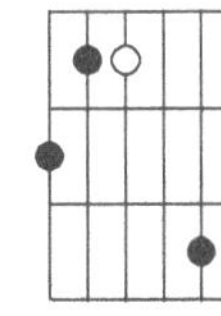

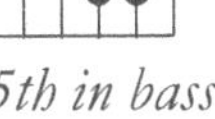

5th in bass

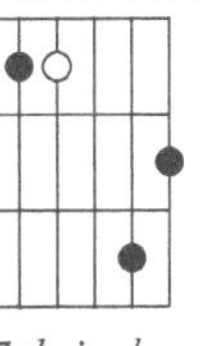
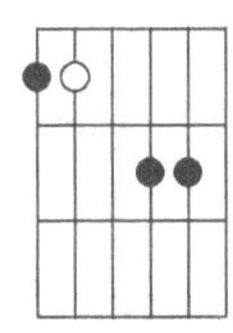

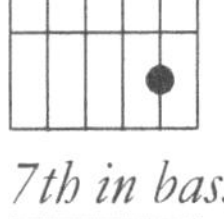

7th in bass

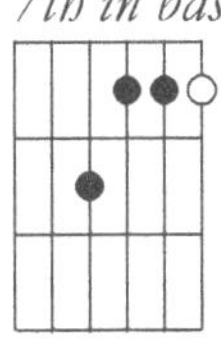
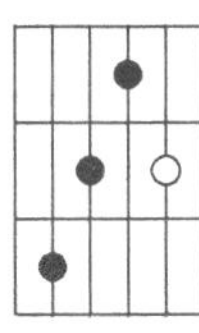
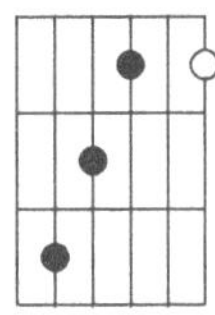
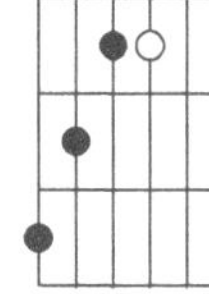
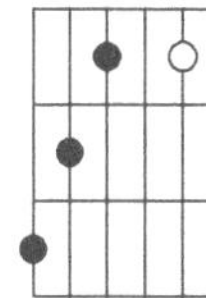
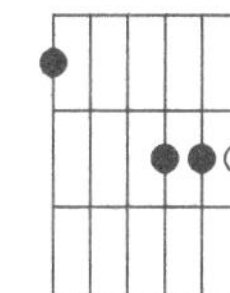
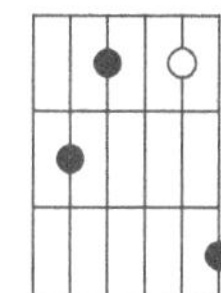
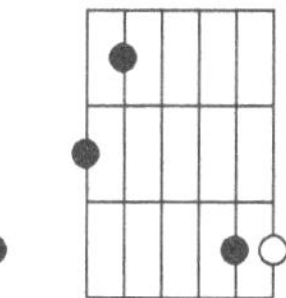

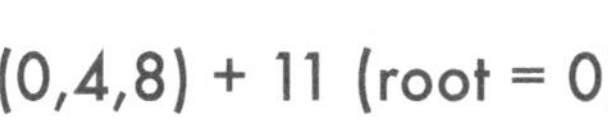

(0,4,8) + 11 (root = 0)

Root in bass

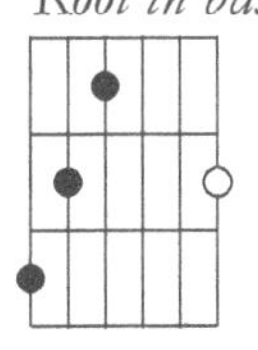
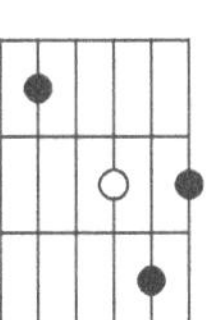
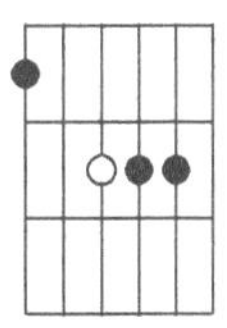
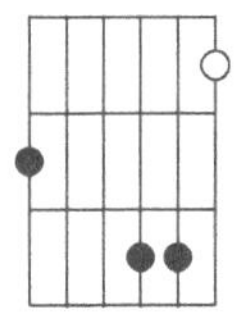
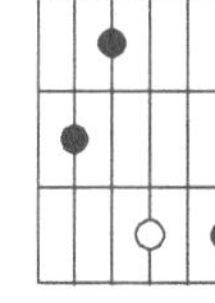
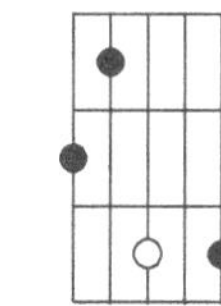
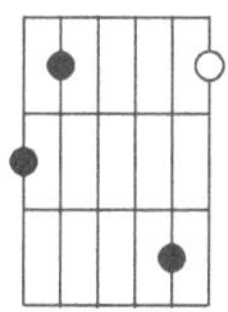

3rd in bass

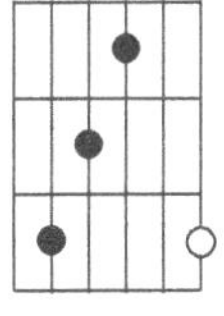
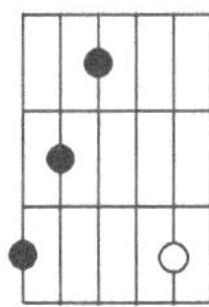
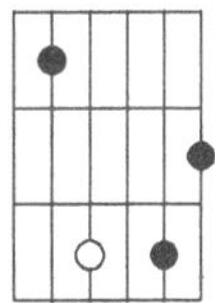
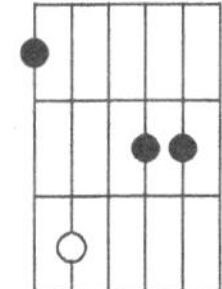

#5th in bass

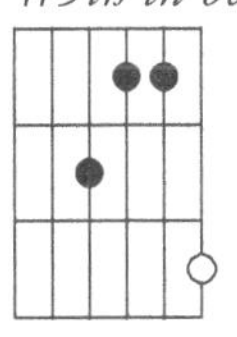
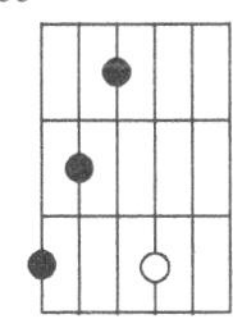
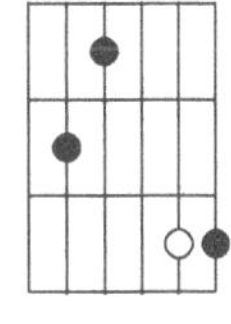
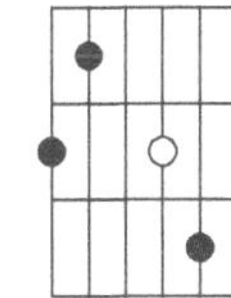

7th in bass

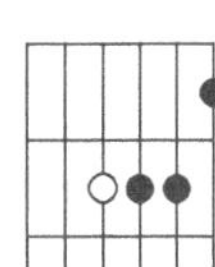
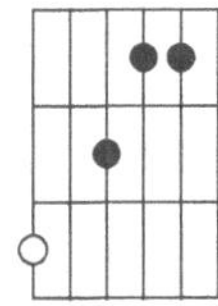
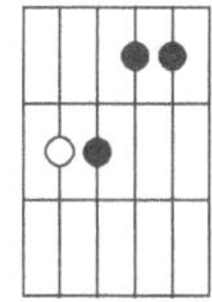
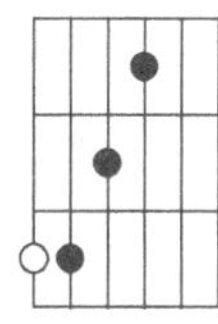
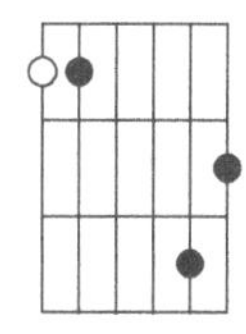
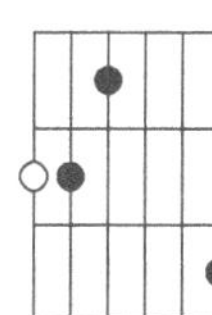

Concept

DOMINANT 7th, DIMINISHED 7th, and MINOR 6th

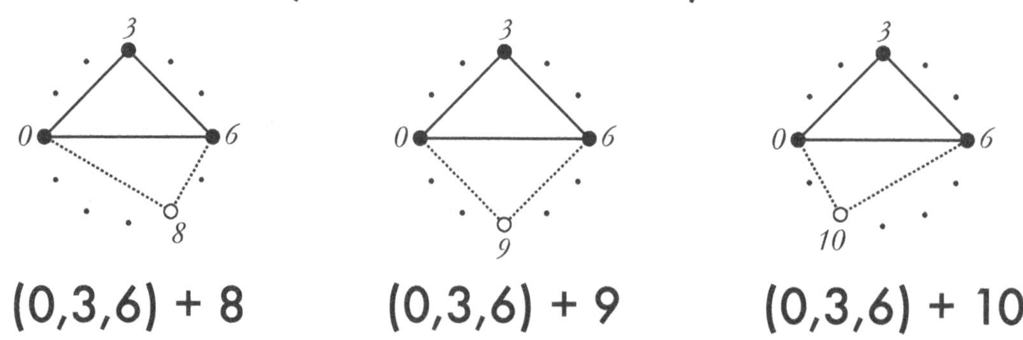

(0,3,6) + 8 (0,3,6) + 9 (0,3,6) + 10

This section will explore the relationship and function of these three structures, which share a common diminished triad.

The *Diminished 7th* (dim7) chord can be found at the 7th degree of the harmonic minor and harmonic major. The *Dominant 7th* (7, or dom7) chord can be found at the 5th degree of all four heptatonic scales, and also at the 4th degree of the melodic minor.

The *Minor 6th* (mi6) is also commonly called *Minor 7 b5,* with a root a minor third lower. For example, Fmi6 *(F, Ab, C, D)* contains the same pitches as Dmi7b5 *(D, F, Ab, C)*. This book will use the convention of calling this structure by the name Fmi6, because of the minor triad which leads the ear to hear F as the root, and because of the this chord's common function as a minor *IV* chord in the key of C. This chord can be found in the diatonic (from the 7th degree), the melodic minor (from the 6th and 7th degree) and in the harmonic minor and harmonic major (from the 2nd degree).
Here is the distribution of Diminished, Dominant 7th, and Minor 6th (Minor 7 b5) chord types in the four heptatonic scales:

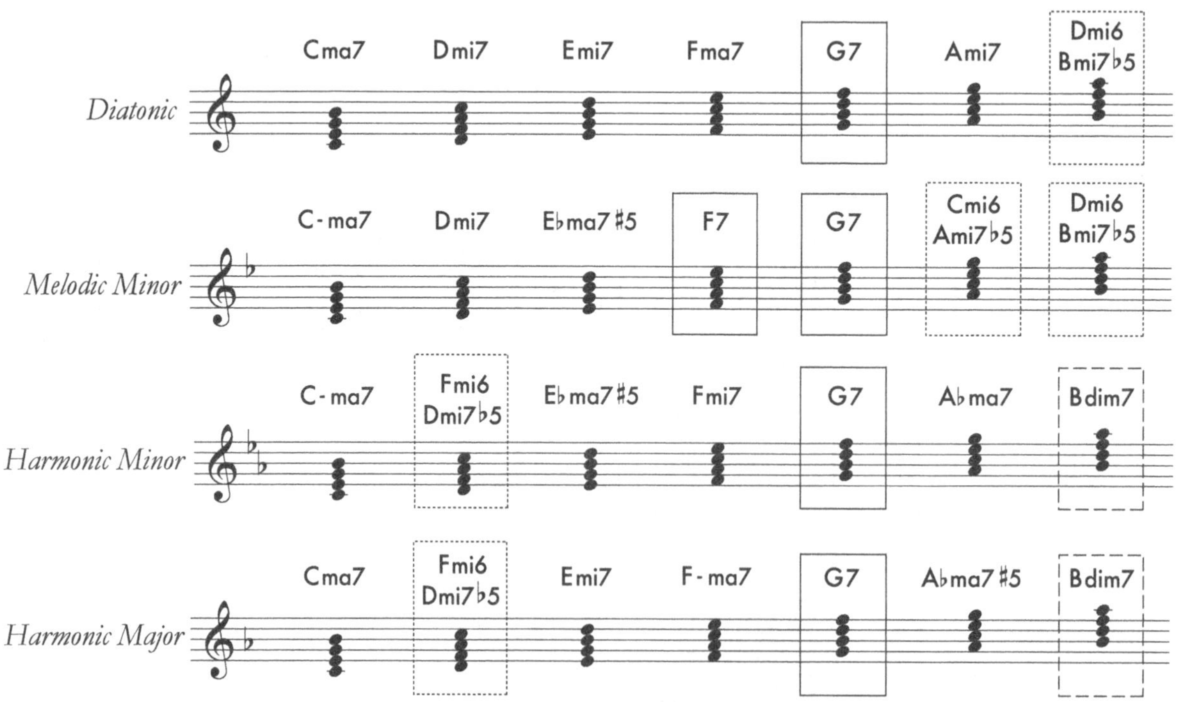

In making the dim7 chord, the pitch that is added creates a completely symmetrical structure that can be named by any of its four pitches (e.g. Bdim7 = Ddim7 = Fdim7 = Abdim7). In making the dom7 chord, the pitch that is added to the diminished triad becomes the root, and in making the mi6 chord, the pitch that is added to the diminished triad becomes the 5th.

Concept

SYMMETRICAL DIMINISHED TRANSFORMATIONS

The subject of harmony is beyond the scope of this book, but it is useful to take a closer look at the relationship between dim7, dom7, and mi6 chords. Notice on these circles how moving any pitch in a dim7 chord down (counterclockwise) by a semitone will make a dom7 chord, and moving any pitch up (clockwise) by a semitone will make a mi6 chord:

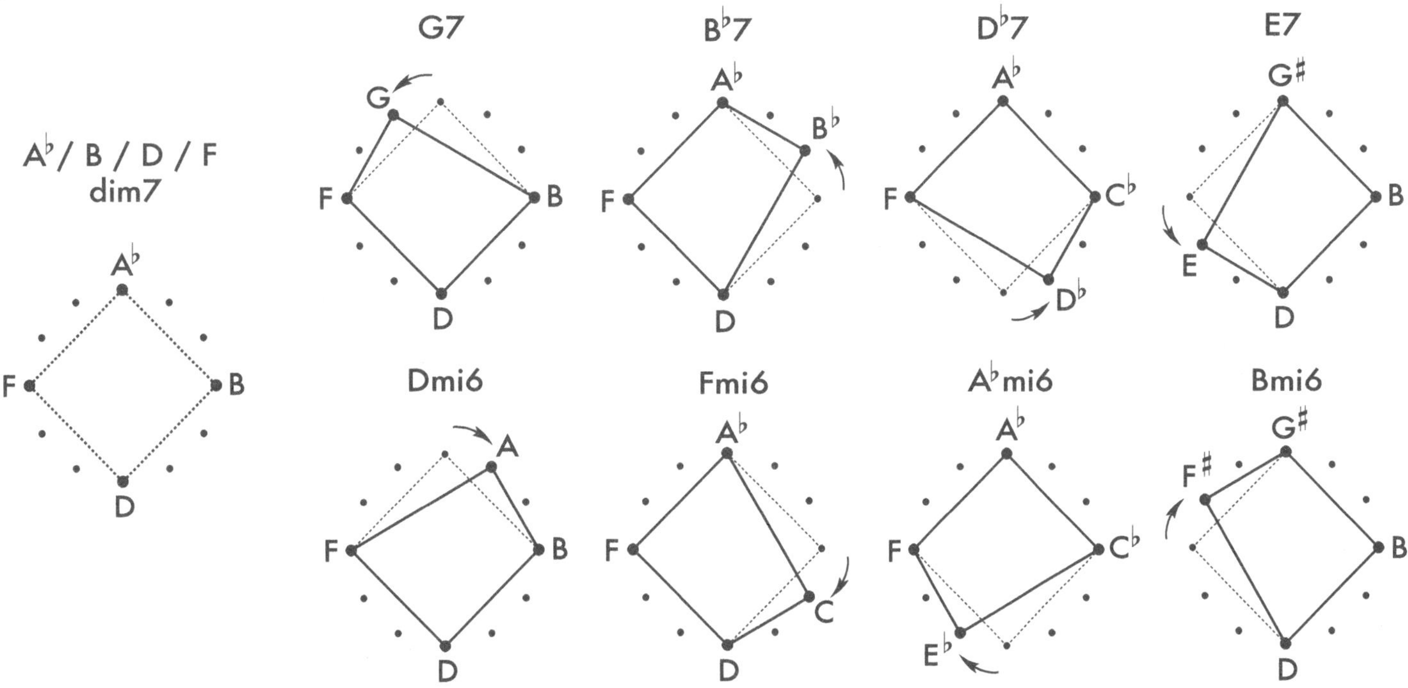

These chords share a family, in the sense that they can all serve as dominants to these tonal centers:

(C major / C minor)

(Eb major / Eb minor)

(Gbmajor / Gb minor)

(A major / A minor)

There are two other dim7 chords *(C, Eb, Gb, A)* and *(Db, E, G, Bb)* that each can produce four dom7 and mi6 chords. This means that the three dim7 chords can produce 24 other structures (12 dom7 and 12 mi6 chords). With some grasp of this idea, a great deal of memorization can be avoided on the guitar, and the idea of families of dominants can also lead to fluid ideas about movement and progression of harmonies.

The dim7 chord can be played on any of the 15 possible sets of four strings (shown on the right).
The last five require the greatest reach.
The first five are the most common because they lay well on the instrument, and the following page shows how to transform each of these into four dom7 and four mi6 chords.

15 voicings of the diminished 7th chord:

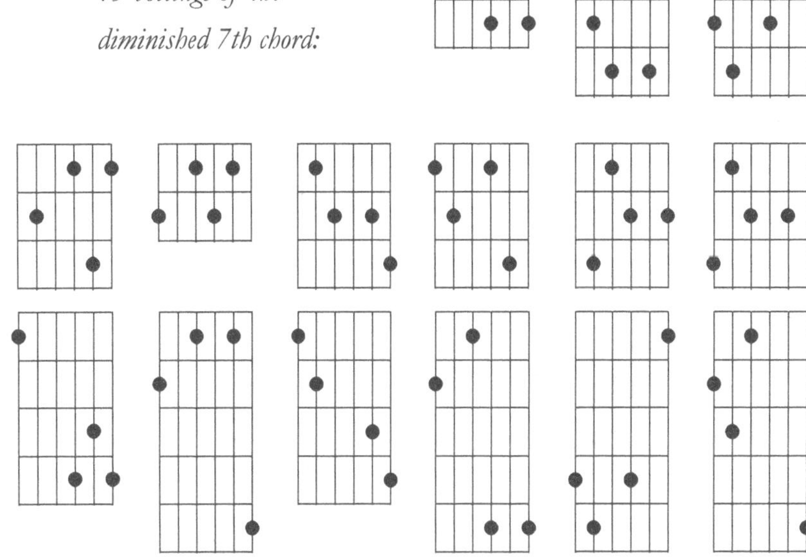

Exercise

DIMINISHED FAMILIES

Each row shows a diminished 7th on the left, and transformations of this shape by one semitone to make 8 other chords. Lowering any pitch of the dim7 produces four dom7 chords, and raising any pitch produces four mi6 chords.
- Move between the diminished 7th chord and each of the other chords in the same row.
- Notice how changing the pitch in each case produces a perfect 5th (or perfect 4th), which indicates the root of the new chord. (root is the lower note of a perfect 5th, or the upper note of a perfect 4th)
- Label the fretboard diagrams with roots and inverions, notice the patterns and symmetry.

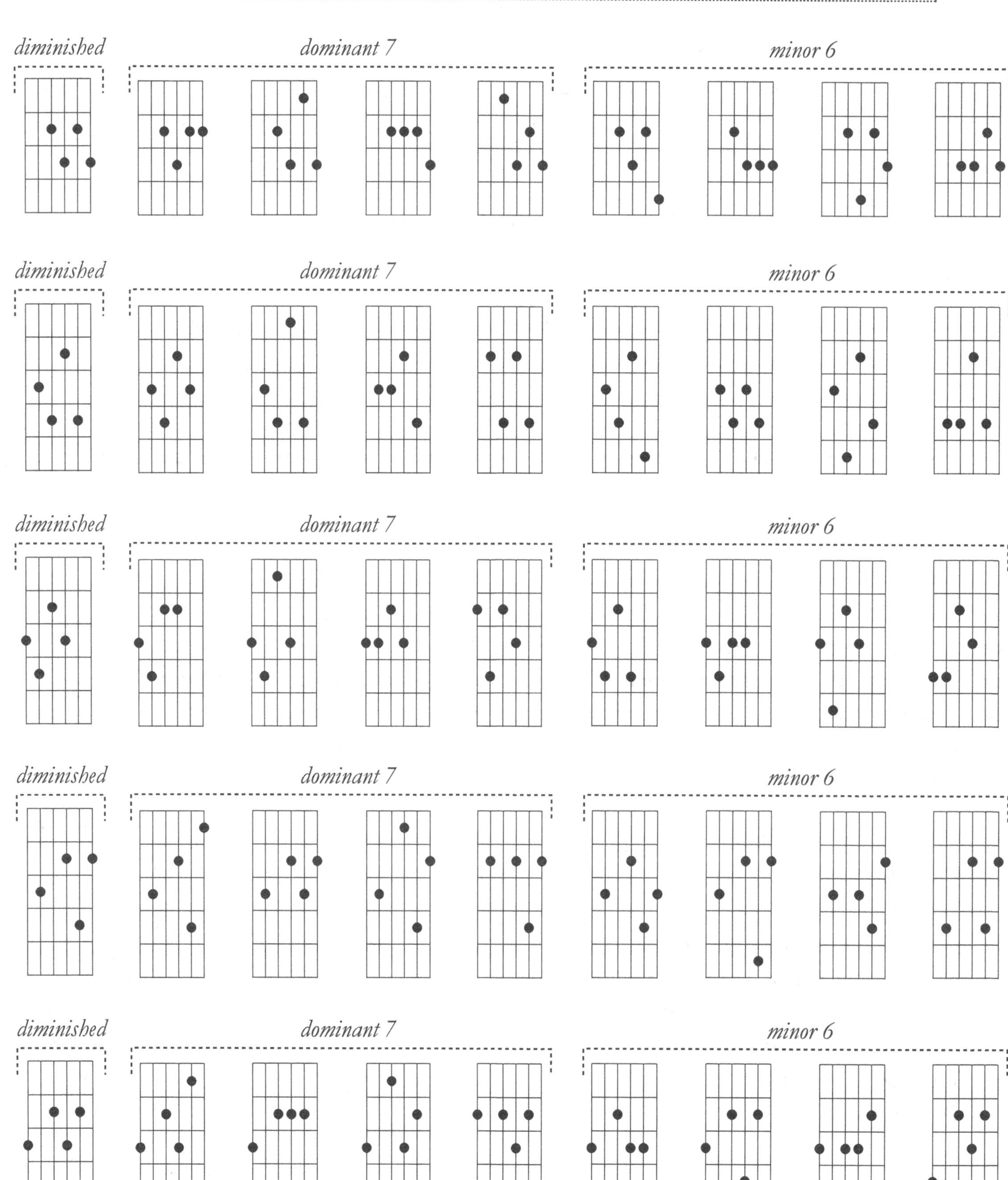

DOMINANT MOVEMENTS

Dominant 7th and minor 6th chords are intervallic mirror images of each other, symmetrically identical combinations of a tritone and a perfect fifth:

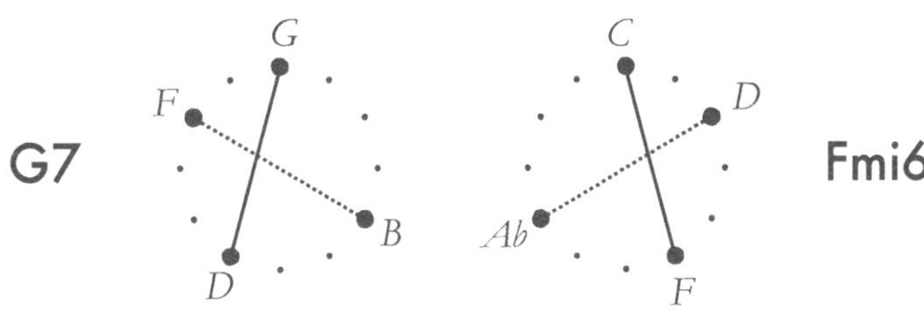

The perfect 5th defines the root, and the tritone contains tonal tension that is the signature color of these two dominant chords. The resolution of this tension can lead to many types of movement. Depending on the inversion and the destination, the tritone can expand or contract during resolution. Based on the previous study of the diminished 7th chord, we can see that either dominant chord can move to four main directions, to tonalities separated by minor 3rds. Here is an example showing how G7 and Fmi6 can both lead to the same destinations. The 5ths are removed from the dominant chords and the tritones are shown with open noteheads to better view this contracting/expanding movement.

G^7 *resolving to:*

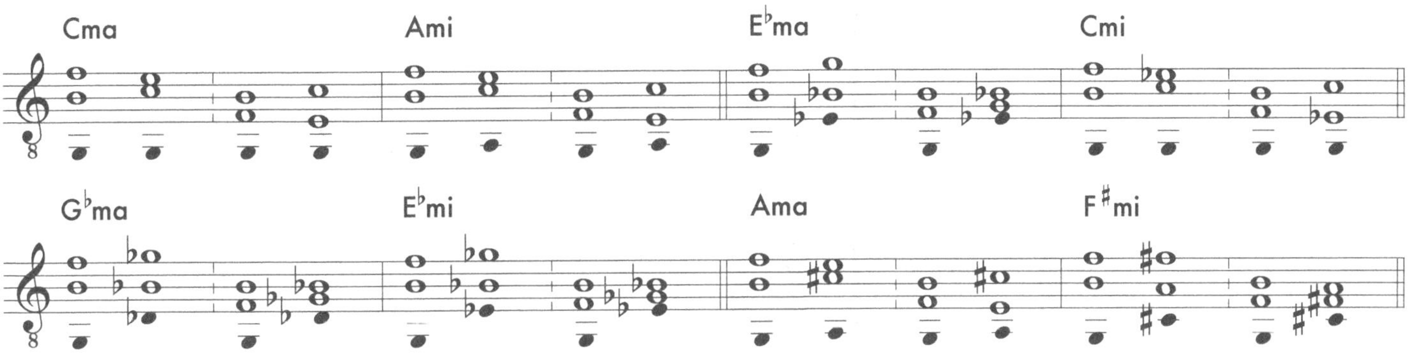

Cma Ami E♭ma Cmi

G♭ma E♭mi Ama F♯mi

Fmi6 *resolving to:*

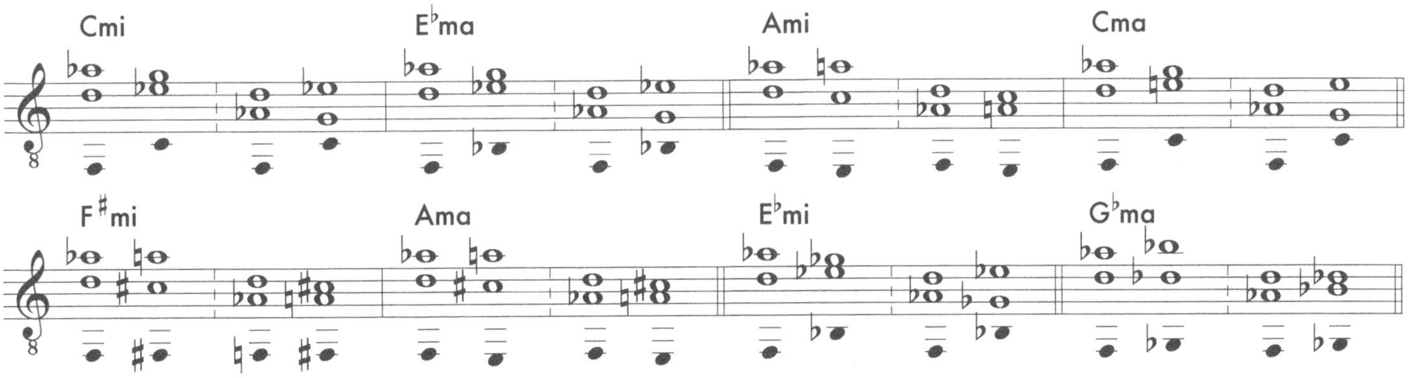

Cmi E♭ma Ami Cma

F♯mi Ama E♭mi G♭ma

These are two dominant chords going to four different key centers. There are 22 other dom7 and mi6 chords and many other types of resolutions. For example, a dominant chord doesn't have to resolve to a major or minor triad - it could just as easily lead to another dominant. And this dominant could lead to another, creating a chain of dominants. Typical chains of dominant 7th and mi6 chords might look like: *G7 , C7, F7, Bb7 . . . etc.* or *Fmi6, Cmi6, Gmi6, Dmi6 . . . etc.*

These chains use only root movements by 4ths and 5ths. Allowing for the four-directional resolutions shown above dramatically increases the possibilities. Long and convoluted progressions can be created with a few simple principles. The exercise on the following page is designed to explore this idea, visually showing all possible pathways for one dominant to another.

Exercise

DOMINANT CHAINS

Possible Dominant progressions. Chords are grouped by fours into families derived from the same diminished 7th structure.
Diagrams show the common name and pitch circle representation with C at "12:00."
Roots are shown as white circles and the master diminished structure with dotted lines.
Move from any chord in a box to any chord in another box along the directional arrows to form dominant progressions.
- *Move straight across the rows from left to right in the upper families (Circle of Fifths)*
- *Change position in the column while moving from left to right in the upper families (Diminished relationships)*
- *Move straight across the rows from right to left in the lower families (opposite Circle of Fifths)*
- *Change position in the column while moving from right to left in the lower families (Diminished relationships)*
- *Include movements between upper and lower families, creating chains of dominant chords.*
- *Improvise melodies using these same movements, using Mixolydian for upper families and Dorian for lower families.*

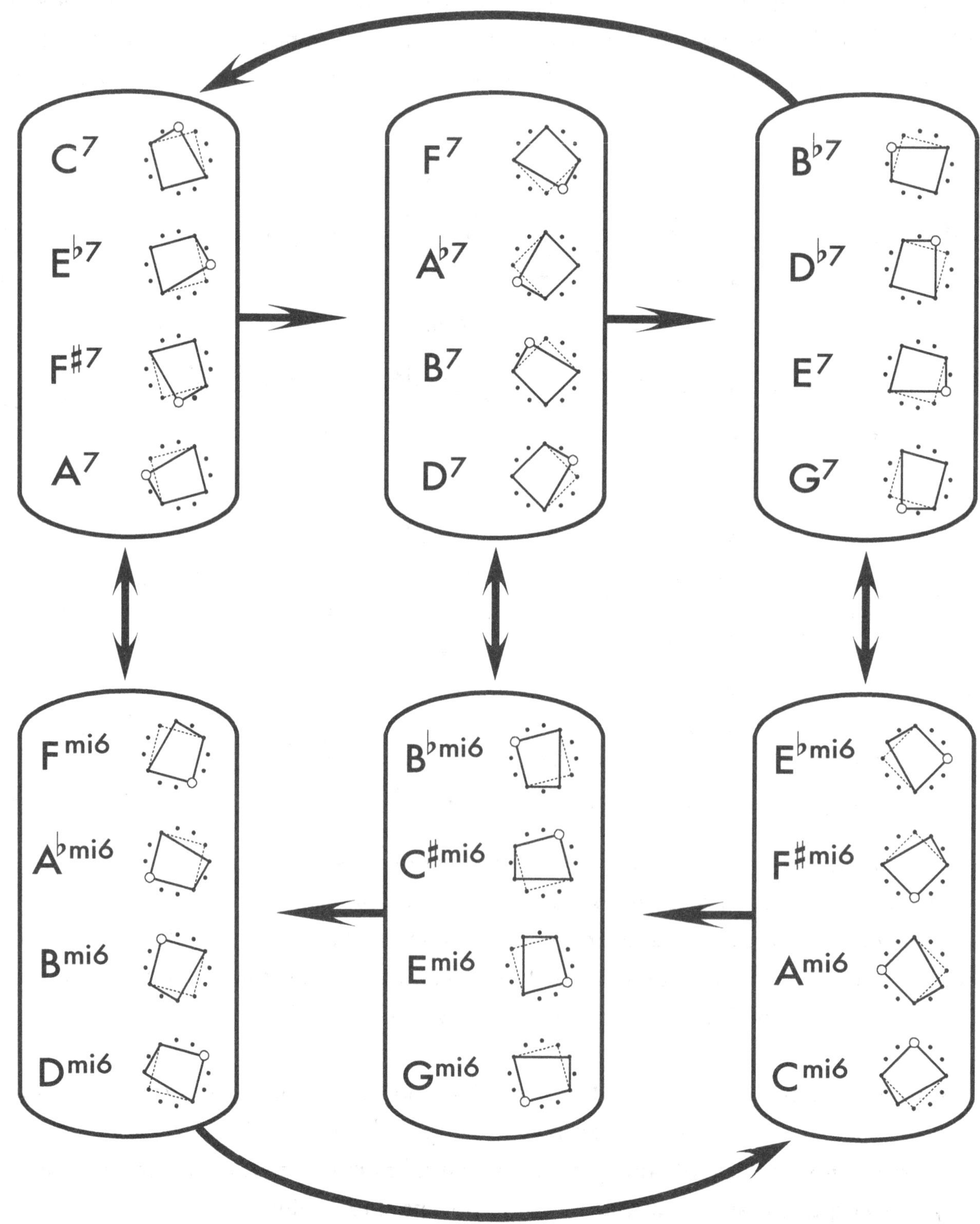

Two examples from the previous exercise.
Shown are two chains of dominant chords derived from pathways in the illustration.

Various movements of Dominant 7th and Minor 6th chords, using a symmetrical pattern on string set {2,3,4,6}. Root movement in 5ths, Major 2nds, Major Thirds, and Semitones.

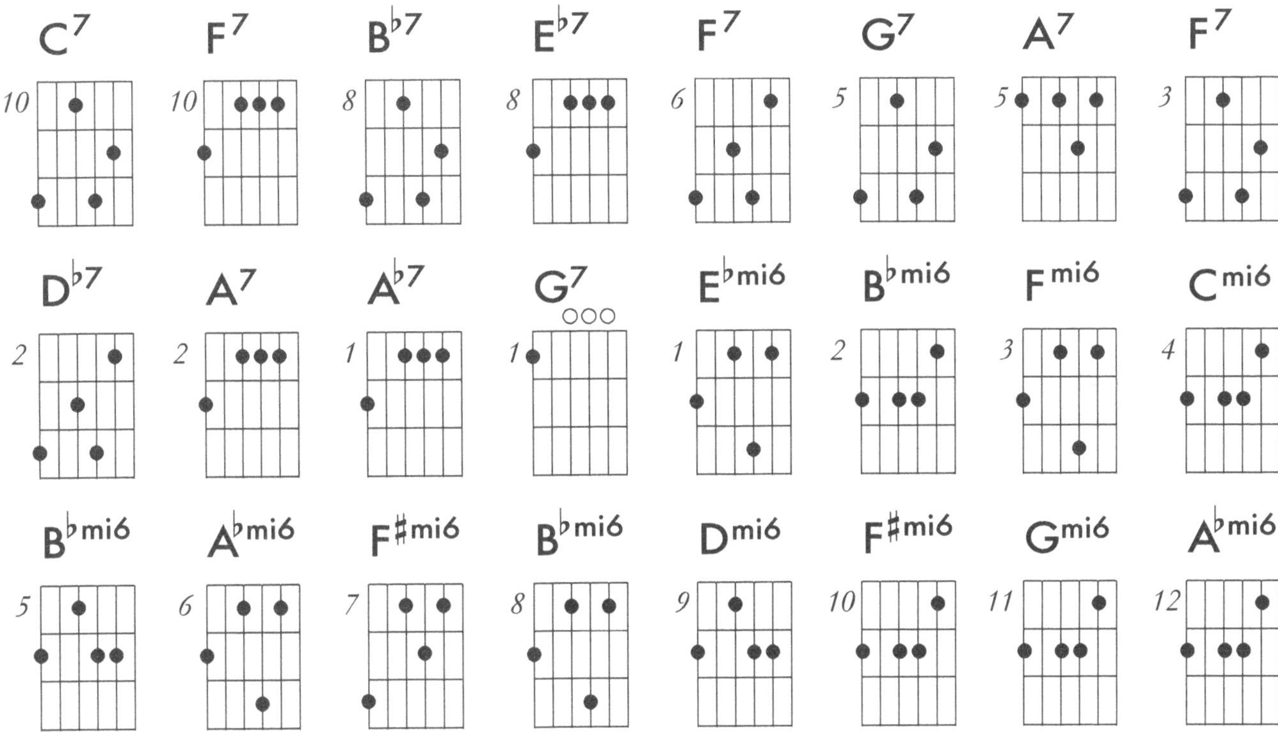

A pattern using all 24 Dominant 7th and Minor 6th chords on string set {2,3,4,6}. Root movement is in major thirds for each set of three chords.

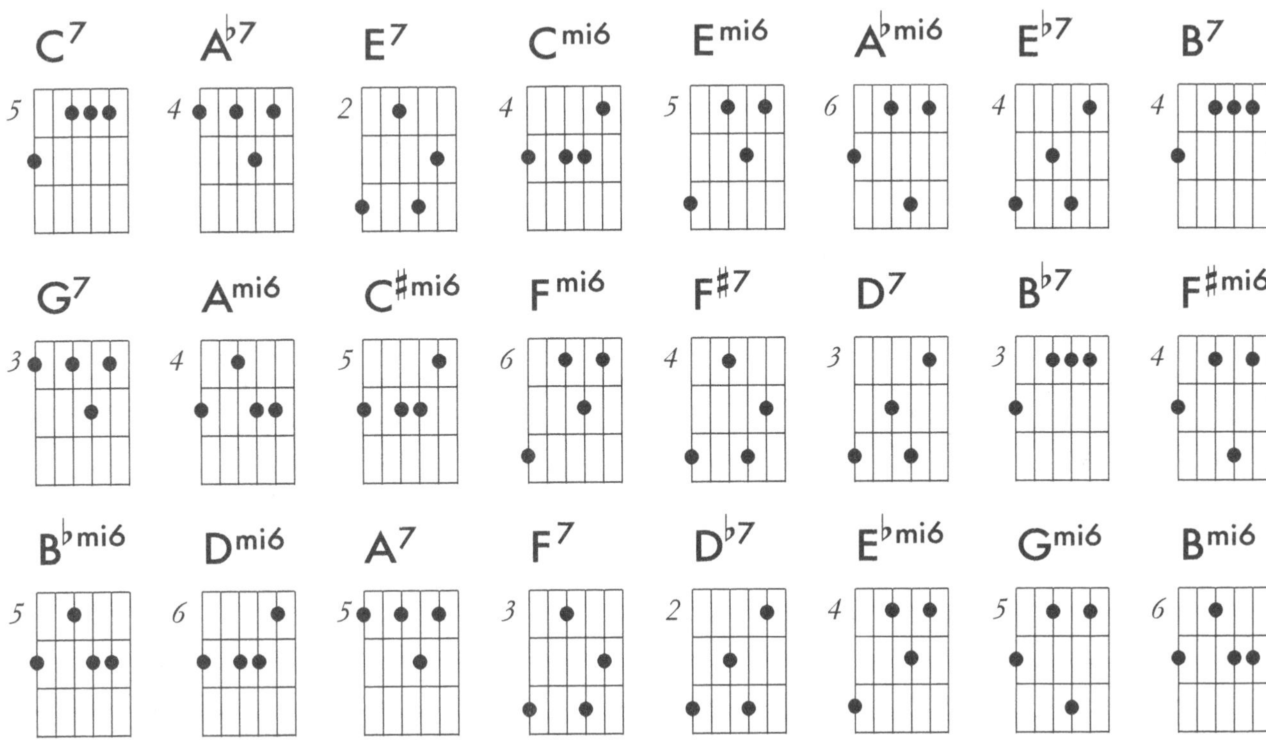

Notes Idea: *Connect any four points, assign pitches to them, play the tetrad in different positions and string sets, analyze it, name it.*

Concept

ALL INTERVAL TETRADS

Take a tritone and combine it with a minor third, wihout doubling any pitches. There are only four ways to do this:

Combination of a Tritone and Minor Third:

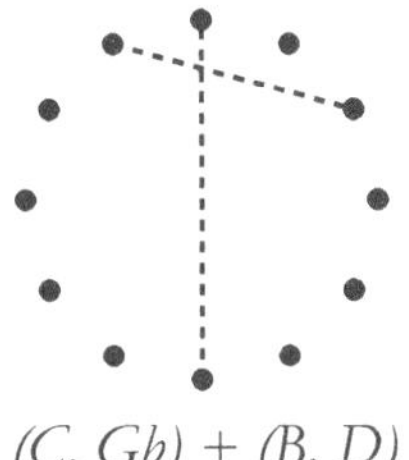

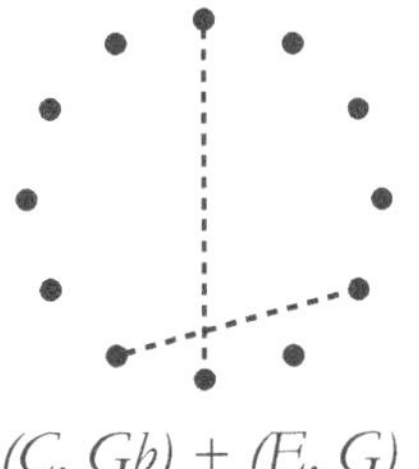

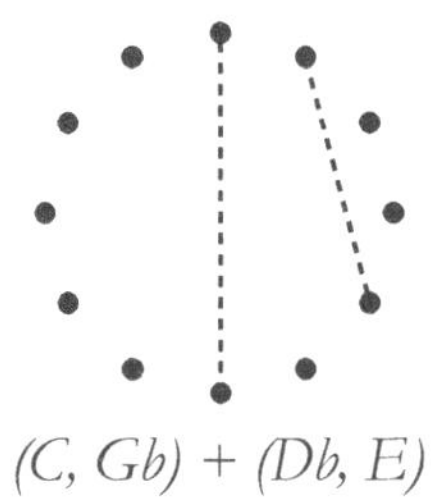

example with C at "12:00": (C, Gb) + (B, D) (C, Gb) + (E, G) (C, Gb) + (Db, E) (C, Gb) + (D, F)

Connecting the pitches gives us these four shapes, the *all interval tetrads*:

The four all-interval tetrads, with tritone in vertical orientation:

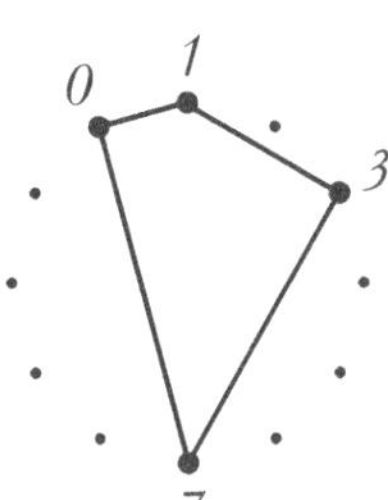

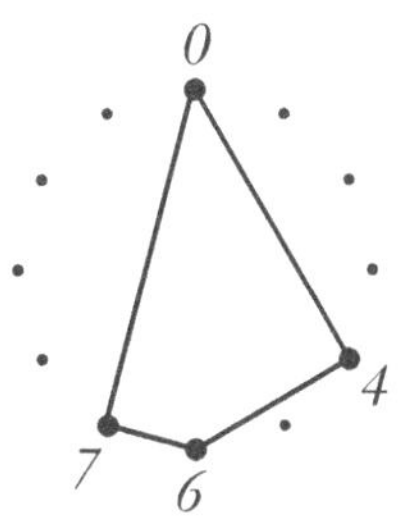

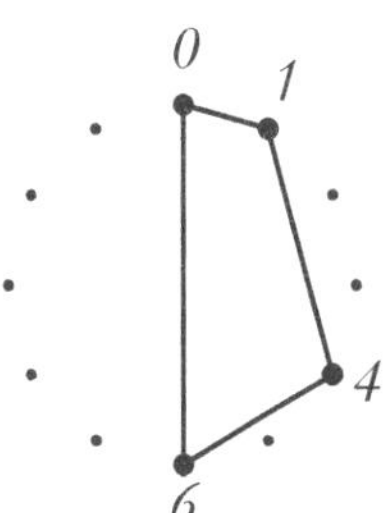

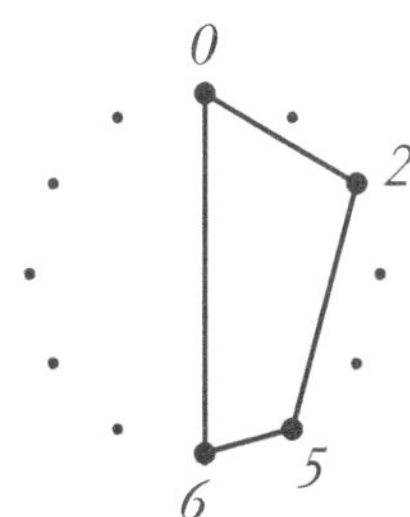

For lack of a better convention, we will name these tetrads with a four-digit number. We arrange the pitches so that they have the smallest possible span (the first two can be bound by a perfect 5th, and the second two by a tritone), and number them in semitones from the bottom up, starting with zero:

The four all-interval tetrads in closest voicings, with numerical labels:

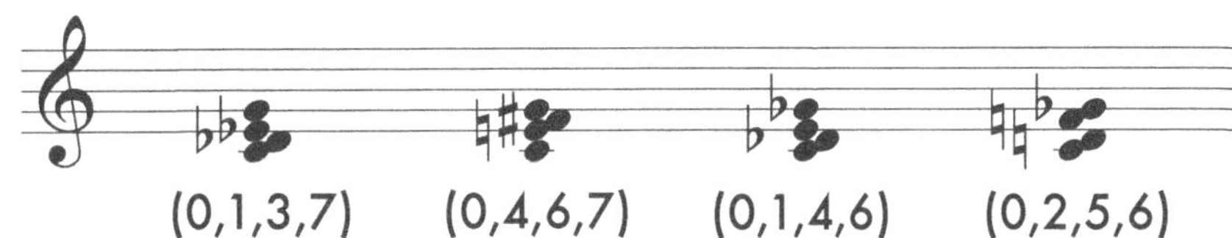

These four pitch sets have a special property: each one of them contains all possible intervals in the chromatic scale. This is shown in the table below (inversion is used for larger intervals):

The all-interval tetrads have a complex and rich sound that changes dramatically upon inversion. The following pages show the most practical voicings for each of them in various inversions and string sets.

Exercise

CHROMA

All interval tetrads, shown with numerical name, traditional pitch names starting on C, pitch circle and fretboard fingerings.
All fingerings are shown that have three adjacent upper strings and lower string 4, 5 or 6 (to limit options and use comfortable voicings).
Rows show common inversions, and columns show common string sets.
Numbers above fretboards show the order of the pitches in the inversion, from low to high.

- *There are 2, 3, 4, and 5 fret fingerings here - choose voicings with a smaller fret span, then work toward longer stretches.*
- *Sing the pitches of a tetrad as a four note melody, either in C (as shown in each example) or transposed to any other key.*
- *Play one of the fingerings, sing the melody. Play another fingering or inversion, sing the melody again.*
- *Notice how the voicing brings out different colors of the melody, and vice versa.*
- *Look for familiar chord forms and notice how they change sonically upon inversion.*
- *Create progressions, improvise.*

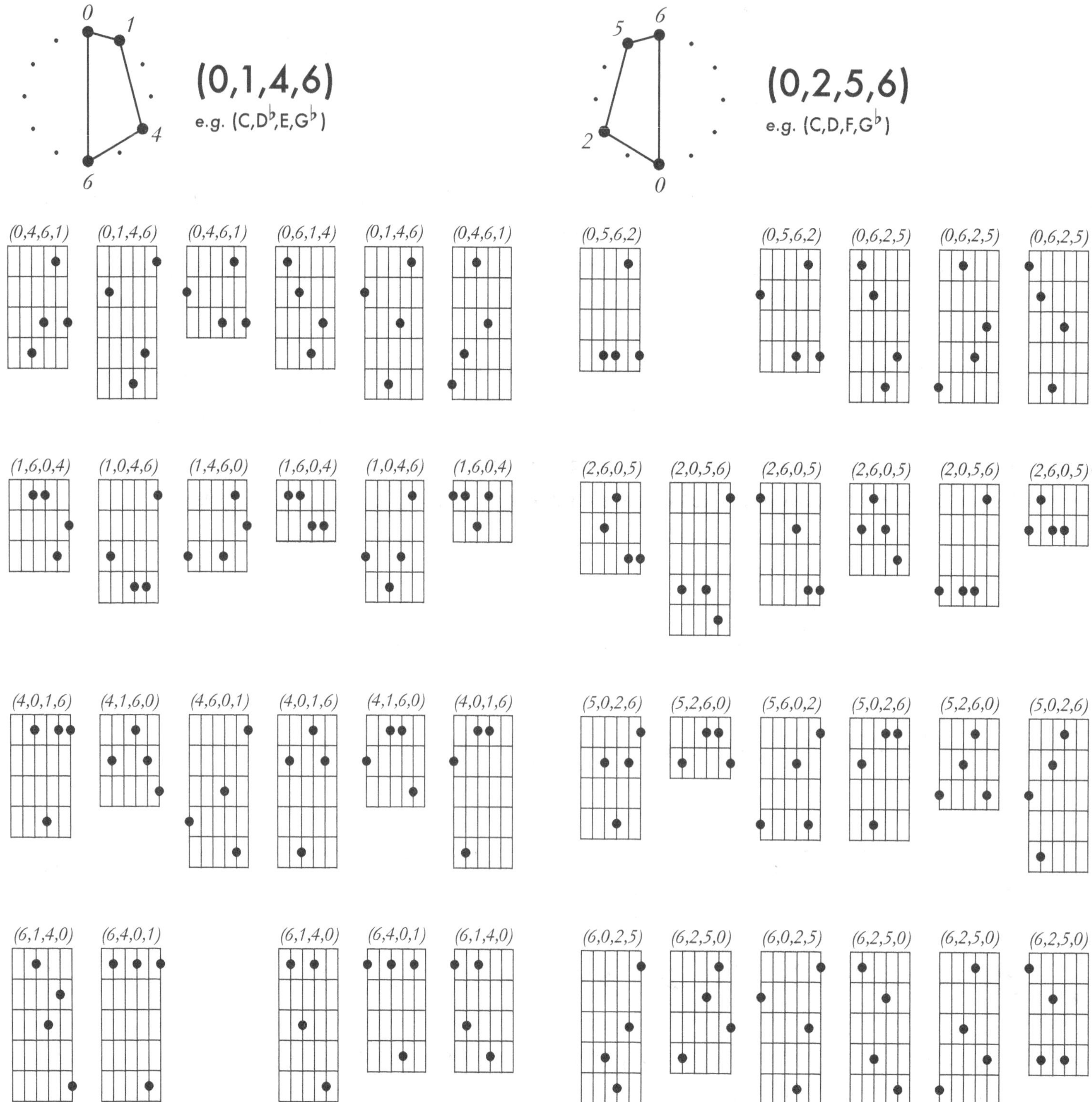

Exercise

0
1
3
7
(0,1,3,7)
e.g. (C,D♭,E♭,G)
6
7
4
0
(0,4,6,7)
e.g. (C,E,F♯,G)
(0,3,7,1) (0,1,3,7) (0,3,7,1) (0,7,1,3) (0,1,3,7) (0,7,1,3)
(0,6,7,4) (0,6,7,4) (0,7,4,6) (0,6,7,4)
(1,7,0,3) (1,0,3,7) (1,3,7,0) (1,7,0,3) (1,0,3,7) (1,7,0,3)
(4,7,0,6) (4,6,7,0) (4,7,0,6) (4,7,0,6) (4,6,7,0) (4,7,0,6)
(3,0,1,7) (3,1,7,0) (3,7,0,1) (3,0,1,7) (3,1,7,0) (3,0,1,7)
(6,0,4,7) (6,4,7,0) (6,7,0,4) (6,0,4,7) (6,4,7,0) (6,0,4,7)
(7,1,3,0) (7,3,0,1) (7,1,3,0)
(7,0,4,6) (7,6,0,4) (7,0,4,6) (7,0,4,6) (7,6,0,4) (7,0,4,6)

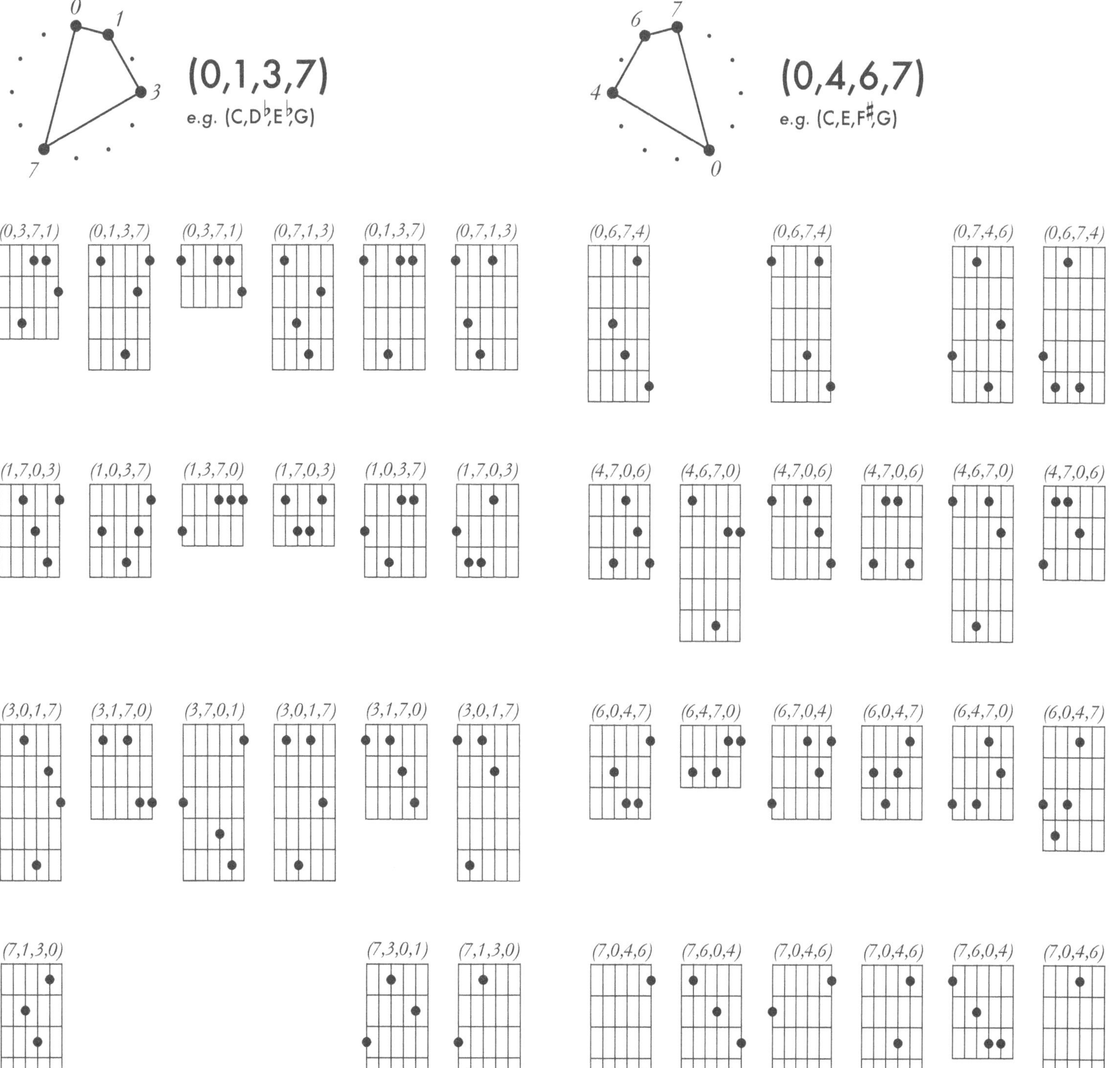

Illustration

TETRAD MANDALA

Showing:

The 43 possible 4-note shapes, transposable to any key.

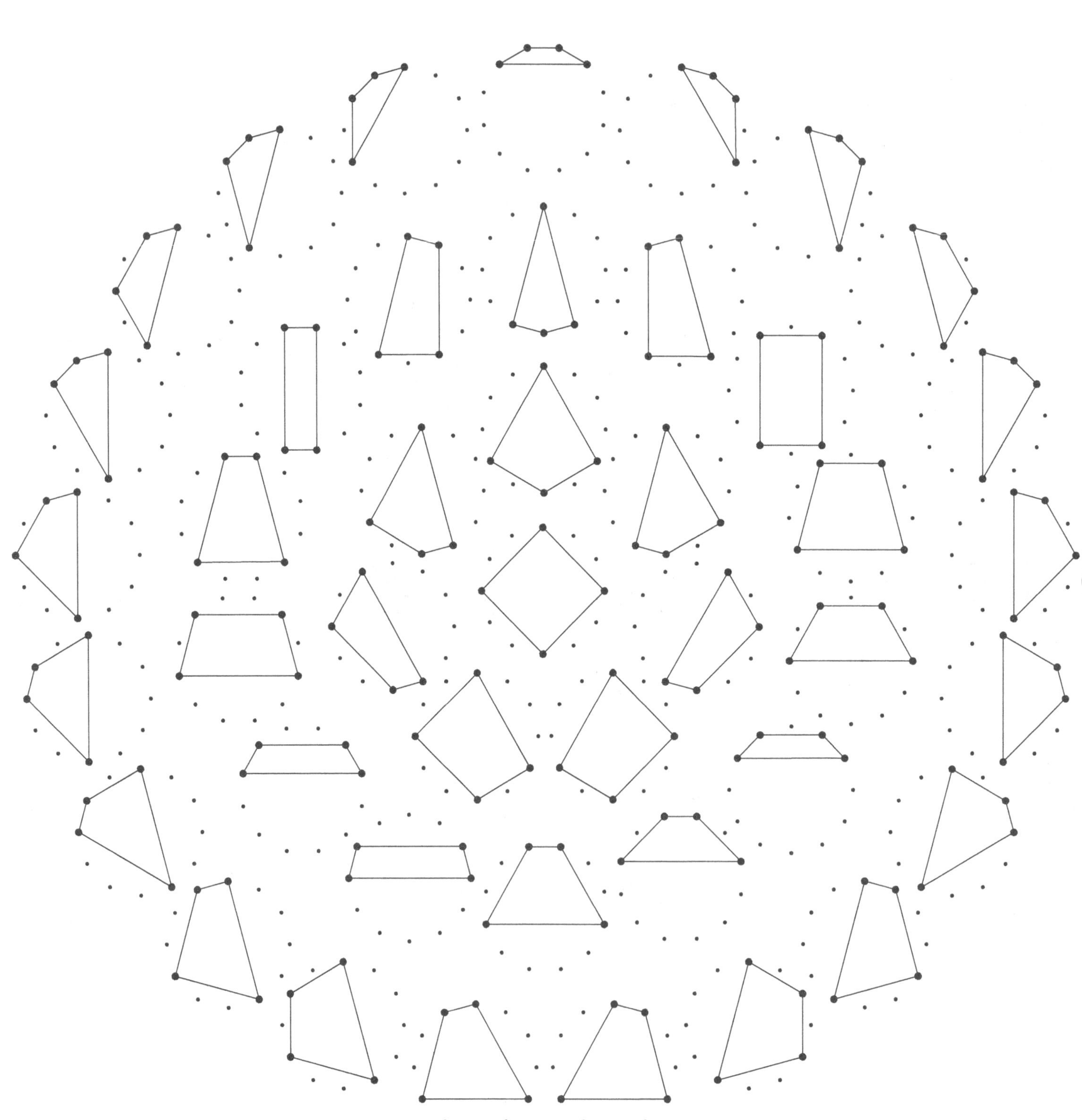

Concept

FURTHER STUDY

All 43 tetrad types are shown in the illustration on the previous page. This chapter has taken a close look at eleven of these - seven derived from stacked thirds in the four heptatonic scales, and four all-interval tetrads. The locations of these on the illustration are here:

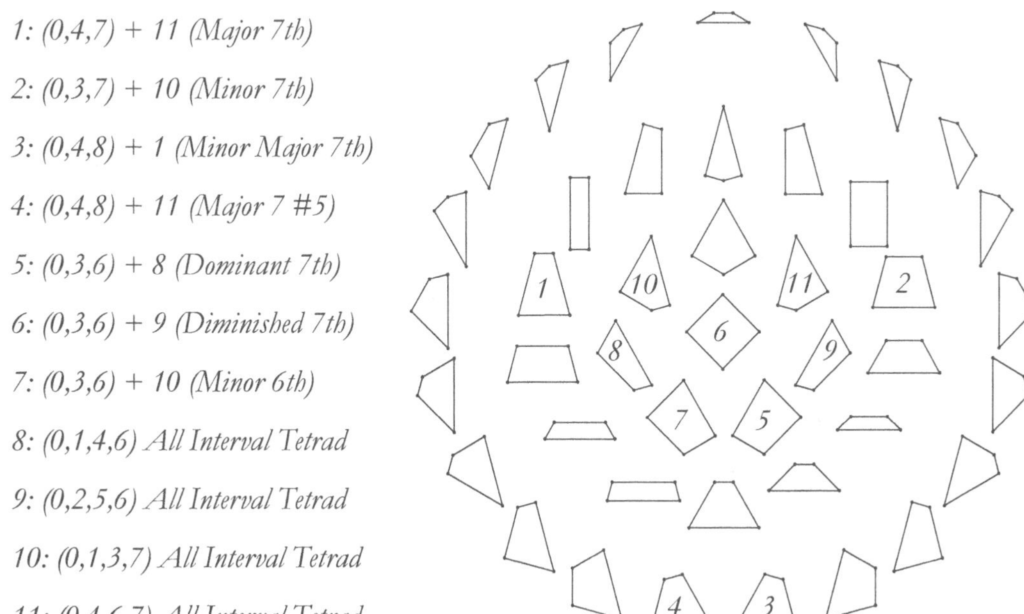

There are 32 remaining tetrads. Remember that any of these can be found by adding a pitch to a triad. Similarly, any 5 note structure can be created by adding a pitch to a tetrad, and so on. This type of study can be overwhelming in the number of possibilities and amount of data involved. Exploring these ideas in an improvisational way can make the work more creative and rewarding. The illustration to the left is meant to give a quick visual summary of what is possible, so that the number of choices, while still large, seems manageable.

The guitar can play up to 6 simultaneous pitches, but fingerings become more limited with each additional pitch. The following pages show complete lists of the 66 *pentads* (5 note structures) and 80 *hexads* (6 note structures). They are written on pitch circles to show the information efficiently (staff notation based transpositions and inversions quickly multiply these numbers to enormous sizes). Explore these shapes, determine which pitches a figure might represent, and find fingerings for various types of chords or scales.

To move beyond 6 pitches, look at the 66 pentads and notice that there are also 66 *heptads* (7 note structures), which are defined by the negative space of the pentads (the dots not connected by lines). For example, the diatonic can be found in the negative space of the pentatonic, which makes them *complementary* pitch sets. The complements of the 43 tetrads are the 43 *octads* (8 notes), the complements of the 19 triads are the 19 *nonads* (9 notes), the complements of the 6 dyads are the 6 *decads* (10 notes), and the complement of single pitch is the single *undecad* (11 notes). The complete chromatic scale (12 notes) is the complement of a scale with zero notes. Altogether, this covers all of the 351 possible structures, from a size of 1 to 12 pitches.

This concludes Part I. This first section has been concerned with "what" (pitches), and the next section will shift the focus to "when" (rhythm).

Illustration

THE 66 PENTADS

Showing:

All possible shapes made by five pitches on a 12-tone chromatic circle (transposable to any key).

Illustration

THE 80 HEXADS

Showing:

All possible shapes made by six pitches on a 12-tone chromatic circle (transposable to any key).

Notes *Idea: Reflections, Observations, and Discoveries related to Part I.*

PART II

Rhythm

Concept

THE PULSE

As far we know, time is an infinite continuum extending from the present in two directions:

We only have control over the events in one direction, from now into the future. In order to keep track of events in time, humans tend to create markers: seconds, minutes, hours, days, years, centuries, millennia, etc. Many of these markers are based on the cycles of nature, the rotation of the Earth, the orbit of the Earth around the Sun, the precession of the equinoxes, the properties of atoms.
The first sound that we hear is a cyclical rhythm - the human heartbeat. In music, a group of people can agree on a common pulse to serve as a marker of the basic temporal unit that they refer to in order to create something synchronized in time. Hours, minutes, and seconds are strict grids based on natural phenomena. A musical pulse is a version of these types of measurements, but with a looser conception - for example, it could be fixed (constant tempo) or variable (changing tempo):

fixed tempo: ● ● ● ● ● ● ● ● ● ● ● → *changing tempo:* ● ● ●●●●● ● ● ● ● ●→

For ease of notation, this book will refer to fixed pulses, with the understanding that any pulse played by humans will inevitably be somewhat variable.

The human ear perceives periodic sounds in a variety of ways. An oscillation occurring 26,400 times a minute sounds to us like the pitch "A 440," but lowering the pitch causes it to gradually lose its tonal quality and begin to sound like distinct pulsations. Five octaves down, the ear may begin to detect individual events (about 14 per second) rather than a continuous flow. After reducing the A 440 by eight octaves, the ear will hear a tempo of 103.125 beats per minute. Pitch and pulse are both versions of cyclic phenomena which exist on the same continuum but are given different names because of the way that we hear.

At high frequencies, the ear hears a periodic return to the same pitch at each doubling of the frequency, or octave. 12-tone equal temperament is a way to divide and organize the continuum of pitch within the octave. At low frequencies, the ear hears periodicity as a regular pulse with space between each event. If the pulsations are slow enough, this continuum of time between each event can be divided and organized into *subpulses*, internal markers that change how the beat "feels." Here is a time line with regular pulses (large dots) and subpulses (small dots), showing an increasing division of the beat into 2, 3, 4, 5, 6, 7, and 8 parts:

● • ● • • ● • • • ● • • • • ● • • • • • ● • • • • • • ● • • • • • • • ●

For the purpose of study, this book will refer to these types of equal divisions of the pulse, with the understanding that there are many ways to feel the inside of the beat that are "off the grid." Swing feel, for instance, could be thought of as an "untempered" division of the beat that is highly variable and personal, yet still recognizable in character. The general idea is that, by agreeing on some ways to measure and describe rhythmic material, it might be possible to develop an internally consistent and functional theory of rhythmic fundamentals.

Concept

THE PICKING HAND

The picking hand is the guitarist's rhythmic engine, and facility with the plectrum or fingers is a fundamental prerequisite for any further study of rhythmic concepts. The following pages contain exercises for increasing control in the movements of this hand. There are many ways to hold and operate a pick, and many approaches are valid. Try to play some of the exercises, ignoring the picking indications. If they seem difficult (especially string skips and accents), consider using some of the ideas from the following course in "Symmetrical Picking." There are only three rules:

1) When moving to a higher string, use a downstroke ⊓ (for example, from the G to B string).
2) When moving to a lower string, use an upstroke V (for example, from the B to G string).
3) When staying on the same string, alternate.

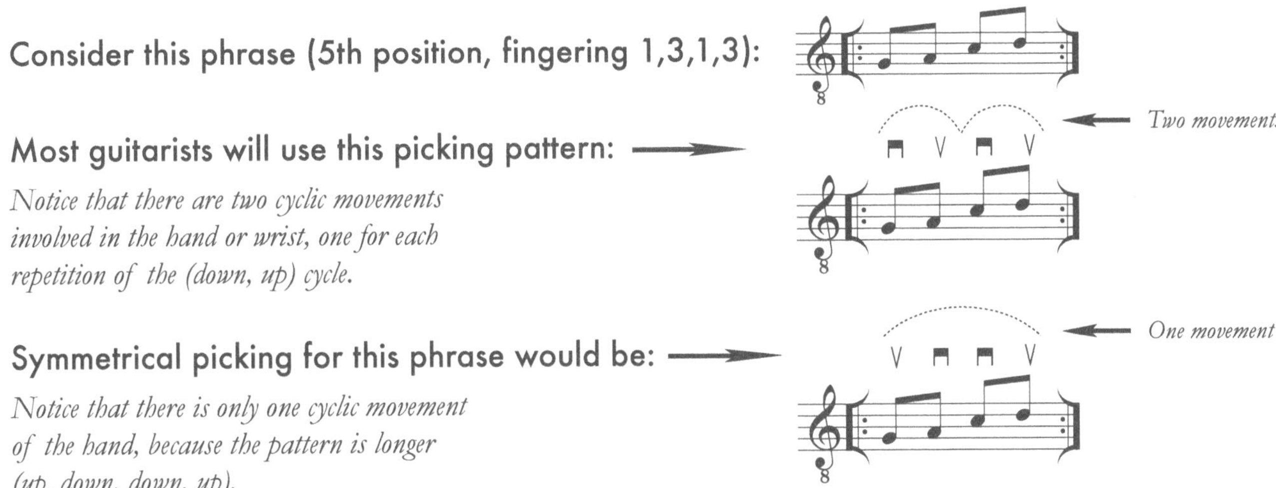

Consider this phrase (5th position, fingering 1,3,1,3):

Most guitarists will use this picking pattern:

Notice that there are two cyclic movements involved in the hand or wrist, one for each repetition of the (down, up) cycle.

Symmetrical picking for this phrase would be:

Notice that there is only one cyclic movement of the hand, because the pattern is longer (up, down, down, up).

With symmetrical picking, issues of velocity, dynamics, accuracy, and endurance shift from the large movements of the arm to the more detailed muscles and joints that control the pick itself. It maximizes small movements in order to increase efficiency and reduce wasted energy. This efficiency becomes magnified with large string skips and leaps. The picking hand can be in continuous motion because it never has to "reset." The main challenge is to produce identical articulations with the pick in either direction. The exercises on the following pages are designed to address this challenge.

When adjusting the picking hand, consider some facts about anatomy: The wrist joint can move in two main directions: flexion and extension (forward and backward) and ulnar and radial deviation (side to side). Try both of these motions repeatedly and notice that flexion and extension has nearly double the range of deviation (about 160 degrees vs. about 50 degrees), and is also stronger and less tiring. A hand position with the wrist resting on the bridge and the palm facing the guitar will primarily use deviation (upstrokes and downstrokes involve a "chopping" motion). Rotating the wrist so that the pinky side of the hand touches the guitar and the palm is visible from above will primarily use flexion (upstrokes and downstrokes involve a "waving" kind of motion). The first position is more suited for micro-details, and the second for power and groove. Symmetrical picking is a method focused on producing strong rhythmic feel, wide dynamic range, large string skips, speed, and endurance. Because of the necessity to perform all articulations in both directions with equal strength, many guitarists will find the flexion/extension hand position to be better suited for this particular study.

Concept

6 RUDIMENTS

A major challenge in picking technique is how to move smoothly from one string to another. The rules of symmetrical picking treat downstrokes and upstrokes as identical, mirror-image movements. To take advantage of this system, the guitarist must be able to produce identical articulations in each direction. In order to work on this methodically, the following pages will borrow some terminology from the rudimental study of percussion. In snare drum studies stickings are notated in binary fashion, "left" or "right." In the rudimental study of picking we will imagine that we are looking down the front of the guitar from the bridge to the nut, where lower strings are to the left and higher strings are to the right. Hitting a higher string and then a lower string is the equivalent of using a right and left stroke on the drum. A secondary function of this method is to remind us that the picking hand is the source of rhythm, so it is sensible to think of the pick as a kind of percussion instrument.

The study will borrow the names of six percussion rudiments, and apply them to the guitar as follows:

1) Single Stroke: one picking stroke (either upstroke or downstroke) on a single string, before moving to a different string.

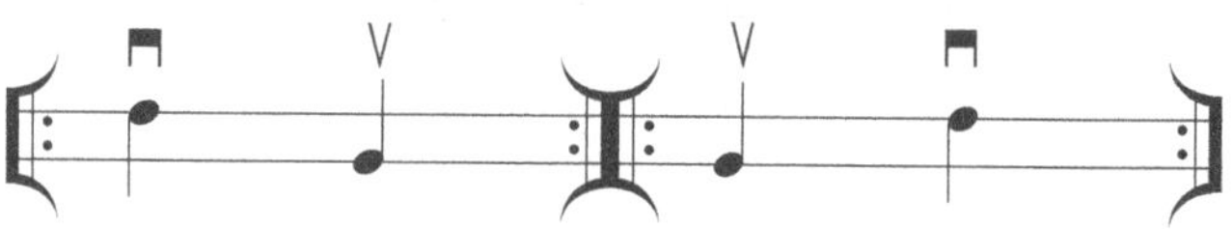

2) Double Stroke: two picking strokes (either upstroke/ downstroke or downstroke/ upstroke) on a single string, before moving to a different string.

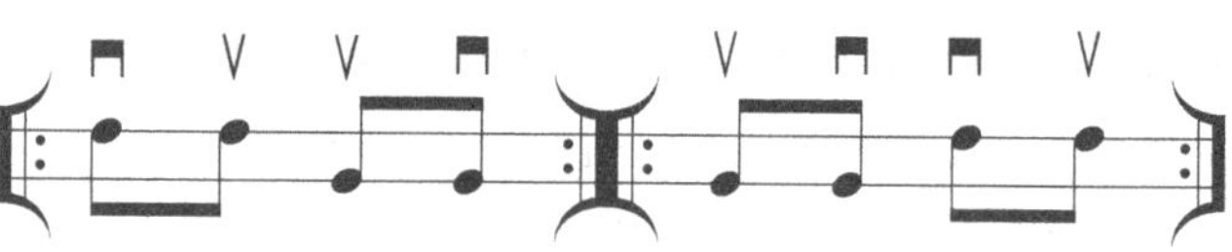

3) Paradiddle: a four stroke pattern between two strings - single, single, double. The direction will be either down/ up/ down/ up or up/ down/ up/ down.

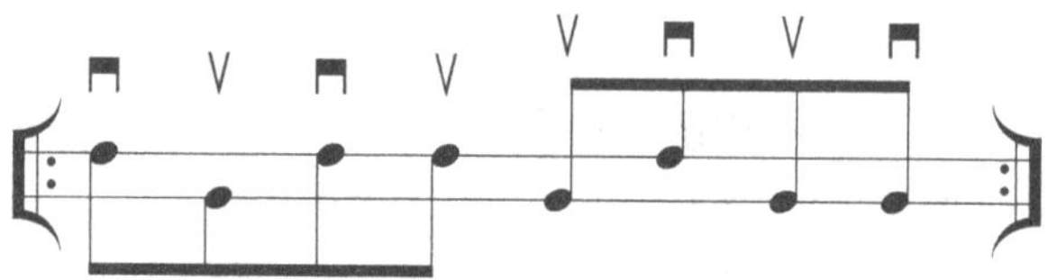

4) Triple Stroke: two picking strokes (either up/ down/ up or down/ up/ down) on a single string, before moving to a different string.

5) Flam: a single stroke on one string preceded by a grace note on another string. The direction will be either down/ down or up/ up.

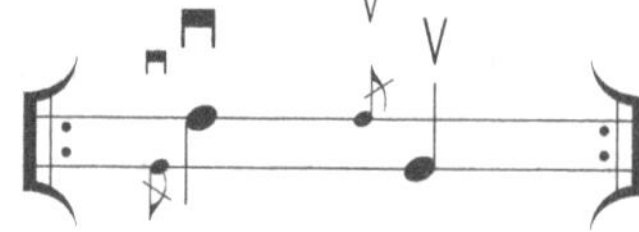

6) Ruff: like a flam, but with two grace notes. The direction will be either up/ down/ down or down/ up/ up

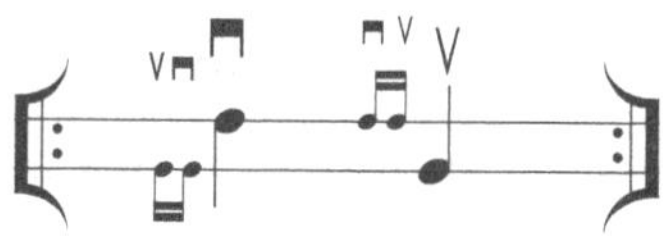

The exercises on the following pages work through each of these movements in detail. The goal of the study is to develop a fluid, relaxed picking technique that can produce controlled articulations regardless of the direction of motion.

Exercise

PICK CONTROL
WARM UP

The five diatonic modes in one position, with picking according to the three rules below.
- Play through the scales, observing the picking articulations, transpose.

Three Rules:

1. *Changing to a higher string:* *Downstroke* ⊓
2. *Changing to a lower string:* *Upstroke* V
3. *Staying on one string:* *Alternate* V ⊓ *or* ⊓ V

Mixolydian

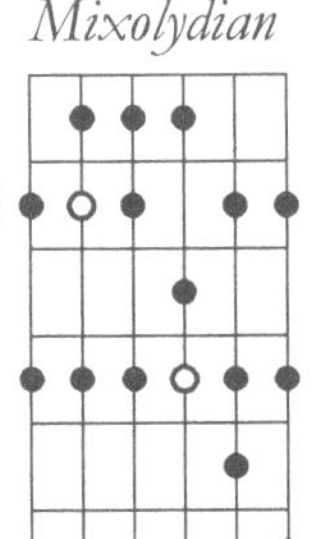

Dorian

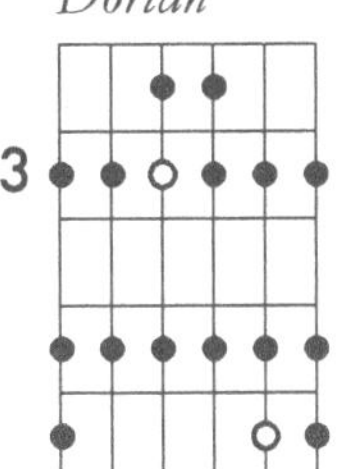

Aeolian

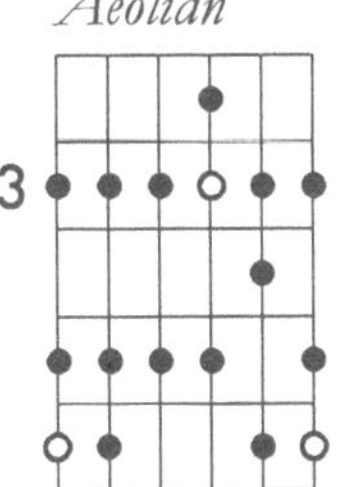

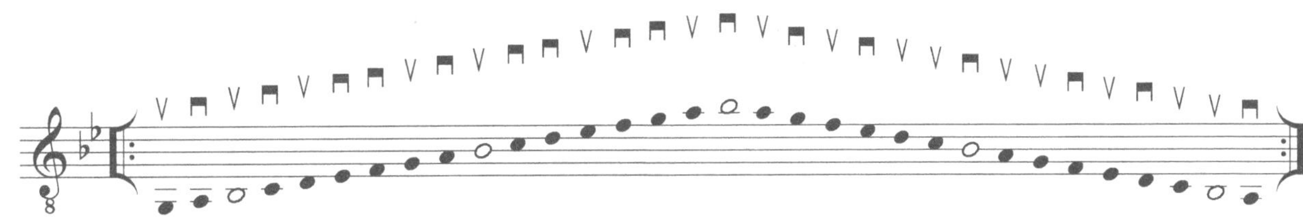

Phrygian + Lydian

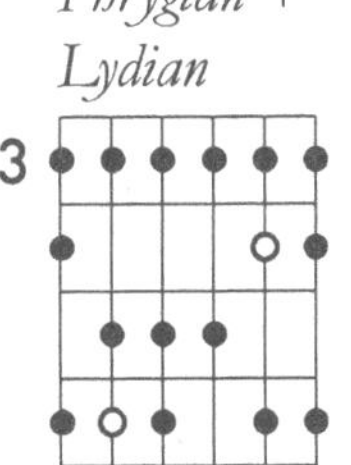

Locrian + Ionian

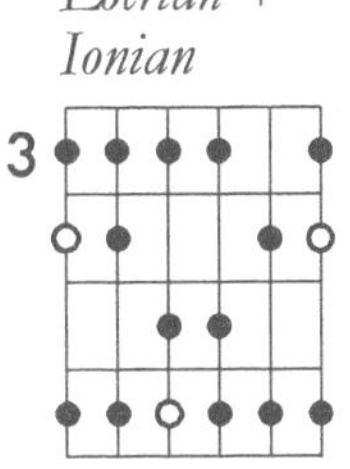

Exercise

PICK CONTROL
SINGLE STROKE

- *Play with slow and clean articulation, then accelerate.*
- *Play with even dynamics, then add accents.*
- *Use other pitch sets (scales, etc).*
- *Don't look at hands.*

⊓ = downstroke

V = upstroke

(5th Position)

Same picking and fingering:

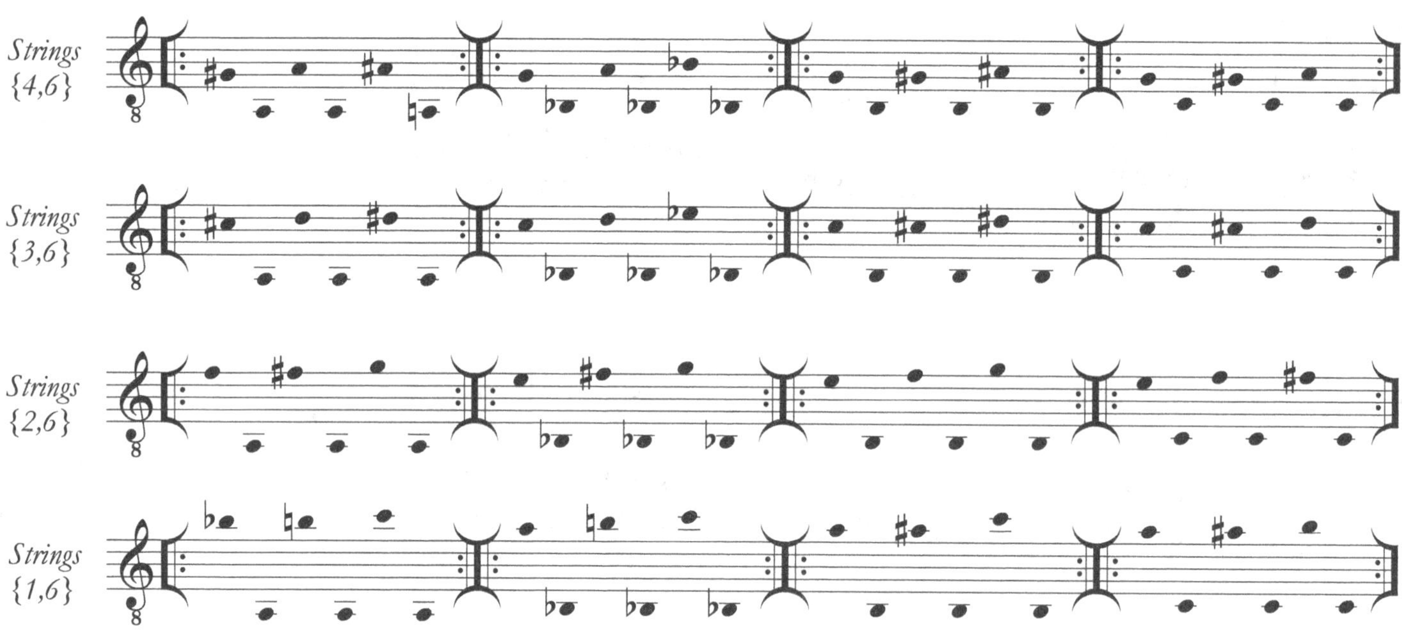

Continue with Strings: {5,4}{5,3}{5,2}{5,1}
{4,3}{4,2}{4,1}
{3,2}{3,1}
{2,1}

Reverse:

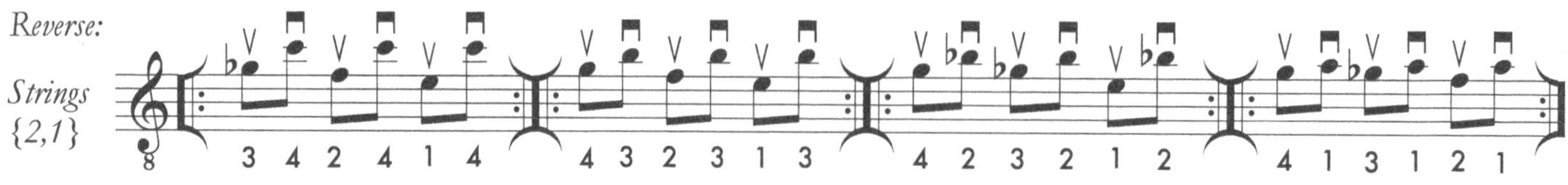

Continue with Strings: {3,1}{4,1}{5,1}{6,1}
{3,2}{4,2}{5,2}{6,2}
{4,3}{5,3}{6,3}
{5,4}{6,4}
{6,5}

Exercise

PICK CONTROL
DOUBLE STROKE

- *Play with slow and clean articulation, then accelerate.*
- *Play with even dynamics, then add accents.*
- *Use other pitch sets (scales, etc).*
- *Don't look at hands.*

⊓ = downstroke

V = upstroke

Same picking and fingering:

Continue with Strings: {5,4} {5,3} {5,2} {5,1}
{4,3} {4,2} {4,1}
{3,2} {3,1}
{2,1}

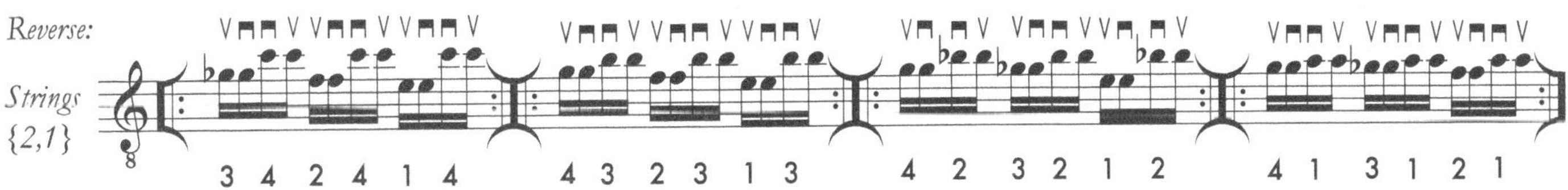

Continue with Strings: {3,1} {4,1} {5,1} {6,1}
{3,2} {4,2} {5,2} {6,2}
{4,3} {5,3} {6,3}
{5,4} {6,4}
{6,5}

Exercise

PICK CONTROL
PARADIDDLE

- *Play with slow and clean articulation, then accelerate.*
- *Start with adjacent string pairs, then increase difficulty by using string pairs with gaps.*
- *Exaggerate accents (hard as possible), then relax and accent only slightly.*
- *Don't look at hands.*

⊓ = downstroke
V = upstroke

Basic Pattern:

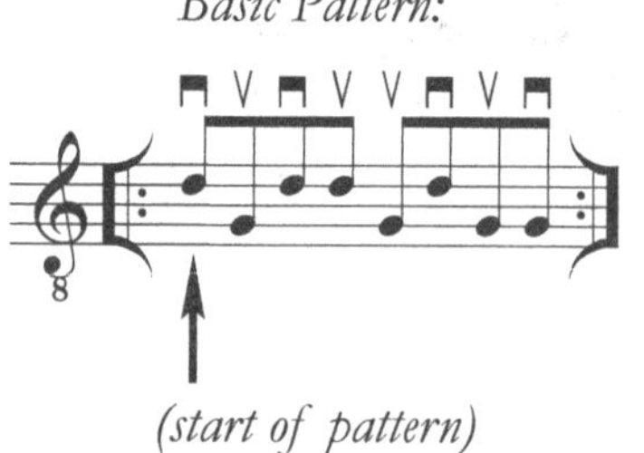

(start of pattern)

Rotations:

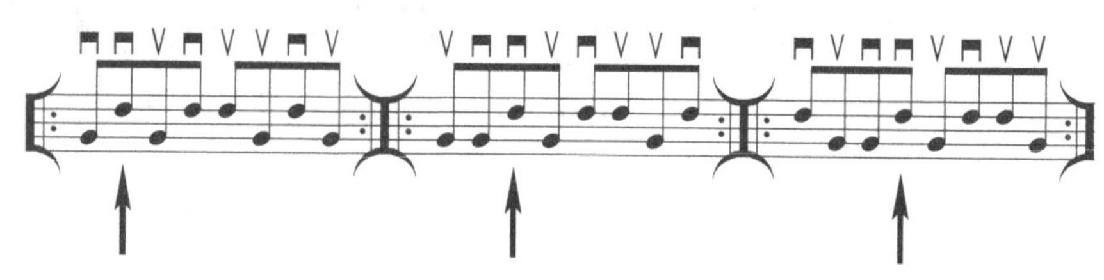

Four accent placements, Four rotations:

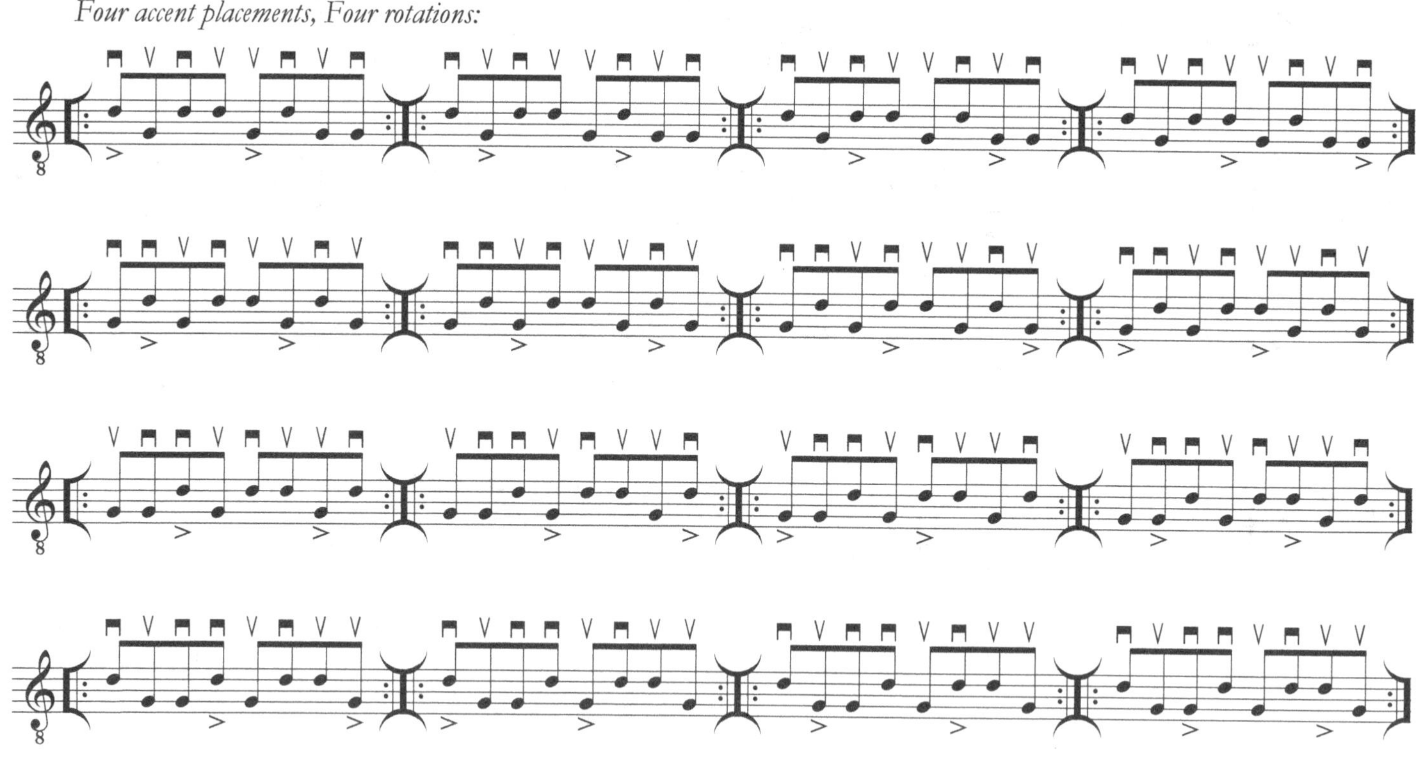

- *This example uses the fingering pair {3,1} with the string pair {3,4} in 5th position*
- *In any position, there are 180 possible combinations of fingering and string pairs:*

12 Finger pairs:	*Combined with:*	*15 String Pairs:*				
{1,2}{1,3}{1,4}		{1,2}	{1,3}	{1,4}	{1,5}	{1,6}
{2,1}{2,3}{2,4}		{2,3}	{2,4}	{2,5}	{2,6}	
{3,1}{3,2}{3,4}		{3,4}	{3,5}	{3,6}		
{4,1}{4,2}{4,3}		{4,5}	{4,6}			
		{5,6}				

← easier *harder →*

Exercise

PICK CONTROL
TRIPLE STROKE

- *Play with slow and clean articulation, then accelerate.*
- *Any single stroke exercise can also be used for triple strokes*
- *Experiment with different accent patterns, combinations of singles, double, and triples.*
- *Don't look at hands.*

⊓ = downstroke
V = upstroke

Basic Pattern:

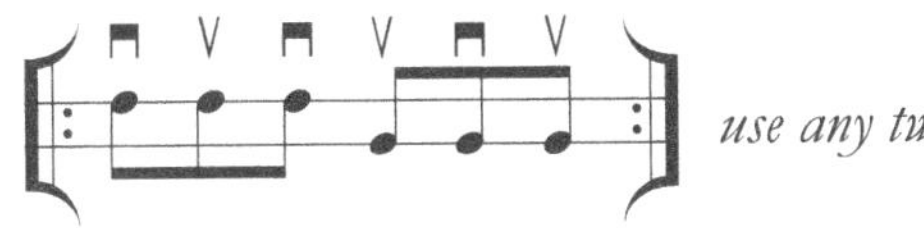

use any two strings

Combinations idea with triples, doubles, and singles:

5 stroke

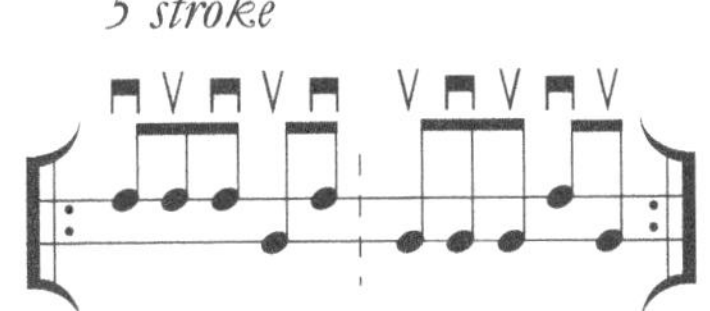

6 stroke

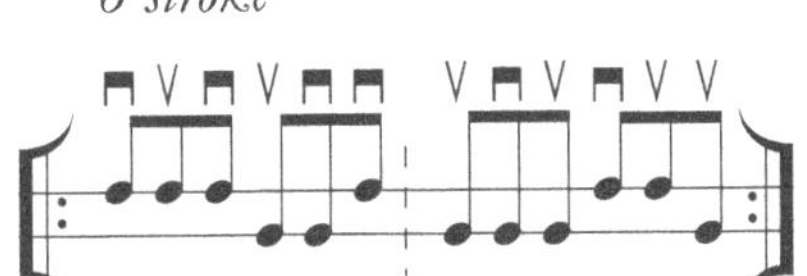

7 stroke

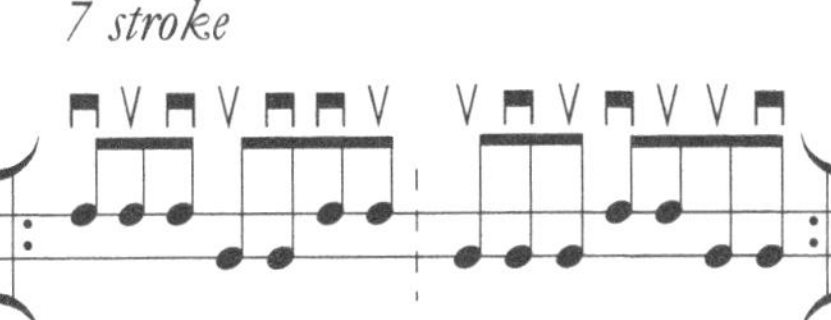

8 stroke

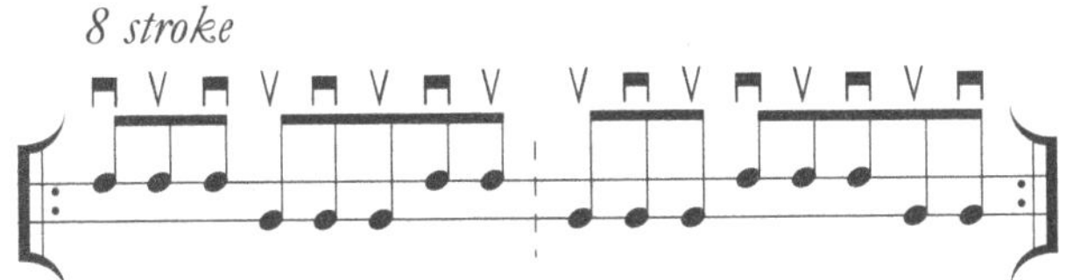

9 stroke

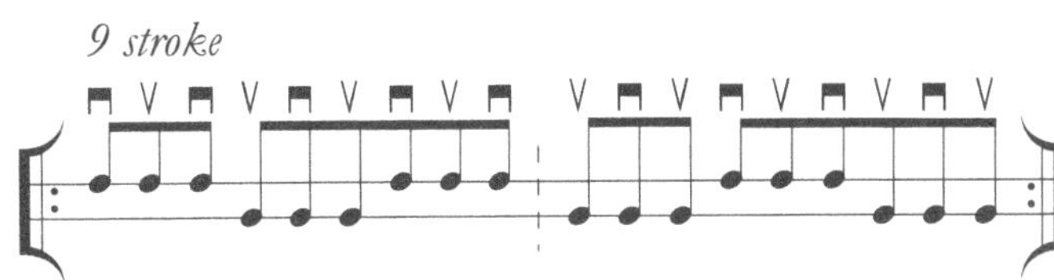

Play 5,6,7,8,9 stroke patterns consecutively, as quintuplets, accenting the figures:

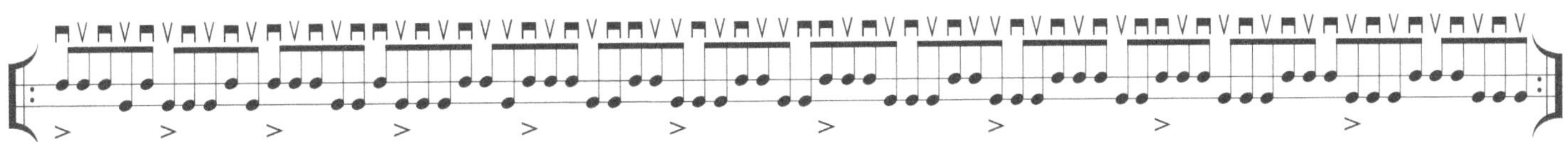

or as septuplets:

or as a continuous flow, with accents every 5th note, or every 7th note:

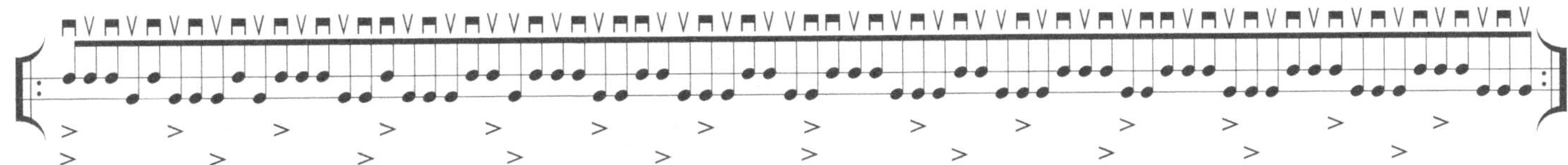

Exercise

PICK CONTROL
FLAM RUDIMENTS

- *Grace note should be as close as possible to the following note without being a "strum"*
- *Grace note should be sounded, not ghosted*
- *Upstroke flam should have identical articulation to downstroke flam (this may involve some hand or pick angle adjustment)*
- *Flams on non-adjacent strings are difficult (try doing these without touching the intervening strings)*
- *If played clearly, a polyrhythmic texture will result between the two strings. For example, the upper string pattern in the last exercise is:*

- *Use any of the 180 finger / string combinations in a single position*
- *Use a variety of accents and rotations*
- *Play with slow and clean articulation, then accelerate*
- *Don't look at hands*

⊓ = downstroke
V = upstroke

(Use any two strings and fingers)

Flam:

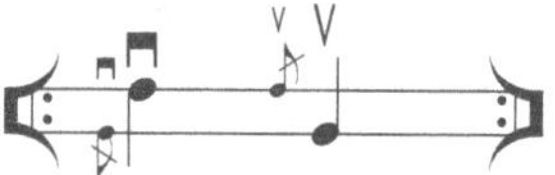

Flam Tap:

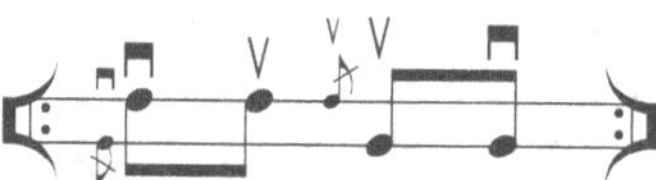

Inverted Flam Tap:

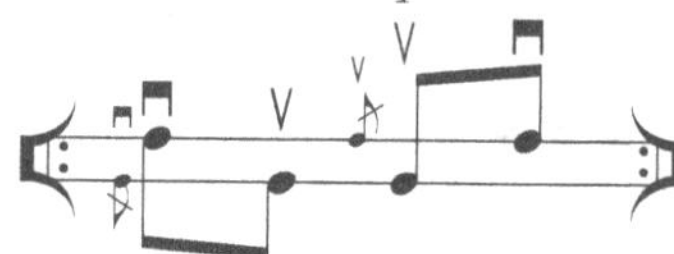

Flam Accent:

Swiss Triplet:

Swiss Triplet (reverse):

Flamadiddle:

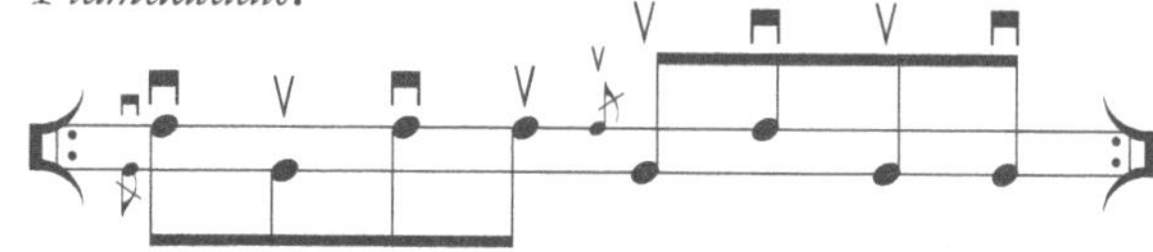

Windmill:

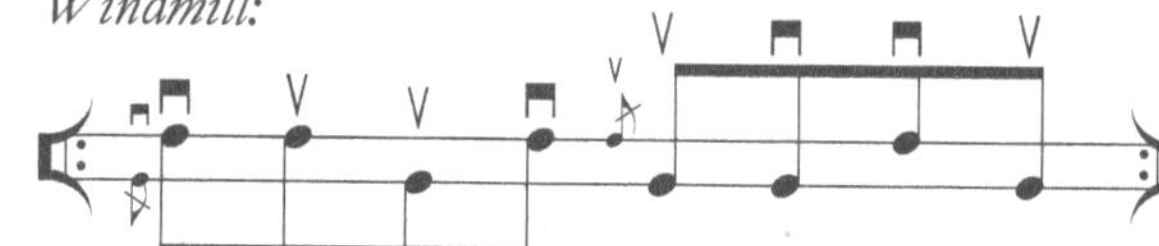

Exercise: 2,3 and 4 stroke patterns

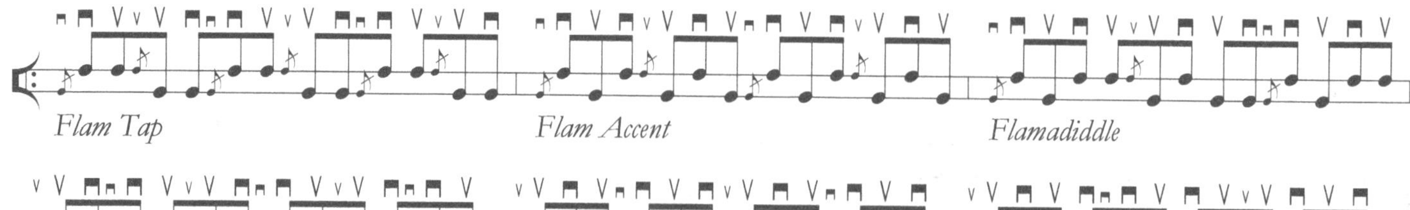

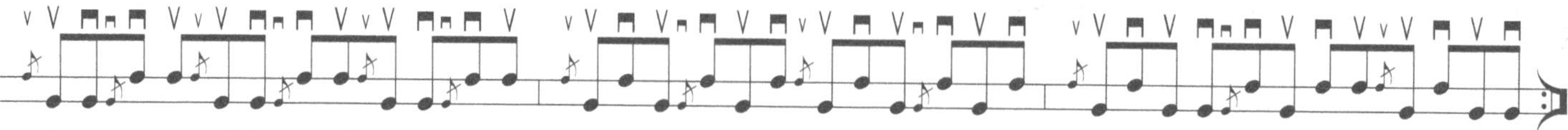

(same pattern, with reversed strings)

Exercise: Windmills and Swiss Triplets

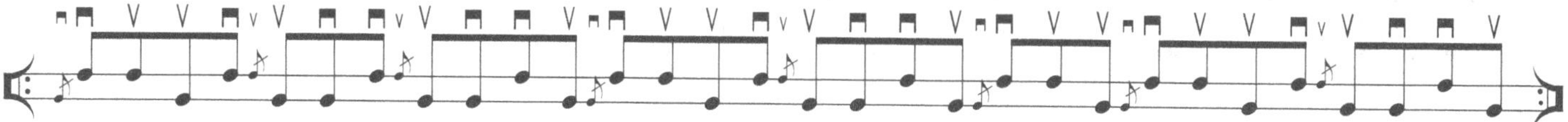

Play as: 8th notes (15 beats)
triplets (10 beats)
quintuplets (6 beats)

Exercise

PICK CONTROL
RUFFS AND DRAGS

- *Grace notes should be as close as possible to the following note without being a "strum"*
- *Grace noted should be sounded, not ghosted*
- *Drags in either direction should have identical articulation*
- *Drags on non-adjacent strings are difficult*
  (try doing these without touching the intervening strings)
- *Use any of the 180 finger / string combinations in a single position*
- *Use a variety of accents and rotations*
- *Play with slow and clean articulation, then accelerate*
- *Don't look at hands*

⊓ = downstroke
V = upstroke

(Use any two strings and fingers)

Half Drag (Ruff):

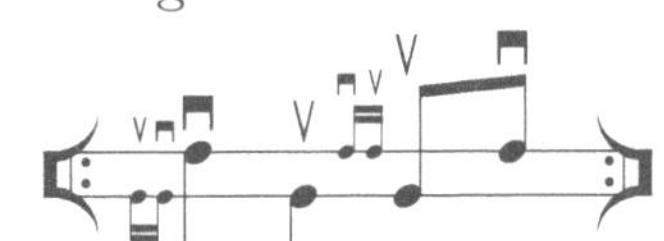

Double Drag:

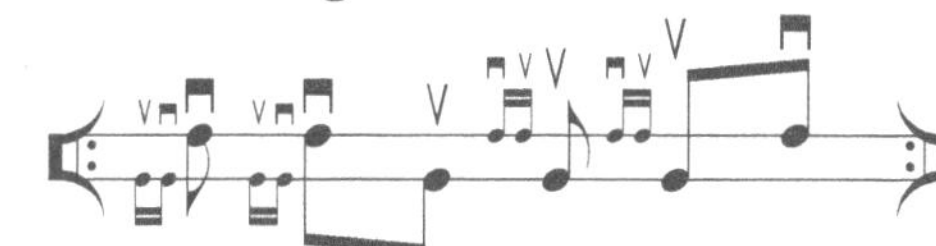

Drag Paradiddle:

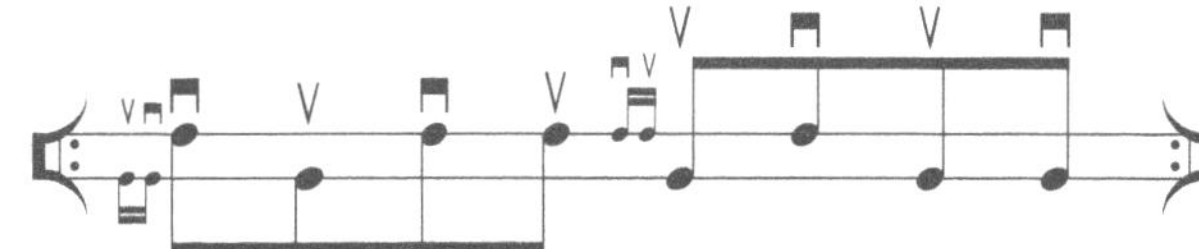

Rotations and accents:

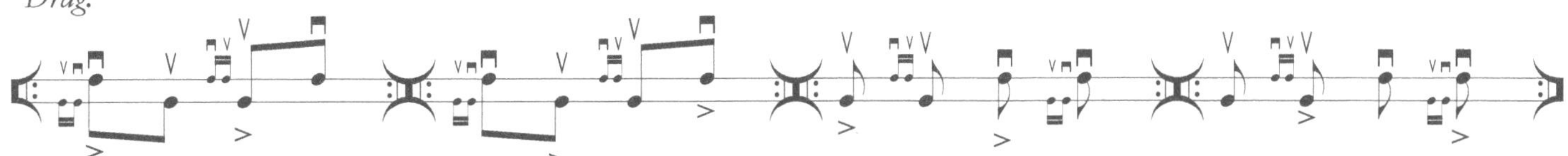

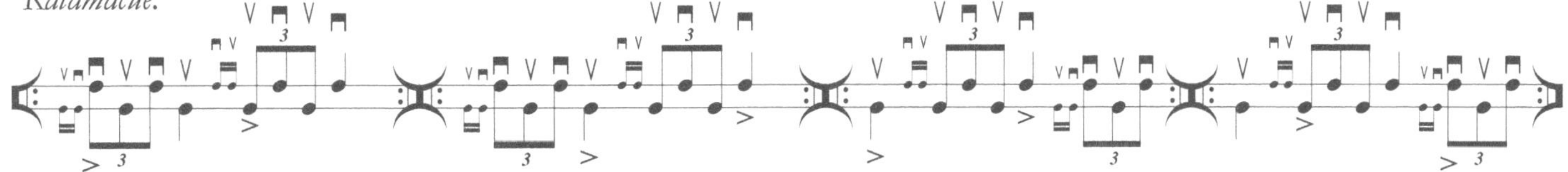

Drag Paradiddle:

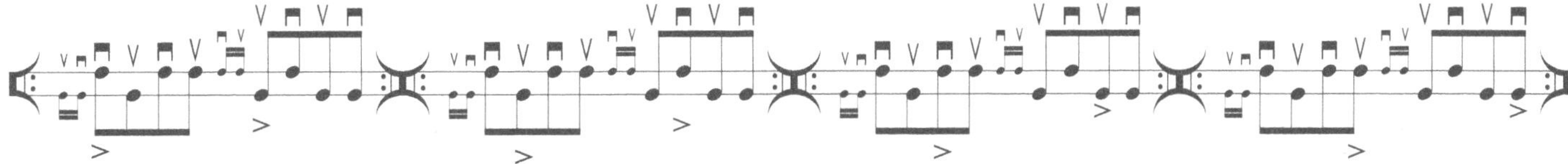

Exercise

RUDIMENTAL WORKOUT

All variations are 16 beats, following the rhythmic pattern (2,2,3,3,4,4,2,2,3,3,4 - repeat with reversed strings).
- Play any or all sections, focusing on producing identical articulations with downstroke and upstroke.
- Use any two strings, where upper staff line is the higher string. Start with adjoining strings, then increase spread.

Exercise

GROOVE IN 144

For Two Musicians

A two part groove in 144, for practicing ghost notes, palm muting, strings skips, alternate and symmetrical picking, and accents. Length of the groove is 144 16th notes, marked with fingerings, positions, picking, and accents. Accents follow these patterns:
Layer 1: (8,7,6,5,4,5,6,7) x 3
Layer 2: (7,7,7,7,6,7,7) (7,7,6,7,7,7,7) (7,7,7,6,7,7,7)
- Play Layer 1 with continuous alternate picking, using the palm to mute the spaces between notes.
- Play Layer 2 with symmetrical picking, trying to get strong upstroke accents.
- Play two Layers together with two musicians, locking the groove. Improvise.

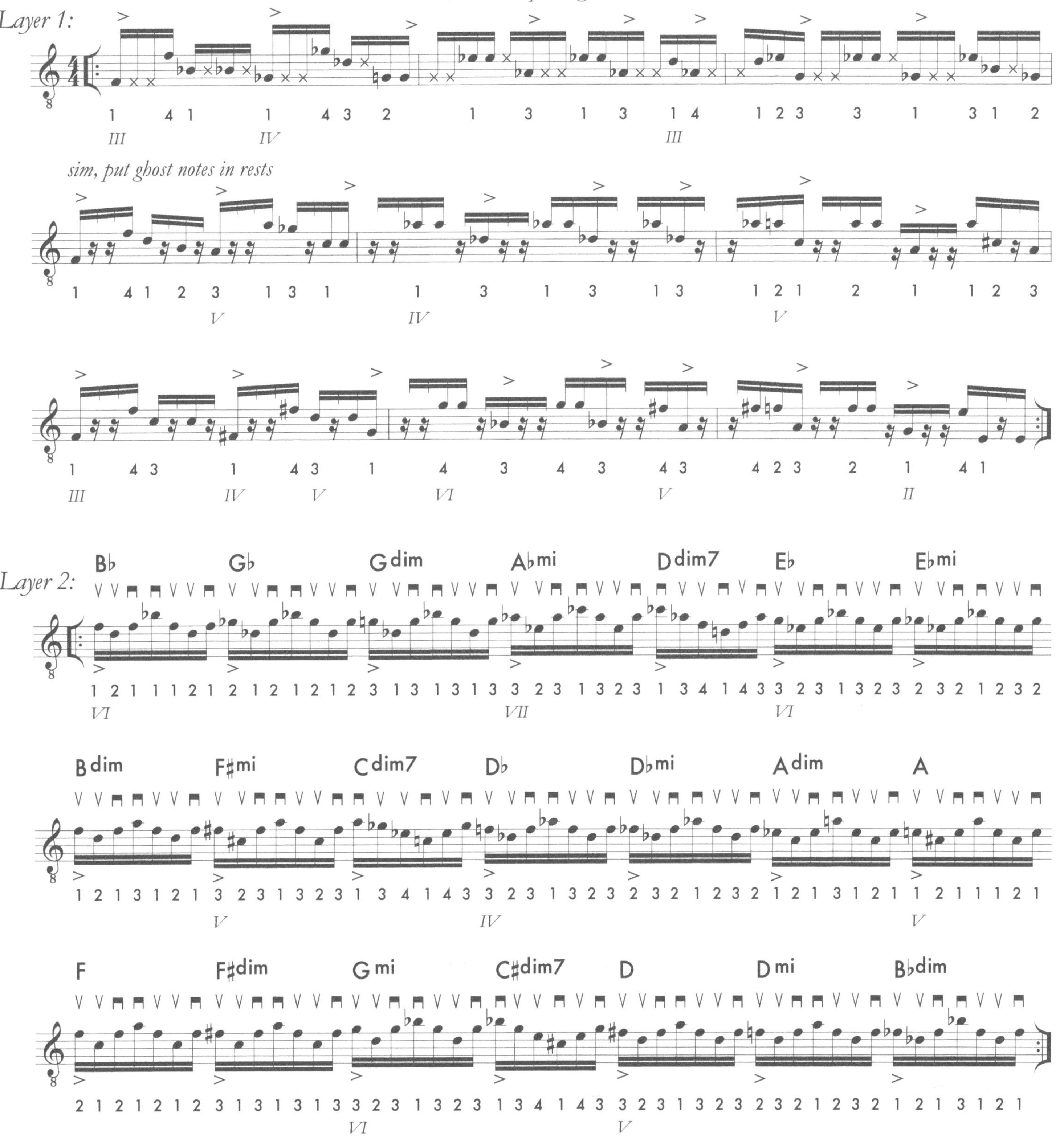

(This is a seciton of the guitar part for "Figurations" on the Miles Okazaki album of the same name.)

Exercise

DYNAMICS

Shown are subdivisions of the pulse from 2-8, with accents on each subpulse.
Work toward an ability to produce eight distinct intensity levels with a single pitch, alternate picking or fingers.
Dynamic range is from the softest possible (barely brushing the string) to the loudest possible (digging in deep, slapping the string).
Traditional dynamic markings are used to distinguish these levels:

Softest → *Loudest*

ppp ***pp*** ***p*** ***mp*** ***mf*** ***f*** ***ff*** ***fff***

- *Play without accents, subdividing the beats as evenly as possible. Use a metronome to maintain consistency (one beat per bar).*
- *Play with accents, making the accents only slightly louder than the other notes (seven examples on lower right).*
- *Play more extreme contrasts in dynamics, use these patterns with a looping scale or melody. Play without the metronome.*
- *Improvise, thinking about including a variety of dynamics. If playing electric, try to play very softly with the amp at high volume.*

Seven Subdivision Levels:

3 3 3

5 5 5 5 5

6 6 6 6 6 6

7 7 7 7 7 7 7

Seven Dynamic Levels:

Unaccented	*Accented*
ppp	***pp***
pp	***p***
p	***mp***
mp	***mf***
mf	***f***
f	***ff***
ff	***fff***

Exercise

ENDURANCE

A meditative exercise for building endurance and patience.

- *Set a metronome to 25 beats per minute.*
- *Play 16 strokes per beat, using any material.*
- *Continue for 25 minutes without stopping to make 10,000 strokes.*

During the 25 minutes:

- *Observe which parts of the hand or body become fatigued, and make adjustments without stopping.*
- *Make the material interesting by adding accents, patterns, rudiments, melodies, or improvisations.*
- *Breathe slowly and try to enter a state of relaxation.*
- *Afterward, take note of any interesting mental and physical effects.*

The material should not be too active in the fingering hand, as the point is to build endurance with the picking hand. For example, this two octave chromatic scale will take one minute. Playing it ascending and descending in 12 positions plus one last ascension will take the entire 25 minutes.

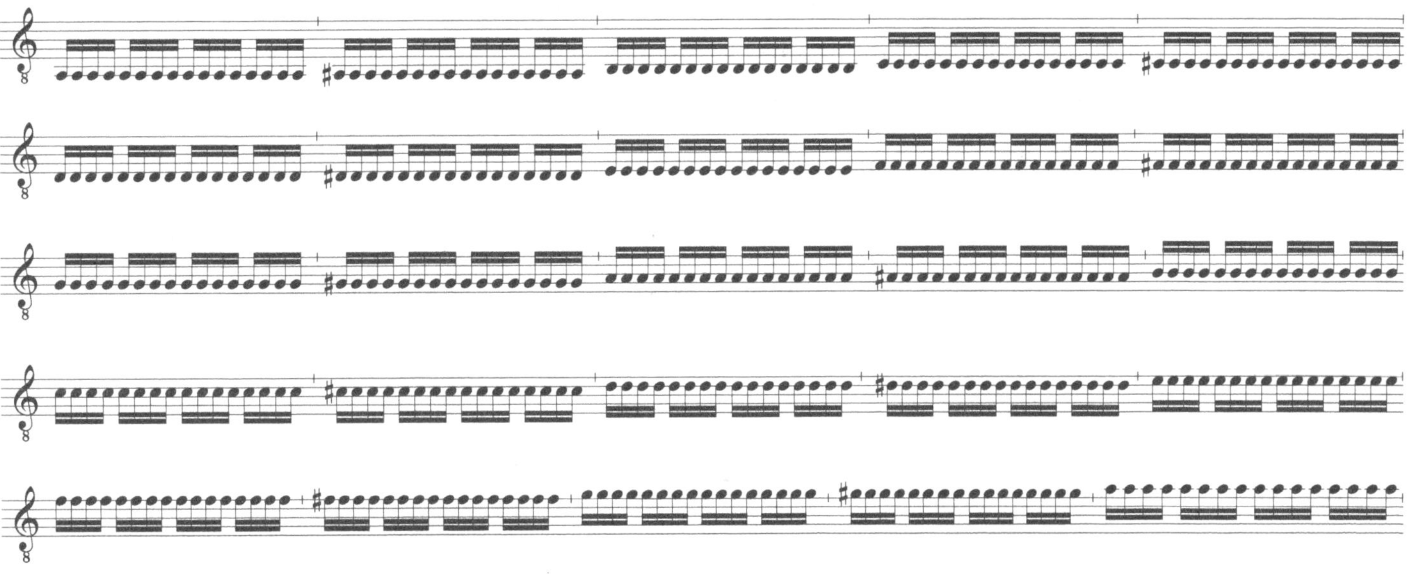

Notes

Concept

CLAVE

In the earlier studies of pitches we saw how the diatonic and pentatonic scales are complementary pairs, mutually filling in each other's negative space to make all 12 tones:

Chromatic Circle:

Interior: Pentatonic
Exterior: Diatonic

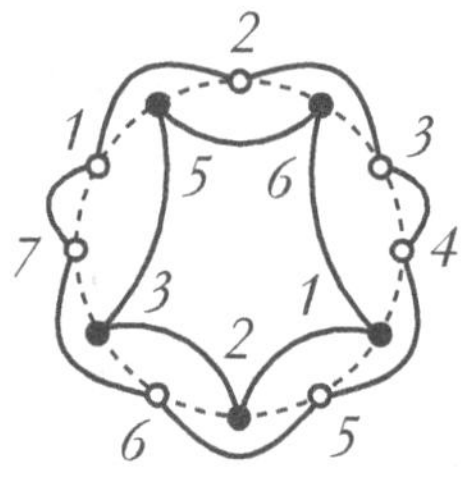

Separated onto two circles, we have the two familiar shapes to the right. Now imagine that, instead of a circle of chromatic pitches, these circles represent a rhythmic cycle of 12 points. The large dots are sounded events and the small dots are rests.

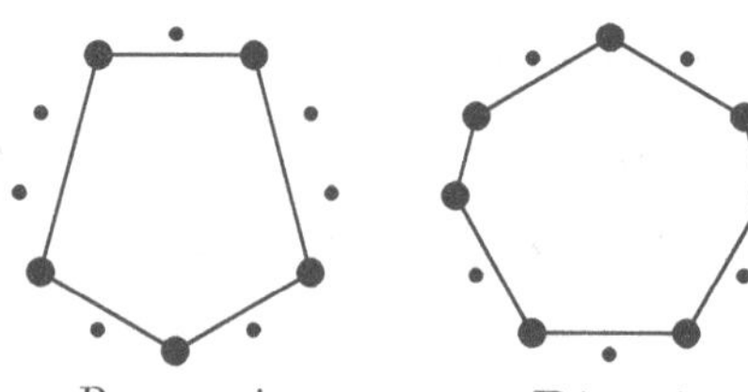

Pentatonic *Diatonic*

Reading these circles clockwise from the dotted circle produces rhythmic figures that are commonly known as a *clave*. It's interesting to notice that two of the most common tonal sounds in the world (pentatonic and diatonic) are structural analogues to two of the most universal rhythmic figures. The study of the clave in the context of various cultures and musical traditions is beyond the scope of the book, but we can use the clave here as a link between pitch and rhythm to help unify these two areas of study.

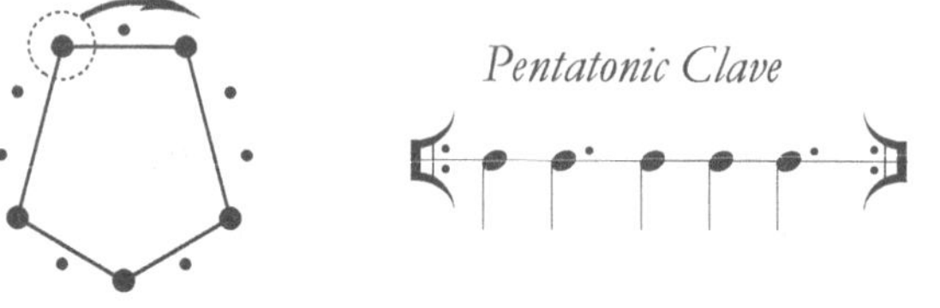

One example of this could be looking at different "modes" of these rhythms, by starting them at different points. Here are five modes of the pentatonic clave and seven modes of the diatonic clave:

Pentatonic Clave, five perspectives:

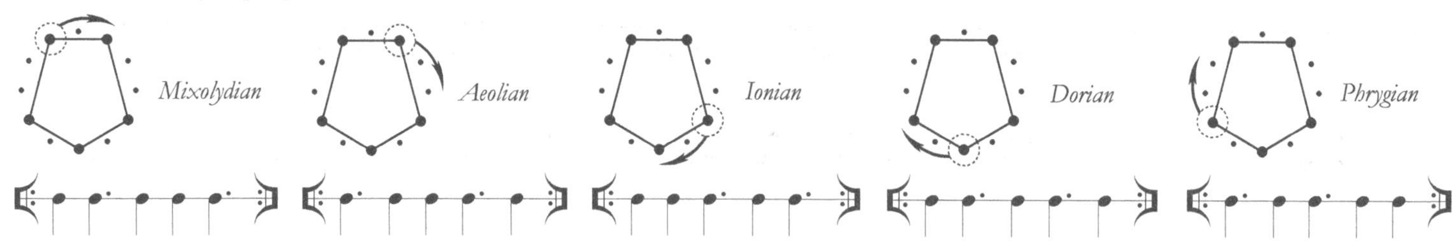

Diatonic Clave, seven perspectives:

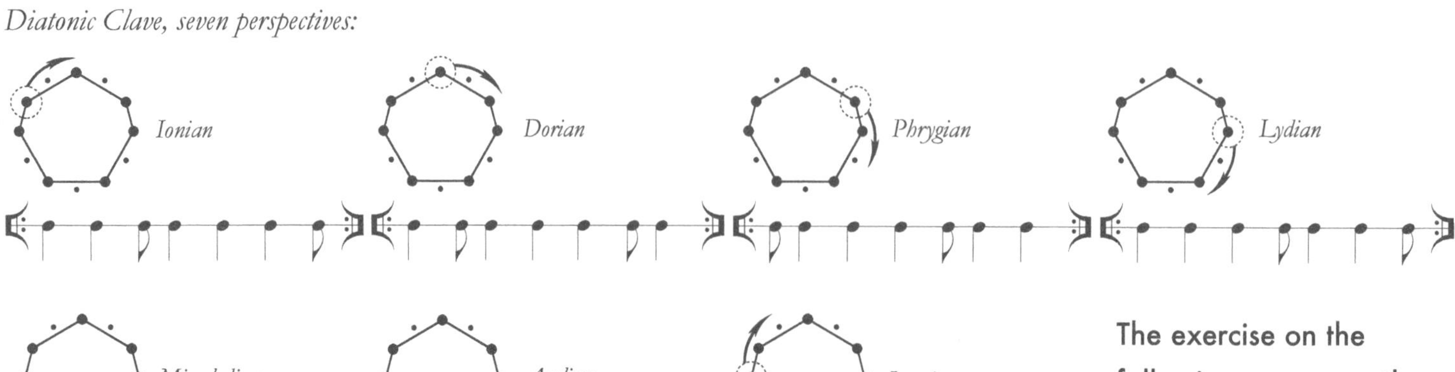

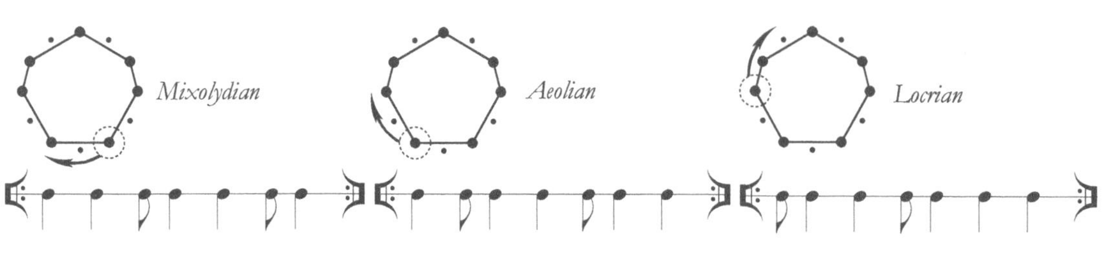

The exercise on the following page uses the diatonic clave as raw material for an exercise to study subdivisions of the beat.

PRIMES

An exercise using a clave figure to work on the first four prime subdivisions of the beat (2,3,5, and 7).
- Without thinking about a time signature, play this rhythmic figure with a single pitch:

- Play the same figure in 8th notes, triplets, quintuplets, and septuplets (shown below).
- Notice that the figure can have two orientations to the beat in duple, 3 in triple, 5 in quintuple, and 7 in septuple.
(similar orientations are grouped in boxes in duple and triple, and in all cases the start of the figure is marked with an arrow)
- Use the same tempo throughout. Play without looking at the page.
- Create other figures and run them through the same transformations.

Duple:

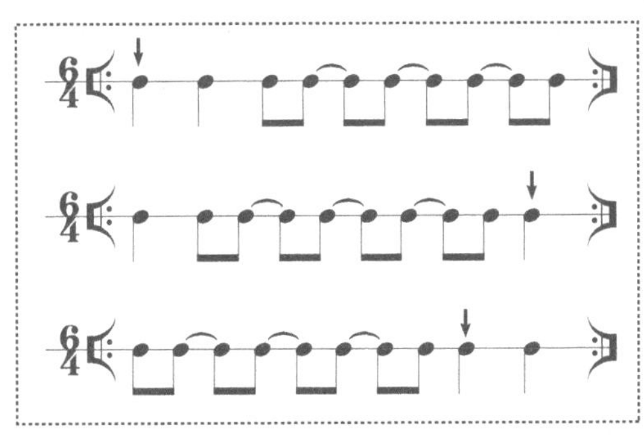
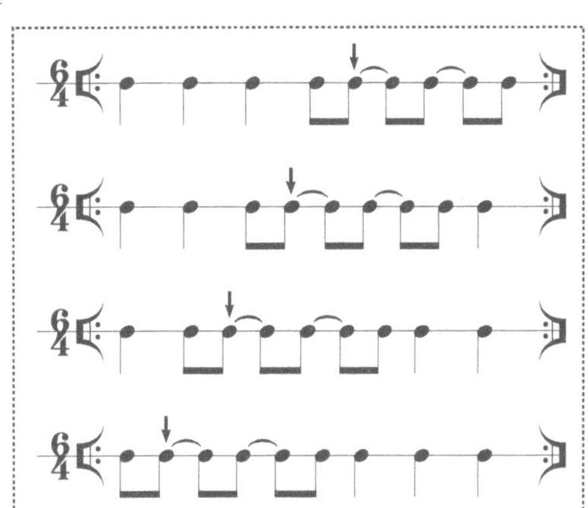

Triple:

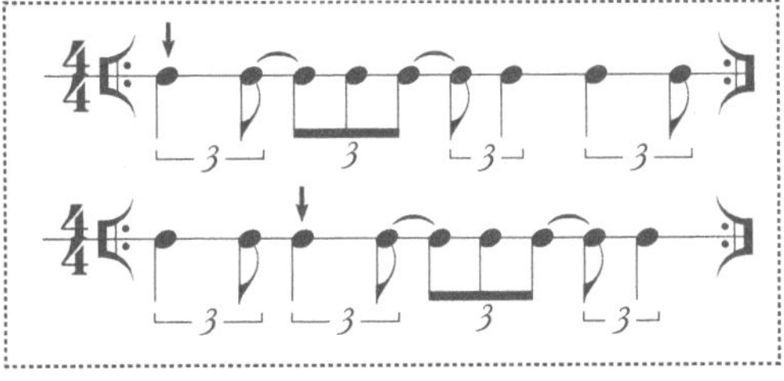
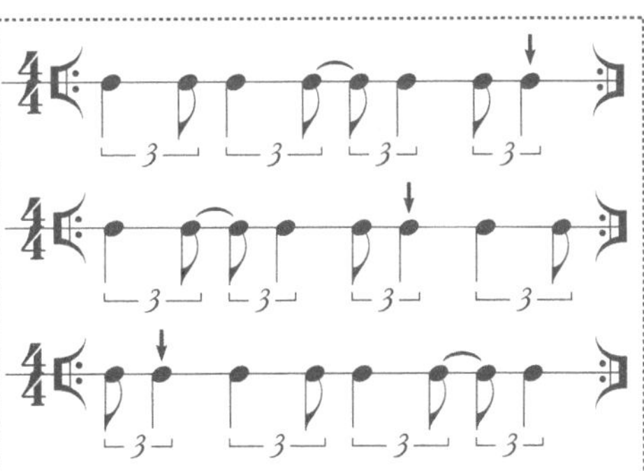
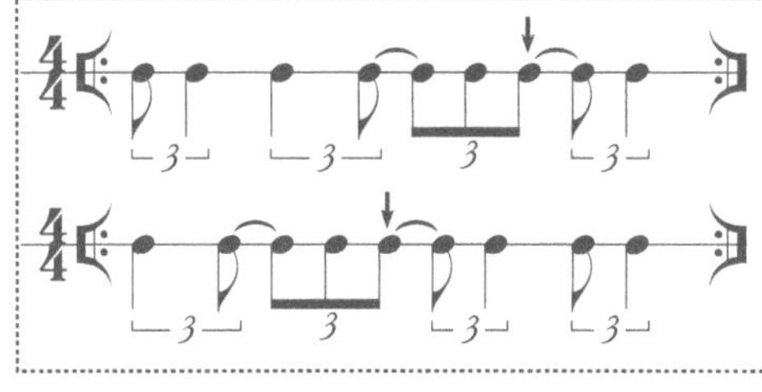

Quintuple:

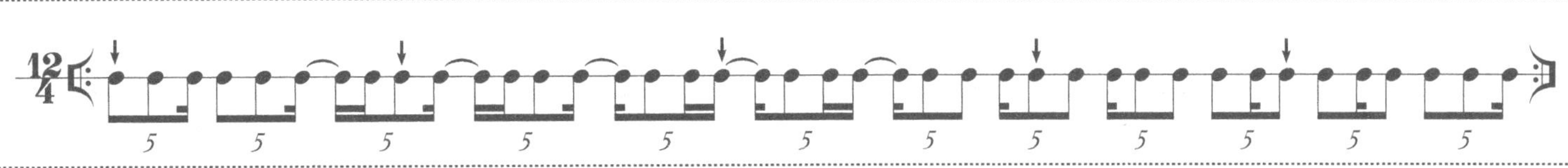

Septuple:

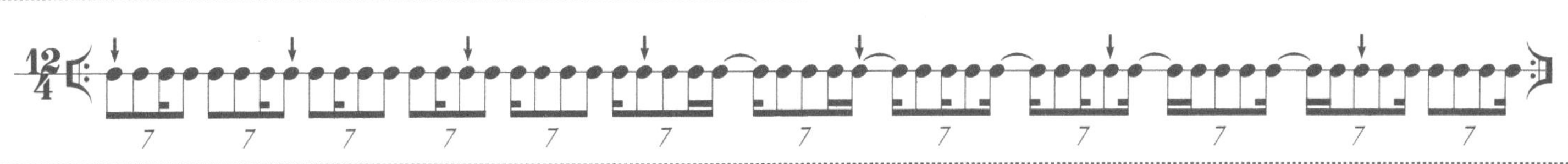

Exercise

KORVAI

A study in quintuple, sextuple, and septuple subdivisions of the beat, using a five stroke phrase with various expansions. Total length is 32 bars, marked with a double line every four bars. "Sim" indicates a continuation of the same tuplet type.
- Use any two pitches. Figure out the pattern and try to play it without reading, then check with the page for accuracy.
- Work on small sections at a time, using a metronome. Change pitch assignments, use five different notes (e.g. a pentatonic scale).
(Note - this is a very difficult exercise)

Form:

(555,666,777,888,999) (55,66,77,88,99) (5,6,7,8,9) in quintuplets (A1, A2, A3), sextuplets (B1, B2, B3), and septuplets (C1, C2, C3).
(77,66,55,2,2,2) in septuplets (D1), (77,66,55,2,2,2) in sextuplets (D2), (77,66,55,2,2) in quintuplets (D3). (32 bars of 4/4)

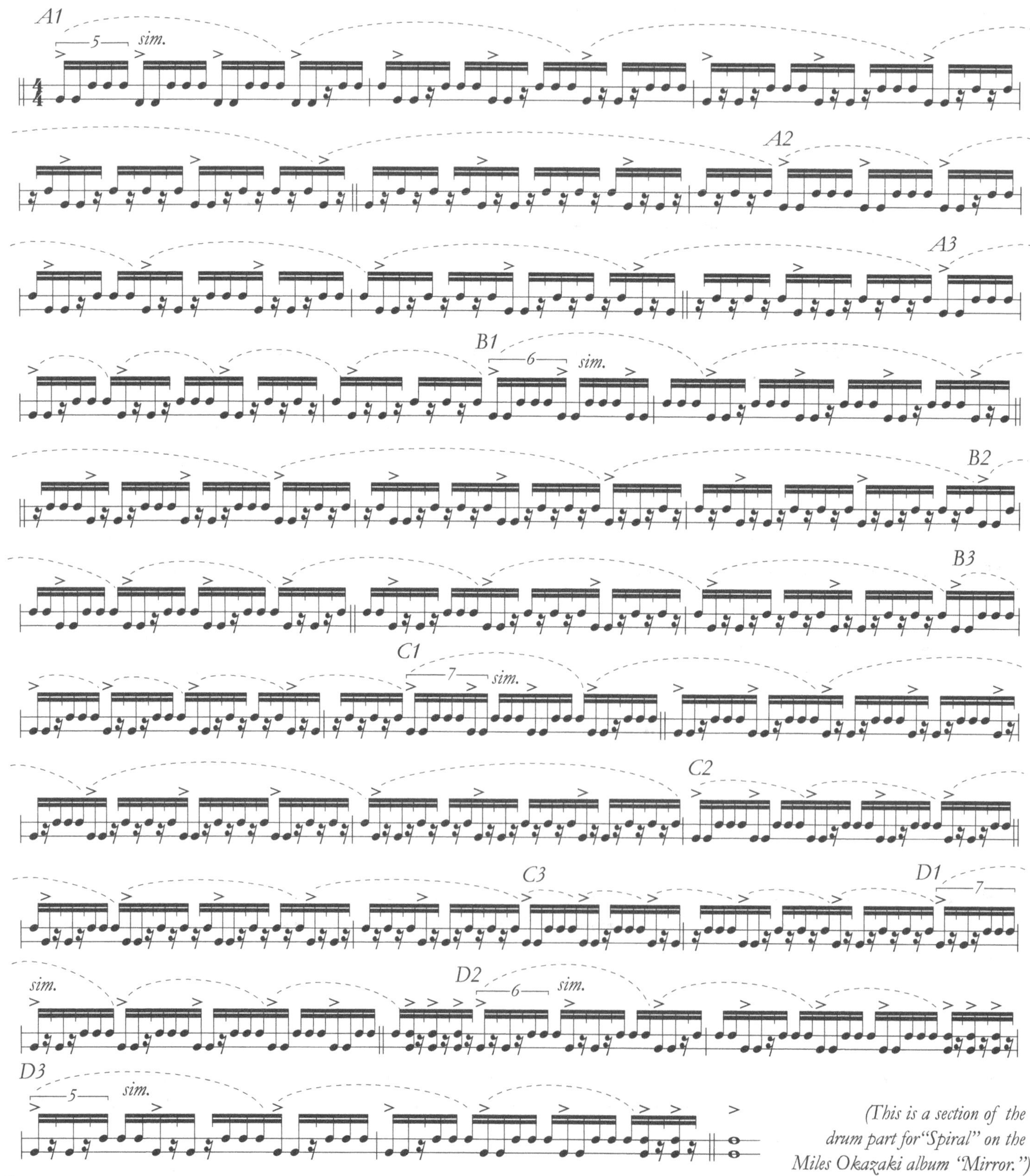

(This is a section of the drum part for "Spiral" on the Miles Okazaki album "Mirror.")

Notes *Idea: Compose two string picking patterns, using combinations of rudiments.*

Exercise

LEGATO DIATONIC MODES

The five diatonic modes in one position, with notes on the same string attached by slurs and symmetrical picking indicated.
- Play through the scales observing the articulations, transpose.

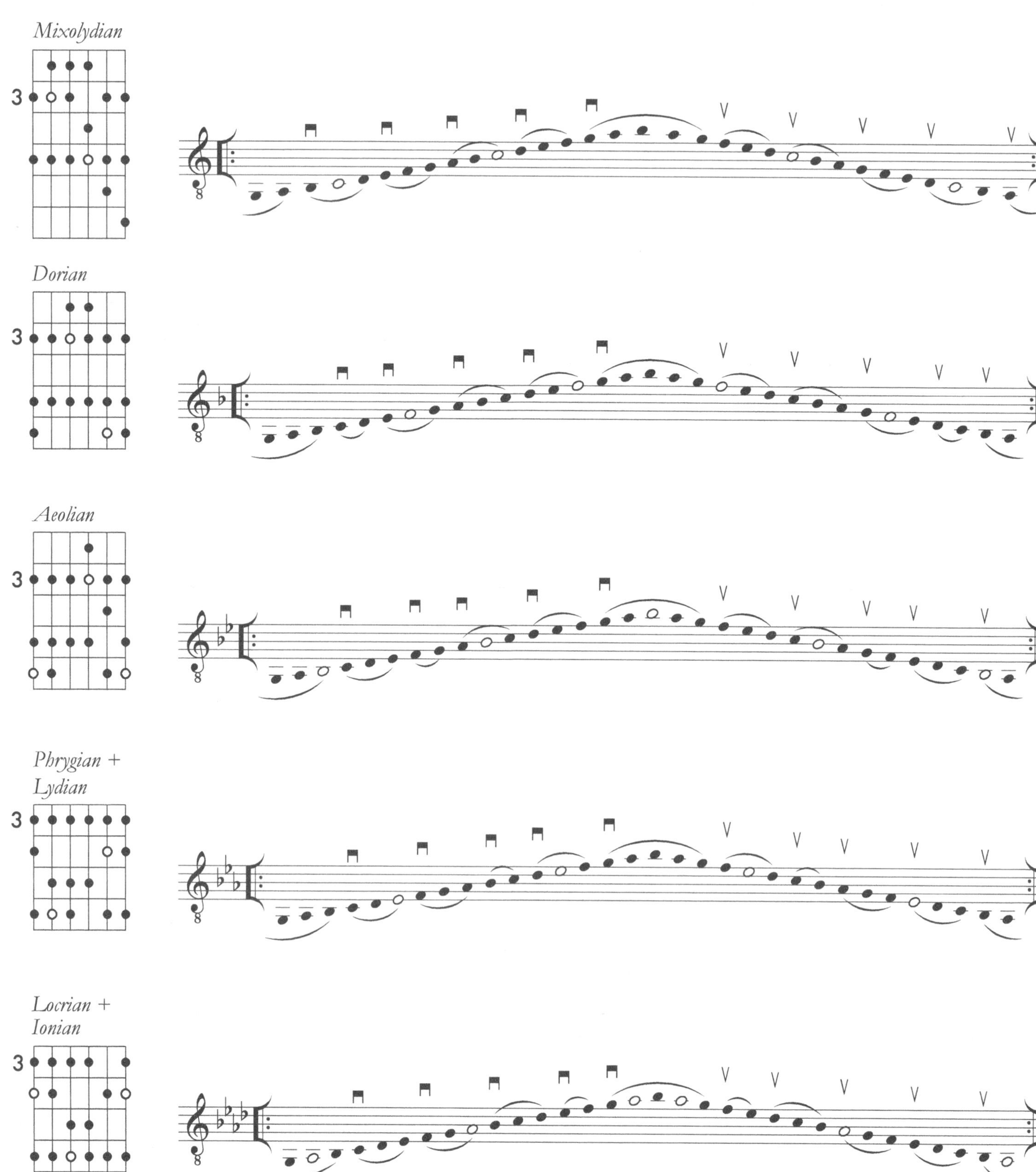

Exercise

DIATONIC ORNAMENTS

Single string exercises. The first two ornaments are written out in full. Ideas for other ornaments follow.
- Play the diatonic scale moving up and down a single string with the indicated ornaments (one picking stroke per slur).
- Play in one key on different strings, and different keys on one string (examples below are in C, on 3rd string)
- Create new ornaments, connect two or more ornaments together, improvise.

one note hammer on and pull off:

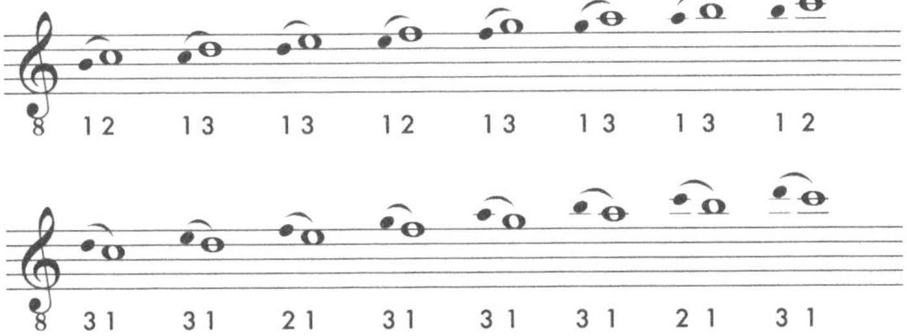

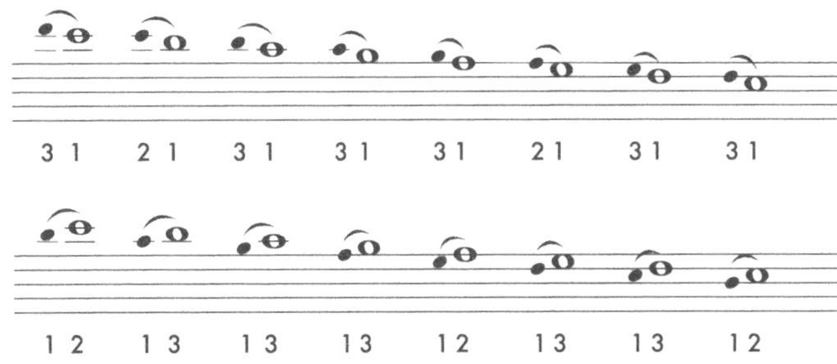

two note surround:

two note mordent:

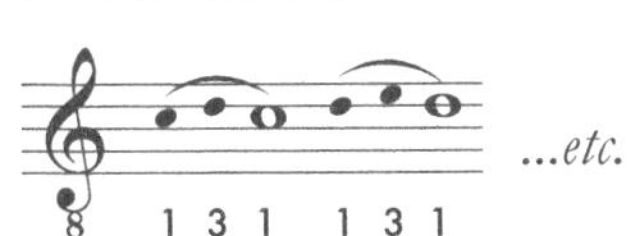

...etc.

...etc.

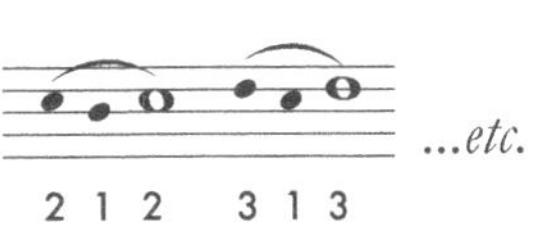

...etc.

...etc.

three note surround:

...etc.

...etc.

...etc.

...etc.

three note approach:

...etc.

...etc.

...etc.

...etc.

four note upper and lower turn:

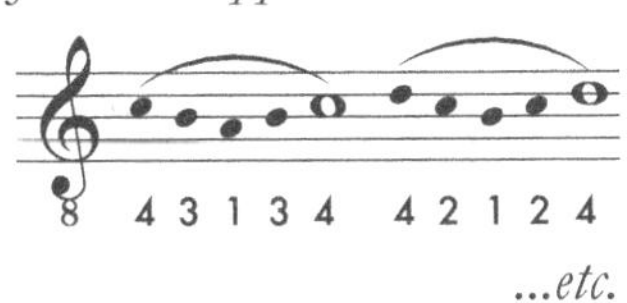

...etc.

...etc.

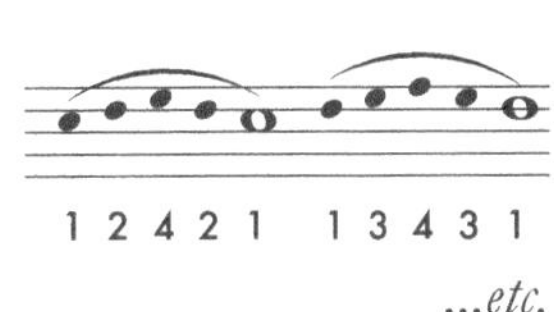

...etc.

...etc.

five note surrounding turn:

...etc.

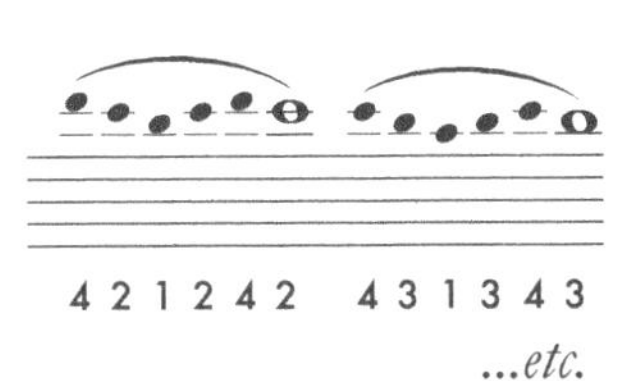

...etc.

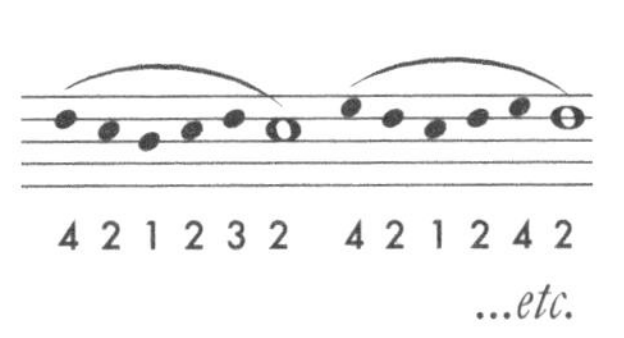

...etc.

...etc.

Exercise

114 CHROMATIC ORNAMENTS

For practicing legato movements on a single string within a range of four frets.
All possible slur patterns of 2, 3 and 4 notes in a 4-fret span are listed.
The initial pitch is colored black. Four fingers fall on consecutive chromatic pitches.
Moving to the right is a hammer-on and to the left is a pull-off.
Order of fingering can be seen in the arcing directional lines, which decrease with each successive pitch (first movement is highest, last is lowest).
Shapes spanning 2 or 3 semitones have multiple possible fingerings, which are listed below the diagram.
- Using any four fret span on any string, play through the movements.
- Combine with slides to move to different positions.

Examples:

In 4th position on the 3rd string (fingers 1,2,3 and 4 covering pitches B, C, C#, D),

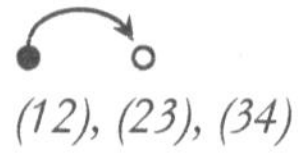
(12), (23), (34)
can represent

or

or

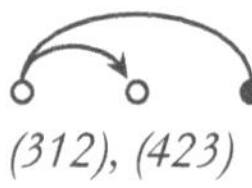
(312), (423)
can represent

or
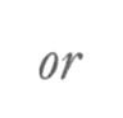
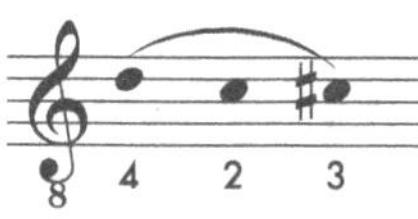

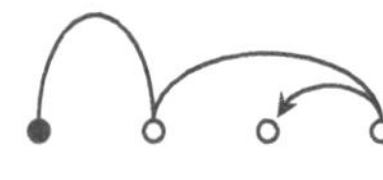
can only be
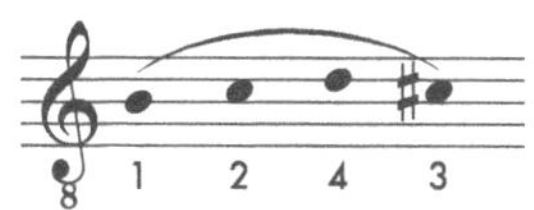

Two Notes:

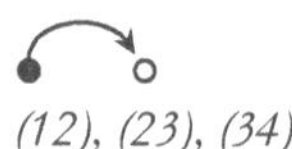
(12), (23), (34)
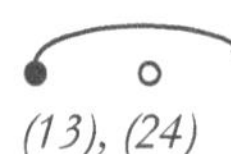
(13), (24)

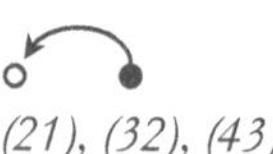
(21), (32), (43)
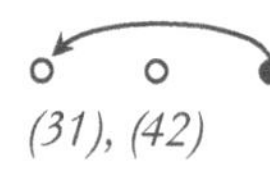
(31), (42)
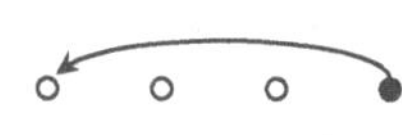

Three Notes:

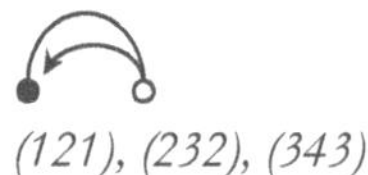
(121), (232), (343)

(123), (234)
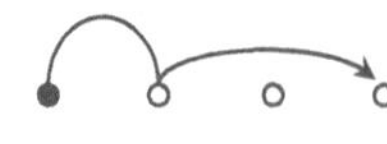
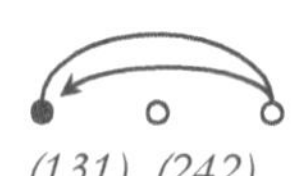
(131), (242)

(132), (243)
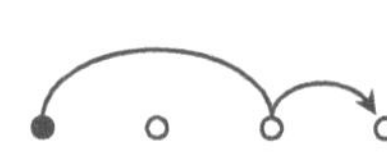

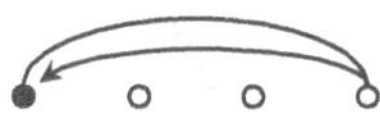
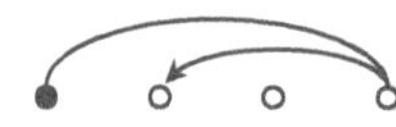
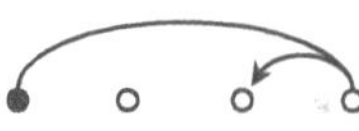

(212), (323), (434)
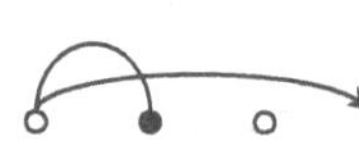
(213), (324)

(231), (342)
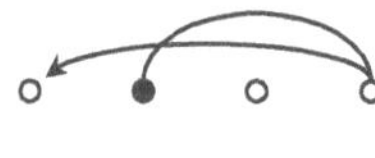
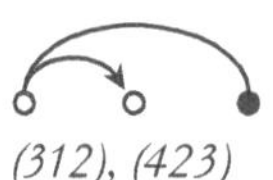
(312), (423)
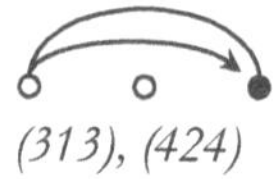
(313), (424)
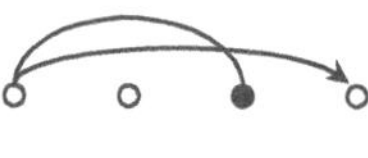
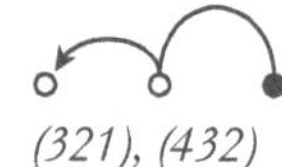
(321), (432)

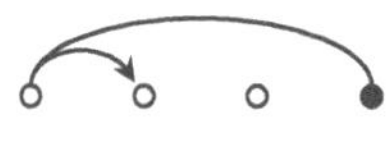
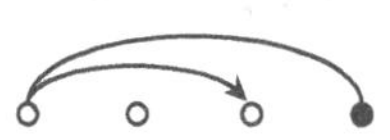
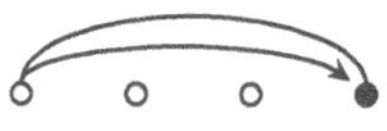
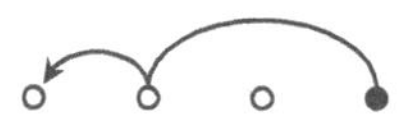
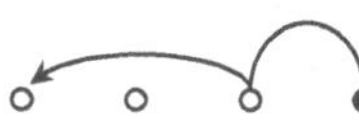

Four Notes:

(1212), (2323), (3434)
(1213), (2324)
(1231), (2342)
(1232), (2343)
(1312), (2423)
(1313), (2424)
(1321), (2432)
(1323), (2434)
(2121), (3232), (4343)
(2123), (3234)
(2131), (3242)
(2132), (3243)
(2312), (3423)
(2313), (3424)
(2321), (3432)
(3121), (4232)
(3123), (4234)
(3131), (4242)
(3132), (4243)
(3212), (4323)
(3213), (4324)
(3231), (4342)

Exercise

SLIDES

Some ideas for working on slides / glissandi and accurately gauging distances along the length of the fretboard.
- *Don't look at hands or guitar. Play in time, to a pulse.*
- *Play any material on one string, sliding from one pitch to another with one finger.*
- *Make the beginning and ending notes of the slide clear, and the intermediate notes a smooth gliding sound.*
- *Make the slide as fast as possible (so that the gliding sound almost disappears).*
- *Make the slide as slow as possible (until it begins to sound more like a chromatic scale).*
- *Change string and location. Change the finger used for the slide.*
- *Shown below are two versions of an F major scale. Some other ideas could include:*
    - *Play a major scale on each string, ascending or descending pitch by pitch. Play patterns, etc.*
    - *Starting on F, play scales in the key of Gb, Db, Ab, Eb, Bb, F, and C.*
    - *Play the four heptatonic scales on each string, or any other scale.*
    - *Slide to all intervals from one pitch (a chromatic scale on one string).*
    - *Slide to one interval from various pitches (e.g., start on random pitches and slide up a perfect 5th).*
    - *Play melodies on one string, trying to get enough motion from the slide to maintain vibration in the string.*

Exercise

BLUES

A study for building skills in legato phrasing with three fingers (hammer-ons, pull-offs, and slides)
Fingerings and positions shown for top staff. Bass line is shown for reference or for a second player.
Entire melody is played on strings 1-4, from frets 3-6.
Aim to end each phrase with the accents shown in the bassline.
Form is a blues in G-sharp minor.
Play at whatever speed is necessary to make all pitches and articulations clear, then work up to ♩ = 180

(This is the melody and bassline of a composition by Miles Okazaki called "Kudzu")

Concept

POLYPULSE

Since the study of rhythms on one string at a time began by looking at pulse, the study of rhythms on multiple strings will take a look at multiple pulses. Consider a time line with a *binary* division of the beat (division into two parts):

Take the subpulses and group them by twos, threes, fours, and larger numbers. Let the beginnings of each group form a new, secondary pulse:

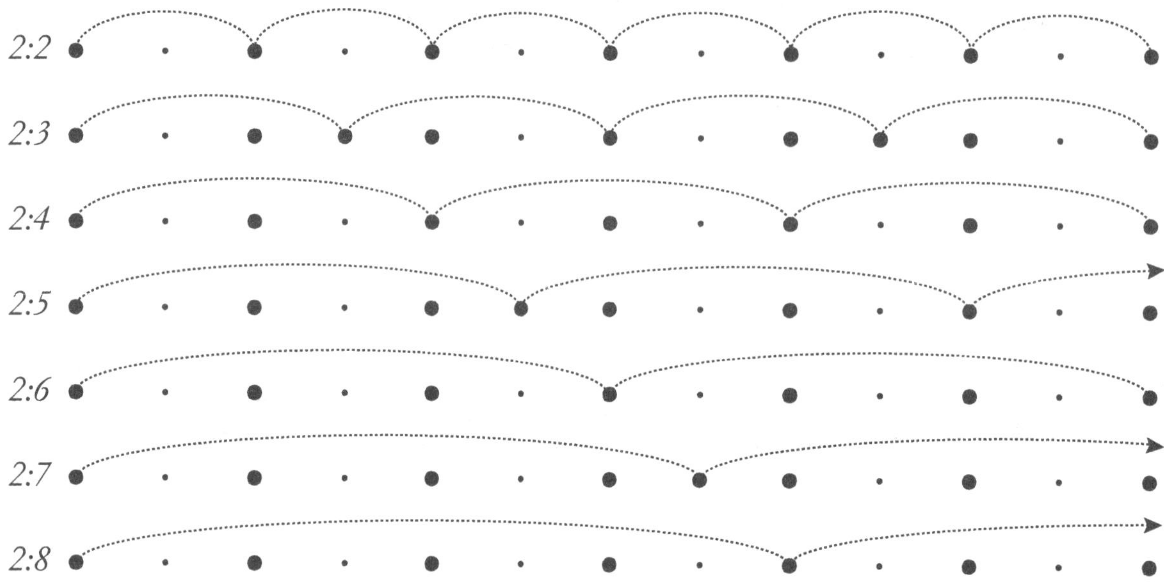

In the figures labeled *2:2, 2:4, 2:6,* and *2:8,* the beginning of each group coincides with the original pulse, producing only unison events. In the figures labeled *2:3, 2:5,* and *2:7,* beginnings of some of the groups fall in the interior of the original pulse, and create a secondary pulse. This demonstrates that, in a binary division of the beat, there are three possible polypulses using groupings of sizes 2-8.

While playing two simultaneous pulses, it's likely that the musician will feel one pulse as a primary point of reference and feel a secondary pulse in relation to it. For example, the polypulse *2:3* could be felt as a three beat cycle with 8th notes in groups of 3. But this same figure could be flipped, making it a two beat cycle with triplets in groups of 2. These are two different perceptions of the same rhythmic sound. It's a similar cognitive phenomenon to the drawing of a cube that changes orientation depending on what area the mind is focused on.

Two perspectives of the combination of 2 and 3 pulses:

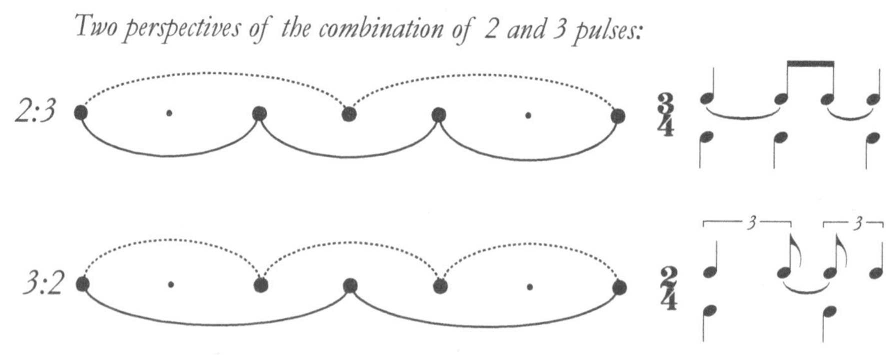

Perspective switching with the Necker Cube:

Continuing this idea through 8 subdivisions of the beat and eliminating all redundancies leads to 14 unique polypulses, each with two perspectives. This is shown in the illustration on the following page.

Illustration

14 POLYPULSES

Showing: *The 14 possible patterns created by combinations of constant pulses in 2-8 subdivisions of the beat. All polypulses are written as reciprocal pairs - read the page upside down to reverse perspective.*

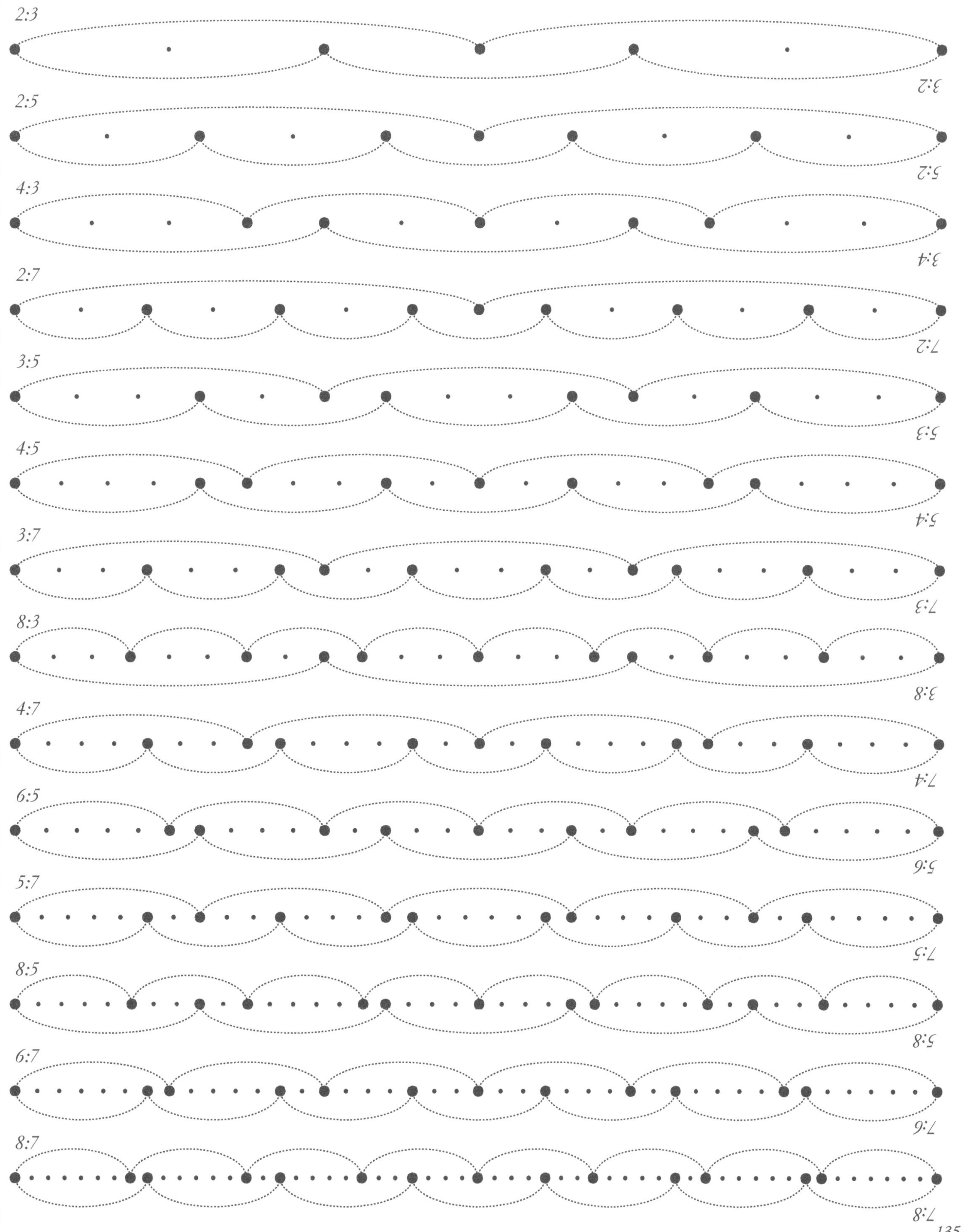

Exercise

PULSE AGAINST PULSE

The 28 possible combinations of two constant pulses, using subdivisions of the beat from 2 to 8. Lower pulse is constant, upper pulse is variable. Two columns show reciprocal pairs. Numbers show relationship of upper to lower pulse (rounded to 3 significant digits).
- Play the two pulses on two strings, using either single pitches or melodies.

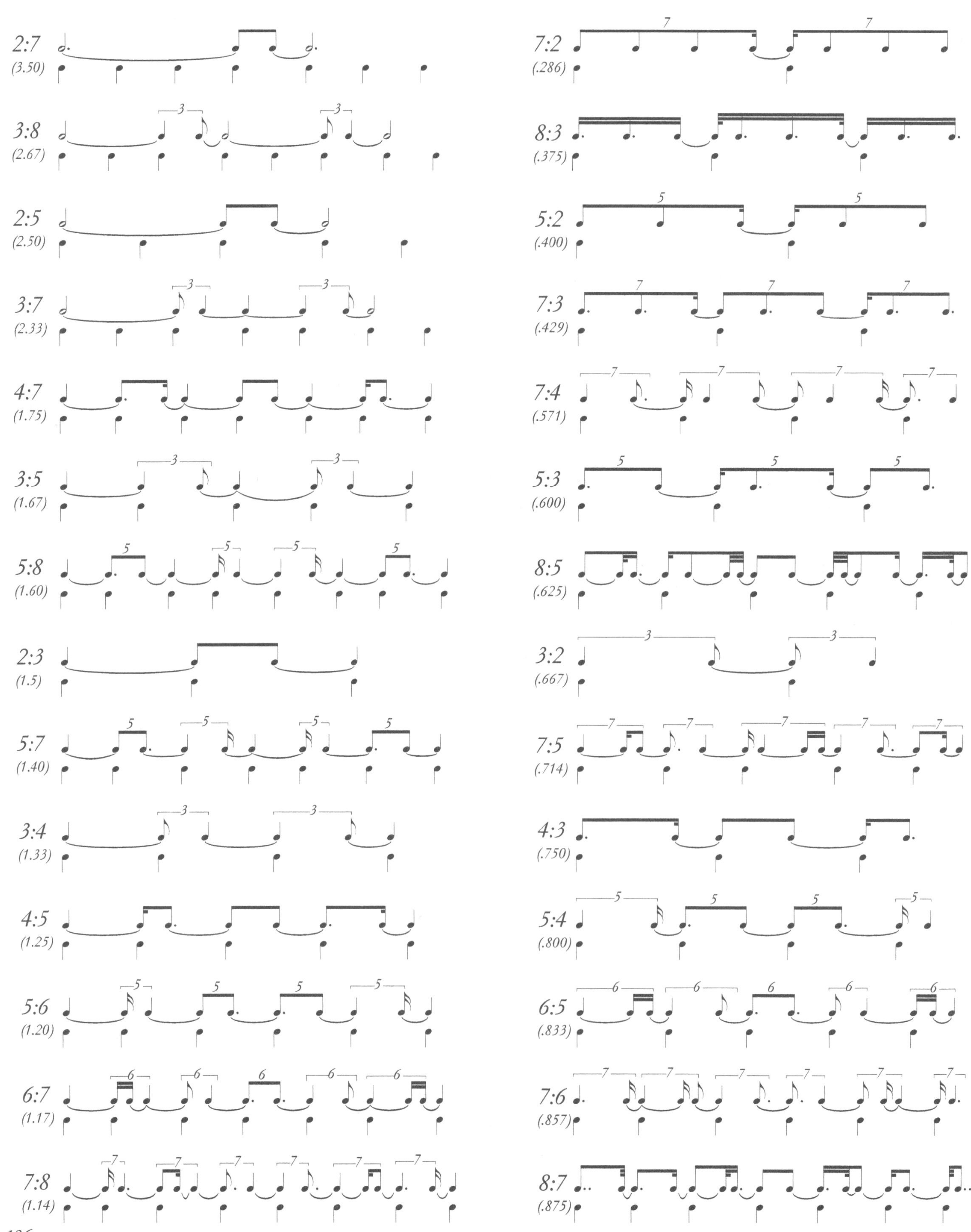

Eight examples of the previous exercise, using pitches.

2:3, static pitches (minor 3rd)

2:3, two pitch alternation (composite is dim7 chord)

3:4, two pitch alternation (composite is Emi7 chord)

4:3, three pitches in each layer, in perfect 5ths (2nd position)

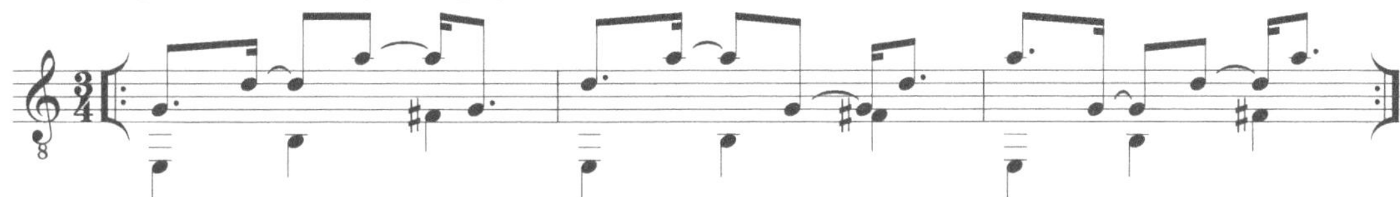

3:5, three pitches in top layer, four pitches in bottom layer (composite is G major scale, 2nd position)

6:5, four triads in top layer, constant pitch in bottom layer (triads are Emi, Dbma, Daug, and Adim, which make 12 tones)

5:4, constant pitch in top layer, triads in bottom layer (triads are Gma, Gdim, Fma, Fdim, use open E for top note)

7:5, Bbmi pentatonic in top layer, E Aeolian in bottom layer (composite makes 12 tones)

...etc. (pattern continues for a total of 35 bars)

Exercise

ILLUSION

A study in polypulses against 4. Form is: (7:4, 5:4), (7:4, 5:4), (7:4, 7:4), (5:4, 5:4), (2 beats rest), (8:4, 7:4, 6:4, 5:4, 4:4)
- Play top note only, feel 4/4 in triplets
- Add polypulses, play both layers together to lock the rhythms.
- Remove the top note but continue to feel the pulse, and notice how the remaining pitches sound like changing tempos in 4/4.

(This is the guitar part for "Halfway," on the Miles Okazaki album "Mirror")

Exercise

THREE PULSES

A study for combining polypulses of 3, 4 and 5. Pulses of 3 and 5 are shown on upper staff, and the pulse of 4 is shown on the lower staff.
- Play any two of the three layers, then introduce the third layer (suggestion: start with 5:4, then add the pulse in 3).
- While playing, listen to each layer in turn to make sure pulse is even.
- Choose one layer and bring it to the foreground by increasing its volume and observing accents (groups of 4 pulses).
- Start as slowly as necessary, work up to ♩ = 80

(This is a section of the guitar part for "Generations," on the Miles Okazaki album of the same name)

Concept

RHYTHMIC DYADS

In the world of equal tempered pitches, we looked at monads (single pitches), dyads (two pitches), triads (three pitches), and so on. We can borrow these terms for the rhythmic world, but we need to clarify what they mean in a new context. We are using a system that describes "where" to build a system that describes "when." Let's say that a constant pulse is something like a rhythmic "monad" - it has no internal shape, and is like a single point in time, cyclically repeating:

A single pitch has no context - it takes two pitches to form a structure with internal dynamics. A perfect fifth establishes a tonality, a tritone contains tension, etc. Similarly, a constant pulse contains no rhythmic variation - because there is no beginning or end, the cyclic length is ambiguous. In a constant pulse, we may hear a cyclic length of one, two, five, seventeen, or any other quantity (these are what might be called *time signatures*), but the shape of the pulse itself does not dictate this number. If a dyad in the pitch world is *a structure with two different notes,* we could say that a rhythmic dyad is *a structure with two rhythmic events of different lengths*. The unevenness of the figure produces something with a definite shape and cyclic length:

This is our most basic rhythm - a cycle of two events, one longer than the other. The human heartbeat itself is an *unquantized* (off the grid) version of this this type of rhythm. For this study, we will use quantized rhythms where the lengths of each event can be measured. The simplest version of the rhythmic dyad would involve the two smallest rhythmic units, which we can call 1 and 2. This cycle could be written on a timeline or a time circle (large dots are sounded events, small dots are rests):

Rhythmic figure [1,2], linear and circular:

1 2 1 2 1 2 1 2 . . .

The time circle is more efficient, and visually expresses cyclicality. For example, if we say that one of the rhythmic units is an 8th note, then we can translate the figure as follows:

= or or = or or

In the same way that a pitch circle does not specify a particular inversion or voicing, a time circle does not specify a time signature or subdivision of the beat. It's merely shorthand for a specific constellation of events in time. This same *[1,2]* rhythm could exist in many different contexts - here it is in six different subdivisions of the beat:

The term "rhythmic figure" in this book will refer the main idea of this page, as *a group of sounded events with at least two events of different length.*

Concept

EXPANSION OF THE DYAD

The rhythmic figure *[1,2]* could be expanded in any number of ways. Examples of two events with different lengths could be *[2,3]*, *[3,5]*, *[5,8]*, *[144,233]*, and any of the other infinite combinations of two numbers. If the two events are the same length, the sound of the rhythm becomes an even pulse. In order to keep this study short, we will take a look at only very small rhythmic values of 1, 2, and 3. The value 1 is our smallest rhythmic building block, a single subpulse. Values of two and three are the next prime (only divisible by themselves and 1) building blocks, and in musical practice these lengths can be felt as single units, without breaking them into component parts. The value of 4 is divisible into two parts, and is usually felt as either *[1,1,1,1]*, *[2,2]*, *[3,1]*, or *[1,3]*. Any value larger than 4 can also be felt as some composite of the first three building blocks. Keeping the values small greatly simplifies this study - we can see that by limiting the elements to lengths of 1, 2, and 3, we can only make three different rhythmic figures with two events. The cycles have lengths of 3, 4, and 5 units. Starting on either of the two hits in each figure produces two "modes" of each dyad:

The three possible rhythmic figures of two events with event length equal to 1, 2, or 3, showing two different starting points.

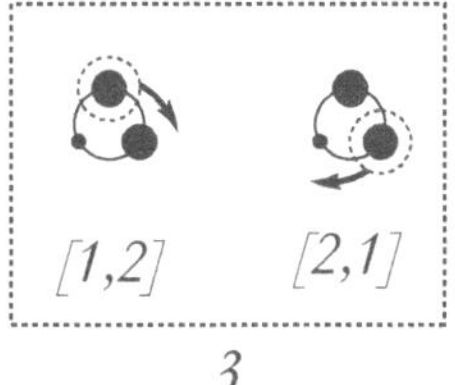

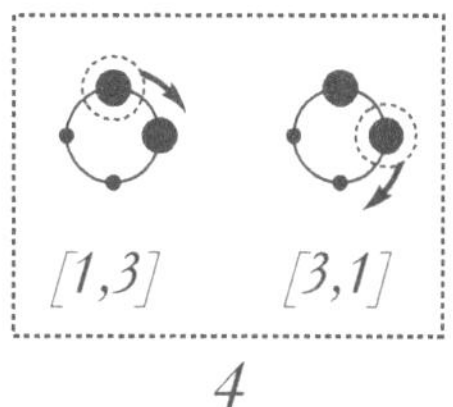

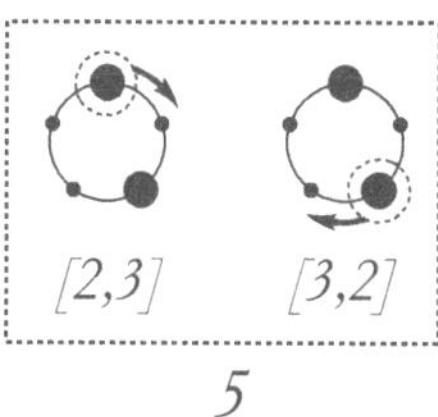

Length: 3 4 5

Now suppose that, using these same building blocks, we want to make rhythmic *triads*. These would be rhythmic figures with three events, with at least two events of different length. After some calculation or trial and error, we would find that there are eight of them:

[1,1,2]

[1,1,3]

[1,2,2]

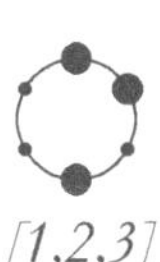
[1,2,3]

[1,3,2]

[1,3,3]

[2,2,3]

[2,3,3]

Each of these rhythmic triads has three modes, and their lengths range in size from 4 to 8 units. We can continue the idea, into rhythmic *tetrads, pentads, hexads,* and so on. For example, the *clave* figures earlier in the book were versions of rhythmic pentads and heptads. The number of possible rhythmic figures increases rapidly with each added event. We can see from the table on the right that these numbers become impractical very quickly. For the purposes of this book, we will stop at 4 events, limiting the number of figures to 29. Layering, combining, and manipulating these rhythms alone could form a lifetime of study. The illustration on the following page shows these 29 basic figures in an arrangement that shows their relationships in terms of number of events and length.

Events:	*Possible Rhythms:*
2	3
3	8
4	18
5	48
6	116
7	312
8	810
9	2,184
10	5,880
11	16,104
12	44,220

Illustration

29 BASIC RHYTHMIC FIGURES

Showing:

Rhythmic figures visualized on cyclical time circles, where large nodes are sounded events and small nodes are rests. Rhythmic intervals are of length 1, 2, or 3. All possible rhythmic shapes of 2, 3 and 4 events are shown. Figures in the same row have the same number of events, and figures in the same column are of equal length. Labels show the rhythmic intervals contained in each figure.

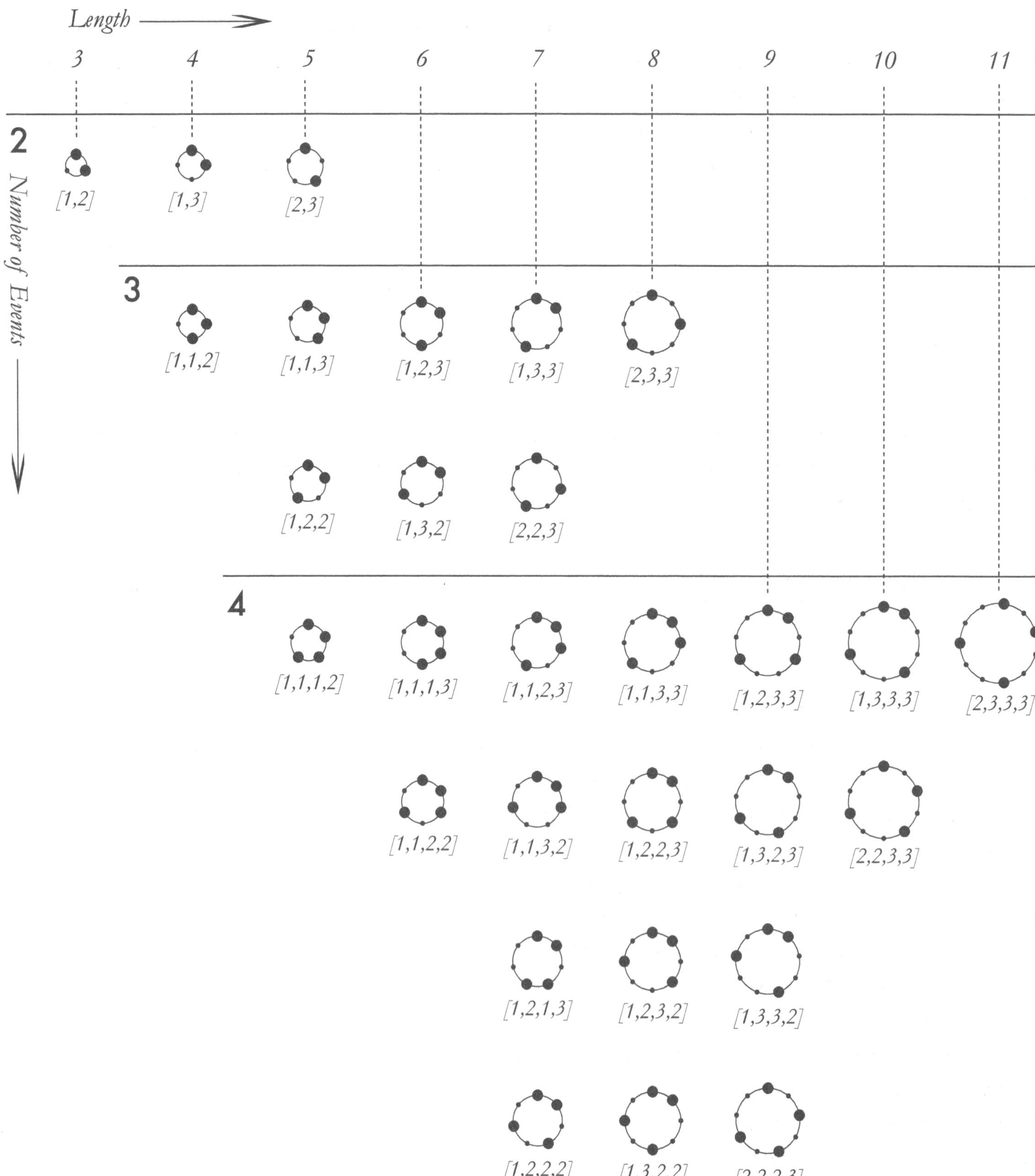

Exercise

THREE HEARTBEATS

For practicing rhythms with two events of length 1, 2 or 3. Each of the three figures is shown in six subdivisions of the beat.
- Play the rhythms with a single pitch, two pitches, or longer melodic material.

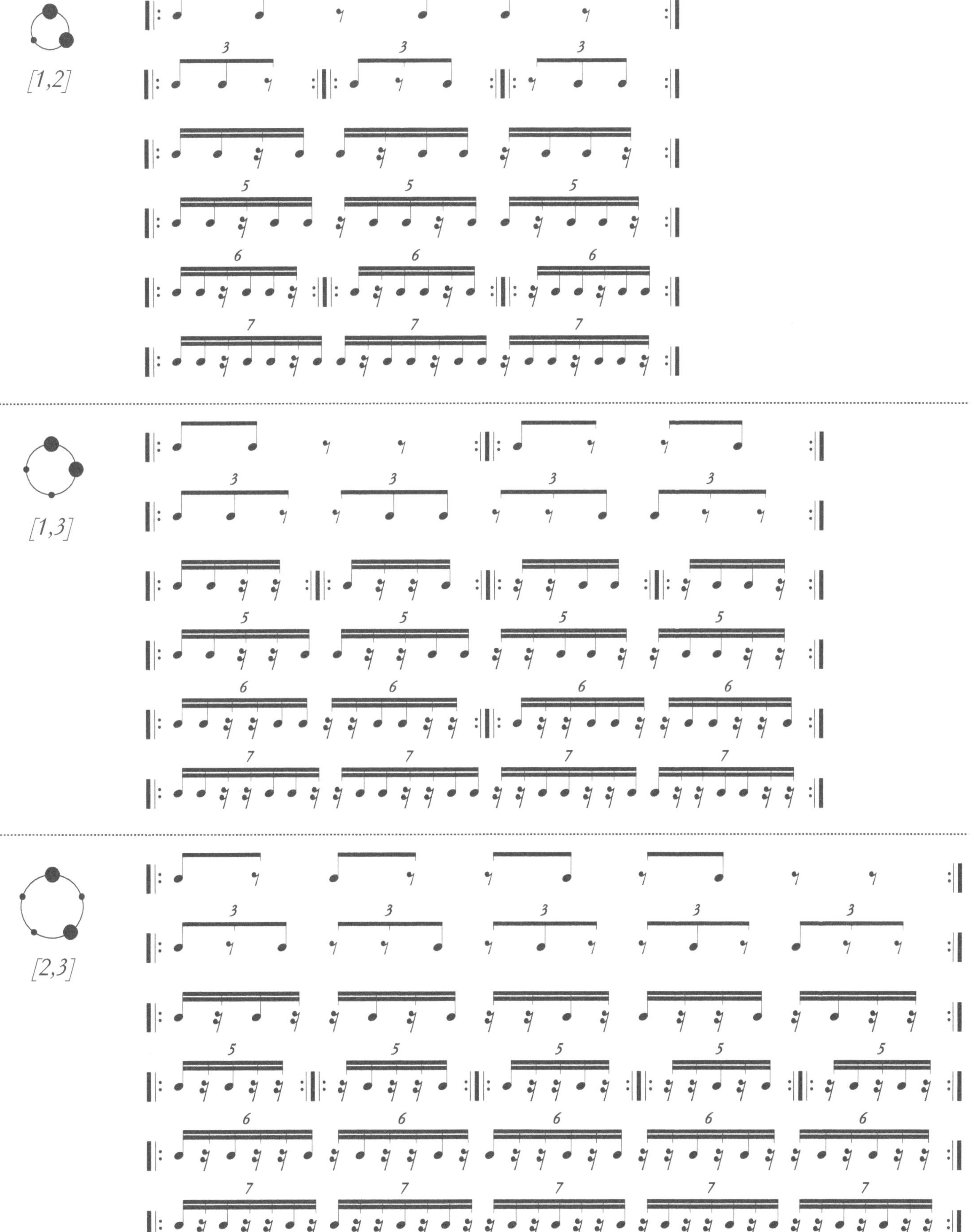

Notes *Idea: Use the time circles (cyclic length from 3-15) to create rhythmic shapes.*

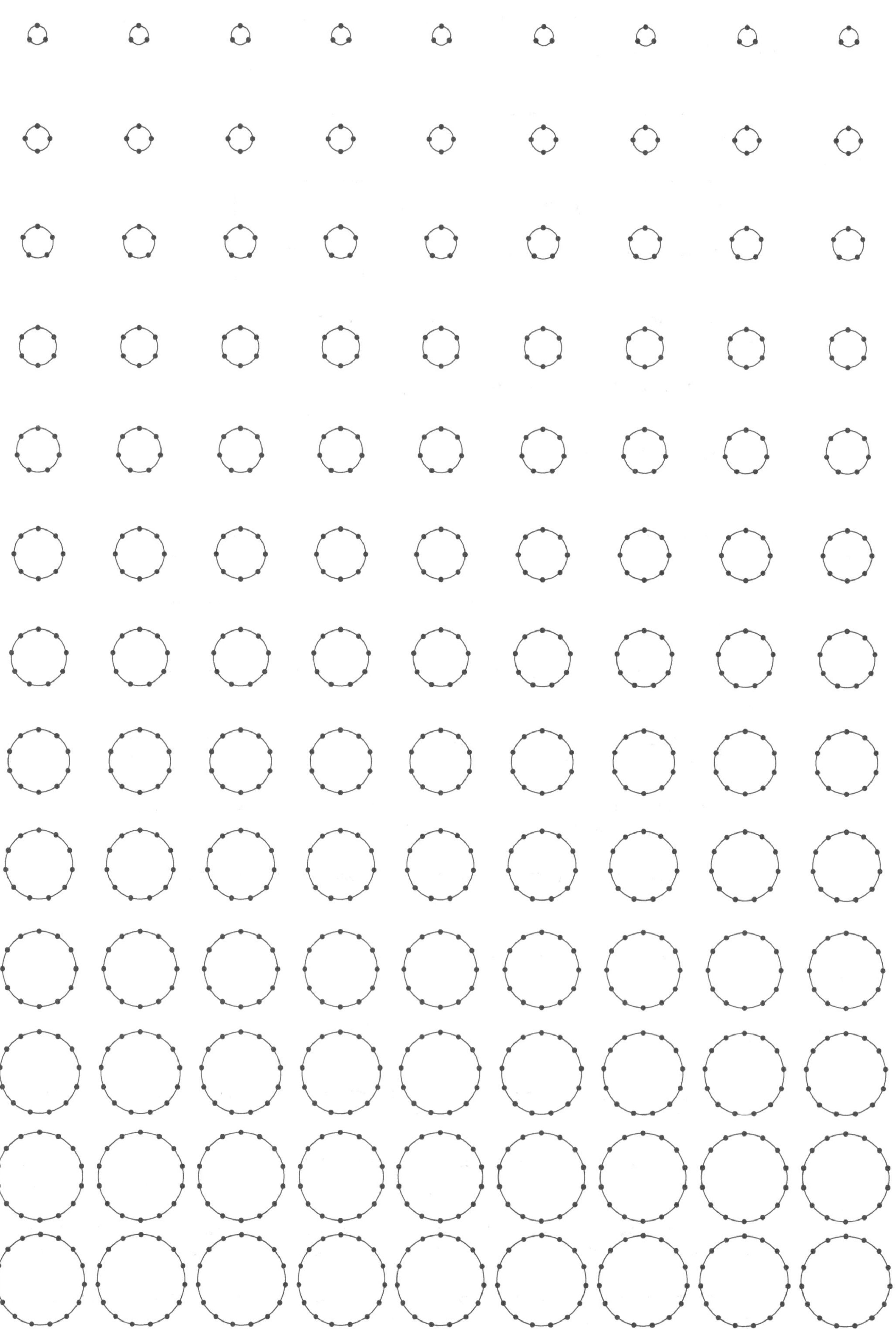

Concept

POLYRHYTHM

Pulse can be thought of as a type of figure where all events have equal length. Layered pulses make polypulses, which appeared earlier in the book. Rhythms can be thought of as types of figures that contain events of unequal length. Layered rhythms make polyrhythms, the final part of this study. Consider the three heartbeat rhythms shown on the previous page. Playing two or more of them simultaneously creates a kind of rhythmic counterpoint. Here are the figures *[1,2]* and *[1,3]*, layered in a duple time feel:

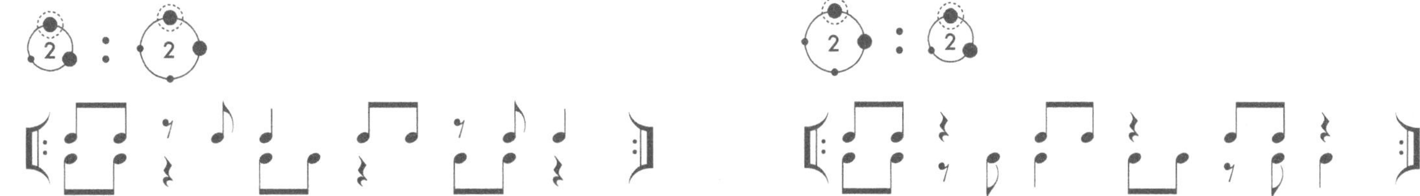

In each example, two time circles are shown, with the figure played on the top layer first. A dotted circle shows the starting point for each rhythm. A number inside each figure shows the subdivision of the beat. The contrapuntal figure is then written out with staff notation.

In these 6-beat patterns, there are four cycles of figure *[1,2]* and three cycles of figure *[1,3]*. Because the rhythms are of different lengths, they move against each other in a phasing type of motion that is reset each time the two figures start at the same point. We can see that any two rhythmic figures of different lengths can be combined in this way to create a larger composite cycle with two voices.

This study of rhythm against rhythm is very challenging on the guitar. Playing two simulataneous rhythmic layers requires developing independence within each hand. The picking hand has a natural division, between the thumb and the opposing fingers. The motions of the fretting hand depend on the choice of melodic material. Beginning with unchanging pitches will allow isolated work on the picking hand. Introducing changing pitches will shift the focus to the fretting hand, and the mental work that has to be done to keep one's place. Consider these three examples of the first rhythm above:

The pitch information acts as a third layer, making longer and longer cycles with each added note. The exercises on the following pages explore polyrhythms between combinations of figures with two events, in duple and triple subdivisions of the beat. Consider the infinite possibilities that can emerge when adding pitches to the rhythms.

Exercise

12 POLYRHYTHMS

Basic rhythmic counterpoint - for developing independence between two simultaneous rhythmic layers.
Shown are all combinations of the first three figures from the 29 Basic Rhythmic Figures in duple and triple pulse.
Time circles and Staff notation show equivalent information.
- Practice without instrument: Sing one layer, clap the other, tap the foot or move the body to the beat.
- Practice with instrument: Let the two layers be two elements (e.g. different strings, a triad with a bass note, etc).
- Use this notation only as a guide to understand how the layers fit together, then avoid reading.
Further Study:
- Explore other figures from the 29 Basic Rhythmic Figures, add melodies to the rhythms, use more than two layers, increase the subdivision of the beat, internalize the pattern so that it is possible to improvise on it without getting lost.

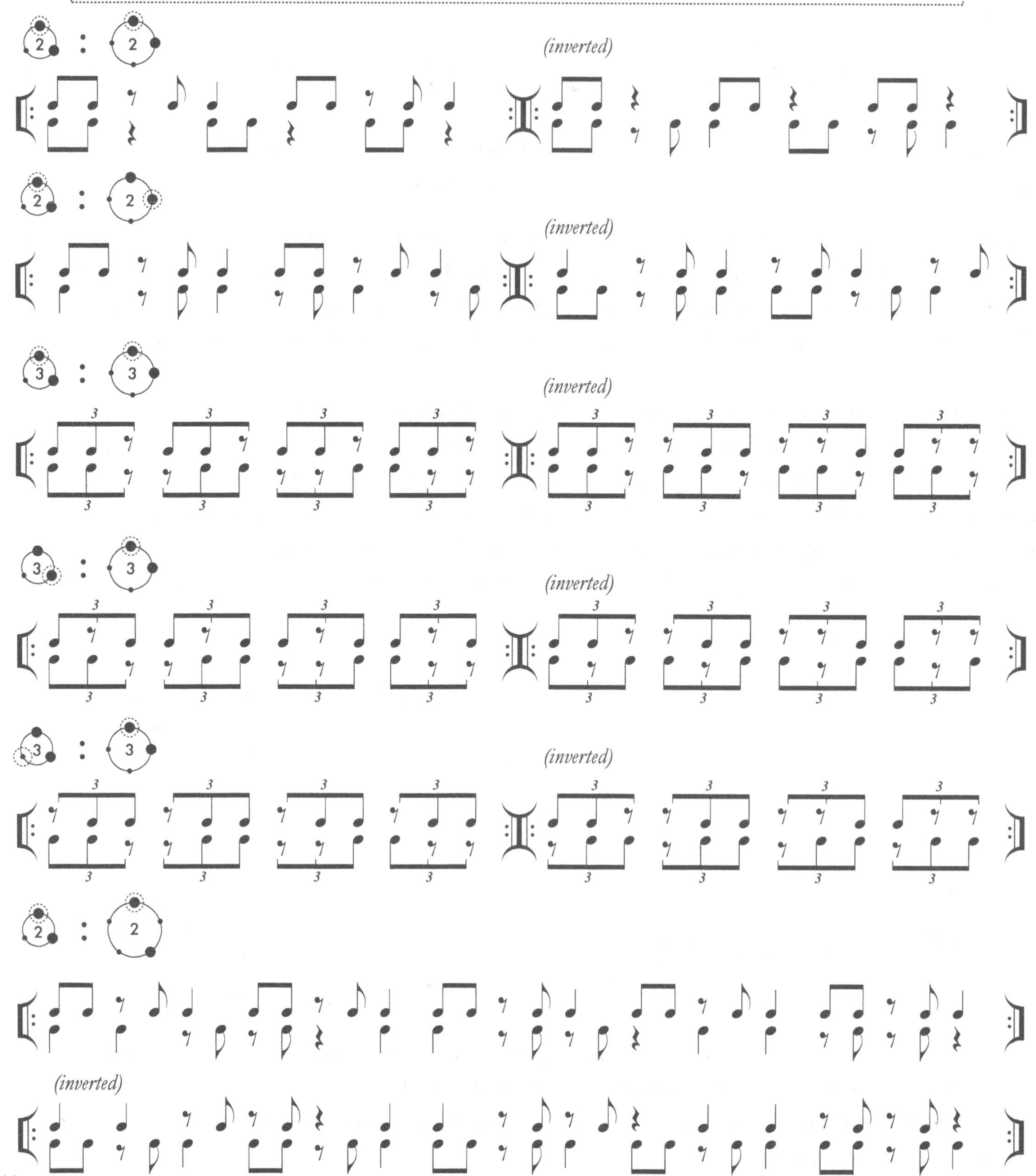

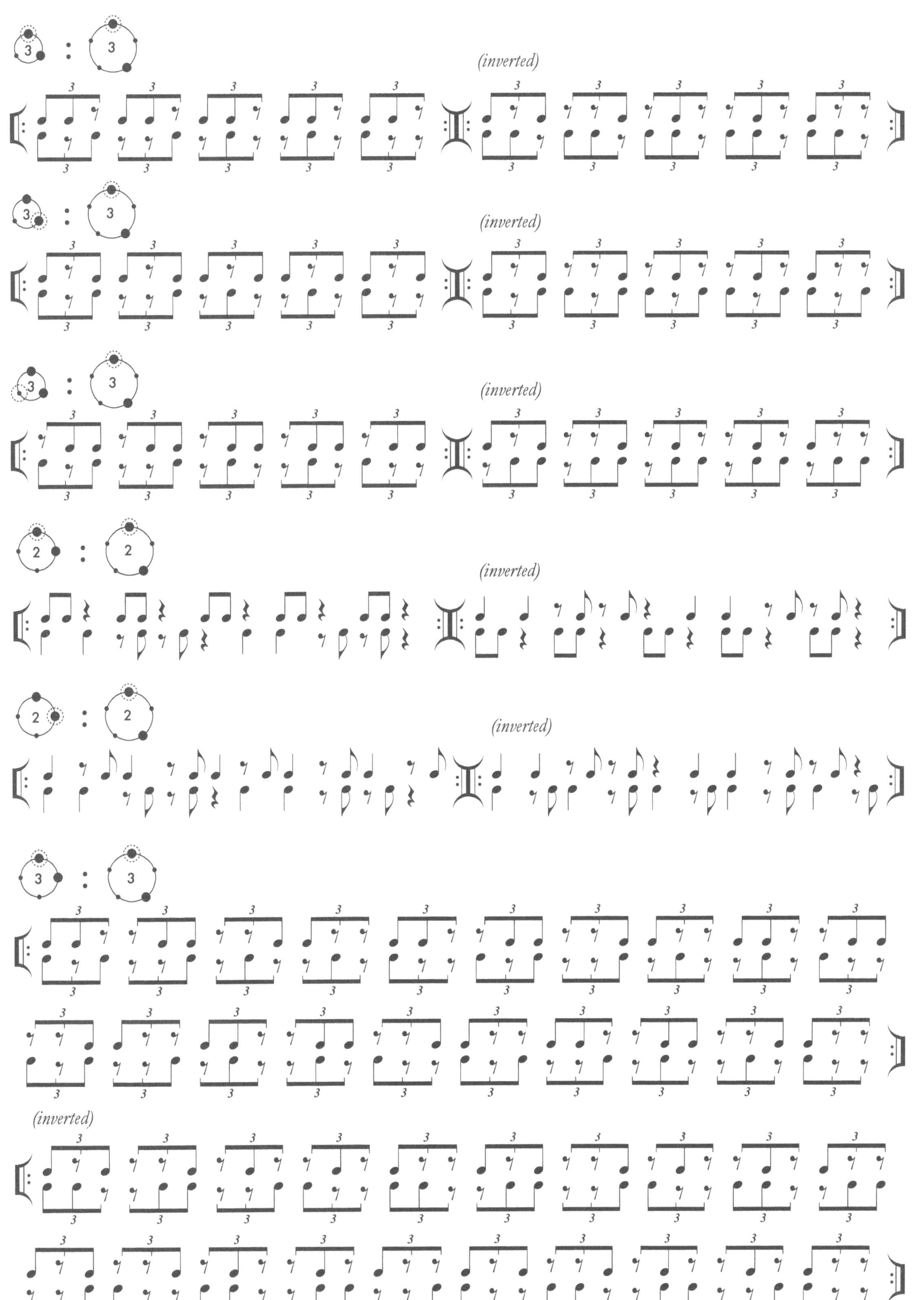
(inverted)
(inverted)
(inverted)
(inverted)
(inverted)
(inverted)

Exercise

POLYRHYTHMIC EXAMPLES

Advanced Polyrhythmic examples, an extension of the previous exercise.
Time circles are from the table of 29 Basic Basic Rhythmic Figures.
Large dots are hits, small dots are rests, dotted circles are initial starting point, and numbers are subdivisions of the beat (clockwise).
Also shown are a verbal description and example on staff notation. Pitch material refers to concepts from Part I of this book.
- Play the examples, trying first to play them without using the staff notation.
- Begin to modify and distort the information, using these ideas as starting points for an improvised rhythmic exploration of the guitar.

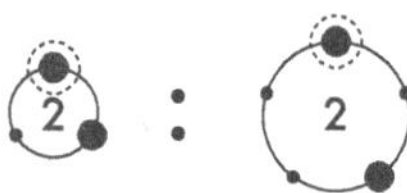

[1,2] against [2,3], duple feel.
Alternating bass note in 4ths with a constant triad (7,0,2) in the top voice (1st position).

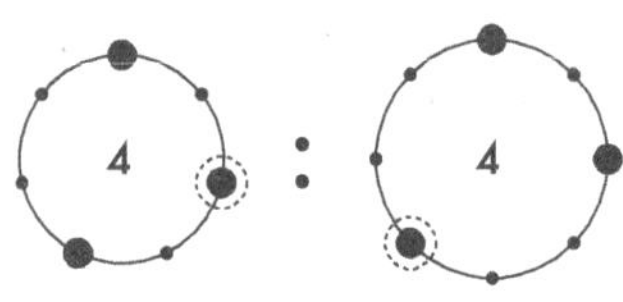

[2,3,2] against [3,2,3], quadruple feel.
Both melodies play triad (2,7,0) (stacked 4ths, 1st position, all open strings except C and F).

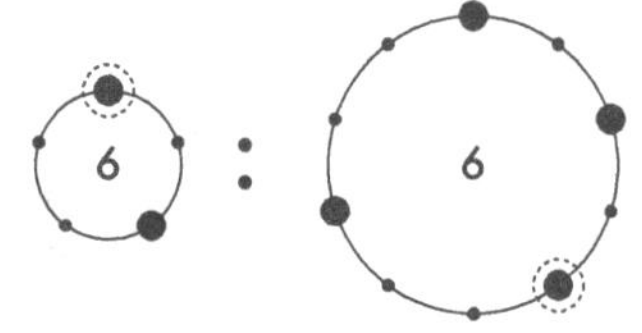

[2,3] against [3,3,2,2], sextuple feel.
Upper melody plays intervals A(0,9), Bb(0,7), Bb(0,8), A(0,9), Bb(0,7), A(0,8).
Lower melody plays 6 hits of D, 6 hits of Db.
The two melodies outline a harmony of: Dma, Bbma, F#ma, F#mi, Bbmi, Dmi.

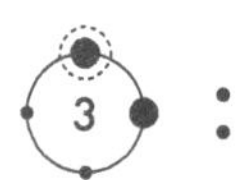

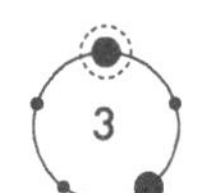

[1,3] against [2,3], triple feel.
Lower melody moves through a chromatic tiling (Fmi, Dma, Gaug, Bbdim).
Upper melody plays all interval tetrad (0,1,4,6) (1st position).

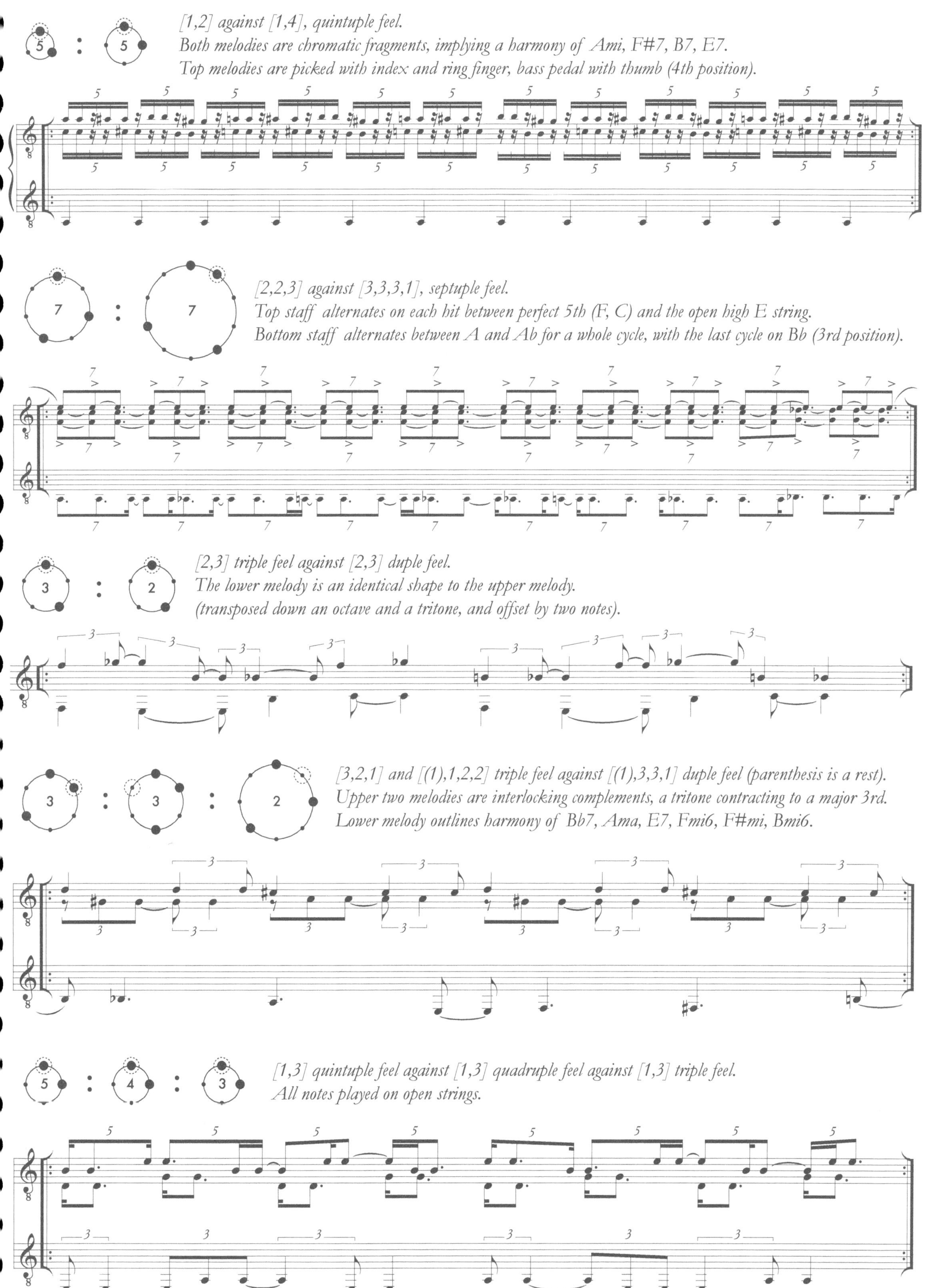

[1,2] against [1,4], quintuple feel.
Both melodies are chromatic fragments, implying a harmony of Ami, F#7, B7, E7.
Top melodies are picked with index and ring finger, bass pedal with thumb (4th position).
[2,2,3] against [3,3,3,1], septuple feel.
Top staff alternates on each hit between perfect 5th (F, C) and the open high E string.
Bottom staff alternates between A and Ab for a whole cycle, with the last cycle on Bb (3rd position).
[2,3] triple feel against [2,3] duple feel.
The lower melody is an identical shape to the upper melody.
(transposed down an octave and a tritone, and offset by two notes).
[3,2,1] and [(1),1,2,2] triple feel against [(1),3,3,1] duple feel (parenthesis is a rest).
Upper two melodies are interlocking complements, a tritone contracting to a major 3rd.
Lower melody outlines harmony of Bb7, Ama, E7, Fmi6, F#mi, Bmi6.
[1,3] quintuple feel against [1,3] quadruple feel against [1,3] triple feel.
All notes played on open strings.

Concept

RHYTHMIC TILING

Make any rhythmic figure that has internal rests. For example: 

Add a second staff with notes that fill in the spaces of the original figure: 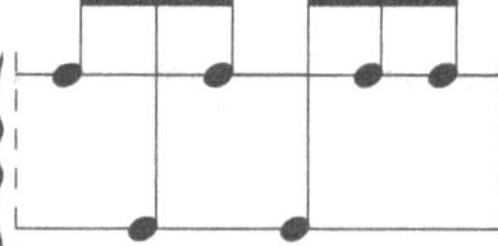

This makes two interlocking figures, positive and negative complements: 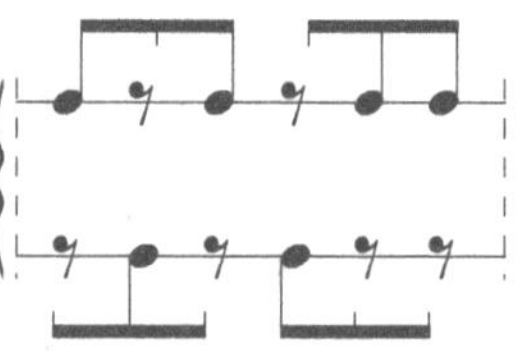

To tile the rhythmic space, append the second rhythmic figure to the first and the first to the second, doubling the length of the pattern and creating a small rhythmic canon:

This idea could be extended to any number of voices and any variety of rhythmic figures. Here is an example with a longer figure, with three voices and a rhythmic cycle of 13:

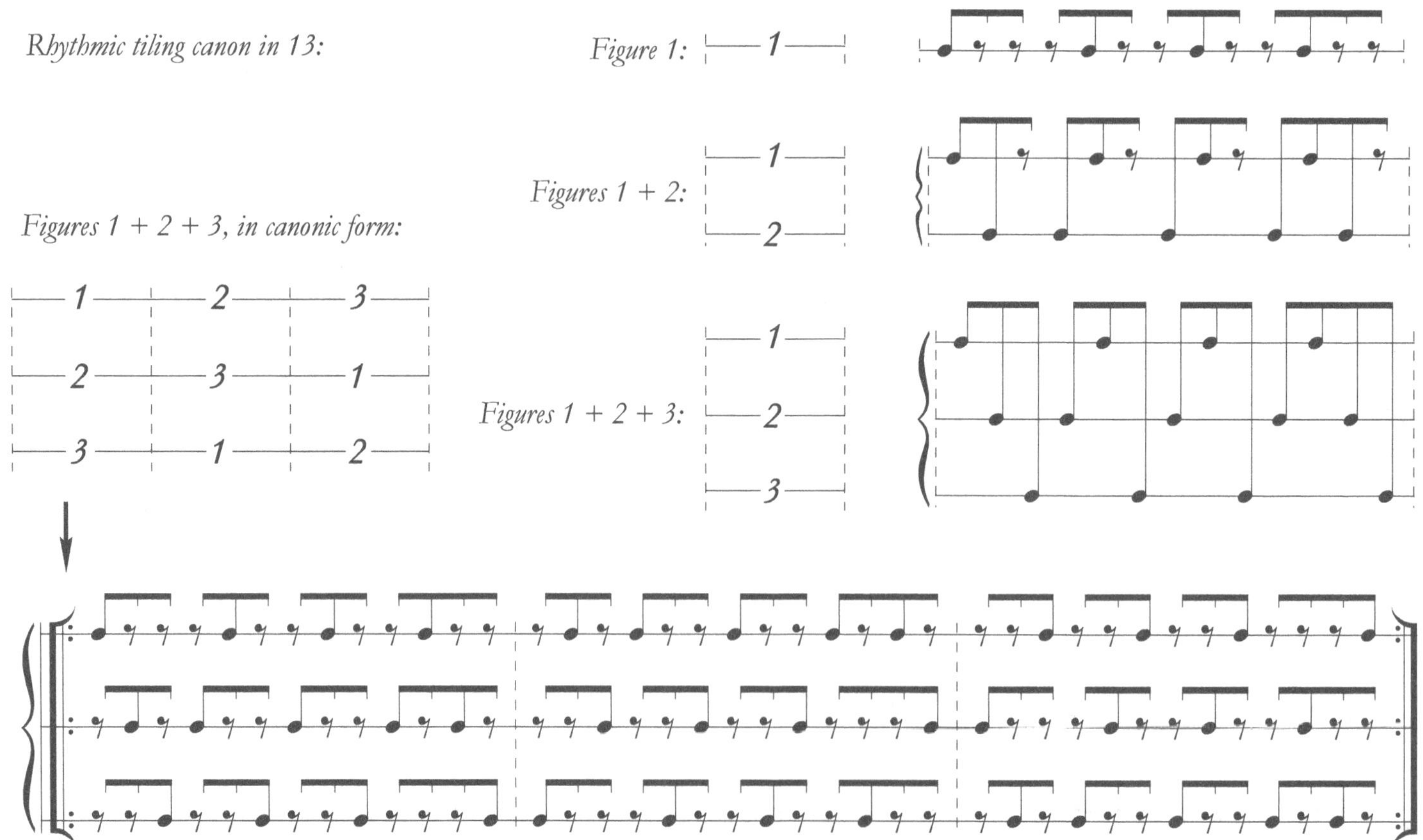

These interlocking patterns can be interesting for guitar practice, creating a variety of unusual picking patterns and fingering stretches. The example on the following page assigns pitches to the pattern above to make a canon in three octaves.

Exercise

CANON

A rhythmic tiling canon with a length of 39 eighth notes. The same melody appears in three octaves.
- Loop A, working to accurately feel the spaces between notes. Play notes long (as written) or short (leaving spaces empty).
- Use the transition to bring in the second voice. Loop B. Use the accents to work toward the sound of two independent melodies.
- Use the transition to bring in the third voice. Loop C. Work toward the sound of three independent melodies.
- Try to let one note ring into the next, holding down pitches as long as possible. This will require significant stretches.
- Improvise on the harmonies created by the interlocking pitches.

A

voice 1:

transition:

entrance voice 2

3 2 1 0 0 3 2 1 0 1

II I

B

voice 1 + voice 2:

0 3 1 2 3 4 3 2 1 3 1 2 0 1 4 0 3 2 1 0 0 3 2 1 0 1

I II I II I

entrance voice 3

transition:

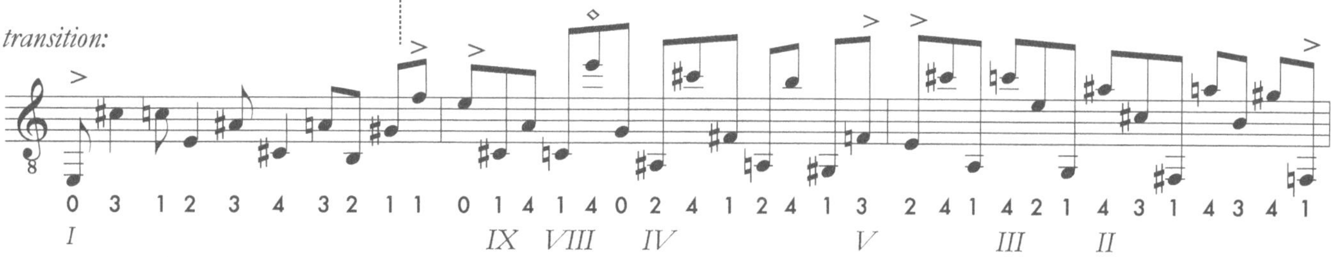

0 3 1 2 3 4 3 2 1 1 0 1 4 1 4 0 2 4 1 2 4 1 3 2 4 1 4 2 1 4 3 1 4 3 4 1

I IX VIII IV V III II

all voices, and composite harmony:

C

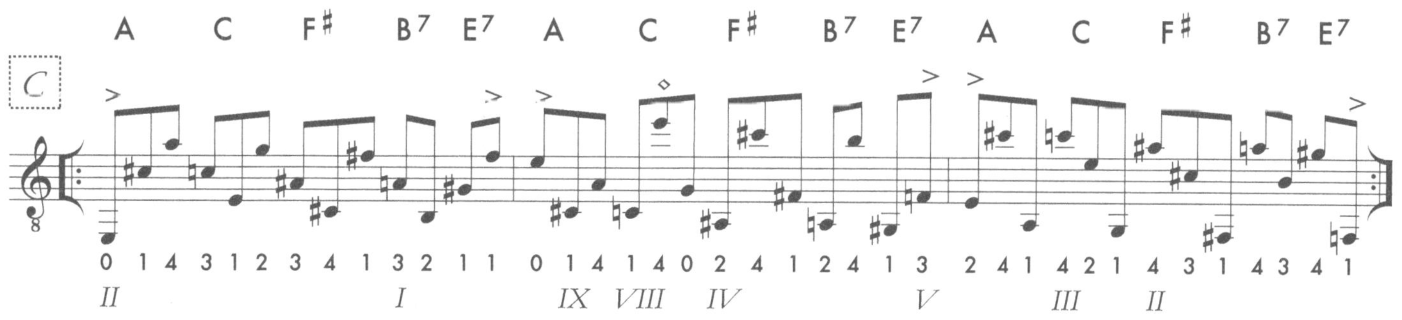

(This is a section of the guitar part for "Wheel" on the Miles Okazaki album "Figurations")

Concept

INFINITE GROWTH

Make two musical phrases, keeping them short and simple. An example is on the right:

In terms of eighth notes, Phrase A has a length of 2, and Phrase B has a length of 3. Now take phrase A and add it to the beginning of phrase B. This makes a new phrase AB, of length 5. Then take phrase B and add it to the beginning of phrase AB. This makes BAB, of length 8. Continue making new phrases by adding the previous phrase to the beginning of the current one. This will create some very interesting patterns governed by the number known as the golden ratio, or ϕ (*phi*), approximately .618. Any two consecutive phrases combine to generate the next phrase, made up of a short and long section. As the phrases grow, the size of the short section in relation to the long section approaches the golden ratio, and the size of the long section in relation to the entire phrase does the same. This happens regardless of the sizes of the first two phrases. For example, the comparative sizes of the last two phrases is 34:55, which approximates phi within 1/100 of one percent. This is a connection through numbers to a fundamental property of nature which has fascinated humans for thousands of years. The idea of the golden ratio can be useful for musicians who are interested in finding conceptual connections between sound and other natural phenomena.

These potentially infinite musical chains can also be useful for any number of physical and mental exercises. For example, here are the 8 phrases above played over a regular cycle of 12/8:

With different raw materials and the length of phrases only limited by the abilities of the memory, the possibilities are endless. The following page shows a visualization of these growing phrases in a linear way and as concentric circles.

Exercise

RHYTHMIC LABYRINTH

A map for generating phrases in golden proportions.
- Starting in the center of the circle, create a phrase to associate with grey. Moving outward, create a phrase to associate with white.
- The third circle begins the process of combining phrases, grey and then white. Put the two phrases together, loop, memorize.
- Continue to move outward, using the illustration as a guide, but reading it as little as possible.
- It may be easier to think in a linear way, in terms of the rules that generate each phrase. This is written at the bottom of the page.
- Transpose the pitches, change the internal rhythms of the cells, play against a pulse or time span, use accents to mark sections.
- Use as test for memory and concentration by moving through as many levels as possible without getting lost. Improvise.

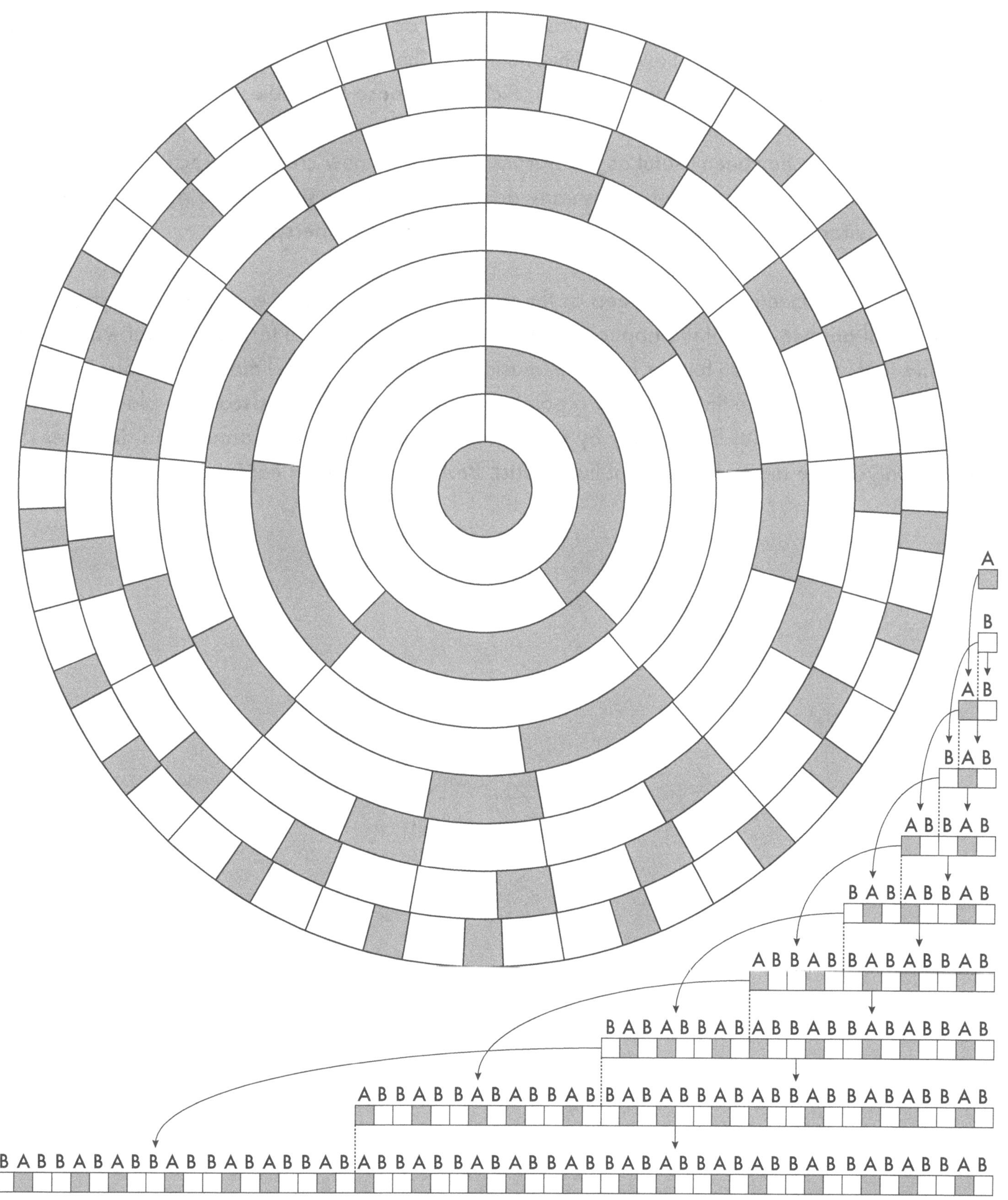

Concept

CONCLUSION

Reaching the end of the book, the reader may notice the absence of many subjects - harmony, counterpoint, sight-reading, composition, technology, acoustics, styles, repertoire, history, business. These are all beyond the scope of this limited study, which has made an effort to stay focused on the topic of musical fundamentals on the guitar. Even in this small area there is a lot of material, potentially a lifetime of study. The amount of information can feel overwhelming to students at any level. For this reason, the book is designed for self-directed practice, with an emphasis on what the player "could" do, rather than what the player "should" do. The principle is to develop your own learning process, rather than following someone else's. The ability to make choices is essential in finding a personal approach to the instrument. Pick and choose the studies that seem interesting - there should be enough variety to accommodate a wide range of personalities. If any particular concept or exercise has been useful as the starting point for a new creative direction, then the book has done its job. Its purpose is not to push any dogma, method, or style, but to open the door to options for guitarists of any background who are looking for new perspectives.

The study of fundamentals goes as deep as the student wants to take it - even the simplest questions have no final answer. Part of the appeal of the search for new musical territory is that we know there is no end to it. As we reach further outward, music teaches us more and more about our inner selves. This book is a map to one tiny corner of a potentially infinite musical landscape, a place filled with sonic creations in varieties limited only by the human imagination, and expanding to distances that depend only on the desire to see what lies ahead. Best of luck in your explorations.

Appendix

This glossary describes how certain words are used in this book. For more detailed and standardized definitions, please refer to an outside source.

GLOSSARY

Augmented: A semitone larger than a major or perfect interval. Can be applied to a major 2nd, 3rd, 6th, 7th, and a perfect unison, 4th, 5th, or octave.
Augmented Triad: Division of the octave evenly into three major 3rds.
Aeolian: The mode beginning on the 6th degree of a major scale.
Beat: A series of sonic events spaced evenly in time, used interchangeably with "pulse."
Binary: Relating to the number two.
Bridge: The stopping point at the upper end of a string, near the picking hand.
Cent: 1/100 of an equal tempered semitone, 1/1200 of an octave. The difference between two consecutive cents is the frequency multiplied by the 1200th root of 2.
Chromatic: Twelve tones to an octave. Also used to designate groups of consecutive semitones, as in a "chromatic cluster."
Clave: A type of cyclic rhythmic figure especially common in music of the African diaspora.
Comma: A small interval between two pitches of the same name that are tuned differently.
Complementary: Two sets of pitches are complementary if, when combined, they fill the entire chromatic scale.
Consonance: A stable sound.
Decad: A set of ten different notes.
Diatonic: The heptatonic scale built by stacking six perfect 5ths from any pitch in equal temperament. The major scale and its modes are diatonic.
Diminished: A semitone smaller than a minor or perfect interval. Can be applied to a minor 2nd, 3rd, 6th, and a perfect unison, 4th, 5th, or octave.
Diminished Triad: Division of the octave into two minor thirds and a tritone.
Dissonance: An unstable sound.
Dodecad: A set of 12 different notes, equivalent to the Chromatic Scale.
Dorian: The mode beginning on the 2nd degree of a major scale.
Downstroke: Movement of a pick across the string in an downward direction.
Dyad: A set of two different notes, an interval.
Dynamics: Volume, controlled by articulation
Equal Temperament: A tuning system that divides the octave into 12 equal parts, based on a logarithmic scale.
Figure: Any group of rhythmic events with at least two events of different lengths.
Frequency: Cycles per second, given in hertz (Hz). The standard frequency of the open A string of the guitar is 110 Hz.
Fundamental: 1) A basic, essential skill. 2) The lowest, generating note of a harmonic series.
Harmonic: The pitch produced by setting a string in motion while lightly touching a point on the string that marks a division of the vibrating part by whole numbers. Used interchangeably with "Partial."
Harmonic Major: The heptatonic scale that differs from the diatonic by a single semitone, a flatted 6th degree.
Harmonic Minor: The heptatonic scale that differs from the diatonic by a single semitone, a raised 7th degree of the Aeolian minor (raised 5th degree of Ionian).
Heptad: A set of seven different notes.
Heptatonic: Containing seven different notes, used here to refer to the scales of the Diatonic, Melodic Minor, Harmonic Minor, and Harmonic Major.
Hexad: A set of six different notes.
Hexatonic: Containing six different notes.
Improvisation: Spontaneous composition.
Interval: The difference between two pitches.
Inversion: A description of the vertical order of simultaneous pitches.
Ionian: The mode beginning on the 1st degree of a diatonic scale.
Just Intonation: A tuning system based on whole number ratios, where pitches are derived from the harmonic series.
Korvai: A type of rhythmic composition found in the Carnatic music of South India.
Legato: Long, attached notes, controlled by articulation.
Locrian: The mode beginning on the 7th degree of a major scale.
Logarithm: Used here to refer to the binary logarithm (base 2), which is used to measure cents and decibels.

Lydian: The mode beginning on the 4th degree of a major scale.
Melodic Minor: The heptatonic scale that differs from the diatonic by a single semitone, a flatted 3rd degree.
Mixolydian: The mode beginning on the 5th degree of a major scale.
Minor: A semitone smaller than a major interval. Can be applied to a major 2nd, 3rd, 6th, and 7th.
Monad: A single pitch.
Monophonic: One pitch at a time.
Node: The point where the finger touches the string.
Nonad: A set of nine different notes.
Nut: The stopping point at the lower end of a string, near the fretting hand.
Octad: A set of eight different notes.
Octatonic: Containing eight different notes. Used here interchangeably with "diminished scale."
Ornament: A phrase on a single string with only one picking stroke, often fast notes that surround or approach a central note.
Overtone: A higher tone produced simultaneously with the fundamental.
Partial: The pitch produced by setting a string in motion while lightly touching a point on the string that marks a division of the vibrating part by whole numbers. Used here interchangeably with "Harmonic."
Pentad: A set of five different notes.
Pentatonic: Containing five different notes. Used here to refer to the set of pitches found by stacking four perfect 5ths. The open strings of the guitar are pentatonic.
Perfect 5th: Used to refer to either the pitch created by the 3rd partial or the equal tempered interval that spans 7 semitones.
Phrygian: The mode beginning on the 3rd degree of a major scale.
Pitch Circle: A circle of 12 points, where pitches ascend chromatically in a clockwise direction. Pitch collections are shown as dots connected by lines. Any pitch can be at "12:00."
Polyphonic: Layered pitches.
Polypulse: Layered pulses.
Polyrhythm: Layered rhythms.
Pulse: A series of sonic events spaced evenly in time, used interchangeably with "beat."
Quantize: Put onto a grid, where everything has a measurable value.
Rhythm: Used here to describe a series of sonic events spaced unevenly in time, often cyclical in nature.
Rotation: Used interchangeably with "transposition," referring to the orientation of a shape on a pitch or time circle.
Rudiment: A fundamental skill, used here to refer to the basic movements of the picking hand.
Semitone: 1/12 of an octave. The difference between 2 consecutive semitones is the frequency multiplied by the 12th root of 2.
Slide: Movement between pitches on a single string with a single finger without rearticulation.
Slur: Movement between pitches on a single string with more than one finger without rearticulation.
Staccato: Short, detached notes, controlled by articulation.
String: The sonic generator of the guitar. The six strings from low to high E,A,D,G,B,E are numbered 6,5,4,3,2,1, respectively.
Subdivision: Division of a pulse into equal parts (e.g. duple, triple, quintuple, etc).
Subpulse: The unit that is a part of an equally divided pulse (e.g. a single triplet, 16th note, etc).
Symmetrical Picking: A picking technique, first presented in this book, designed for speed, accuracy, power, and groove.
Symmetry: A mirror-image relationship within the visualized geometry of a collection of pitches or rhythms.
Ternary: Relating to the number three.
Tetrad: A pitch collection with four notes.
Tiling: Filling a complete pitch space or interval of time with interlocking pieces that have no gaps or overlaps.
Timbre: The tonal color of an instrument.
Time Circle: Cyclic rhythmic notation, where the number of dots represents the length of the cycle, sounded events are written as large dots, and rests are written as small dots. Time proceeds in a clockwise direction, starting at any point.
Tone: Whole tone, 1/6 of an octave, two semitones. Also, the quality of the sound produced on an instrument.
Tonnetz: A visual representation of pitch relationships in just intonation.
Triad: A set of three different notes.
Tritone: 1/2 of an octave, spanning three whole tones.
Undecad: A set of eleven different notes.
Upstroke: Movement of a pick across the string in an upward direction.
Whole Tone Scale: The scale made entirely of whole tones, which divides the octave into six equal parts.

SHORT SUBJECTS

This book has mostly avoided advice and opinion, but here are a few informal thoughts.

On Practice:
It's likely that you will play things in performance that are similar to what you've practiced. To play creatively, it's necessary to practice creatively. When your practice sounds more like a performance, your performances will sound less like someone practicing.

On Patience:
Take your time. You learn how to play fast by practicing slowly. The process of internalization can't be forced - reflexes can only be built with repetition. There are no short cuts.

On Discipline:
Discipline doesn't have to be painful - it can mean doing a little bit of something every day. Consistency is the key. A small task performed consistently can acheive huge results. Five minutes of focused practice is more productive than an hour of noodling around.

On Technique:
Technique doesn't have to mean "chops." It can mean knowing how to use the tools you've chosen for your personal musical goals. Musicians can build a whole career on a small, well-honed skill set. That being said, expertise with more tools gives a player more options. If you have the feeling that your ideas are ahead of your ability to execute them, it's time to sharpen the tools you have, or find some new ones.

On Gear:
Guitarists are buried in options for tone enhancement - endless varieties of instruments, pedals, processors, and other devices. At its best, the right gear can allow the guitarist to build a highly personalized sound world, but at its worst it can be a distraction in performance and serve as a crutch for substandard technique. The sound still originates from the hands. If the raw sound coming from the guitar doesn't have a strong tone and feel, no amount of fancy gear can make it speak.

On Excuses:
Don't complain, don't explain. If you honestly do the best you can in any situation, then your work needs no justification.

On Sight Reading:
It's not more difficult to sight read on the guitar than on other instruments - sometimes the number of choices just gets in the way. Try limiting choices for any particular pitch. For sight-reading music cold, try starting in the middle of the neck, around 5th position. From here, you can reach about 2 1/2 octaves without duplicate pitches. Change positions if the range is awkward, and work out ideal fingerings when you have time. Normally guitar is written up an octave, but it's useful to also be fluent at reading concert pitch in both treble and bass clefs.

On Metronomes:
Be mindful of what you learn from machines. A metronome is just a measuring device - it serves a specific purpose, but isn't useful for all tasks. Metronomes don't teach about flow, feel, or groove, but they do measure quantities very accurately, so for the musician who wants to chart progress on a task with data they are invaluable. To work on natural time, play with other humans.

On Composition and Improvisation:
Just because something is made slowly and deliberately doesn't mean that it can't have elements of spontaneity and passion, and just because something is made quickly and extemporaneously doesn't mean that it can't have detail, structure, and architecture.

On Looking:
Guitarists who constantly look at their hands while performing are telling people, "I'm more interested in what I'm saying than what you're saying." If you have this tendency, look at the people you are playing with, look out into the audience, pay attention to something that is outside of yourself. Notice how this changes the way you listen.

On Listening:
You can listen to yourself, or you can listen to others, or you can listen to yourself and others at the same time. The last thing usually works the best. Imagine removing your ears and putting them somewhere else in the room, where you have the advantage of distance to hear the balance of your instrument in a larger context. This can also work if you are playing alone.

On Style and Repertoire:
Music exists in a cultural context, and usually it has a social purpose. Learning, internalizing, and performing material from a musical tradition is a way of saying "this is where I'm coming from." When the audience understands this, you can take them to many places.

On Feel:
Feel is a subject beyond this or any book. All the study in the world will be useless without some sense of feel in performance. This includes the intangibles - groove, timing, phrasing, flow, touch, vibe, personality, soul. A core idea in this book is that a solid grasp of fundamentals allows the musician to be relaxed, and a relaxed musician can forget about the guitar and focus on communicating a feeling to others.

A detailed list of the influences on the various sections of this book.

SOURCES

Page 2, "The String": This chapter (pages 1-12) was influenced by several works that use the monochord as a tool to look at tuning systems, acoustics, and the philosophy of Harmonics, including Helmholtz' *On the Sensations of Tone,* Kayser's *Textbook of Harmonics,* and McClain's *The Myth of Invariance,* and Partch's *Genesis of a Music.*

Page 8, "Building a Chromatic Scale in Just Intonation": The lattice seen on this page was influenced by the methodology and visualization of pitch relationships in Mathieu's *Harmonic Experience: Tonal Harmony from its Natural Origins to its Modern Expression.*

Pages 34-35, "Diatonic Magic Square" and "The Scrambler": In the ancient design of a magic square the sum of each row, column, and diagonal are identical. A relative of the magic square is the Latin square and the modern Sudoku puzzle, which cannot repeat an element in any row, column, or constrained area. These two exercises use pitches instead of numbers to make pitch sequences without repeated notes.

Page 36, "Tonal Cycloid": This is a roulette curve inspired by the type of geometric patterns made by tracing a point on wheel rolling within another wheel, similar to the children's toy known as *Spirograph.*

Page 40, "16 Symmetrical Shapes": These shapes are arrived at by a purely combinatorial process and then applied to the guitar in a theoretical way. For an extensive study of the application of symmetrical structures to the guitar, readers are advised to purchase guitarist Pat Martino's *The Nature of Guitar.*

Page 46, "The Chromatic Scale": The image in the upper right is a 12 sided polygon with all vertices connected to each other. Versions of this diagram have been used for many purposes for hundreds of years, including Marin Mersenne's version from 1648 with the pitches in cycle of 5ths order in his *Harmonicorum Libri XII.* The total number of pitch sets and the sequence of numbers to the left of the diagram is the answer to a basic problem of combinatorics. A complete lists of pitch class sets using various algorithms can be found in many sources, including Forte's *The Structure of Atonal Music*, Rahn's *Basic Atonal Theory,* Carter's *Harmony Book*, and Yamaguchi's *Complete Thesaurus of Musical Scales.* In pitch-class set theory it is most common to categorize groups of pitches that are inversionally equivalent (i.e. a major and minor triad) as belonging to the same "set class." In this system there are a total of 223 unique set classes. This book is more concerned with sound than abstract structure and does not use inversional equivalence, which leads to a total of 351 unique pitch sets.

Pages 49-56, "The Dyad": Working through the possibilities of intervals on adjacent and non-adjacent strings is an idea inspired by Mick Goodrick's classic *The Advancing Guitarist.* Goodrick's work has an a more general influence over this work in terms of its method of inquiry and focus on practical application to the instrument.

Pages 59-79, "The Triad": Most 20th century music theorists (Forte, Rahn, Carter, etc) list twelve possible triads, or "trichords." This collection of nineteen was arrived at after discussions with saxophonist Steve Coleman, arriving at the opinion that the ear does not really detect inversional equivalence (i.e. major = minor, because of identical interval content). This is only one perspective. For example, O'Gallagher's *Twelve Tone Improvisation* is an extensive study of 12 trichord types, where inversion is one of the devices used to transform the trichord. In the diagrams used in this book, the geometry of the connected points on the circle makes 19 different triangles. This trichord geometry, using similar diagrams, is the basis for an entire compositional system in Schat's *The Tone Clock.*

Page 82, "Triadic Mutation Pathways": The phrase "Triad Mutations" appears in titles on Steve Coleman's 2006 album *Weaving Symbolics.* The title of this page is similar, but the concept is different than the one used on the album.

Page 95, "Symmetrical Diminished Transformations": This and the next four pages involve a topic of symmetrical harmony that has been explored in depth and taught for years by saxophonist Steve Coleman. Coleman's work draws on a long history of theorists in musical polarity including Hans Kayser, Ernst Levy, Hugo Riemann, and Johannes Lippius, but has focused on application in the context of spontaneous composition. The pages in this book show how some of these concepts translate to formations on the guitar. Similar visualizations of a parent diminished structure transformed into four dominant chords can be found in Pat Martino's *The Nature of Guitar,* and this concept is also central to harmonic concepts taught by pianist Barry Harris.

Page 104, "Tetrad Mandala": The arrays on this page as well as the following three pages were arrived at through manipulation of geometric shapes. The numbers and intervallic content were checked against various sources, most notably Rahn's *Basic Atonal Theory.*

Page 110, "The Pulse": This page contains a very cursory description of auditory perception. For a detailed and scholarly study of this subject, readers are referred to Sethares' *Rhythm and Transforms*

Page 111, "The Picking Hand": The three rules listed here are not a new concept. The system is called "symmetrical picking" here, but has also had various names in the past, including "economy picking," "efficiency picking," and "directional picking." It is really just a common sense way of moving from string to string that has been used by dozens of guitarists before it ever had a name. The important part of the entire picking section is approaching the picking hand like a drummer, which requires a symmetrical approach as a prerequisite.

Page 112, "6 Rudiments": The section on rudiments that continues for the next 8 pages is indebted to studies with drummer Dan Weiss, an expert on improvisation using rudimental technique. The title "Pick Control" is borrowed from George Lawrence Stone's *Stick Control for the Snare Drummer*, and the title "Rudimental Workout" is a play on Alan Dawson's famous "Rudimental Ritual."

Page 124, "Clave": The connection of diatonic scales to typical clave patterns is an analogy often mentioned by saxophonist Steve Coleman. Coleman has done extensive work in this area of translating the language of pitch into the rhythmic world. For extensive and authentic studies of clave, readers are encouraged to read Dafnis Prieto's *A World of Rhythmic Possibilities.*

126, "Korvai": The title is a type of rhythmic composition from Carnatic music in the South of India. This page and the studies of quintuple and septuple division of the beat are influenced by a long period of study with Carnatic percussionist Ganesh Kumar.

Page 129, "Diatonic Ornaments": The idea for this study came from the preface to J.S. Bach's *Klavierbüchlein,* which contains a table of ornaments and their corresponding symbols.

Page 134, "Polypulse": The cube drawn in the lower right takes its name from Swiss cystallographer Louis Albert Necker, who described this optical illusion in 1832.

Page 135, "14 Polypulses": This page has some kinship with the "interference patterns" found in Joseph Schillinger's *The Schillinger System of Musical Composition.* The main difference is that the the study in this book works on feeling multiple simultaneous tempos, and not in creating composite rhythms.

Page 140, "Rhythmic Dyads": Rhythmic figures from this point on in the book are written using "necklace notation," which has a history in both music and mathematics. The concepts of circular rhythms in this book were most influenced by the work of Willie Anku. Other theorists using necklace notation include Godfried Toussaint and William Sethares. Sethares cites Safi al-Din al-Urmawi's 13th century *Book of Cycles* to note that the notation of rhythmic cycles on a circle is a very old idea (*Rhythm and Transforms,* p. 28).

Page 141, "Expansion of the Dyad": The table in the bottom right shows the number of rhythms possible with increasing numbers of events. The author arrived at the numbers from 1-7 events through making manual lists. These numbers were checked by mathematician and bassist Francois Moutin, who then provided a general equation for any number of events. This series of numbers can also be found at the Online Encyclopedia of Integer Sequences, where it is described as "the number of aperiodic necklaces with n beads of 3 colors."

Page 143, "Three Heartbeats": This and the following five pages use the heartbeat as a primordial rhythm to explore fundamental rhythmic principles. This is inspired by conversations with master drummer Milford Graves, who has done pioneering work for decades in connections between biology and music.

Page 150: "Rhythmic Tiling": This and the following page draw ideas from email correspondence with mathematician and music theorist Rachel Wells Hall.

Page 152: "Infinte Growth": This and the following page are influenced by the aperiodic tiling patterns created by mathematician Roger Penrose.

Publication information for works cited in "Sources," as well as other works that served as more general inspiration for this book.

BIBLIOGRAPHY

Anku, Willie. *"Inside a Master Drummer's Mind: A Quantitative Theory of Structures in African Music."* Trans-Cultural Music Review, 2007.

Bach, Johann Sebastian. *Klavierbüchlein für Anna Magdalena Bach.* 1725.

Carter, Elliott. *Harmony Book.* Edited by Nicholas Hopkins and John F. Link. New York: Carl Fischer, 2002.

Coleman, Steve. *"Regarding the Sonic Symbolism of When and Where." Arcana V.* New York: Hips Road/Tzadik, 2010.

DeVito, Chris, ed. *Coltrane on Coltrane: The John Coltrane Interviews.* Chicago: A Cappella Books, 2010.

Forte, Allen. *The Structure of Atonal Music.* New Haven, CT: Yale University Press, 1973.

Goodrick, Mick. *The Advancing Guitarist.* Milwaukee, WI: Hal Leonard Books, 1987.

Haeckel, Ernst. *Art Forms in Nature.* Munich: Prestel Verlag, 2004, ©1904

Hall, Rachel W. and Paul Klingsberg. "Asymmetric Rhythms and Tiling Canons." *American Mathematical Monthly 113* (2006), no. 10, 887–896

Helmholtz, Hermann. *On the Sensations of Tone.* New York: Dover Publications, 1954, ©1885.

Hindemith, Paul: *Elementary Training for Musicians (2nd ed.)* London: Schott & Co, 1946.

Kayser, Hans. *Textbook of Harmonics.* Trans. Ariel Godwin. USA, Sacred Science Institute, 2006, ©1950.

Knuth, Donald E. *The Art of Computer Programming, Vol 4a, Combinatorial Algorithms.* Boston, MA: Pearson Education, 2011.

Lateef, Yusef A. *Repository of Scales and Melodic Patterns.* Amherst, MA: FANA Publishing, 1981.

Lee, Bruce. *The Art of Expressing the Human Body.* North Clarendon, VT: Tuttle Publishing, 1988.

Martino, Pat. *The Nature of Guitar.* www.truefire.com/pat-martino/the-nature-of-guitar, 2016.

Mathieu, W.A. *Harmonic Experience: Tonal Harmony from its Natural Origins to its Modern Expression.* Rochester: Inner Traditions International, 1997.

McClain, Ernest G. *The Myth of Invariance: The Origin of the Gods, Mathematics, and Music from the Rg Veda to Plato.* York Beach, ME: Nicolas-Hays, Inc., 1976.

Mersenne, Marin. *Harmonicorum Libri XII,* Paris: Guillaume Baudry, 1648.

Necker, Louis Albert. "Observations on some remarkable phenomenon which occurs in viewing a figure of a crystal or geometrical solid." *London and Edinburgh Philosophical Magazine and Journal of Science, vol 1*, 1832.

O'Gallagher, John. *Twelve-Tone Improvisation: A Method for Using Tone Rows in Jazz.* Rottenburg, Germany: Advance Music, 2013.

Partch, Harry. *Genesis of a Music, (2nd ed.)* New York: Da Capo Press, 1974, ©1949.

Penrose, Roger. "Set of tiles for covering a surface." Patent US 4133152 A, 1979.

Prieto, Dafnis. *A World of Rhythmic Possibilities.* Dafnison Music, 2016

Rahn, John. *Basic Atonal Theory.* New York: Schirmer Books, 1987, ©1980.

Schat, Peter. *The Tone Clock. Contemporary Music Studies, Book 7.* Routledge, 1993.

Schillinger, Joseph. *The Schillinger System of Musical Composition.* Perseus Books, 1941

Sethares, Willaim A. *Rhythm and Transforms.* London: Springer-Verlag London Limited, 2007.

Stone, George Lawrence. *Stick Control for the Snare Drummer.* Afred Music Publishing, 2009, ©1935.

Tarkovsky, Andrey. *Sculpting in Time.* Austin: University of Texas Press, 2005, ©1986.

Tufte, Edward R. *The Visual Display of Quantitative Information (2nd ed.).* Cheshire, CT: Graphics Press, 2001.

Van Eps, George. *Harmonic Mechanisms for Guitar, Volume One.* Pacific, MO: Mel Bay Publications, 1980.

Wilcoxon, Charley. *Modern Rudimental Swing Solos for the Advanced Drummer.* Grafton: Ludwig Music, 1979, ©1941.

Yamaguchi, Masaya. *The Complete Thesaurus of Musical Scales.* New York: Masaya Music Services, 2006.

ACKNOWLEDGMENTS

This book is the summation of many years of study, and many people have helped me along the way. The visual approach of the book comes from my Mother, Father, and Stepfather, who all make things of beauty with the highest possible level of craftsmanship. Michael Townsend was my first mentor, a guitarist and musicologist who introduced me to the idea of improvisation and opened the door to musical traditions from all over the world. The ideas about music as a universal human activity come from these early studies. The importance of fundamentals, rhythm, feel, and musical identity come from my second mentor, guitarist Rodney Jones, who helped me strengthen my basic skills, navigate through the musical world of New York City, and find my own direction. Saxophonist Steve Coleman has been my third mentor, whose influence is everywhere in this book. His methodology is something that I've deliberately tried to emulate - a search for universal musical principles, a focus on the study of music as a process of self-discovery, an uncompromising standard of musicianship, an exhaustive and logical approach to fundamentals grounded in a respect for the unknowable complexities of nature and the individual human mind. The sections on symmetrical dominant movements and rhythmic counterpoint with unequal cycles are direct descendants of his work. The exploratory nature of the exercises, open-ended and focused on creativity, comes from pianists Anthony Davis and Kenny Barron, who provided a great amount of the nuts and bolts of my primary training in composition and improvisation, teaching through example. Many possibilities in rhythm opened up to me while studying with percussionist Ganesh Kumar, who showed me the intricacies of South Indian music for a number of years. The ideas about subdivision of the beat and rhythmic shapes come largely from these studies. Drummer Dan Weiss is my longest collaborator, and a tireless student of music. The entire section on Symmetrical Picking is based on things that he has shown me on the drumset, and his relentless drive toward improving musicianship is the attitude behind many of the exercises. The idea of organizing my thoughts and notes into book form first occurred to me while teaching at the Banff Centre under the direction of the visionary musician and educator Vijay Iyer. He demonstrated to me that a clear presentation of ideas can inspire people, and that the exchange of ideas can build communities. The desire for optimal ways of presenting information in this book led to many unconventional solutions that made sense to me, but not necessarily to anyone else. This led to a painstaking process of testing out various pages, rewriting, clarifying, and editing out nearly half of the book. This would not have been possible without extensive proofreading and feedback from (in alphabetical order): Harold Bott, Marius Duboule, Matthew Hough, James Hurt, Sergio Krakowski, Alex Levine, Fred Lyra, Francois Moutin, John O'Gallagher, Travis Reuter, Dan Schmidt, Aaron Shorr, Vaughn Stoffey, Rajna Swaminatham, Ohad Talmor, and Dan Weiss.

Most of all, thanks to my wife Pavani Thagirisa, for her endless patience and support.

ABOUT THE AUTHOR

American guitarist Miles Okazaki grew up in Port Townsend, Washington, in the Pacific Northwest of the United States. He discovered the guitar at age 6, and began playing gigs at age 14. He has toured the world for 20 years in a variety of groups, and has taught for the Banff Centre, the University of Michigan, The Juilliard School, Queens College, the New Jersey Performing Arts Center, and The New School. He has released four albums of original compositions, and holds degrees from Harvard University, Manhattan School of Music, and The Juilliard School. He currently lives in Brooklyn, New York, with his wife and children. This is his first book.

Notes

Notes

MEL BAY